LIBRARY OF NEW TESTAMENT STUDIES
612

Formerly the Journal for the Study of the New Testament Supplement Series

Editor
Chris Keith

Editorial Board
Dale C. Allison, John M.G. Barclay, Lynn H. Cohick, R. Alan Culpepper,
Craig A. Evans, Robert Fowler, Simon J. Gathercole, Juan Hernandez Jr.,
John S. Kloppenborg, Michael Labahn, Love L. Sechrest, Robert Wall,
Catrin H. Williams, Britanny Wilson

THE MEDIA MATRIX OF EARLY JEWISH AND CHRISTIAN NARRATIVE

Nicholas A. Elder

LONDON • NEW YORK • OXFORD • NEW DELHI • SYDNEY

T&T CLARK
Bloomsbury Publishing Plc
50 Bedford Square, London, WC1B 3DP, UK
1385 Broadway, New York, NY 10018, USA
29 Earlsfort Terrace, Dublin 2, Ireland

BLOOMSBURY, T&T CLARK and the T&T Clark logo
are trademarks of Bloomsbury Publishing Plc

First published in Great Britain 2019
Paperback edition first published 2021

Copyright © Nicholas Elder, 2019

Nicholas Elder has asserted his right under the Copyright,
Designs and Patents Act, 1988, to be identified as Author of this work..

For legal purposes the Acknowledgements on p. x constitute
an extension of this copyright page.

All rights reserved. No part of this publication may be reproduced or
transmitted in any form or by any means, electronic or mechanical,
including photocopying, recording, or any information storage or retrieval
system, without prior permission in writing from the publishers.

Bloomsbury Publishing Plc does not have any control over, or responsibility for,
any third-party websites referred to or in this book. All internet addresses given
in this book were correct at the time of going to press. The author and publisher
regret any inconvenience caused if addresses have changed or sites have
ceased to exist, but can accept no responsibility for any such changes.

A catalogue record for this book is available from the British Library.

Library of Congress Cataloging-in-Publication Data
Names: Elder, Nicholas A., author.
Title: The media matrix of early Jewish and Christian narrative /
by Nicholas A. Elder, B.A., M.A., Ph.D.
Description: 1 [edition]. | New York: T&T Clark, 2019. | Series: Library of New Testament
studies; volume 611 | Includes bibliographical references and index.
Identifiers: LCCN 2019020062 (print) | ISBN 9780567688101 (hardback)
Subjects: LCSH: Bible. Mark–Criticism, interpretation, etc. | Joseph and
Aseneth–Criticism, interpretation, etc. | Narration (Rhetoric)
Classification: LCC BS2585.52 .E43 2019 (print) | LCC BS2585.52 (ebook) |
DDC 226.3/06–dc23
LC record available at https://lccn.loc.gov/2019020062
LC ebook record available at https://lccn.loc.gov/2019981220

ISBN: HB: 978-0-5676-8810-1
PB: 978-0-5677-0154-1
ePDF: 978-0-5676-8811-8
eBook: 978-0-5676-8813-2

Series: Library of New Testament Studies, 2513-8790, volume 612

Typeset by Deanta Global Publishing Services, Chennai, India

To find out more about our authors and books visit
www.bloomsbury.com and sign up for our newsletters.

CONTENTS

Preface	viii
Acknowledgments	x
Abbreviations	xi

Chapter 1
MARK AND ASENETH 1

Chapter 2
MEDIA THEORY, ANCIENT MEDIA, AND ORALLY COMPOSED
NARRATIVES FROM THE PAPYRI 11
  Mixed-media theory 11
  Features of oral and literary registers 16
    Criterion #1: Parataxis, apposition, and the idea unit 16
    Criterion #2: Repetition of syntactical patterns, words,
      phrases, and ideas 19
    Criterion #3: Verb employment 20
    Criterion #4: Multiform tradition 23
    Criterion # 5: Embedded textuality and intertextuality 25
  Composition by dictation in Greco-Roman antiquity 28
  Orally composed papyri narratives 32
    BGU I.27 32
    P.Oxy. 903 36
  The purposes, features, and semantic range of ὑπομνήματα in
    Greco-Roman antiquity 43
  Ecclesiastical testimony to Mark's composition 48
  Conclusion 50

Chapter 3
LINGUISTIC ORAL RESIDUES 53
  Textual traditions, recensions, and reconstructions of
    Joseph and Aseneth 53
  Bilingual influence 58
  Residually oral linguistic characteristics 61
    Criterion #1: Parataxis, apposition, and the idea unit 62
    Apposition, copulative constructions, and the "hitching post" ... 64
    Absence of literarily conceived syntax 65

Parataxis, apposition, and the idea unit in Mark	66
Criterion #2: Repetition of syntactical patterns, words, phrases, and ideas	72
Criterion #3: Verb employment	84
Conclusion	93

Chapter 4
METALINGUISTIC ORAL RESIDUES — 95

Criterion #4: Multiform traditions	95
The multiform tradition of *Joseph and Aseneth*	95
The multiform tradition of Mark	98
Linguistic characteristics of Mark's longer ending	101
Criterion #5: Intertextuality	103
Intertextuality in *Joseph and Aseneth*	104
Joseph and Aseneth 1:3 and Gen. 41:46-49	105
Joseph and Aseneth 4:9 and Gen. 41:38	106
Joseph and Aseneth 27–29 and 1 Samuel 17	106
Intertextuality in Mark	115
Mark 2:23-28 and 1 Sam. 21:2-10	119
Mark 14:27 and Zech. 13:7	120
Mark 4:35-41, Jon. 1:1-15, and Psalm 106 LXX	123
Mark 5:1-20 and the Book of the Watchers (1 En. 1–36)	126
The geographical mistake in the setting of Mark 5:1-20	129
Conclusion	132

Chapter 5
LINGUISTIC TRAJECTORIES OF *JOSEPH AND ASENETH* AND MARK — 133

Introduction	133
Redacting parataxis and simplicity of clauses	135
Redacting parataxis and simplicity of clauses in *Joseph and Aseneth*	135
Redacting parataxis and simplicity of clauses in Mark	137
Redacting verbal mood, tense, and voice	140
Redacting verbal mood, tense, and voice in *Joseph and Aseneth*	140
Redacting verbal mood, tense, and voice in Mark	145
Redacting repetitive syntactical patterns, words, phrases, and ideas in Mark	150
Intercalations in Mark, Matthew, and Luke	151
The media forms of the Synoptic Gospels	156
Mark's Gospel (εὐαγγέλιον)	157
Matthew's book (βίβλος)	161
Luke's historical prologue	163

CONCLUSION	167
Results of reading *Joseph and Aseneth* as a textualized oral narrative	168
Results of reading Mark as a textualized oral narrative	174
Results of reading antique textualized oral narratives	177
Works Cited	179
Subject and Author Index	198
Index of Scripture and Other Ancient Literature	200

PREFACE

The seeds for this book were planted when I first read Christoph Burchard's introduction to *Joseph and Aseneth* in James H. Charlesworth's *Old Testament Pseudepigrapha*. Toward the beginning of his introduction he indicates that *Joseph and Aseneth* is "a little longer than the Gospel of Mark."[1] As I continued through Burchard's introduction and then the narrative itself, several other similarities to Mark's Gospel became clear, prompting the question "why?"[2]

Possessing an interest in media criticism of the New Testament, and particularly the Second Gospel, I suspected that this burgeoning field would be of consequence for *Joseph and Aseneth*, given its similarities with Mark. At that point, without any reference to Mark's Gospel I argued that orality theory does productively inform interpretation of the pseudepigraphon in an article published in the *Journal for the Study of Judaism*.[3] My intent was to explore the similarities between Mark and *Joseph and Aseneth* at greater length later on. My dissertation, completed under the direction of Julian V. Hills and Joshua Ezra Burns in the Department of Theology at Marquette University, and this book, which is a revised version of that dissertation, are the fruit of that intent.

I wish to make it clear from the outset that I do not consider *Joseph and Aseneth* some kind of "background" narrative for interpreting Mark. While I first came to the former because of my interest in the latter, I have developed an appreciation for

---

1. Christoph Burchard, introduction to "*Joseph and Aseneth*: A New Translation and Introduction," in *The Old Testament Pseudepigrapha*, ed. James H. Charlesworth, vol. 2 (Garden City: Doubleday, 1985), 177. This is true of his reconstruction of the Greek text, but is not true of Marc Philonenko's, which is 2,992 words shorter than Mark and will be prioritized in what follows (*Joseph et Aséneth: Introduction, Texte Critique, Traduction, et Notes*, StPB 13 [Leiden: Brill, 1968]). I address my preference for Philonenko's version in Chapter 3.

2. The following from Burchard's introduction particularly stood out: *Joseph and Aseneth* was originally written in Greek but linguistically betrays Aramaic or Hebrew influence ("New Translation," 181, 185); the plot is straightforward and lacks vivid details (ibid., 182); sentences are paratactically structured with infrequent use of particles other than "and" (ibid., 184); this results in a "rigidity of style" that is difficult for the modern reader to appreciate (ibid., 186); the majority of *Joseph and Aseneth*'s manuscripts were "made to be read aloud" (ibid., 195).

3. Nicholas A. Elder, "On Transcription and Oral Transmission in Aseneth: A Study of the Narrative's Conception," *JSJ* 47 (2016): 119–42.

Joseph and Aseneth that rivals my appreciation for the Gospel of Mark. It is a story worth experiencing and studying on its own accord. And because it is worthy of study on its own accord, it ought to be studied with reference to contemporaneous narratives, just as Mark should. This is why I study the two narratives in tandem in what follows. They throw interpretive light on one another.

ACKNOWLEDGMENTS

I owe a debt of gratitude to the many people who have been involved in this project. First, to Julian V. Hills and Joshua Ezra Burns, who oversaw my dissertation of which this book is a revised version. There scarcely could have been a better combination of advisors for the nature of that project. The text that follows has been improved greatly by their feedback on both its content and its rhetoric. Any deficiencies are, of course, my own. Michael Cover and Andrei A. Orlov also provided substantial feedback on the manuscript that has made its way into what follows. I am also grateful for the financial and academic support that I have received from the Marquette University Department of Theology before and during the process of completing this project.

Early versions of the arguments made here were presented in various regional and national meetings of the Society of Biblical Literature. The Synoptic Gospels, Pseudepigrapha, Performance Criticism of Biblical and Other Ancient Texts, and the Intertextuality in the New Testament sections at the national meeting all served as productive venues to present this work in, as did the Midwest and Upper Midwest regional meetings. Thank you to the chairs and participants of all of these sections.

Countless hours of music have been drumming in my ears in the time that it took to complete the research and writing for this project. I know well that what plays in the writing process has no small effect on what is produced. The medium and what influences the mode of production does indeed affect the message. More than any other album, I have frequently returned to Sufjan Steven's ode to the Brooklyn-Queen's Expressway, *The BQE*, a postmodern orchestral masterpiece that ambles electro-symphonically through seven melodically eclectic and lyricless movements, as motivation and background noise for writing this book.

Most importantly, my family has sacrificed a great deal to make this book a reality, not least uprooting from the Front Range of Colorado to move to Milwaukee, WI. Relinquishing three hundred days of sunshine a year to face the reality of something called "polar vortices" is perhaps the best evidence of their unflagging support. Beth, Brooks, Kit James, Nettie, and Lucy, thank you.

ABBREVIATIONS

AB	Anchor Bible
AGJU	Arbeiten zur Geschichte des antiken Judentums und des Urchristentums
AJP	*American Journal of Philology*
BDAG	Danker, Frederick W., Walter Bauer, William F. Arndt, and F. Wilbur Gingrich. *Greek-English Lexicon of the New Testament and Other Early Christian Literature*. 3rd ed. Chicago: University of Chicago Press, 2000 (Danker-Bauer-Arndt-Gingrich)
BDB	Francis Brown, S.R. Driver, and Charles A. Briggs, *A Hebrew and English Lexicon of the Old Testament* (Oxford: Clarendon Press, 1907)
BDF	Friedrich Blass, A. Debrunner, and Robert W. Funk, *A Greek Grammar of the New Testament and Other Early Christian Literature* (Cambridge: Cambridge University Press, 1961)
BETL	Bibliotheca ephemeridum theologicarum lovaniensium
BR	*Bible Review*
BT	*The Bible Translator*
BTB	*Biblical Theology Bulletin*
BZ	*Biblische Zeitschrift*
CBQ	*Catholic Biblical Quarterly*
ClQ	*Classical Quarterly*
CurBR	*Currents in Biblical Research*
EJL	Early Judaism and Its Literature
ETL	*Ephemerides theologicae lovanienses*
ExpTim	*Expository Times*
FRLANT	Forschungen zur Religion und Literatur des Alten und Neuen Testaments
GRBS	*Greek, Roman, and Byzantine Studies*
HTR	*Harvard Theological Review*
HUCA	*Hebrew Union College Annual*
ICC	International Critical Commentary
JANESCU	*Journal of the Ancient Near Eastern Society of Columbia University*
JBL	*Journal of Biblical Literature*
JECS	*Journal of Early Christian Studies*
JR	*Journal of Religion*
JSJ	*Journal for the Study of Judaism in the Persian, Hellenistic, and Roman Period*
JSJSup	*Journal for the Study of Judaism in the Persian, Hellenistic, and Roman Period*, Supplement Series
JSNT	*Journal for the Study of the New Testament*

JSNTSup	*Journal for the Study of the New Testament*, Supplement Series
JSOTSupp	*Journal for the Study of the Old Testament*, Supplement Series
JSP	*Journal for the Study of the Pseudepigrapha*
JSPSup	*Journal for the Study of the Pseudepigrapha*, Supplement Series
LCL	Loeb Classical Library
LEC	Library of Early Christianity
LNTS	The Library of New Testament Studies
LSJ	H.G. Liddell, Robert Scott, and H. Stuart Jones, *Greek-English Lexicon* (Oxford: Clarendon Press, 9th ed., 1968)
NETS	*A New English Translation of the Septuagint*. Edited by Albert Pietersma and Benjamin G. Wright. New York: Oxford University Press, 2007
NovT	*Novum Testamentum*
NovTSup	*Novum Testamentum*, Supplements
NTL	New Testament Library
NTS	*New Testament Studies*
NTTS	New Testament Tools and Studies
NTTSD	New Testament Tools, Studies, and Documents
PVTG	Pseudepigrapha Veteris Testamenti graece
RSV	Revised Standard Version
RTR	*Reformed Theological Review*
SBLDS	SBL Dissertation Series
SBLRBS	SBL Resources for Biblical Study
SBLSP	SBL Seminar Papers
SemeiaSt	Semeia Studies
SNTSMS	Society for New Testament Studies Monograph Series
SP	Sacra Pagina
StPB	Studia Post-biblica
SVTG	Studia in Veteris Testamenti pseudepigrapha
TDNT	Gerhard Kittel and Gerhard Friedrich (eds), *Theological Dictionary of the New Testament* (trans. Geoffrey W. Bromiley; 10 vols.; Grand Rapids: Eerdmans, 1964)
TENTS	Texts and Editions for New Testament Study
Them	*Themelios*
TQ	*Theologische Quartalschrift*
TSAJ	Texte und Studien zum antiken Judentum
VC	*Vigiliae christianae*
WBC	Word Biblical Commentary
WUNT	Wissenschaftliche Untersuchungen zum Neuen Testament
WUNT 2	Wissenschaftliche Untersuchungen zum Neuen Testament 2
ZNW	*Zeitschrift für die neutestamentliche Wissenschaft*
ZPE	*Zeitschrift für Papyrologie und Epigraphik*

Chapter 1

MARK AND ASENETH

A paradox has emerged during the past thirty years of Markan scholarship. With the rise of narrative criticism, many deem the gospel a well-crafted and even sophisticated story. Mark creates a narrative world into which its audience is invited to enter. According to David Rhoads and Donald Michie in the opening words of *Mark as Story*, this is "a world full of conflict and suspense, a world of surprising reversals and strange ironies, a world of riddles and hidden meanings."[1] As interpreters began to read Mark as a unified whole in the early 1980s, interest shifted from the world behind the text to the world of the text.[2] The Second Gospel, which was previously judged an artless collection of sources, became a literary achievement written by an artist par excellence.[3]

But Mark's style has not changed during this time and neither have assessments of it.[4] Linguistically, many consider the narrative terse and

---

1. David Rhoads and Donald Michie, *Mark as Story: An Introduction to the Narrative of a Gospel* (Philadelphia: Fortress, 1982), 1.

2. Christopher W. Skinner examines the far-reaching influence of Rhoads and Michie's monograph, especially with respect to the shifting methodological landscape of the late 1970s through the early 1990s ("Telling the Story: The Appearance and Impact of *Mark as Story*," in *Mark as Story: Retrospect and Prospect*, ed. idem and Kelly R. Iverson, SBLRBS 65 [Atlanta: Society of Biblical Literature, 2011], 1–16).

3. Mark's literary acumen was granted before the publication of *Mark as Story* by William L. Lane, *The Gospel of Mark*, NICNT (Grand Rapids: Eerdmans, 1974), 26. It began to be more frequently mentioned following its publication (Urban C. Von Wahlde, "Mark 9:33–50: Discipleship: The Authority that Serves," *BZ* 29 [1985]: 50; Larry W. Hurtado, "The Gospel of Mark in Recent Study," *Them* 14 [1989]: 48; Rob Starner, *Kingdom of Power, Power of Kingdom: The Opposing World Views of Mark and Chariton* [Eugene: Pickwick, 2011], 6–7).

4. Evaluations of Mark's language as crude or simplistic prior to 1980 include Martin Dibelius, *From Tradition to Gospel*, trans. Bertram Lee Woolf (New York: Scribner, 1965), 3; trans. of *Die Formgeschichte des Evangeliums* (Tübingen: Mohr Siebeck, 1919); A. E. J. Rawlinson, *The Gospel according to St. Mark*, Westminster Commentaries (London:

unpolished.[5] Those who claim that Mark writes sophisticated Greek are few.[6] This is the heart of the paradox. On the one hand, the gospel is narratively effective, even artistic. On the other, its style is literarily unadorned. Mark is a compelling story written in unaccomplished Greek.[7]

There is a growing consensus that this incongruity results from Mark existing at the borderland between orality and textuality. The preface to the third edition of *Mark as Story* exemplifies this new development in Markan studies. There, Rhoads, Michie, and Joanna Dewey claim that the Second Gospel is an "oral/aural composition."[8] Yet there is little clarity about what it means for a narrative to be an "oral/aural composition." It is common for other nebulous terms such as "residual orality" and "oral literature" to be applied to Mark, as if merely evoking these categories settles the matter about the gospel's distinct style.

One of my objectives in this book is to bring precision to these terms. I agree with those who argue that Mark is an oral composition and that the gospel exhibits a preponderance of residual orality. But these terms will not be employed without

---

Metheun, 1942), xxxii; Morton Smith, "Comments on Taylor's Commentary on Mark," *HTR* 48 (1955): 38; D. E. Nineham, *St. Mark*, Pelican New Testament Commentaries (Philadelphia: Westminster, 1963), 215; Theodore J. Weeden, *Mark: Traditions in Conflict* (Philadelphia: Fortress, 1971), 140; John C. Meagher, *Clumsy Construction in Mark's Gospel: A Critique of Form- and Redaktionsgeschichte*, Toronto Studies in Theology 3 (Lewiston: Mellen, 1979).

5. Passing remarks about Mark's unpolished style can be found in Dean W. Chapman, *The Orphan Gospel: Mark's Perspective on Jesus*, The Biblical Seminar 16 (Sheffield: JSOT Press, 1993), 20; John Painter, *Mark's Gospel* (London: Routledge, 1997), 8; Joel Marcus, *Mark: A New Translation with Introduction and Commentary*, 2 vols., AB 27–27A (New York: Doubleday, 2008), 2:60; Ben Witherington III, *The Gospel of Mark: A Socio-Rhetorical Commentary* (Grand Rapids: Eerdmans, 2001), 19.

6. Lane and Mary Ann Beavis nearly make this contention. Both concede that Mark writes in a simple style, but they argue that this is a deliberate choice. Lane lauds the narrative's unadorned language as a product of "conscious literary or even theological intention" and concludes that the gospel was written "with consummate skill" (*Gospel of Mark*, 28). Beavis insists that Mark shows rhetorical sophistication and that the gospel's style, while second-rate, displays some elements of literary flourish that will have been appreciated by educated readers (*Mark's Audience: The Literary and Social Setting of Mark 4:11–12*, JSNTSup 33 [Sheffield: JSOT Press, 1989], 42–44).

7. To this end Craig A. Evans writes, "For all the evangelist's shortcomings in matters of literary style and polish, it must be admitted that his literary achievement is nonetheless remarkable and should be viewed as successful" ("How Mark Writes," in *The Written Gospel*, ed. Markus Bockmuehl and Donald A. Hagner [Cambridge: Cambridge University Press, 2005], 148).

8. Michie Rhoads and Joanna Dewey, preface to *Mark as Story: An Introduction to the Narrative of a Gospel*, 3rd ed. (Minneapolis: Fortress, 2012), xi–xii.

situating them within ancient media culture, which I will do in Chapter 2. It is one thing to claim that a narrative exhibits residual orality and to categorize it as oral literature. It is another to offer a reason why it exhibits residual orality. I will contend that Mark displays style and syntax characteristic of oral storytelling because it is an oral tradition that was committed to the written medium via dictation.

By proposing this explanation for the orality that abides in Mark's written form, I am intentionally distancing myself from the so-called Great Divide approach to orality and textuality. The Great Divide perspective considers orality and textuality to be two modalities of communication that are competing or mutually exclusive. It also tends to exaggerate the importance of orality in antiquity while minimizing the functions of textuality. By painting orality with such broad strokes, scholars adopting this outlook have not paid adequate attention to why a *written* text might exhibit features characteristic of oral discourse.

Werner H. Kelber is often charged with first generating this Great Divide approach in his seminal monograph *The Oral and the Written Gospel*.[9] Therein Kelber does not contend that the Gospel of Mark is oral literature itself, as many other Markan interpreters have argued since the publication of this book.[10] The

---

9. Werner H. Kelber, *The Oral and the Written Gospel: The Hermeneutics of Speaking and Writing in the Synoptic Tradition, Mark, Paul, and Q* (Bloomington: Indiana University Press, 1983). Kelber is often cited as the first biblical interpreter who utilized orality studies to interpret NT texts. This is not strictly accurate, as others had published less technical studies applying the oral-formulaic theory of Albert Lord and Milman Parry to biblical texts, such as Leander E. Keck ("Oral Traditional Literature and the Gospels: The Seminar," in *The Relationships Among the Gospels: An Interdisciplinary Dialogue*, ed. William O. Walker [San Antonio: Trinity University Press, 1978], 103–22). Kelber himself states that Johann Gottfried Herder was "the originator of the thesis of the oral gospel" (Kelber, *Gospel*, 77; Herder, "Vom Erlöser der Menschen: Nach unsern drei ersten Evangelien," in *Herders Sämmtliche Werke*, ed. Bernhard Suphan, vol. 19 [Berlin: Weidmann, 1880], 135–252). While Kelber might not have originated the theory about the "oral gospel" he does more influentially argue than anyone previously that "the Gospels were composed and received in a world dominated by oral communication" (Richard A. Horsley, introduction to *Performing the Gospel: Orality, Memory, and Mark*, ed. idem et al. [Minneapolis: Fortress, 2006], viii). While *The Oral and the Written Gospel* proved to be more influential, Kelber's article "Mark and Oral Tradition" (*Semeia* 16 [1979]: 7–55) had already explored the gospel's oral—or non-oral—tradition. Kelber notes that *The Oral and the Written Gospel* is very much an expansion of the hypothesis laid out in "Mark and Oral Tradition" (preface to *Gospel*, xvii).

10. The claim that Mark is oral literature is made, in one form or another, in Joanna Dewey, "Oral Methods of Structuring Narrative in Mark," *Int* 43 (1989): 32–44; Pieter J. J. Botha, "Mark's Story as Oral Traditional Literature: Rethinking the Transmission of Some Traditions about Jesus," *Hervormde Teologiese Studies* 47 (1991): 304–31; Joanna

opposite is the case. Kelber maintains that Mark did *not* extend an oral tradition but resisted many of its constituent aspects.¹¹ According to him, the first written gospel was an attempt to silence the pre-Synoptic tradition that was heavily influenced by orality.¹² In Kelber's treatment, Mark's exploitation of the written medium is an intentional break with the oral medium. But he affirms that oral forms and conventions "gained admittance into the written document."¹³ Oral features made their way into the written text because of the prominence of oral tradition.¹⁴ According to Kelber, these features include parataxis, formulaic phrases such as καὶ ἐγένετο and καὶ γίνεται ("and it happened"), the speed at which the narrative progresses, the ubiquity of the third-person plural, the dominance of active verbs, a high number of instances of the historical present, and the frequency of direct speech.¹⁵

In his final analysis, Kelber finds Mark's evocation of the oral gospel tradition hostile and destructive.¹⁶ Mark retains aspects of an antecedent oral tradition only to supersede it in written form. Mark's Gospel takes a polemical stance against the prophetic voice that promoted "the oral metaphysics of [Jesus's] presence."¹⁷ By writing a gospel that relegates Jesus's authority to the past rather than the prophetic present, the author of Mark harnesses the modality of writing to support an ideological agenda that silenced its oral predecessors. Mark intentionally creates a Great Divide between oral and textual traditions.¹⁸

Dewey, "The Gospel of Mark as Oral Hermeneutic," in *Jesus, the Voice, and the Text: Beyond The Oral and the Written Gospel*, ed. Tom Thatcher (Waco: Baylor University Press, 2008), 71–87; Richard A. Horsley, "Oral and Written Aspects of the Emergence of the Gospel of Mark as Scripture," *Oral Tradition* 25 (2010): 93–114; idem, "The Gospel of Mark in the Interface of Orality and Writing," in *The Interface of Orality and Writing: Speaking, Seeing, Writing in the Shaping of New Genres*, ed. Annette Weissenrieder and Robert B. Coote, WUNT 260 (Tübingen: Mohr Siebeck, 2010), 144–65.

11. Kelber, new introduction to *The Oral and the Written Gospel: The Hermeneutics of Speaking and Writing in the Synoptic Tradition, Mark, Paul, and Q* (Bloomington: Indiana University Press, 1997), xix.

12. Ibid., 17.

13. Ibid., 44.

14. Ibid.

15. Ibid., 65–66. As I shall show in Chapter 2, some of the features that Kelber identified as evidence of Mark's indebtedness to the oral lifeworld are substantiated as features of oral discourse by sociolinguists. Those working in this field had not yet reached substantive conclusions about the differences between oral and written narratives when Kelber first published *The Oral and the Written Gospel*.

16. Ibid., 94.

17. Ibid., 99.

18. Kelber has contested the allegation that his perspective in *The Oral and the Written Gospel* and subsequent publications falls prey to the much-maligned Great Divide approach

By arguing his case in this forceful and dichotomous form, Kelber exposes a deep-seated bias of modern biblical criticism. Exposing the chirographic-typographic hegemony in biblical scholarship remains Kelber's principal contribution to the field of NT interpretation, as it ushered in the current era of orality studies that considers seriously the oral lifeworld in which NT texts were produced and received.[19]

Discussions about this oral lifeworld have until recently tended to exclude the possibility that orally influenced discourses were also textually influenced, even when the object of inquiry itself is a written document. For example, Joanna Dewey writes, "the gospel [Mark] remains fundamentally on the oral side of the oral/written divide."[20]

Responding to this overemphasis on orality in the first-century context, Rafael Rodríguez attempts to deconstruct the binarial relationship that orality and textuality is often constructed in, arguing that NT scholarship needs a more complete understanding of both, particularly when it comes to their cultural and social functions.[21] For Rodríguez, the essentialization of both orality and textuality, and especially oral cultures and literate cultures, has led

---

to orality and textuality. In his updated introduction, Kelber writes, "I do not myself use the term *the Great Divide*, nor was it part of our vocabulary in the late seventies and early eighties when the book was written" (new introduction, xxi). He argues that his "strong" thesis was necessary to overcome the chirographic and typographic biases that reigned in biblical scholarship (ibid., xxi–xxii).

19. Kelber's contribution has been praised as "the single most important and influential work on oral tradition" (Terence C. Mournet, *Oral Tradition and Literary Dependency: Variability and Stability in the Synoptic Tradition and Q*, WUNT 195 [Tübingen: Mohr Siebeck, 2005], 86). Kelly R. Iverson similarly lauds this text, writing, "There is little doubt that when thinking about the history of orality studies in Gospels research, terms such as 'watershed' and 'turning point' are justifiably applied to *The Oral and the Written Gospel*" ("Orality and the Gospels: A Survey of Recent Research," *CurBR* 8 [2009]: 82). Finally, Rafael Rodríguez writes that "we exaggerate only slightly if we speak of a 'Kelber revolution' in NT scholarship" (*Oral Tradition and the New Testament: A Guide for the Perplexed* [London: Bloomsbury, 2014], 39).

20. Dewey, "Gospel of Mark," 86. It is worth noting that in 2013 Dewey softened her dichotomous argument and distanced herself from the Great Divide position ("The Gospel of John in Its Oral-Written Media World," in *The Oral Ethos of the Early Church: Speaking, Writing, and the Gospel of Mark*, ed. idem, Biblical Performance Criticism Series 8 [Eugene: Cascade, 2013], 31–49). Now she argues that the first-century environment was characterized by orality *and* textuality. She still affirms that orality undergirded all composition and performance, but also concedes that writing played a significant role in the gospel's media setting.

21. Rodríguez, "Reading and Hearing in Ancient Contexts," *JSNT* 32 (2009): 151–78, esp. 159.

NT scholars to misunderstand the complex relationship between the two.[22] As a remedy, he proposes that NT scholars exploring the effects of orality and textuality need to acknowledge that these modalities vary in different cultures. Understanding the roles of orality and textuality in any given context is the most significant task of the interpreter, according to Rodríguez.[23] This entails investigating texts along with the social, historical, and cultural worlds in which they were produced.

Rodríguez has called his a "contextual" approach to orality and textuality.[24] This perspective considers the mutual effect of textuality and orality to be central. Scholars promoting this contextual methodology maintain that neither orality nor textuality is a monolithic reality. The two modalities work differently in various social and cultural contexts. These interpreters want to avoid making summative claims about orality and textuality. Instead, they attempt to understand the communication systems of respective ancient contexts before investigating the implications of orality and textuality within those communicative environments. They also affirm that the two modalities are interrelated. It is from this contextual outlook that I argue that the residual orality present in the written text of Mark results from the gospel being an oral tradition, of which one instantiation was textualized via dictation.

That Mark is an oral tradition composed in this manner is evidenced by its beginning, its ending, and elements in between the two. The first words of the narrative designate it "orally proclaimed news" (εὐαγγέλιον).[25] In a novel way, this oral message now abides in written form. "Gospel" (εὐαγγέλιον) was originally a media term, but, under Mark's influence, it came to connote content about the life, death, and resurrection of Jesus the Nazarene in a variety of forms. I will argue in Chapter 5 that "gospel" (εὐαγγέλιον) in Mk 1:1, as a meta-generic category, indicates more about the narrative's medium than its genre. Furthermore, Mark's successors, Matthew and Luke, also signal their media affiliations at the beginnings of their narratives.

Just as Mark's relationship to the oral lifeworld is intimated in its opening words, so also is it revealed in its closing words. The gospel infamously ends on an anticlimactic note. Mark 16:8 disappointed readers as early as the second century, at which point tradents appended what they must have determined to be more satisfying endings. They were able to do so because Mark was considered an open tradition that could be expanded. In Chapters 2 and 4, I shall argue that there are certain media conditions under which a narrative is more likely to be augmented.

---

22. Rodríguez is concerned less with the essentialization of orality or textuality per se than with the essentialization of oral and literate cultures (ibid., 160).

23. Ibid., 172.

24. Rodríguez, *Oral Tradition and the New Testament*, 71–85.

25. In Chapter 5 I discuss the various meanings of the term εὐαγγέλιον and how its connotations changed from the first to second centuries CE.

Mark, as a textualized oral tradition, meets these conditions. We shall also see that the ending "for they were afraid" (ἐφοβοῦντο γάρ) is not so curious in view of media-critical considerations.

Between the gospel's beginning and end, its style hints at its medium and mode of composition. Anacolutha, for example, are frequent in Mark.[26] These occasions of ruptured syntax and their close counterparts, parenthetical insertions, bespeak oral composition. When visualized in writing they appear awkward or jarring, but when heard they serve as oral punctuation.[27] As Robert M. Fowler writes, "The spoken word readily forgives and perhaps even favors anacoluthon."[28] This is but one way that oral composition and aural reception shed light on a characteristic of Mark's grammar.

Many other linguistic features that make Mark stylistically distinct from the later gospels are the very features that are characteristic of spoken stories. This raises old questions about how Mark relates to vernacular Greek and the Koine of the papyri that were addressed by the likes of Adolf Deissmann and Albert Thumb at the turn of the twentieth century. These questions will be revisited in Chapters 2 and 3. In the latter, we shall also see that several Markan idiosyncrasies follow normal patterns of spoken narrative. For example, the word εὐθύς, which is typically, and I will argue often improperly, translated "immediately," makes better sense as a multifunctional discourse marker, which is a sequencing device common in oral narrative, than as an adverb that connotes immediacy. Other Markan particularities, such as the historical present, intercalations, parataxis, and repetition, likewise suggest that the gospel is an oral tradition composed via dictation.

Mark was not the only narrative composed this way in early Judaism and Christianity. A near contemporary of the gospel, the Hellenistic Jewish narrative *Joseph and Aseneth*, appears to have been written similarly. This text presents a quandary similar to that of the Second Gospel. It is also an effective story told in a

---

26. C. H. Turner lists Mk 1:1-4; 2:10-11, 15-16, 22, 26b; 3:22-30; 6:14-15; 7:2, 3-4, 18-19, 25-26a; 8:14-17; 9:36-42; 12:12a; 13:9-11; 14:36; 16:3-4, 7 as instances of parenthetical insertion in the gospel ("Marcan Usage: Notes, Critical and Exegetical on the Second Gospel," in *The Language and Style of the Gospel of Mark: An Edition of C. H. Turner's "Notes on Marcan Usage" Together with Other Comparable Studies*, ed. J. K. Elliott, NovTSup 71 [Leiden: Brill, 1993], 23–35). These are not as disruptive as the anacolutha, which Robert M. Fowler lists as Mk 1:2-3; 2:10-11, 22; 3:30; 7:2-5, 19; 11:31-32; 14:49 (*Let the Reader Understand: Reader-Response Criticism and the Gospel of Mark* [Harrisburg: Trinity Press International, 2001], 112 n. 52). Herbert Weir Smyth notes that anacoluthon can be either natural or a literary affectation (*Greek Grammar*, revised by Gordon M. Messing [Cambridge: Cambridge University Press, 1956], §3007).

27. Fowler, *Let the Reader Understand*, 113.

28. Ibid.

simple style.²⁹ Moreover, many of the linguistic characteristics exhibited in Mark are also present in *Joseph and Aseneth*.

As it happens, this pseudepigraphon has never been systematically compared with Mark.³⁰ Presumably this is because the two narratives are dissimilar on many counts. *Joseph and Aseneth* is a Jewish text.³¹ Mark is literature from the early Jesus

---

29. That *Joseph and Aseneth* is written in unadorned Greek is noted by Burchard ("New Translation," 185–86) and Patricia Ahearne-Kroll ("*Joseph and Aseneth*," in *Outside the Bible: Ancient Jewish Writings Related to Scripture*, ed. Louis H. Feldman, James L. Kugel, and Lawrence H. Schiffman, vol. 3 [Philadelphia: Jewish Publication Society, 2013], 2526). Neither of them suggests an underlying cause for the narrative's style.

30. However, Christoph Burchard has taken up the task of assessing how *Joseph and Aseneth* has been utilized for interpreting the NT. He details six different ways ("The Importance of *Joseph and Aseneth* for the Study of the New Testament: A General Survey and a Fresh Look at the Lord's Supper," NTS 33 [1987]: 102–34). First, *Joseph and Aseneth* has been referenced to interpret aspects of the Lord's Supper. Burchard observes that the first modern treatments of *Joseph and Aseneth* by NT scholars were concerned with the phrases ἄρτος εὐλογημένος ζωῆς, ποτήριον εὐλογημένον ἀθανασίας and χρῖσμα εὐλογημένον ἀφθαρσίας in *Jos. Asen.* 8:5 and their potential for interpreting the Last Supper. See George D. Kilpatrick in "The Last Supper," *ExpTim* 64 (1952): 4–8; Joachim Jeremias, "The Last Supper," *ExpTim* 64 (1952): 91–92. Second, *Joseph and Aseneth* provides another data point for interpretive problems of NT Greek. Burchard notes that Jeremias's reading of the ambiguous question τί γὰρ οἶδας εἰ in 1 Cor. 7:16 was "the first attempt to solve a problem of NT Greek by appealing to JosAs" ("The Importance of *Joseph and Aseneth* for the Study of the New Testament," 106); Jeremias, "Die missionarische Aufgabe in der Mischehe (1 Cor 7:16)," in *Neutestamentliche Studien für Rudolf Bultmann: Zu seinem siebzigsten Geburtstag am 20. August 1954*, ed. Walther Eltester, BZNW 21 [Berlin: Töpelmann, 1954], 255–60). Others would follow Jeremias's lead. See Christoph Burchard, "Ei nach einem Ausdruck des Wissens oder Nichtwissens Joh 9:25, Act 19:2, 1 Cor 1:16, 7:16," *ZNW* 52 (1961): 73–82; idem, "Fußnoten zum neutestamentlichen Griechisch," *ZNW* 61 (1970): 157–71; Edgar W. Smith, *Joseph and Aseneth and Early Christian Literature: A Contribution to the Corpus Hellenisticum Novi Testamenti* (PhD diss., Claremont Graduate School, 1975). Third, the pseudepigraphon informs treatments of conversion in early Judaism and Christianity. Fourth, the narrative helps elucidate NT eschatology. Fifth, it provides comparative material for NT ethics. And sixth, the grammar of the narrative has been the subject of short notes. After explicating these six ways *Joseph and Aseneth* has been referenced by NT scholars, Burchard then offers some "fresh suggestions" as to how *Joseph and Aseneth* can aid NT interpretation: He reads *Jos. Asen.* 8:5-7 in conversation with sacramental rites in the NT; determines that *Joseph and Aseneth* is of little help in uncovering the symbolic antecedents to the Lord's Supper; reads John 6 in view of the phrase "bread of life" (ἄρτος [εὐλογημένος] ζωῆς [σου]) in *Jos. Asen.* 8:5, 9; 15:5; 16:16; 19:5; 21:21; and intertextually interprets Paul's discussion of the Lord's Supper in 1 Corinthians 10–11 with reference to the narrative ("Importance," 102–28).

31. The consensus about the Jewish or Christian provenance of *Joseph and Aseneth* has swung back and forth in the history of scholarship. Questions of provenance began with the *editio princeps* of the narrative by Pierre Batiffol, wherein he argued that the story was a Christian text from the fifth century CE constructed from a haggadic tale from the preceding

movement. Generically, *Joseph and Aseneth* is a product of, or at least influenced by, ancient romance novels; Mark by the βίοι ("Lives").[32] *Joseph and Aseneth* has a feel-good, romantic ending: The hero and heroine live happily ever after in marital bliss. Mark's ending, in contrast, is stark. The protagonist, abandoned by his followers, is tortured and dies. He is raised, but his devotees fail to tell anyone

century ("Le Livre de La Prière d'Aseneth," in *Studia Patristica: Études d'ancienne Littérature Chrétienne*, vols. 1–2 [Paris: Leroux, 1889], 1:36–37). The influence of Batiffol's assessment is indicated by the fact that *Joseph and Aseneth* was not included in early twentieth-century collections of Jewish pseudepigrapha by Emil Kautzch and R. H. Charles (Kautzch, *Die Apokryphen und Pseudepigraphen des Altens Testaments*, 2 vols. [Tübingen: Mohr Siebeck, 1900]; Charles, *The Apocrypha and Pseudepigrapha of the Old Testament in English*, vols. 2 [Oxford: Clarendon, 1913]). Shortly thereafter the consensus shifted, and the narrative began to be considered a Jewish text from the Hellenistic period. This reversal was the result of Burchard's and Marc Philonenko's influences. Both scholars, working with the textual witnesses of the narrative to construct critical editions, contended that *Joseph and Aseneth* had Jewish origins (Burchard, *Untersuchungen zu Joseph und Aseneth: Überlieferung—Ortsbestimmung*, WUNT 8 [Tübingen: Mohr Siebeck, 1965], 99–100; Philonenko, *Joseph et Aséneth*, 100–9). And presently, while most still consider the narrative Jewish, there is a vocal minority that maintains Christian authorship, emboldened by Ross S. Kraemer's arguments against the necessity of early and Jewish authorship (*When Aseneth Met Joseph: A Late Antique Tale of the Biblical Patriarch and His Egyptian Wife, Reconsidered* [New York: Oxford University Press, 1998]). Christian authorship is argued by Michael Penn ("Identity Transformation and Authorial Identification in Joseph and Aseneth," *JSP* 13 [2002]: 178–83) and Rivka Nir (*Joseph and Aseneth: A Christian Book*, Hebrew Bible Monographs 42 [Sheffield: Sheffield Phoenix, 2012]). Recent works arguing for Jewish authorship include Angela Standhartinger, *Das Frauenbild im Judentum der hellenistischen Zeit: Ein Beitrag anhand von "Joseph und Aseneth,"* AGJU 26 (Leiden: Brill, 1995), 205–40; Gideon Bohak, *Joseph and Aseneth and the Jewish Temple in Heliopolis*, EJL 10 (Atlanta: Scholars Press, 1996), xiii; Erich S. Gruen, *Heritage and Hellenism: The Reinvention of Jewish Tradition* (Berkeley: University of California Press, 1998), 92–96; Patricia Ahearne-Kroll, "Joseph and Aseneth and Jewish Identity in Greco-Roman Egypt" (PhD diss., University of Chicago, 2005), 175; John J. Collins, "Joseph and Aseneth: Jewish or Christian?" *JSP* 14 (2005): 97–112; Angela Standhartinger, "Recent Scholarship on Joseph and Aseneth (1988–2013)," *CurBR* 12 (2014): 369–71. I concur with the majority that the narrative was originally of Jewish provenance and was later edited and transmitted by Christians.

32. *Joseph and Aseneth*'s relationship to the novels is addressed in Chapter 4. Mark's similarity to the βίοι is assessed in Johannes Weiss, *Das älteste Evangelium: Ein Beitrag zum Verständnis des Markus-Evangeliums und der ältesten evangelischen Überlieferung* (Göttingen: Vandenhoeck & Ruprecht, 1903), 11–14; Clyde Weber Votaw, "The Gospels and Contemporary Biographies," *American Journal of Theology* 19 (1915): 45–73, 217–49; reprinted as *The Gospels and Contemporary Biographies* (Philadelphia: Fortress, 1970); Charles H. Talbert, *What is a Gospel? The Genre of the Canonical Gospels* (Philadelphia: Fortress, 1977); Richard A. Burridge, *What are the Gospels? A Comparison with Graeco-Roman Biography*, SNTSMS 70 (Cambridge: Cambridge University Press, 1992); David E. Aune, "Genre Theory and the Genre-Function of Mark and Matthew," in *Mark and Matthew I*, ed. Eve-Marie Becker and Anders Runesson, WUNT 271 (Tübingen: Mohr Siebeck, 2011), 145–75.

about it.[33] *Joseph and Aseneth* unashamedly promotes Jewish monotheism over Egyptian idolatry. The gospel aims to convince its audience of Jesus's messianic identity and that the Jewish deity has inaugurated a new age through this agent. *Joseph and Aseneth* features a female main character, while Mark's is a male with a band of mostly male disciples. In short, Mark and *Joseph and Aseneth* differ as to theology, ideology, content, and, most importantly, genre.

Despite these differences, the two narratives exhibit remarkable similarities. Chief among these is the enigma of being compelling stories written in unsophisticated Greek. As I shall argue, *Joseph and Aseneth* and Mark are also comparable with respect to length, language, overall structure, how they evoke intertexts, and how they were textually reappropriated by later tradents. The central argument of this book is that these two nearly contemporaneous narratives are oral traditions that were committed to the written medium via dictation. Recent sociolinguistic research has shown that speaking and writing stories involve different psychological processes and result in different syntax. I draw on these studies to show that Mark and *Joseph and Aseneth* exhibit a style characteristic of oral storytelling.[34] I also engage media theory and studies of ancient media to show that these narratives share two metalinguistic features, further indicating that they are oral literature codified in writing. On the basis of this sociolinguistic research and media theory, I propose five criteria as a heuristic apparatus for comparing *Joseph and Aseneth* and Mark *ex hypothesi*. These criteria aid in determining the density of the narratives' residual oralities and assessing the ways in which Mark and *Joseph and Aseneth* bear the marks of both orality and textuality.

Moving toward these criteria, there is something I wish to be clear about from the outset: claiming that these narratives exhibit residual orality as a result of their composition by dictation is *not* to imply that they are divorced from textuality. *Mark and Joseph and Aseneth are written texts.* As written documents that were composed via dictation, they represent one way that orality and textuality function in tandem in the Greco-Roman world. They exist at the borderland between these two modalities. Recognizing that this is the case better equips the interpreter when it comes to understanding why features characteristic of orality show up in these texts, how Mark and *Joseph and Aseneth* are related despite their dissimilitude in genre, and the ways that each narrative's medium and mode of composition matters for its interpretation.

---

33. This assumes that the shorter and longer endings of Mark are secondary, which remains the scholarly consensus and will be addressed in Chapter 4.

34. It is in this sense that I use the phrase "residual orality." By residual orality I do *not* mean modes of thought and expression exclusive to primary oral cultures. This is one way that Walter J. Ong first employed the phrase (*Rhetoric, Romance, and Technology: Studies in the Interaction of Expression and Culture* [Ithaca: Cornell University Press, 1971], 25–26; idem, *Orality and Literacy: The Technologizing of the Word* [London: Routledge, 1982], 31–76). Lack of clarity on the part of interpreters has led to confusion about the semantic range of residual orality in orality studies and biblical performance criticism.

Chapter 2

MEDIA THEORY, ANCIENT MEDIA, AND ORALLY COMPOSED NARRATIVES FROM THE PAPYRI

Mixed-media theory

A mixed-media approach that is attuned to the cooperative nature of orality and textuality in the ancient Mediterranean world is more constructive than the Great Divide perspective that has permeated much biblical scholarship concerned with orality and performance. In this chapter, I outline this mixed-media perspective, propose five criteria for evaluating the degree to which Koine Greek narratives display elements characteristic of orality and textuality, address how, why, and by whom texts were composed via dictation in Greco-Roman antiquity, assess the utility of the five proposed criteria by reading narratives from the papyri that were almost assuredly composed via dictation with the criteria, and propose a media category from Greco-Roman antiquity that *Joseph and Aseneth* and Mark are closest to, namely, ὑπομνήματα, which I will be translating as "oral memoirs."

By adopting a mixed-media approach, I take as axiomatic Ruth H. Finnegan's claim that most cultures possess and employ various forms of media.[1] Both orality and textuality played their roles in the ancient Mediterranean environment. Additionally, these modalities overlap and work in concert.[2] A given discourse can begin life as an oral narrative and be transcribed into a written medium. In contrast, a written narrative can be read orally. John Lyons calls this phenomenon "media transferability."[3] The boundaries between media are permeable from this complex media-transfer perspective.[4]

---

1. Ruth H. Finnegan, *Literacy and Orality: Studies in the Technology of Communication* (Oxford: Blackwell, 1988), esp. 141.

2. Ibid., 143.

3. John Lyons, *Language and Linguistics: An Introduction* (Cambridge: Cambridge University Press, 1981), 11.

4. Werner H. Kelber argues that prior media heritages shape new media contexts and that clear-cut distinctions between oral and literary modalities of communication are illusory ("Modalities of Communication, Cognition, and Physiology of Perception: Orality, Rhetoric, and Scribality," *Semeia* 65 [1994]: 193–216, esp. 194).

While media have permeable boundaries and discourses are often transferred into new forms, features of a tradition's media history imprint themselves upon a given narrative. These are particularly observable when a narrative undergoes media transformation. When oral literature is transferred to a written medium, oral psychodynamics are often detectable in the written medium. Werner H. Kelber describes such discourses as "intermedial."[5] Such narratives possess several characteristic features that, as we shall see, are present in both Mark and *Joseph and Aseneth*.[6] Conversely, a literarily conceived discourse can be read aloud without being edited for oral recitation, and the psychodynamics of writing are readily recognizable in the written discourse's oral reading. But when a discourse moves further away from its original conception and media form, the traces of that medium become increasingly faint.

Egbert J. Bakker offers an apparatus for analyzing the oral and literate conceptions of discourses.[7] According to him, those investigating the intersection of oral and written traditions ought to distinguish between the conception and the medium of a discourse.[8] Certain qualities are normally associated either with speaking or with writing because the two modalities require different hermeneutic activities.[9] Bakker places the conception of a discourse and the conception of that discourse's writing, its medium, on parallel continua:[10]

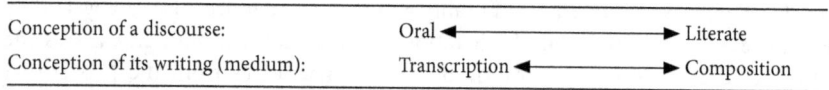

Conception of a discourse:	Oral ◄─────►	Literate
Conception of its writing (medium):	Transcription ◄─────►	Composition

Both writing and orality, in Bakker's view, are variegated activities. There is not one purpose or operation of orality, nor is there just one of writing. Both have diverse roles that overlap. Any given discourse can exhibit features that are more oral or

---

5. Werner H. Kelber, "The Comparative Study of Oral Tradition," in *Dictionary of the Bible and Ancient Media*, ed. Tom Thatcher, Chris Keith, Raymond E. Person Jr., and Elsie R. Stern (New York: Bloomsbury T&T Clark), 253.

6. These are "rhymically shaped diction, repetitive techniques, parallelisms, audience cues, typical scenes, stock phrases, epithets, and countless other features that were fashioned in response to performative imperatives and memorial needs" (ibid., 253).

7. Egbert J. Bakker, "How Oral Is Oral Composition?" in *Signs of Orality: The Oral Tradition and Its Influence in the Greek and Roman World*, ed. Anne E. Mackay (Leiden: Brill, 1999), 29–47.

8. Ibid., 30. Many sociolinguists differentiate between the conception and medium of a discourse, though often using different terminology. Wulf Oesterreicher lists several of these scholars and their preferred terminologies ("Types of Orality in Text," in *Written Voices, Spoken Signs: Tradition, Performance, and the Epic Text*, ed. Egbert J. Bakker and Ahuvia Kahane [Cambridge: Harvard University Press, 1997], 257 n. 2).

9. Bakker, "How Oral?" 30.

10. Reproduced with slight alteration from ibid., 31.

more literary. One of the advantages of this model is that it appreciates both the complex relationship between orality and writing and the detectable differences between the two modalities. By conceiving of narratives on a sliding scale of oral to literate, the interpreter is not forced into making totalizing claims about textual traditions, nor must he or she see orality and textuality as mutually exclusive or competing categories. Rather, narratives exist on this sliding scale, some exhibiting more oral, and some exhibiting more literary, psychodynamics.

But Bakker's model remains imprecise in some respects. It supplies little information about the different functions of orality and textuality and does not indicate the ways that they work in tandem. The methodological work of John Miles Foley and Paul Zumthor can help fill this theoretical gap.[11] Zumthor provides a more precise description of oral tradition. He first outlines five phases of a discourse: (1) Production; (2) Transmission; (3) Reception; (4) Storage; and (5) Repetition.[12] An oral tradition is any discourse wherein operations one, four, and five are carried out in the oral mode.[13] That is, if a discourse begins life orally, is stored mnemonically by tradents, and then is reactivated by subsequent tellings, it is categorized as an oral tradition. It is in Zumthor's sense that I consider Mark and *Joseph and Aseneth* to have antecedent oral traditions.[14] Before they were committed to writing, both were produced, stored, and repeated orally.

Whereas Zumthor helps determine what constitutes oral tradition, Foley's theoretical notions of how orality and textuality inform one another provides categories in which the different relationships between these modalities might be placed. For him, verbal art falls into four types: oral performance, voiced texts, voices from the past, and written oral poems.[15] Where a discourse falls within

---

11. John Miles Foley, *The Singer of Tales in Performance* (Bloomington: Indiana University Press, 1995), 60–98; idem, *How to Read an Oral Poem* (Urbana: University of Illinois Press, 2002), 38–53; idem, "Plentitude and Diversity: Interactions between Orality and Writing," in Weissenrieder and Coote, *Interface*, 103–18; Paul Zumthor, *Oral Poetry: An Introduction*, trans. Kathy Murphy-Judy, Theory and History of Literature 70 (Minneapolis: University of Minnesota Press, 1990), 3–56.

12. Zumthor, *Oral Poetry*, 22.

13. Ibid., 23.

14. There is no incontrovertible evidence that *Joseph and Aseneth* had an oral existence before the narrative was transferred to the written medium. But Bakker's theory of the conceptions and media of discourses make the possibility more likely than not. Furthermore, the narrative exhibits several folkloristic themes, and some of its interpretive difficulties are resolved if it first existed as an oral tradition. This is especially the case with Aseneth's name change in 15:6, as I have argued elsewhere (Elder, "On Transcription," 140–41).

15. Foley, *How to Read*, 38–52; idem, "Plentitude and Diversity," 107–9.

these types depends on how it is composed, performed, and received. Foley and Rodríguez visualize the categories in a table:[16]

	Composition	Performance	Reception
Oral Performance:	Oral	Oral	Aural
Voiced Texts:	Written	Oral	Aural
Voices from the Past:	Oral/written	Oral/written	Aural/written
Written Oral Poems:	Written	Written	Written

Voices from the Past is the type germane to the gospels and *Joseph and Aseneth*. In this category, the discourse is derived from oral tradition. It can be composed orally via dictation or by way of writing as a literate composition. Similarly, the oral tradition can be performed and received orally or textually. Voices from the Past is a broad category into which any discourse that derives from an oral tradition might fall.[17] I hold that we can be more precise about Mark's and *Joseph and Aseneth*'s place in this particular category. They are oral traditions, specifically oral narratives, that were produced, stored, and transmitted orally. Eventually, they were committed to the written medium. This was initially done via dictation, likely in an effort to maintain continuity with their past medium and because their tradents were not scribally literate. After being transferred to a new medium, they could be, and were, altered textually. Thus Mark and *Joseph and Aseneth* fall within Foley's Voices from the Past category, but they are of a similar, more specific type in this group. In long form, I'd call this type an *orally textualized oral-narrative tradition*. This mouthful expresses (1) that the oral tradition was committed to a textual medium; (2) how it was committed to its new medium, namely, orally; and (3) that the tradition is narrative in form. Henceforth I will refer to this category in short form as *textualized oral narrative*.

This type contrasts with oral traditions that were committed to the written medium in a more literary mode. Matthew, Luke, and some later recensions of *Joseph and Aseneth*, while still to be categorized as Voices from the Past insofar as they are derived from antecedent oral traditions and might have been orally performed and aurally received, were not orally composed. This being the case, they are not in the same subcategory as their predecessors as to their medium. Transposing Foley's categories onto Bakker's continuum, oral performance is on the left end and written oral poems on the right, as such:

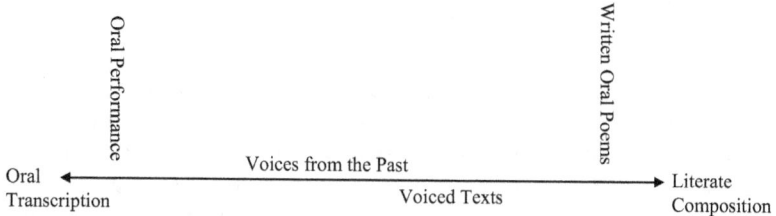

16. Rodríguez, *Oral Tradition*, 81; Foley, "Plentitude and Diversity," 108.

17. Foley indicates that "parts of the Hebrew Bible and the New Testament" should be placed in this category, though he doesn't indicate which parts (*How to Read*, 46).

I categorize Mark and the early recensions of *Joseph and Aseneth* as Voices from the Past, as I do Matthew, Luke, and the *a*-text family of *Joseph and Aseneth*. The latter three are further to the right on the continuum than the former.

But are we to think of Matthew and Luke as wholly separate traditions from Mark? Are they altogether different "books" than their predecessor? Recently Matthew D. C. Larsen has answered both of these questions in the negative, suggesting that early readers of the Synoptics will not have considered what we now know as the Gospel according to Matthew and the Gospel according to Mark as two different texts authored by two different persons.[18] Instead, "they would have regarded them as the same open-ended, unfinished, and living work: the gospel—textualized."[19] On the basis of ancient media practices and early testimony about the production of the gospels, Larsen compellingly argues that we ought not to treat the Gospel of Mark as a closed tradition and a finished "book."[20] Rather, Mark is "an unfinished collection of notes," that Matthew and Luke "finish," or as I prefer, "literaturize."[21]

If Larsen is correct, then we ought to relabel our plotted points on the oral-literal continuum. The Markan gospel tradition, as carried forward and "finished" or "literaturized" by Matthew and Luke, itself now exists further to the right on the continuum. Though, in my estimation, this does imply that we *move* and replot Mark on the right of this continuum. Rather, new instantiations of the Markan tradition are established:

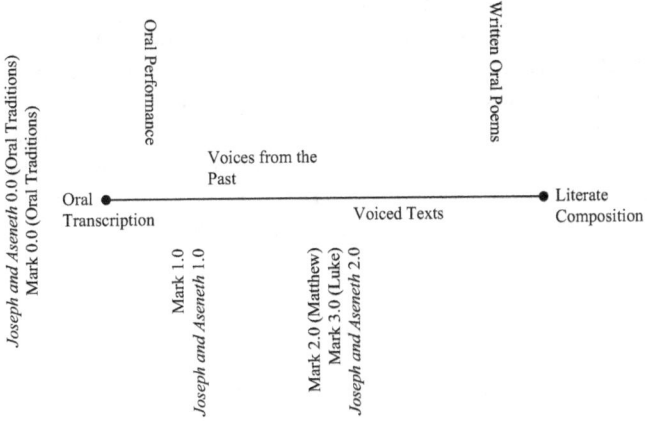

18. Larsen, *Gospels Before the Book* (Oxford: Oxford University Press, 2018), esp. 79–120. I agree with Larsen's claim that Matthew and Luke are part of the same fountaining *tradition* as Mark, though I part ways with him when it comes to not regarding Matthew and Luke as separate books or texts than the Gospel of Mark. Matthew and Luke are different kinds of texts than Mark and were produced and received in different ways than their predecessor.

19. Ibid., 4.

20. Ibid., 100.

21. Ibid., 106. "Literaturize" is a verbal form derived from David E. Aune's claim that Matthew and Luke are a "literaturization" of the Markan Jesus tradition (*The New Testament in Its Literary Environment*, LEC [Philadelphia: Westminster, 1987], 65–66). That is, Matthew and Luke improve Mark's oral style and more firmly establish their accounts as part of the βίοι ("biographies") genre.

Thus far, this continuum and the points on it have only represented the textual instantiations of Mark. If the gospel tradition, or at least portions of it, existed in oral form(s) before being composed as a continuous written narrative, a claim that has a long history in *formgeschichte*, then any other number of instantiations of the tradition might be plotted to the left of the entire continuum, as I have done immediately above for both Mark and *Joseph and Aseneth*.

When it comes to *Joseph and Aseneth*, similar media dynamics to Mark are at work. However, with the pseudepigraphon, later instantiations of the narrative are unquestionably a part of the same open tradition. There is no debate that, however different certain versions of the story might be, various texts of *Joseph and Aseneth* represent the same "book." In Chapter 5 we will look to the ways that *Joseph and Aseneth* is edited and find that later instantiations of the tradition, above labeled "*Joseph and Aseneth* 2.0," literaturize their predecessors in ways similar to Matthew and Luke's literaturization of Mark.

As yet there is no serviceable apparatus for hypothesizing whether or not a Koine Greek narrative was composed via dictation, appraising how it exhibits residual orality, and determining on which side of this continuum it leans. Given this absence, in what follows I will marshal sociolinguistic research concerned with the differences between writing and speaking a narrative to establish three linguistic criteria by which these assessments can be made with greater acuity. Sociolinguists acknowledge that speaking and writing entail different psychological processes that respond to variegated social, linguistic, and cultural situations. For this reason, there are features *characteristic* of oral and literary registers. Since the invention of the tape recorder, sociolinguists have been able to observe the unique features of oral narratives and compare these to the features of written narratives.[22] I have distilled these differences into three categories and created three criteria from them: (1) parataxis, apposition, and the idea unit; (2) repetition of syntactical patterns, words, phrases, and ideas; and (3) verb employment.

Features of oral and literary registers

Criterion #1: Parataxis, apposition, and the idea unit

Parataxis with the coordinating conjunction καί, particularly in Mark's Gospel, has been noted as a feature of the Greek vernacular by several biblical

---

22. The classic study that uses the tape recorder is Wallace L. Chafe's edited volume *The Pear Stories: Cognitive, Cultural, and Linguistic Aspects of Narrative Production* (ed. idem, Advances in Discourse Processes 3 [Norwood: Ablex], 1980). It is a collection of essays by sociolinguists who observe the differences between oral narrative and written narrative. First, individuals were shown a short film with no dialogue and were tape-recorded orally retelling the narrative depicted in the film. They were then asked to write the narrative. The articles in the collection compare the differences and similarities between these oral retellings and the written retellings in a variety of languages.

scholars.[23] Nonetheless, most of these interpreters do not hypothesize *why* parataxis is a feature of the vernacular. Sociolinguistic research suggests that this is a common feature of oral storytelling in most languages, demarcating what is called, among other designations, the idea unit.[24]

It is because of the idea unit that spoken discourse, especially when transferred and examined in a written medium, appears to advance in short, additive bursts. Bakker writes that an idea unit "is usually four to seven words long; it can be a complete syntactic unit, such as a clause, but it can also be something that needs to be complemented to make sense syntactically; and in spoken language it is marked by intentional boundaries, and often by pauses."[25] Short idea units make oral discourse easier for the speaker to produce and the hearer to process. Rather than exerting mental energy attempting to comprehend how clauses and entire segments of a discourse are related, the hearer focuses on the single ideas contained within each unit. They often determine the units' relationship to one another by means other than grammar, such as prosody and chronological sequencing. This does not imply that there are no logical relationships between events or idea units,

---

23. Ernest Best, "Mark's Narrative Technique," *JSNT* 37 (1989): 49; Antoinette Clark Wire, *The Case for Mark Composed in Performance*, Biblical Performance Criticism Series 3 (Eugene: Cascade, 2011), 80–84; Dewey, "Oral Methods," 37–38; Mournet, *Oral Tradition*, 177 n. 83; James D. G. Dunn, "Altering the Default Setting: Re-Envisaging the Early Transmission of the Jesus Tradition," in *The Oral Gospel Tradition*, ed. idem (Grand Rapids: Eerdmans, 2013), 70; Richard A. Horsley, *Jesus in Context: Power, People, and Performance* (Minneapolis: Fortress, 2008), 103–4; Fowler, *Let the Reader Understand*, 113.

24. Chafe addresses the idea unit at length (*Discourse, Consciousness, and Time: The Flow and Displacement of Conscious Experience in Speaking and Writing* [Chicago: University of Chicago Press, 1994], 53–70; idem, "Linguistic Differences Produced by Differences between Speaking and Writing," in *Literacy, Language, and Learning: The Nature and Consequences of Reading and Writing*, ed. David R. Olson, Nancy Torrance, and Angela Hildyard [Cambridge: Cambridge University Press, 1985], 106–11). Ong uses the nomenclature "adding structure" to refer to idea units in oral narrative (*Rhetoric*, 38–39).

25. Bakker, "How Oral?" 39. Chafe similarly observes that "a prototypical idea unit has the following properties: (1) It is spoken with a single coherent intonation contour, ending in what is perceived as a clause-final intonation; (2) it is preceded and followed by some kind of hesitation, ranging from a momentary break in timing to a filled or unfilled pause lasting several seconds; (3) it is a clause — that is, it contains one verb and phrase along with whatever noun phrases, prepositional phrases, adverbs, and so on are appropriate; and (4) it is about seven words long and takes about two seconds to produce. Idea units do not always conform to this prototype, but on the whole they are clearly identifiable elements of spoken language, and deviations from the prototype are usually explainable in interesting ways" ("Linguistic Differences," 106).

but that these relationships are signaled by means other than syntax.[26] Hearers and speakers work out the relationship between events that are paratactically structured through the tools provided by physical copresence. The coordinating conjunction, in spoken discourse, possesses a wider range of meaning than simple coordination.[27] The result is that *and* occurs far more frequently in oral narrative than in written. Karen Beaman finds that it appears about twice as often in the former than in the latter.[28] Similarly, Zumthor notes that parataxis is a defining characteristic of all oral genres.[29]

In contrast to the paratactic structuring found in residually oral narratives, literarily conceived narratives possess more complex syntactical relationships between clauses, sentences, and paragraphs.[30] These types of narrative still employ idea units, but the units are longer and are related to one another in more complex syntactical relationships. This is because writers are able to spend more time mentally and physically crafting their sentences into longer and more intricate units.[31] As a result, complex sentences are the norm in most forms of written narrative.[32]

Writers use a variety of tools to create more complex sentences that can better communicate the nuance of their thought and fill in the existential void between writer and reader. Participial phrases, prepositional phrases, relative clauses, adverbs, indirect questions, attributive adjectives, constituents joined in pairs, and complement clauses are but a few of these devices.[33] An abundance of these features in a discourse is evidence that it has been well planned syntactically and was conceived for a written medium. The absence of them is an oral residue.

---

26. Suzanne Fleischman notes that the relationships between clauses in oral literature are non-explicit (*Tense and Narrativity: From Medieval Performance to Modern Fiction* [Austin: University of Texas Press, 1990], 186).

27. Karen Beaman, "Coordination and Subordination Revisited: Syntactic Complexity in Spoken and Written Narrative," in *Coherence in Spoken and Written Discourse*, ed. Deborah Tannen, Advances in Discourse Processes 12 (Norwood: Ablex, 1984), 60–61.

28. Ibid., 61.

29. Zumthor, *Oral Poetry*, 107.

30. According to Ong, written discourse is more complex because it must fill in the existential void left when a reader is not in physical proximity to the author (*Orality and Literacy*, 38).

31. On this Deborah Tannen writes, "The use of complex constructions, relative clauses, and formal cohesive devices reflects what has been called the literate strategy of establishing cohesion by lexicalization" ("Oral and Literate Strategies in Spoken and Written Narratives," *Language* 58 [1982]: 7).

32. Wallace Chafe and Jane Danielwicz, "Properties of Spoken and Written Language," in *Comprehending Oral and Written Language*, ed. Rosalind Horowitz and S. Jay Samuels (San Diego: Academic Press, 1987), 104.

33. Chafe provides a full list with discussion of each ("Linguistic Differences," 108–10).

In Koine Greek, the idea unit and parataxis are produced by the simple coordinating conjunction καί. They can also be created by apposition. Because paratactic structuring is easily noticed, it will be the first criterion applied to *Joseph and Aseneth* and Mark. My research suggests that Mark and *Joseph and Aseneth*'s paratactic structures are initial indicators that the narratives will contain other residually oral qualities. When paratactic structuring and a shorter average length of clauses is prominent in a narrative, other features that are characteristic of oral storytelling, such as repetition, are to be expected. As we shall see, this is precisely the case with these two narratives.

Criterion #2: Repetition of syntactical patterns, words, phrases, and ideas

Oral narrative is more repetitive than written narrative.[34] This is because, in comparison with spoken narrative, written narrative is produced more slowly and is editable.[35] While repetition can work rhetorically in literature, oral narrative is more repetitive than written narrative on three different levels: individual lexemes, syntactical structure, and entire episodes and concepts. Repetition in literarily conceived texts is usually on the grammatical level, rather than on all three.

There are two reasons for the redundancy of words and phrases that is inherent to oral storytelling: (1) clarity of expression and (2) rapidity of production. Regarding the first, Walter Ong argues that redundancy in oral discourse is a result of an audience's inability to back loop the "evanescent" spoken word.[36] Speakers are naturally more redundant than writers in order to articulate clearly their message to their audience. Redundancy is also a result of the speed at which oral discourse is produced in comparison with written discourse. This allows planned, written discourse to possess a richness of vocabulary that is rare in oral discourse.[37] While colloquial language often exhibits a narrow range of vocabulary, speakers compensate for this fact by "assigning a premium to freshness."[38] For this reason, colloquial registers often employ words that are less common or even considered ungrammatical in written discourse.

---

34. Zumthor suggests that repetition is the "universally definitive feature" of oral literature (*Oral Poetry*, 111).

35. According to Chafe, handwriting takes at least ten times longer than speaking does ("Integration and Involvement in Speaking, Writing, and Oral Literature," in *Spoken and Written Language: Exploring Orality and Literacy*, ed. Deborah Tannen, Advances in Discourse Processes 9 [Norwood: Ablex, 1982], 36–38). On the effect of written narrative's editability see Ong, *Orality and Literacy*, 103.

36. Ong, *Orality and Literacy*, 40. See also Zumthor, *Oral Poetry*, 29; Werner H. Kelber, "Jesus and Tradition: Words in Time, Words in Space," in idem, *Imprints, Voiceprints, and Footprints of Memory: Collected Essays of Werner Kelber* (Atlanta: Society of Biblical Literature, 2013; orig., 1994), 117.

37. Chafe and Danielwicz, "Properties," 91.

38. Ibid., 92.

The second area in which oral narrative is more redundant than written narrative is syntactic structure. Once again, this is a result of the rapidity of production characteristic of spoken discourse.[39] The repetition of syntactic constructions can also have a rhetorical effect, since repetition allows the hearer to track with the speaker and to immerse himself or herself in the narrative. Repetition creates "a mesmerizing rhythm which sweeps the hearer along."[40] To literate sensibilities, repeating the same sentence structure can seem rhetorically ineffective and makes for unaccomplished writing. Yet, from an oral perspective a repetitive structure is an effective tool for communication.

Finally, oral narrative is more prone to repeat entire episodes or concepts. Ong argues that this is because of the redundancy inherent to thought.[41] The technology of writing obviates this redundancy by creating a physical text that can be critically scrutinized by its author and reader. By restating entire episodes, or the point of an episode in different words, speakers communicate their message more effectively with the *copia*, or fullness, that is natural to oral narrative.

When the criterion of repetition is applied to *Joseph and Aseneth* and Mark, we shall find that they are repetitive in word choice, syntactical constructions, and the concepts they are conveying. Further, we will see that they contain words that are found less frequently in literarily conceived discourse. In contrast, literarily conceived discourse is not as repetitive in vocabulary or syntactical constructions. Sentences may follow some consistent patterns as a result of a given author's literary style, but there is a wider variety of syntactical configurations than in narrative that is orally conceived. We will also find that literarily conceived narratives possess a greater range of literary forms and genres. While orally conceived narratives primarily have direct narration of events and direct discourse, literarily conceived narrative supplements the narration of events with other forms.

Criterion #3: Verb employment

In some ways, oral narratives are more complex than written narratives with respect to their employment of verbs. In other ways, oral narratives show simplicity in verbal tense, voice, and mood. On the one hand, oral narrative often switches between tenses in a manner that appears ungrammatical to literate sensibilities, exhibiting a more complex, even sophisticated, use of verbal tense. On the other hand, oral narrative does not usually make full use of the variety of tenses, voices, and moods that are available in any language in the same way that literarily conceived narratives do.

---

39. Tannen, "Oral and Literate Strategies," 7. See also Elinor Ochs, "Planned and Unplanned Discourse," in *Discourse and Syntax*, ed. Talmy Givón, Syntax and Semantics 12 (New York: Academic Press, 1979), 70–72.

40. Tannen, "Oral and Literate Strategies," 7.

41. Ong, *Orality and Literacy*, 40.

Sociolinguists have found that oral narrative often begins in the past tense but will move into the present as the narrative progresses.[42] This makes the event a speaker is narrating more immediate to his or her audience. Concerning this immediacy, Wallace Chafe distinguishes between the represented event and the representing consciousness.[43] In oral narrative, the present tense "present[s] the event or state [of the represented consciousness] as if its time coincided with that of the representing consciousness."[44] The historical present and the imperfective aspect are common in oral narrative and provide a direct connection between the speaker's consciousness and the hearer's consciousness, presenting the event as immediate.

It is not the present tense alone that accomplishes this immediacy. The effect is also created by direct speech.[45] The past progressive tense, often in conjunction with the present tense, does the same.[46] The result is that oral narrative exhibits an even distribution of the simple past tense, the past progressive, and the present tense. In Koine Greek, this is the aorist tense, the imperfect tense, and the present tense, respectively.

In contrast to the even distribution of these three tenses in oral narrative, literarily conceived narrative generally possesses past tense verbs and the other tenses supplement these for artistic effect. Supplemental tenses do not function to represent the producer's consciousness in an immediate mode because written discourse does not instinctively transport the represented event into the

---

42. Ochs, "Planned and Unplanned Discourse," 70. See also Judith Walcutt, "The Topology of Narrative Boundedness," in *Discourse Across Time and Space*, ed. Elinor Ochs Keenan and Tina Bennett, Southern California Occasional Papers in Linguistics 5 (Los Angeles: University of Southern California Press, 1977), 51–68.

43. Chafe, *Discourse*, 198.

44. Ibid., 208.

45. For this reason, the historical present and direct discourse often co-occur. Deborah Schiffrin writes, "A verb of saying (along with a reference to the original speaker) usually precedes quoted material. Using the present tense with that verb is another way in which the narrative framework replaces the situation of speaking to make the reported material more immediate. Thus, we would expect the [historical present] to be more frequent in our data with direct than indirect quotes..." ("Tense Variation in Narrative," *Language* 57 [1981]: 58). In his research, Chafe finds that direct speech occurs about three times more frequently in oral than in written discourse ("Integration and Involvement," 48; idem, *Discourse*, 210). The most common historical present verb in Koine Greek narratives is λέγω ("to say") employed in conjunction with direct speech. In Chapter 3 we shall see how this historical present tense verb functions in Mark and *Joseph and Aseneth*.

46. Schiffrin observes that there are functional reasons that the historical present and the past progressive mutually support one another in oral narrative ("Tense Variation," 59), as does William Labov ("The Transformation of Experience in Narrative Syntax," in *Language in the Inner City: Studies in the Black English Vernacular* [Philadelphia: University of Pennsylvania Press, 1972], 387–88).

representing consciousness, as spoken narrative does. Rather, "when writing removes copresence and interaction [between producer and receiver], the hold [of the representing consciousness] is weakened and the represented consciousness is free to migrate to a different time and place."[47] This different time and place is the past and the written document, respectively. Migrating the represented consciousness to the past better facilitates artistic and complex employment of the verbal tenses and moods. In writing, narrative events can be represented by their temporal or aspectual relationship to one another. For this reason, the past tense is predominantly employed, and a full range of other tenses and moods accompany it for artistic effect. In Koine Greek, this translates into a heavy dose of the aorist tense, accompanied by less frequent employment of the imperfect, present, future, perfect, and pluperfect tenses. The full range of the Koine verbal tense system will be found in narratives that are literarily conceived more often than in narratives that are orally conceived. The other verbal moods, especially subjunctives, infinitives, and participles, occur more frequently in literarily conceived narrative, as these also accomplish the complex syntax that is inherent in written narrative but not in oral.[48]

Finally, writers make recourse to the passive voice more frequently than speakers do. Chafe found that passive verbs occur about five times more often in writing than in speaking.[49] This higher frequency is the result of two phenomena. First, speakers are often more involved in their narrative than writers are, bringing the represented consciousness in line with the representing consciousness. Active verbs facilitate this better than passives do. Second, writers present events and clauses in complex relationships to one another, because both writers and readers lack temporal constraints for producing and experiencing a discourse. A full engagement with the options available for verbal voice attests to this complexity. In Koine Greek, narratives literarily conceived are more likely to exhibit the passive voice than narratives orally conceived. Be that as it may, because narrative in general naturally commends the active voice, the rise in the passive in literarily conceived discourse is usually not as pronounced as the differences between oral and written narrative in verbal tense and mood.[50]

In short, we will see a movement between the aorist, imperfect, and present tense in Koine Greek narratives orally conceived. This is a movement between represented and representing consciousness. Authors of orally conceived narratives do not avail themselves to the full tense, voice, and mood systems as authors

---

47. Chafe, *Discourse*, 227. Chafe calls this phenomenon "displaced immediacy."

48. Chafe finds that participles are used four times more often in written discourse than in spoken discourse ("Integration and Involvement," 40–41).

49. Ibid., 45. Tina Bennett's findings ("An Extended View of Verb Voice in Written and Spoken Personal Narratives," in Ochs and Kennan, *Discourse Across Time and Space*, 43–49), as well as Ochs's ("Planned and Unplanned Discourse," 69–70), are similar to Chafe's.

50. Ochs, "Planned and Unplanned Discourse," 69.

of literarily conceived discourse do. The latter are more likely to employ aorist tense verbs primarily, supplementing them with the imperfect, present, future, and perfect tenses to create a more distal and syntactically complex represented consciousness. This entails engagement with a wider range of the different verbal voices and moods available to the writer.

These first three criteria have been concerned with the differing language and style of oral and written narratives. But there are also differences between these two modalities at the metalinguistic level. The last two criteria are concerned with how narratives that are composed via dictation from an antecedent oral tradition relate to that tradition and how they recall other texts and traditions.

Criterion #4: Multiform tradition

Oral literature is equiprimordial.[51] Every instance of a narrative, whether spoken or written, is equally original. Past tellings of a tale may shape future instantiations, but each representative of the tradition is itself of interest. Equiprimordial traditions are "characterized by similar and different meanings," and each declamation is a "freshly autonomous event."[52] Here, orality theory dovetails with social memory theory. Memory theorists profess that tradition is nothing less than a memorial process reactivated in and reshaped by new contexts.[53] Both the historical past and present exigencies exert influence on the tradition that is reproduced and received in a new setting.[54] From this perspective, texts and traditions do not necessarily develop linearly.[55] It is not as though their original provenance or

---

51. Equiprimordial (*gleichursrünglich*) is a Heideggerian term that Werner H. Kelber appropriates to address the "simultaneity of multiple originals" of speech acts ("The Works of Memory: Christian Origins as MnemoHistory—A Response," in *Memory, Tradition, and Text: Uses of the Past in Early Christianity*, ed. Alan Kirk and Tom Thatcher, SemeiaSt 52 [Leiden: Brill, 2005], 237; idem, "In the Beginning were the Words: The Apotheosis and Narrative Displacement of the Logos," in idem, *Imprints*; orig., 1990, 77–80).

52. Kelber, "Works of Memory," 238.

53. Jan Assmann claims that tradition "refers to the business of handing down and receiving, as well as the continued existence of what has been received" ("Introduction: What is Cultural Memory?" in idem, *Religion and Cultural Memory: Ten Studies*, trans. Rodney Livingstone [Stanford: Stanford University Press, 2006], 25). Tradition is therefore concerned with the received past as it exists in the present. According to Tom Thatcher and Alan Kirk, social memory theorists "refuse to authorize any sharp distinction between memory and tradition" ("Jesus Tradition as Social Memory," in Kirk and Thatcher, *Memory, Tradition, and Text*, 32).

54. Kirk names the salient past and present social realities "potent variables" in the construction of social memory ("Memory Theory and Jesus Research," in *Handbook for the Study of the Historical Jesus*, ed. Tom Holmén and Stanley E. Porter, 4 vols. [Leiden: Brill, 2011], 1:817).

55. Kelber, "Works of Memory," 239.

historical core can be recovered in some pure, untainted form if we could just peel back subsequent layers of tradition. Traditions are contiguous with their past, but diverging memorial trajectories and refractions are also to be interpreted in their own right.[56]

The equiprimordiality of oral literature leads to another one of its properties, which Zumthor has called *mouvance*. *Mouvance* refers to the "radical instability" of an oral tradition.[57] Oral traditions are, by their nature, open to changes. Zumthor writes, "The oral text, for the most part, is multiple, cumulative, many-colored, sometimes diverse to the point of being contradictory."[58] When oral traditions are transferred into the written medium, they often continue to exhibit *mouvance*. This is a holdover from the equiprimordiality of oral literature. From the multiform textual tradition of the *Actus Vercellenses*, Christine M. Thomas argues that this tradition must have existed and developed within an oral milieu, since textual multiforms are a "smoking gun" of oral transmission.[59] Narratives that have a background in oral performance, she proposes, are more textually fluid than those that don't.[60] She goes so far as to propose that each manuscript might be viewed as a performance, and calls this the "performance attitude toward written texts."[61]

The more a text linguistically bears the marks of its oral predecessors, the more pluriform its textual tradition is likely to be. If a narrative existed as an oral tradition before moving into the textual medium, its oral form is likely to persist even after its transference to the new modality.[62] Texts that are more residually oral exhibit a more multiform textual tradition because the attitude applied to the oral

---

56. Anthony Le Donne, *The Historiographical Jesus: Memory, Typology and The Son of David* (Waco: Baylor University Press, 2009), 73.

57. Zumthor, *Oral Poetry*, 202; idem, *Essai de poétique médiévale* (Paris: Seuil, 1972), 68–72.

58. Zumthor, *Oral Poetry*, 103.

59. Thomas, *The Acts of Peter, Gospel Literature, and the Ancient Novel: Rewriting the Past* (Oxford: Oxford University Press, 2003), 69. Similarly, others have argued that multiformity is characteristic of oral traditions, including Albert B. Lord (*The Singer of Tales* [Cambridge: Harvard University Press, 1960], 99–100) and Raymond F. Person (*The Deuteronomic History and the Book of Chronicles: Scribal Works in an Oral World*, AIL 6 [Atlanta: Society of Biblical Literature, 2010], 69–86).

60. Thomas, *Acts of Peter*, 78–86.

61. Ibid., 85. Similarly, Martin S. Jaffee notes, "A given book normally circulated in a variety of textual forms, some longer and some shorter, one copy distinct in a variety of ways from any other. [...] To the degree that the book *was* its oral declamation and aural appropriation (rather than its mere material copy), the manuscript substrate of the book bore the influence of the performative contexts in which it was shared" (*Torah in the Mouth: Writing and Oral Tradition in Palestinian Judaism 200 BCE-400 CE* [Oxford: Oxford University Press, 2001], 18; emphasis original).

62. Zumthor, *Oral Poetry*, 26.

tradition likewise applies to their existence in the textual medium.[63] There are, in this situation, multiple receptions of the tradition. When oral and written media of the same narrative exist simultaneously, both possess a more fluid existence, and there is not the same concern for the original as there is when a narrative is conceived literarily.

When it comes to ancient narratives, we'll see that residually oral texts are more likely to possess a textual tradition that is voluminous, multiform, and living. There will be different versions of the same narrative extant. The general storyline will be maintained, but there will often be significant differences between the versions. The "original" form of the story may not be precisely preserved. Authors and redactors will add, remove, and change aspects of the narrative as they please. This is not ill-intended editorial activity but simply the result of altering a narrative for a new mode and context of reception.

Criterion # 5: Embedded textuality and intertextuality

Words spoken are more ephemeral than words written. As Finnegan puts it, "The most obvious property of writing is that it gives permanence to verbal expression. Words can be transmitted through space and over time in permanent and unchanging form."[64] This leads to another phenomenon that characterizes literarily conceived narrative, as opposed to orally conceived narrative: embedded textuality.

Written narratives can manipulate and transmit other texts, embedding them within their narrative. This is what Jacques Derrida calls the iterability of writing.[65] Because writers have freedom of time not afforded to speakers, they are able to examine other texts, determine how they will be utilized within their own discourse, and then reproduce the text within their narrative. The result is that literarily conceived narratives show intertextual precision. These narratives can more accurately reproduce their intertexts as they exist in time and space.[66]

Oral narratives also evoke intertexts, but not in the same way that literarily conceived narratives do. Producers of oral narratives can embed other texts in their discourses by recalling the text, or a portion of the text, mnemonically. This is a less exact process than when a physical text is reproduced in a literarily conceived discourse. The amount of text reproduced mnemonically will always be limited by the speaker's memorial reservoir. Textuality can deepen this reservoir significantly by externally storing a discourse. Producers of oral narrative can then utilize

---

63. Thomas, *Acts of Peter*, 85.
64. Finnegan, *Literacy and Orality*, 17.
65. Jacques Derrida, "Signature Event Context," in *Margins of Philosophy*, trans. Alan Bass (Chicago: University of Chicago Press, 1982), 7.
66. I do not intend to imply that oral narrative is not influenced by and does not utilize a variety of intertexts. My point here is simply that intertextuality functions differently in oral narrative than in written.

textual traditions by having those texts on hand and reading them aloud. This requires a level of preparation on the speaker's part and is another demonstration of the overlap between orality and textuality.

Jan Assmann's work on cultural and communicative memory provides a theoretical entry point for considering intertextuality in ancient media culture.[67] Assmann expands the boundaries of what constitutes a text. As (post)modern people conditioned by the fixity of printed texts, we tend to think of them as single, stable entities.[68] They are ink, formed into readable signs, printed on bound pages that can be reproduced with absolute accuracy. But Assmann, assessing the differences between ancient and modern memory and textuality, considers a text a "retrieved communication."[69] Written words themselves are not necessarily texts. Rather, writing is an externalization of memory for the reactivation of what he calls "cultural texts."[70] Cultural texts come in a variety of forms. Writings, oral storytelling traditions, rituals, and customs are but a few examples.

When a cultural text is recalled, it is not necessarily evoked by embedding words from a written text verbatim. Rather, ideas, themes, or key phrases signal that a certain cultural text is alluded to. This familiarity with and recall of cultural texts in the oral-mnemonic mode is similar to what has been called secondary orality. This term was originally coined by Ong who used it to refer to electronic media, such as radio and television, that are dependent on writing and print but are not themselves writing or print.[71] Whereas primary orality is, for Ong, completely independent of textuality, secondary orality only exists within a literate culture and is directly dependent on it. In recent biblical research, the term secondary orality refers to something different from Ong's notion. In this context, it has connoted

---

67. See especially the aforementioned collection, *Religion and Cultural Memory*; originally *Religion und Kulturelle Gedächtnis*, 3rd ed. (Münich: Beck, 2000). Assmann's research has recently garnered much attention in the nascent field of New Testament media criticism. Kelber has applied Assmann's *Traditionsbruch* concept to Mark ("Works of Memory," 228–29, 243–44) and Chris Keith similarly employs Assmann's *zerdehnte Situation* ("Prolegomena on the Textualization of Mark's Gospel: Manuscript Culture, the Extended Situation, and the Emergence of the Written Gospel," in *Memory and Identity in Ancient Judaism and Early Christianity: A Conversation with Barry Schwartz*, ed. Tom Thatcher, SemeiaSt 78 [Atlanta: SBL Press, 2014], 175–81).

68. Elizabeth Eisenstein's monumental work, *The Printing Press as an Agent of Change: Communications and Cultural Transformations in Early Modern Europe*, 2 vols. (Cambridge: Cambridge University Press, 1979), details the far-reaching psychological, cultural, and technological influence of the printing press.

69. Jan Assmann, "Cultural Texts Suspended Between Writing and Speech," in idem, *Religion and Cultural Memory*, 108.

70. Jan Assmann, "Remembering in Order to Belong: Writing, Memory, and Identity," in idem, *Religion and Cultural Memory*, 85–87.

71. Ong, *Orality and Literacy*, 3.

"indirect familiarity with texts through oral tradition."[72] That is, if a text was heard in a public reading rather than read individually, it was experienced through secondary orality.[73] It has been especially employed in this way with reference to the Gospel of Thomas, in the study of which secondary orality is the concept that suggests that the Synoptics were mediated to the author of that gospel orally rather than textually.[74] The problem with applying the concept in this manner is, as Mark S. Goodacre notes, twofold. First, it imports a new connotation to Ong's phrase that already expresses something totally different.[75] And second, it commends a Great Divide approach to orality and textuality, conceiving of the influence of these modalities as unidirectional.[76]

It would be possible to expand the semantic range of "secondary orality" to include cultural texts in whatever form they exist. But I consider this unnecessary for our purposes not only because the term is already freighted, but also because Foley's "communicative economy" and "metonymy" are concepts that signify this kind of expanded mnemonic recall of cultural texts.[77] According to Foley, performers of a tradition can evoke "an enormous wellspring of meaning" with a familiar phrase, theme, or scene.[78] Once a communicative node metonymically activates the wellspring of tradition, in whatever form the tradition exists, the performer continues his or her tale with that tradition in the audience's mind.[79] Speakers can recall a cultural text or tradition without precisely reproducing long strings of words from a written text verbatim but by evoking themes, ideas, or catchphrases from the more expansive cultural text.

When reading texts with an eye to their embedded textuality and intertextuality, we will find that authors of orally conceived narratives do not reproduce other texts in the same way that authors of literarily conceived narrative do. Intertextuality in these narratives is more likely to be more general, mnemonic, and echoic. To employ Richard B. Hays's well-known taxonomy of intertextuality, allusions and echoes will abound in orally conceived narratives.[80] In texts that are

---

72. Mark S. Goodacre, *Thomas and the Gospels: The Case for Thomas's Familiarity with the Synoptics* (Grand Rapids: Eerdmans, 2012), 137; similarly, Rodríguez, *Oral Tradition*, 26–27.

73. Kelber, *Gospel*, 217–18.

74. Review of how studies on the Gospel of Thomas apply this concept in Goodacre, *Thomas*, 138–39.

75. Goodacre, *Thomas*, 138–39.

76. Ibid.

77. Foley, *Singer of Tales*, 53–56.

78. Ibid., 54.

79. Ibid.

80. Hays details the differences between allusions and echoes in his seminal monograph, *Echoes of Scripture in the Letters of Paul* (New Haven: Yale University Press, 1989; repr., 1993), 29. He offers methodological considerations for detecting allusions and echoes in ibid., 29–33 and *The Conversion of the Imagination: Paul as Interpreter of Israel's Scripture* (Grand Rapids: Eerdmans, 2005), 34–45. In contrast to quotations, allusions and echoes do

literarily conceived, we will find a higher presence and a greater cross-section of intertextuality, manifested in lists, exact representations of other texts, and texts quoted verbatim from antecedent sources.

In conclusion to this section, the five criteria outlined above will serve as tools that measure the density of Mark's and *Joseph and Aseneth*'s residual orality. This density suggests that both are related to an antecedent oral tradition. I will argue that the differences between telling a story orally and writing a story shed light on these narratives and their subsequent reception. But I wish to go beyond the simple claim that Mark and *Joseph and Aseneth* exhibit features of oral literature and possess dense residual orality to offer a theory as to *why* they do so. They were composed via dictation by scribally illiterate persons. If this claim is to be substantiated, we need to move toward the media *realia* of the world in which these narratives were produced. I will first consider composition by dictation in this context and the purposes for which scribally illiterate persons might have dictated a text. To demonstrate the utility of the three linguistic criteria proposed above, I read two papyrological texts that were almost assuredly composed in this manner with these criteria as compositional lenses.

Composition by dictation in Greco-Roman antiquity

Composition by dictation was a ubiquitous practice in the Greco-Roman world.[81] Both the literati and those who were not "grapho-literate" wrote this way.[82] As to the former, it was a privilege of wealthy, literate men, though also some women, who could afford to hire or purchase a secretary to produce texts. Nicholas Horsfall notes that transcription by dictation was practiced for the initial stages of literary composition by, among others, Caesar, Pliny the Elder, Pliny the Younger, and Vergil.[83] This mode of composition for literary texts had several practical advantages to it. First, it could greatly increase the amount of time a person spent writing and thus also his or her literary output. Pliny the Elder was particularly adept at using transcription to this end. He would dictate as he walked, sunbathed, ate, and traveled.[84] Another frequently overlooked advantage of dictation is that

not necessarily possess verbatim repetition of words. If they do, the repetition is of only a few words, often in different grammatical forms.

81. E. Randolph Richards, *The Secretary in the Letters of Paul*, WUNT 2/42 (Tübingen: Mohr Siebeck, 1991), 15–23; idem, *Paul and First-Century Letter Writing: Secretaries, Composition, and Collection* (Downers Grove: InterVarsity Press, 2004), 59–64.

82. "Grapho-literacy" is a term Keith uses to refer to the relatively few individuals who could write, copy, and compose literary texts (*Jesus Against the Scribal Elite: The Origins of the Conflict* [Grand Rapids: Baker Academic, 2014], 24–25).

83. Nicholas Horsfall, "Rome without Spectacles," *Greece & Rome* 42 (1995): 52.

84. Ibid.

it allowed an individual to continue to write after his or her eyes began to fail.⁸⁵ This is particularly consequential in the ancient context where ophthalmia, a condition that causes inflammation of the eyes and makes many everyday tasks more difficult, was common.⁸⁶

Despite its advantages, composition by dictation produced a less polished literary product, and so had its detractors. Quintilian, for example, disparages the practice. In *Inst*. 10.3.17–18, he criticizes those who write a rough draft as quickly as they can, calling it their "raw material" (*silvam*) that will later be worked into proper form. The better practice, he suggests, is to write carefully from the start. From this critique of rough drafts, Quintilian moves immediately to his opinion of dictation (*dictandi*), noting that it should be clear to his reader what he thinks, given his judgment on impromptu writing. Because the mind moves faster than the hand, writing *sua manu* produces a more refined product, according to Quintilian. Dictating allows the speaker to pour forth his or her thoughts more rapidly, resulting in writing that is "crude and casual" (*rudia et fortuita*).⁸⁷ Quintilian recommends a different modus operandi for writing: a writer should work alone in a secluded, unadorned study at night by the light of a single lamp (*Inst*. 10.3.25–27).

Quintilian had the luxury to choose between writing *sua manu* and dictating his texts. The case was similar for many of his wealthy, educated colleagues. But the vast majority of people in the Greco-Roman world could produce texts only through a proxy. Even those who had received a basic Jewish education were not likely to be trained in writing and composition.⁸⁸ These skills were separately acquired from

---

85. Ibid., 49–51. That this was a very real concern is indicated by Quintilian's concession that those with weak eyesight can use papyrus for writing. He judged that writing on wax tablets was preferable because they were more conducive to a steady, uninterrupted flow of thought. A writer using papyrus had to disrupt his flow frequently to dip the pen in ink. Ink on papyrus was apparently much easier to see and did not strain the eyes as reading from wax tablets did. Quinitilian supposes this is papyrus's primary advantage over tablets (*Inst*. 10.3.31–32).

86. Horsfall, "Rome without Spectacles," 49.

87. Chafe notes that, because handwriting takes approximately ten times longer than speaking, in the act of writing, the flow of consciousness is slowed down and "we have time to mold a succession of ideas into a more complex, coherent, integrated whole, making use of devices we seldom use in speaking" ("Integration and Involvement," 37). Quintilian's recognition that speaking a discourse results in "crude and casual" writing coheres with sociolinguistic theory, which finds that speaking is produced in spurts of "idea units" that are only loosely connected syntactically (ibid., 37).

88. Nathan Morris, *The Jewish School: An Introduction to the History of Jewish Education* (London: Eyre and Spottiswoode, 1937), 14–15; Birger Gerhardsson, *Memory and Manuscript with Tradition and Transmission in Early Christianity*, trans. Eric J. Sharpe (Grand Rapids: Eerdmans, 1998), 58; Christine Schams, *Jewish Scribes in the Second-Temple Period*, JSOTSupp 291 (Sheffield: Sheffield Academic, 1998), 308 n. 102; Catherine Hezser, *Jewish Literacy in Roman Palestine*, TSAJ 81 (Tübingen: Mohr Siebeck, 2001), 88, 474; eadem, "Private and Public Education," in *The Oxford Handbook of Jewish Daily Life in*

writing through specialized instruction.[89] The ability to compose an original text was the highest form of literacy a person, Jewish or otherwise, could attain.[90]

Even elementary writing skills were a commodity in relatively short supply in Greco-Roman antiquity. Recent research has shown that there were different types and gradations of literacy in the ancient world. Reading and writing were separate skills.[91] The ability to write simple documents or even sign one's name was not presupposed in this context. There was a large population of "semi-literates" who could do so, but also a substantial number of "illiterate" people who could not.[92] The former, though they could write, often chose not to. This is evidenced by the practice common in antiquity of appending a greeting written in one's own hand to a letter transcribed by an amanuensis.[93] Illiterate people were no doubt

---

Roman Palestine, ed. eadem (Oxford: Oxford University Press, 2010), 471; Chris Keith, *The Pericope Adulterae, the Gospel of John, and the Literacy of Jesus*, NTTSD 38 (Leiden: Brill, 2009), 72–79; idem, *Jesus' Literacy*, 100–4; idem, *Jesus*, 24–25.

89. Morris, *Jewish School*, 55, 81–83; Meir Bar-Ilan, "Writing in Ancient Israel and Early Judaism Part Two: Scribes and Books in the Late Commonwealth and Rabbinic Period," in *Mikra: Text, Translation, Reading and Interpretation of the Hebrew Bible in Ancient Judaism and Early Christianity*, ed. Martin Jan Mulder (Philadelphia: Fortress, 1988), 22; Harry Y. Gamble, *Books and Readers in the Early Church: A History of Early Christian Texts* (New Haven: Yale University Press, 1995), 7; Keith, *Jesus*, 25; idem, *Pericope*, 77.

90. Raffaella Cribiore, *Writing, Teachers, and Students in Graeco-Roman Egypt*, American Studies in Papyrology 36 (Atlanta: Scholars Press, 1996), 10; Keith, *Pericope*, 53. It is sometimes supposed that the Markan evangelist was a "poor writer" and that this accounts for the gospel's unique style. But the ability to compose a narrative presupposes a level of education that is incommensurate with being a poor writer. If the Markan evangelist could write, he will not likely have written as he spoke. This supposition imports an anachronistic model of training in reading and writing, one that assumes grapho-literacy as the basis of elementary education.

91. Cribiore, *Writing*, 9–10, 148; eadem, *Gymnastics of the Mind: Greek Education in Hellenistic and Roman Egypt* (Princeton: Princeton University Press, 2001), 177; Keith, *Pericope*, 53–94; idem, *Jesus*, 24–26.

92. According to William V. Harris, "semi-literates" are "persons who can write slowly or not at all, and who can read without being able to read complex or very lengthy texts" (*Ancient Literacy* [Cambridge: Harvard University Press, 1989], 5). He also uses the nomenclature "craftsman's literacy" (ibid., 7–8). He is followed by John P. Meier in this respect (*The Roots of the Problem and the Person*, vol. 1 of *A Marginal Jew: Rethinking the Historical Jesus* [New York: Doubleday, 1991], 272–73). Semi-literacy and craftsman's literacy are categories also employed by Herbert C. Youtie ("βραδέως γράφων: Between Literacy and Illiteracy," *GRBS* 12 [1971]: 239–61) and Keith (*Pericope*, 57–59). The fact that most people in the first-century Mediterranean world were functionally illiterate is noted by Harris (*Ancient Literacy*, 5–7) and Keith (*Pericope*, 59–62). All of these studies suggest that it is best to think of degrees of literacy in antiquity.

93. Cribiore, *Writing*, 4–5.

familiar with the roles and impact of writing, but they lacked the requisite skillsets to participate in the literary environment on their own.

Lack of grapho-literacy did not prevent people from accessing and writing texts. They could do so via intermediaries.[94] There are hundreds of occasions of the phrases ἔγραψα ὑπὲρ αὐτοῦ ἀγραμμάτου ("I wrote for him who is illiterate"), ἔγραψα ὑπὲρ αὐτοῦ μὴ εἰδότος γράμματα ("I wrote for him who does not know letters"), and ἔγραψα ὑπὲρ αὐτοῦ βραδέως γράφοντος ("I wrote for him who writes slowly") in the nonliterary papyri.[95] Those who were unlettered could participate in the literary culture by dictating texts to a scribe or informing the scribe what kind of texts they wanted produced.[96] This meant that secretaries had varying levels of involvement in the texts they wrote. E. Randolph Richards places secretarial control on a spectrum.[97] On one end, an amanuensis had little responsibility for a text's content, transcribing verbatim what was spoken to him. In this function, secretaries were "recorders."[98] On the other end of the spectrum, they could be "composers." That is, they produced the discourse's entire contents. This was especially common in the production of stereotyped letters and business documents.[99] In between these two ends, secretaries could play the role of editor or coauthor.[100]

In sum, composition by dictation was a common practice in Greco-Roman antiquity. It was employed by the highly educated to produce initial drafts of literary texts, by those who were functionally or semi-literate as a convenience, and out of necessity by those who were illiterate. Because scribes had varying levels of control over the content of a dictated text, we should not assume that writing by dictation will have produced a unique and recognizable register, nor even residual orality, every time it was employed. Educated individuals who frequently dictated literary texts will have been able to speak in a literary register, and thus minimize literary infelicities characteristic of the vernacular even during their first drafts.[101]

---

94. Harris, *Ancient Literacy*, 33–34; Kim Haines-Eitzen, *Guardians of Letters: Literacy, Power, and the Transmitters of Early Christian Literature* (Oxford: Oxford University Press, 2000), 29–30; Keith, *Pericope*, 59–62.

95. Representative lists for each formula in Thomas J. Kraus, "[Il]literacy in Non-Literary Papyri from Graeco-Roman Egypt: Further Aspects to the Educational Ideal in Ancient Literary Sources and Modern Times," in *Ad Fontes: Original Manuscripts and Their Significance for Studying Early Christianity*, ed. idem, TENTS 3 (Leiden: Brill, 2007), 110–11. R. A. Derrenbacker similarly catalogues references to the ἀγράμματοι (*Ancient Compositional Practices and the Synoptic Problem*, BETL 186 [Leuven: Leuven University Press, 2005], 23 n. 16).

96. Haines-Eitzen, *Guardians*, 29–32.

97. Richards, *Secretary*, 23–53; idem, *Paul*, 64–79.

98. Richards, *Secretary*, 23–43; idem, *Paul*, 64–74.

99. Horsfall, "Rome without Spectacles," 51; Richards, *Secretary*, 49–53; idem, *Paul*, 77–79.

100. Richards, *Secretary*, 43–49.

101. On this, Ong observes, "Once the chirographically initiated feel for precision and analytic exactitude is interiorized, it can feed back into speech, and does" (*Orality and Literacy*, 103). In other words, the practice of writing and the ability to do so affects one's speech.

When there were errors, they will have been edited out in later stages of the composition process. Dictation was most frequently employed during the initial stage of composition by the Greco-Roman literati and most literary texts underwent multiple rounds of revision.[102] But this does not mean that composition by dictation never produced residual orality. It would have resulted in an oral register when the scribe took dictation as a direct transcript. Certain types of texts were more prone to be transcriptions and closer to the Koine Greek vernacular than others. By probing those texts and investigating them with the linguistic criteria generated above, we can better determine the probability that a text was composed by dictation. My suggestion is that Mark and *Joseph and Aseneth* were both composed in such a manner and initially were not substantially altered to read as literary documents.

Before moving toward the two primary narratives that this book addresses, two others will be examined. In what follows, I analyze two texts from the papyri as test cases for the utility of the linguistic criteria I have proposed above. These two texts have been chosen for this task because they are of the type very likely to be composed via dictation and they report actions in a story-like manner.[103] That is, they possess "narrativity."[104]

Orally composed papyri narratives

BGU I.27

Epistolary texts from the papyri, of which BGU I.27 is a representative, are especially illuminating examples of the Greek vernacular. For Basil Mandilaras, letters from the papyri are the best samples of everyday speech and colloquial forms that we possess

---

102. Horsfall, "Rome without Spectacles," 52; Myles McDonnell, "Writing, Copying, and Autograph Manuscripts in Ancient Rome," *ClQ* 46 (1996): 474; Rex Winsbury, *The Roman Book: Books, Publishing and Performance in Classical Rome*, Classical Literature and Society (London: Duckworth, 2009), 102; Eric Eve, *Writing the Gospels: Composition and Memory* (London: SPCK, 2016), 54.

103. I do not wish to give the impression that these two texts were chosen completely at random. There was an element of subjectivity in their selection. Reading through nonliterary papyri, I looked for texts that possessed narrativity, were more than a few lines, and had generic features that suggested they might be oral transcriptions. The features that indicate that each of these two texts was composed in this manner are noted below. Very few papyri met all three of these conditions.

104. Literary theorists, following the influential work of Monica Fludernik, typically judge the extent to which a discourse possesses narrativity with respect to its evocation of real-life experience (*Towards a "Natural" Narratology* [London: Routledge, 1996], 20–38). Theoretical considerations of narrativity in Marie-Laure Ryan, "Toward a Definition of Narrative," in *The Cambridge Companion to Narrative*, ed. David Herman (Cambridge: Cambridge University Press, 2007), 22–36; H. Porter Abbott, "Narrativity," in *Handbook of Narratology*, ed. Peter Hühn (Berlin: de Gruyter, 2009), 309–28.

of Hellenistic and Koine Greek.¹⁰⁵ This is particularly apposite to those letters that are personal and do not appear to be premeditated. Letters that are "quick communications" are more likely to represent the vernacular because letters in general were typically dictated and this type of letter in particular will have been only lightly modified for the textual medium.¹⁰⁶ BGU I.27 is of this type. It is a letter dated to the second or third century CE from Irenaeus to his brother, Apollinarius. In its entirety, it reads:¹⁰⁷

(1) [Εἰρηναῖος Ἀπολιναρίωι τῶι φιλτάτ]ωι ἀδε[λ]φ[ῶι] πολ[λ]ὰ χαίρει[ν]. καὶ διὰ π[α]ντὸς εὔχομαί σε ὑγιένεν, καὶ ἐ[γὼ] αὐτὸς ὑγιένω. γινώσ- (5) {σ}κειν σε θέλω ὅτει εἰς γῆν ἐλήλυθα τῇ ς τοῦ Ἐπεὶφ μηνὸς καὶ ἐξεκενώσαμεν τῇ ιη τοῦ αὐτοῦ μηνός. ἀνέβην δὲ εἰς Ῥώμην τῇ κε τοῦ αὐ- (10) τοῦ μηνὸς καὶ παρεδέξατο ἡ- μᾶς ὁ τόπος ὡς ὁ θεὸς ἤθελεν, καὶ καθ᾽ ἡμέραν προσδεχόμ[ε-] θα διμαισσωρίαν, ὥστε ἕως σήμερον μηδέναν ἀπολε- (15) λύσθαι τῶν μετὰ σίτου. ἀσπάζομαι τὴν σύνβιόν σου πολλὰ καὶ Σερῆνον καὶ πάν- τες τοὺς φιλοῦντάς σε κατ᾽ ὄνο- μα. (20) ἔρρωσ[[θ]]ο. Μεσορὴ θ.	Irenaeus to Apollinarius his dearest brother many greetings. I pray continually for your health, and I myself am well. I wish you to know that I reached land on the 6th of the month Epeiph and we unloaded our cargo on the 18th of the same month. I went up to Rome on the 25th of the same month and the place welcomed us as the god willed, and we are daily expecting our discharge, it so being that up till to-day nobody in the corn fleet has been released. Many salutations to your wife and to Serenus and to all who love you, each by name. Goodbye. Mesore 9. (Addressed) To Apollinarius from his brother Irenaeus.¹⁰⁸

Verso: Ἀπολιναρί(ωι) ἀπὸ Εἰρηναίου ἀδελφοῦ.

The letter briefly narrates Irenaeus's travels and does not appear to possess literary ambition. Given the ubiquity of the practice of dictating letters to scribes and the hand that this letter is written in, it is likely a dictated text. An application of the sociolinguistic criteria proposed above supports this claim.

---

105. Mandilaras, *The Verb in the Greek-Non-Literary Papyri* (Athens: Hellenic Ministry of Culture and Sciences, 1973), 46.

106. Haines-Eitzen suggests that the employment of scribes for letters was so ubiquitous that scribes did not identify themselves as the transcribers of the text (*Guardians*, 29–30).

107. Reproduced from A. S. Hunt and C. C. Edgar, trans., *Select Papyri*, Non-Literary Papyri Private Affairs, 5 vols., LCL (Cambridge: Harvard University Press, 1932), 1:306. This letter is widely available. See Ulrich Wilcken, ed., *Grundzüge und Chrestomathie der Papyruskunde*, vol. 1, Part 2: *Chrestomathie*, 4 vols. (Hildesheim: Olms, 1963), 445; George Milligan, *Selections from the Greek Papyri* (Cambridge: Cambridge University Press, 1912), 41. Also translated in John Garrett Winter, *Life and Letters in the Papyri* (Ann Arbor: University of Michigan Press, 1933), 38–39. I have not normalized the Greek text here or in the text that follows.

108. Trans. Hunt and Edgar, *Select Papyri*, LCL.

Criterion #1: Parataxis, apposition, and the idea unit The prevalence of parataxis with καί in the nonliterary papyri is well documented. Nigel Turner writes, "The papyri provide ample evidence that popular speech favours parataxis."[109] Adolf Deissmann notes this phenomenon of the papyri and its similarity to the NT, as does Mandilaras.[110] Mandilaras further observes that καί is commonly followed by an indicative verb, where a participial phrase might have been expected.[111] He maintains that this phenomenon results from the colloquial form of letters.[112] This comports well with sociolinguistic theory. Narratives that are comprised of popular speech or are themselves transcribed speeches will be structured paratactically, utilizing idea units and avoiding complex syntactical relationships.

In the present example, parataxis is prominent. In this short letter of 86 words, καί appears seven times. Lines 3–15 constitute the narrative portion of the letter, wherein καί coordinates clauses five times and never individual words. This, along with other syntactical features, breaks the narrative into short idea units, suggesting that it leans to the oral side of the oral-literary continuum. Excising the greeting and farewell and organizing the narrative portion of the letter by these units is revealing:

καὶ διὰ π[α]ντὸς εὔχομαί σε ὑγιένεν,	And I pray continually for your health,
καὶ ἐ[γὼ] αὐτὸς ὑγιένω.	and I myself am well.
γινώσ{σ}κειν σε θέλω ὅτει	I wish you to know that
εἰς γῆν ἐλήλυθα τῇ ς τοῦ Ἐπεὶφ μηνὸς	I reached land on the 6th of the month,
καὶ ἐξεκενώσαμεν τῇ ιη τοῦ αὐτοῦ μηνός.	And we unloaded on the 18th of the same month. I went up to Rome on the 25th of the same month,
ἀνέβην δὲ εἰς Ῥώμην τῇ κε τοῦ αὐτοῦ μηνὸς	
καὶ παρεδέξατο ἡμᾶς ὁ τόπος ὡς ὁ θεὸς ἤθελεν,	and the place welcomed us, as the god willed,
καὶ καθ' ἡμέραν προσδεχόμ[ε-]θα διμαισσωρίαν,	and we are daily expecting our discharge,
ὥστε ἕως σήμερον μηδέναν ἀπολελύσθαι τῶν μετὰ σίτου.	it so being that up till to-day nobody in the corn fleet has been released.[113]

109. Nigel Turner, *Syntax*, vol. 3 of *Grammar of New Testament Greek* (Edinburgh: T&T Clark, 1963), 334.

110. Adolf Deissmann, *Light from the Ancient East: The New Testament Illustrated by Recently Discovered Texts of the Graeco-Roman World*, trans. Lionel Richard Mortimer Strachan (London: Hodder & Stoughton, 1910), 127–52; Mandilaras, *Verb*, 46.

111. Mandilaras, *Verb*, 366.

112. Ibid. Mandilaras lists the following papyri as illustrative examples of this phenomenon: BGU 1079, 6-9 (41 CE); P.Hamb 86, 14-15 (second century CE); P.Oxy. 528, 14-15 (second century CE); P. Lond 418, 12 (346 CE); P. Lond 243, 9-11 (346 CE); P. Lond 244, 20-22 (fourth century CE).

113. The translation here is my own, altered from Hunt and Edgar, *Select Papyri*, LCL. On the occasions where they have chosen to omit a translation of καί, I have translated it "and."

When broken down in this manner, half of the idea units in the narrative begin with καί. This is to be expected of stories in the vernacular. In addition, the length of the units in this breakdown, at an average of six words each, is in line with sociolinguistic studies, which find that most idea units are four to seven words long.[114] The idea units are loosely connected and make sense on their own, rarely requiring a complement clause.

Criterion #2: Repetition of syntactical patterns, words, phrases, and ideas The size of this text is not sufficient to permit significant conclusions about the criterion of repetition, but two observations are worth mentioning briefly. First, there is some level of syntactical repetition accomplished by parataxis and the idea unit. Second, there is ideological and verbal repetition as Irenaeus expresses the chronology of his travels. In the central portion of the letter he relates three different dates with the genitive τοῦ μηνός.

Criterion #3: Verb employment This brief narrative's employment of verbs reflects what is expected of spoken narrative. I previously noted that oral narrative tends to have an even distribution of present and past tense verbs. This is a result of the distinction between the represented and the representing consciousness. On the one hand, the past tense narrates events that have happened in order "to orient the addressee to the temporal and spatial context of the event related."[115] On the other hand, the present tense accomplishes a sense of immediacy between the speaker and the hearer. Speakers tend to use present tense verbs to align temporally their own consciousness with their hearers' consciousness. A fairly even distribution of past tense and present tense verbs occurs in this text. In the indicative mood, four present tense verbs are used along with five past tense verbs.[116] This even distribution of the past and present in the indicative mood is consonant with what we expect to find in oral narrative.

It is also significant that most verbs in this text are in the indicative mood. There are ten indicative verbs, two complementary infinitives, and one infinitive with an accusative subject. There is also a conventional infinitive and imperative in the letter's greeting and closing, respectively. Significantly, there is only one participle in the entire text, τοὺς φιλοῦντας, and this is a substantival participle.

---

114. Chafe, "Linguistic Differences," 106.
115. Ochs, "Planned and Unplanned," 70.
116. The present tense verbs are εὔχομαι, ὑγιένω, θέλω, and προσδεχόμεθα. The past tense verbs are ἐλήλυθα, ἐξεκενώσαμεν, ἀνέβην, παρεδέξατο, and ἤθελεν. While ἐλήλυθα is technically a perfect tense form, it surely carries an aoristic function. This is what Smyth calls a "perfect of dated past action," which "is used of a past action whose time is specifically stated" (*Greek Grammar*, §1949). This is the case here, as the verb is followed by a specific date.

In lines 4, 7–8, and 10–11 καί precedes an indicative verb where a participial phrase would likely have been utilized by an author who conceived his or her text literarily. This is illustrative of the fact not only that spoken discourse prefers the indicative mood, but also that it does not place its clauses in varying degrees of relation, as written discourse does. One of the most common tools for indicating the relationship between clauses in written discourse is participial construction.[117]

Finally, the narrative also possesses verb employment that is characteristic of an oral register regarding its consistent use of the active and middle-deponent voices. The result is that the passive is nearly nonexistent in the text. There are only two verbs in the passive voice: the infinitive ἀπολελύσθαι and the standard farewell, ἔρρωσθο. The other thirteen verbal forms are all in the active or middle. This is representative of the fact that speakers are more involved in their narratives than writers are and are not constructing a discourse wherein thought is displaced onto the written text.

P.Oxy. 903

P.Oxy. 903 is an affidavit by an unnamed wife lodging complaints against her husband, who has purportedly mistreated both her and his household.[118] The account is exceptional in its length and the depth of details it provides. The petition is pertinent for our purposes not only because it possesses narrativity but also because it is likely a transcription of oral speech. This is suggested by three factors. First, the verb προεῖπον ("I said before") in line 25 implies that the unnamed wife has been speaking these accusations aloud and not writing them. Second, given the social distribution of literacy in the context of the affidavit, it is less likely that this woman had the ability to write the petition herself.[119] Finally, even among

---

117. Chafe, "Linguistic Differences," 112.

118. Bernard P. Grenfell and Arthur S. Hunt note that "the present document [...] was presumably a kind of affidavit used in proceedings taken against the husband; it is written in vulgar Greek ..." (Grenfell and Hunt, eds., *The Oxyrhynchus Papyri*, vol. 6 [London: Egypt Exploration Fund, 1908], 239).

119. As Harris notes, there is some evidence that girls could have been educated at the elementary level in the late Empire, but "it is overwhelmingly probable [...] that without any improvement in the social position of women girl pupils continued to be heavily outnumbered by boys" (*Ancient Literacy*, 310). While female literacy rates were not uniform across all times and locales, they will have generally been lower than male literacy rates in antiquity (ibid., 22–24).

those who were grapho-literate, petitions of this sort were typically dictated to scribes.[120] The account, in its entirety, reads:[121]

περὶ πάντων ὧν εἶπεν κατ' ἐμοῦ ὕβρεων.
ἐνέκλεισεν τοὺς ἑ[α]υτοῦ δούλους καὶ τοὺς
ἐμοῦ ἅμα τῶν τροφίμ[ω]ν μου καὶ τὸν προνοητὴν καὶ τὸν
υἱὸν αὐτοῦ ἐπὶ ὅλας ἑ[πτ]ὰ ἡμέρας εἰς τὰ κατάγαια αὐτοῦ,
(5) τοὺς μὲν δούλους αὐτ[οῦ κ]αὶ τὴν ἐμὴν δούλην Ζωὴν ὑβρίσας
ἀποκτίνας αὐτοὺς τῶν π[λ]ηγῶν, καὶ πῦρ προσήνεγκεν ταῖς τρο-
φίμαις μου γυμνώσας αὐ[τὰ]ς παντελῶς ἃ οὐ ποιοῦσι οἱ νόμοι, καὶ
λέγων τοῖς αὐτοῖς τροφίμοις ὅτι δότε πάντα τὰ αὐτῆς, καὶ εἶπαν
ὅτι οὐδὲν ἔχει παρ' ἡμῶν, τοῖς δὲ δούλοις λέγων μαστιγ{γ}ο<υ>μένοι<ς> ὅτι
(10) τί ἤρκεν ἐκ τῆς οἰκίας μου; βασανιζόμενοι οὖν εἶπαν ὅτι οὐδὲν
τῶν σῶν ἤρκεν ἀλλὰ σῶά ἐστιν πάντα τὰ σά.
ἀπήντησεν δὲ αὐτῷ Ζω[ΐλ]ος ὅτι καὶ τὸν τρόφιμον αὐτοῦ ἐνέ-
κλισεν, καὶ εἶπεν αὐτῷ ὅτ[ι] διὰ τὸν τρόφιμόν σου ἦλθας ἢ διὰ τὴν
τοίαν ἦλθας λαλῆσαι ἐπάνω αὐτῆς;
(15) καὶ ὤμοσεν ἐπὶ παρουσίᾳ τῶν ἐπισκόπων καὶ τῶν ἀδελφῶν αὐτοῦ
ὅτι ἀπεντεῦθεν οὐ μὴ κρύψω αὐτή<ν> πάσας μου τὰς κλεῖς καὶ ἐπέχω \καὶ τοῖς δούλοις/
\αὐτοῦ ἐπίστευσεν κἀμοὶ οὐκ ἐπίστευσεν/[122] οὔτε ὑβρίζω αὐτὴν ἀπεντεῦθεν. καὶ
γαμικὸν γέγονεν, καὶ μετὰ

120. Benjamin Kelly, *Petitions, Litigation, and Social Control in Roman Egypt* (Oxford: Oxford University Press, 2011), 42. Kelly offers a two-stage mode of composition for official petitions by scribes: "First, the person wanting to write the petition could presumably have gone in person to a scribe and given an oral account of the dispute. The scribe (or a group of scribes collaboratively) would have then reduced the complaint to writing, putting it into what was regarded to be the proper form for this type of document" (ibid., 44). Kelly cites BGU IV 1139, BL VII 42 as an example of this oral to literate movement. He writes, "In these [additions and interlinear additions to the text] we can see both the breathless and emotive oral performance of the petitioners (whose daughter had allegedly been kidnapped), and the attempts by the scribe to cast the story in a more conventional form" (ibid.). It is probable that P.Oxy. 903 is also the result of a similar process, as the text is written in the vernacular and there are interlinear additions at lines 15–16.
121. Greek text reproduced from Grenfell and Hunt, *Oxyrhynchus Papyri*, 6:239–40. Also available in Lincoln H. Blumell and Thomas A. Wayment, eds., *Christian Oxyrhynchus: Texts, Documents, and Sources* (Waco: Baylor University Press, 2015), 446–50. I have translated the text myself, as Grenfell and Hunt's translation smooths over many of the residually oral features of the petition, especially its parataxis. I have also chosen in this case not to present the Greek and English side by side so that I might retain the lines of the text.
122. This is a supralinear insertion that serves as a parenthetical explanation about the keys.

τὰς συνθήκας ταύτας καὶ τοὺς ὅρκους ἔκρυψεν πάλιν ἐμὲ τὰς κλεῖς
εἰς ἐμέ. καὶ ἀπελθοῦσα [εἰ]ς τὸ κυριακὸν ἐν Σαμβαθώ, καὶ ἐποίησεν
(20) τὰς ἔξω θύρας αὐτοῦ ἐνκλισθῆναι ἐπάνω μου λέγων ὅτι διὰ τί ἀπῆλ-
θας εἰς τὸ κυριακόν; καὶ πολλὰ ἀσελγήματα λέγων εἰς πρόσωπόν
μου καὶ διὰ τῆς ῥινὸς αὐτο[ῦ,] καὶ περὶ σίτου (ἀρτάβας) ρ τοῦ δημοσίου τοῦ
ὀνόματός μου μηδὲν δεδωκὼς μηδὲ ἀρτάβ(ην) μίαν. ἐνέκλεισεν δὲ
τοὺς τόμους κρατήσας αὐτ[ο]ὺς ὅτι δότε τὴν τιμὴν τῶν (ἀρταβῶν) ρ, μηδὲν
(25) δεδω[κὼς] ὡς προεῖπον. καὶ εἶπεν τοῖς δούλοις αὐτοῦ ὅτι δότε συμμά-
χους ἵνα καὶ αὐτὴν ἐνκλείσωσι. καὶ ἐκρατήθη Χωοῦς ὁ βοηθὸς αὐτοῦ
εἰς τὸ δημόσιον καὶ παρέσχεν αὐτῷ Εὐθάλαμος ἐνέχυρον καὶ οὐκ ἠρκέσθη.
ἦρκα κἀγὼ ἄλλο μικρὸν καὶ παρέσχον τῷ αὐτῷ Χωοῦτι. ἀπαντήσας δὲ
αὐτῷ εἰς Ἀντινόου ἔχουσα τὸ πρὸς βαλανίόν μου μεθ᾽ ὧν ἔχω κοσμαρι-
(30) δίων, καὶ εἶπέν μοι ὅτι εἴ τι ἔχεις μετ᾽ ἐσοῦ αἴρω αὐτὰ δι᾽ ὃ δέδωκες τῷ
βοηθῷ μου Χωοῦτι ἐνέχυρον διὰ τὰ δημόσια αὐτοῦ. μαρτυρῆσαι δὲ
περὶ τούτων πάντων ἡ μήτηρ αὐτοῦ. καὶ περὶ Ἀνίλλας τῆς δούλης
αὐτοῦ ἔμεινεν θλίβων τὴν ψυχήν μου καὶ ἐν τῇ Ἀντινόου καὶ ἐνταῦθα
ὅτι ἔκβαλε τὴν δούλην ταύτην ἐπειδὴ αὐτὴ οἶδεν ὅσα κέκτηται, ἴσως
(35) θέλων μοι καταπλέξαι καὶ ταύτῃ τῇ προφάσει ἆραι εἴ τι ἔχω· κἀγὼ οὐκ
ἠνεσχόμην ἐκβαλεῖν αὐτήν. καὶ ἔμεινεν λέγων ὅτι μετὰ μῆναν
λαμβάνω πολιτικὴν ἐμαυτῷ. ταῦτα δὲ οἶδεν ὁ θ(εός).

Concerning all the abuses he spoke against me.
He locked his own servants, as well as mine,
together with my foster children and his agent and
his son for seven whole days in his cellars,
(5) having tortured his servants and my servant Zoe,
nearly killing them with blows, he also burned my foster-daughters with fire,
    stripping them completely, which the laws don't allow,
and he said to the same foster children, "Give me all the things that are hers!" And
    they said, "She doesn't have anything with us." But to the servants he said, while
    they were being
(10) beaten, "What has she taken out of my house?" The tormented ones then said,
    "She hasn't taken anything of yours, but all your property is safe."
Zoilus went to meet him because he had also locked up his foster child, and he
    said to him, "Have you come on account of your foster child or have you come
    on account of the woman, to talk about her?"
(15) And he swore in front of the bishops and his brothers,
"From now on I will not hide all my keys from her and I will stop \and he trusted
    his servants but he did not trust me/ and not insult her from now on." And a
    marriage certificate was made, and after these
agreements and oaths he again hid the keys
from me. And when I went to church at Sambatho, he again had
(20) the outer-doors locked from me, saying, "Why did you go
to church?" And he spoke many abusive insults to my face
and through his nose. And concerning the 100 artabae of wheat due to the state

in my name, he has not paid anything, not a single artaba! But he locked up
the account books, grasping them [saying], "Pay the price of the 100 artabae!"
(25) He paid nothing, as I previously said. And he said to his servants, "Provide
helpers to shut her up as well." And Choous, his helper,
was taken to prison, and Euthalamus provided bail for him and it wasn't enough.
And I took a little more and gave it to this same Choous. But when I met him at
Antinoopolis, having my bathing-bag with me and my ornaments,
(30) he said to me, "If you have anything with you, I'll take them on account of
what you gave to my assistant Choous for his pledge due to the state." And his
mother will witness about all these things. And concerning Anilla, his servant,
he continued vexing my soul, both in Antinoopolis and here, [saying],
"Throw this servant out since she knows how much she has acquired," probably
(35) wishing to get me involved and by this excuse to take all that I have. And I
refused to throw her out. And he persisted, saying, "After a month
I will take a concubine." God knows these things.

Criterion #1: Parataxis, apposition, and the idea unit As in the previous account, καί is abundant in P.Oxy. 903. The connective appears 36 times out of a total 395 words, or 1 in 10.97 words.[123] It functions conjunctively on nine occasions, adverbially on two, and paratactically on twenty-five. Moreover, on the basis of Grenfell and Hunt's punctuation, the connective begins exactly half of the text's sentences. As has already been noted, spoken discourse utilizes the common connective at the beginning of clauses far more frequently than written discourse does, since literarily conceived discourse prefers subordination to coordination.

Also indicative of the oral syntactical structuring of this text is the tendency to string multiple clauses together, often with the connective καί. Beaman finds that spoken discourse has a greater tendency to join multiple clauses together into one sentence with coordination.[124] Writers of narrative will not typically coordinate more than three or four clauses in a sentence, whereas speakers will sometimes coordinate over ten clauses in a single sentence.[125] In this respect, the first sentence in the text is instructive. It encompasses all of lines two through ten and contains eight clauses. Many of the times when the editors have opted for periods could be changed to commas, because, as I have noted, half of the sentences in this text begin with the coordinating conjunction καί. It is significant that καί functions paratactically and is immediately followed by a verb on eight of the twelve occasions that the editors have opted to punctuate with a comma. For this speaker, as is the case for most speakers, the distinction between a sentence and a clause

---

123. δέ is used in this text in a manner and syntactical position similar to καί on six occasions. It is not always the case that in Koine texts δέ operates in a paratactic manner similar to καί, but in this text there seems to be little semantic difference between the two connectives.

124. Beaman, "Coordination and Subordination," 58.

125. Ibid.

is ambiguous. This is why sociolinguists prefer to utilize the nomenclature "idea unit" rather than "sentence" when it comes to speech units in oral narrative.

Lastly, the text is highly disjointed from the beginning. As Richard Alston has observed, it begins in medias res, which is characteristic of oral narrative.[126] The speaker often moves to new ideas without providing a syntactical or ideological transition. For example, at line 15, after recounting her husband's conversation with Zoilus, she abruptly moves into a narration about the oath her husband took in front of the bishops and brothers. The two accounts are entirely unrelated, and she transitions by simply saying, "And he swore ..." (καὶ ὤμοσεν ...). There are similar abrupt transitions at lines 7, 12, 21, 22, 26, and 32. Part of this results from the petition being an enumeration of her husband's abuses against her and the household. But it is also the result of her oral narration, as oral discourse often does not utilize logical and grammatical transitions between episodes being relayed.[127]

Criterion #2: Repetition of syntactical patterns, words, phrases, and ideas The letter from Irenaeus was not a large enough sample to observe repetition outside of familiar syntactical patterns. In this text, however, we find superfluous repetition not only of syntax but also of words, phrases, and ideas. Spoken narrative tends to be repetitive for at least two reasons. First, repetition helps reiterate the point that a speaker is making.[128] Second, the rapidity of production of spoken discourse results in a constricted variety of lexemes. For this reason, when it comes to speaking, certain lexemes are frequently repeated. With writing, the situation is different because of the possibility of editing and pausing to consider word choice. As a result, written narrative tends to be less repetitive in terms of specific lexical choices.[129]

The speaker in P.Oxy. 903 is repetitive in terms of her syntax, lexical choices, and the ideas she is portraying. Regarding syntax, she tends to structure her sentence with καί followed by an indicative verb. She usually dictates the object of the verb, in the accusative case, immediately following the verb. On a few occasions, she inserts a dative prepositional phrase before the object of the verb. She is also predictably repetitive about implying the subject of the verb in the verbal form

---

126. Richard Alston, *The City in Roman and Byzantine Egypt* (London: Routledge, 2002), 307. Ong suggests that beginning in medias res is the norm for oral literature ("The Psychodynamics of Oral Memory and Narrative: Some Implications for Biblical Studies," in *The Pedagogy of God's Image: Essays on Symbol and the Religious Imagination*, ed. Robert Masson [Chico: Scholars Press, 1982], 59).

127. As Dewey notes, "In oral narrative *and* links not only clauses and sentences but also whole pericopes" ("Oral Methods," 37). Similarly, Beaman writes, "In spoken narratives, the common *and then* is more frequent for detailing the sequence of events [than relating them with different time adverbials]" ("Coordination and Subordination," 76). Beaman further notes that the phrase "and then" is nearly ten times more frequent in oral narrative than written narrative (ibid., 77).

128. Ong, *Orality and Literacy*, 39–40.

129. Chafe and Danielwicz, "Properties," 91.

itself, rather than stating the subject of the verb explicitly, which she does on only a few occasions.

There is also repetition in her lexical choices. Several words appear on multiple occasions. There is a threefold repetition of ἐνέκλεισεν in lines 2, 12–13, 23, and the subjunctive form of the verb, ἐνκλείσωσι, appears in line 26. When reporting the words of her abusive husband in direct discourse, she employs the second-person plural present imperative active form δότε in lines 8, 24, and 25. In lines 10 and 11 the verb ἦρκεν appears twice, once on the lips of her husband and once on the lips of those being tormented, to restate the fact that she has not taken anything from his house. This kind of repetition and redundancy is obvious throughout the text, so the point need not be belabored here.[130]

Along with lexical repetition, there is a significant amount of ideological redundancy throughout the affidavit. Two instances are noteworthy. The first concerns the repeated participial phrase δεδωκὼς μηδέν in lines 23 and 24–25. Here, the accusation is made that the cruel husband has not paid any of the artabae of wheat due to the state on the wife's behalf. The accuser mentions this fact in line 23 and verbally punctuates it with the appositional phrase μηδὲ ἀρτάβην μίαν ("not a single artaba!"). She then self-consciously repeats the fact in lines 24–25, after reporting how her husband commanded her to pay the 100 artabae: ὅτι δότε τὴν τιμὴν τῶν (ἀρταβῶν) ρ, μηδὲν δεδω[κὼς] ὡς προεῖπον.[131] This makes a threefold repetition concerning the payment, or lack thereof, of the artabae. Second, the wife is repetitive about the identity of her husband as an insolent man. This is indicated by the nature of the complaint and the repetition of ὑβρ- root words, which function both nominally and verbally. A nominal form appears in the first line: περὶ πάντων ὧν εἶπεν κατ' ἐμοῦ ὕβρεων. A participial form, ὑβρίσας, is then used in line 5, followed finally by a verbal form, ὑβρίζω, placed on the lips of the husband himself, in line 17. This repetition suggests that this is the mental category that this wife has for her husband and that it is the charge that she is trying to bring against him.

Criterion #3: Verb employment This speaker uses a wider variety of verbal forms than Irenaeus did in the preceding example. Nonetheless, the employment of verbs in this text shows signs of an oral register more than it does a literary one. These signs are seen in the speaker's preference for the indicative mood, general disuse of the passive voice, and the present tense in direct discourse.

---

130. The following repetitions are also notable: the verb ἐπίστευεν in the supralinear additions in lines 16–17; the frequent use of forms of ἔχω throughout the petition; ἀπεντεῦθεν in lines 16 and 17; the frequent use of aorist forms of ἔρχομαι; Χωοῦτι in line 28 and 31, which redundantly clarifies who was in prison; the indication, by apposition, that Choous is the husband's assistant in lines 26 and 31; perfect forms of δίδωμι in lines 23, 25, and 30; ἔμεινεν in lines 33 and 36; forms of ἐκβάλλω in lines 33 and 36.

131. The use of the plural form, δότε, is somewhat puzzling here, since the abuser is seemingly addressing his wife individually. It could be that the repetition of δότε, as previously noted, caused the wife to report the husband's speech in this way.

The speaker prefers the indicative mood in this petition, as there are forty-six instances of it.[132] As to the other moods, there are five infinitives, one subjunctive, one optative, four imperatives, and seventeen participles.[133] The consistency of the indicative mood further establishes the paratactic structuring and rhythm of the narrative. The recurrent structure of καί followed by an indicative verb is a feature of the Koine vernacular.[134] Hypotactic constructions in the petition are infrequent, though the speaker does use participles more often than Irenaeus did. Frequently, the participle is only loosely related to the verb that it modifies and can nearly stand on its own as a verb in its clause. This is particularly noticeable in lines 21, 23, and 25, where the participles λέγων and δεδωκώς are not modifying any verb but serve as the main verb in their respective clauses. This more independent participial function is also manifested in the three other instances of λέγων that introduce direct discourse and is characteristic of the coordinative rather than subordinative nature of oral narrative.

It is also noteworthy that the passive voice is sparse in P.Oxy. 903.[135] Speakers are more active participants in their discourse than writers are.[136] There are only three passives in the petition: the substantival participle βασανιζόμενοι in line 10, the infinitive ἐνκλισθῆναι in line 20, and the aorist indicative passive ἠρέσθη in line 27.

Finally, direct discourse, which itself can be an indication of transcribed orality, occurs frequently in the text with present tense verbs. Speakers often employ present tense verbs throughout their discourse to portray it more vividly to their hearers.[137] This is what Chafe calls the immediate mode of speaking, which attempts to bring the speaker's extroverted consciousness in line with the time of the representing consciousness.[138] Speakers do not always operate in the

---

132. Depending on how the verb μαρτυρῆσαι is understood in line 31, this number may increase to forty-seven. As it stands, the verb is a 3rd person singular aorist optative active, but Grenfell and Hunt suggest that it is itacized and should be rendered μαρτυρήσει, making it a 3rd person singular future indicative active (*Oxyrhynchus Papyri*, 6:240). In this case the discrepancy results from either the pronunciation by the speaker or the transcription by the scribe. Either way, the future makes better grammatical sense in the passage and is probably the correct reading.

133. As indicated in the previous note, the optative may be better understood as a future indicative. It is also significant that the ratio of participles to indicative verbs in this narrative is identical to the ratio in the Gospel of Mark. This account uses 17 participles compared to 46 indicative verbs, or 1 for every 2.7 indicative verbs. Mark uses 541 participles compared to 1,496 verbs, or, again, 1 for every 2.7 indicative verbs.

134. Mandilaras, *Verb*, 366.

135. Bennett's findings are relevant here. She observed that the passive voice appears far more frequently in written narrative than in oral narrative ("Extended View," 45–49).

136. Chafe, "Linguistic Differences," 117; Ong, *Orality and Literacy*, 45–46.

137. Chafe notes that direct discourse is one of two ways that this is accomplished in spoken discourse. The historical present is the other way, and the two often appear in conjunction (*Discourse*, 208).

138. Ibid., 205–6.

immediate mode, though. They often speak in what Chafe calls the displaced mode to verbalize their consciousness. In the displaced mode, the past tense is more common than the historical present, though the present often occurs when direct speech is reported.[139] This is what we find in the text at hand. Of the nine present indicative forms, six are in direct discourse. The present imperative δότε occurs on three occasions in direct discourse, and the present participle λέγων introduces direct discourse on four occasions. That direct discourse is introduced without a speaking lexeme, but simply with ὅτι in lines 24 and 34, is also suggestive of the narrative's transcriptive nature.

In sum, this petition, which was almost assuredly dictated to a scribe, exhibits the linguistic features expected of an orally composed narrative. This, along with supralinear additions in lines 16–17, suggests that it had not yet been thoroughly edited literarily. As noted above, petitions usually began as oral transcripts dictated to a scribe and were subsequently edited into a more suitable written form by the same scribe or a scribal community.[140] Thus the text exhibits an interfacial relationship with orality and textuality, leaning to the oral side of the oral-literal continuum. It possesses oral syntax in its written form as a "written reminder" of things spoken. For this reason, it can be classified in the versatile category of ὑπομνήματα. I will suggest that *Joseph and Aseneth* and Mark also fit within this classification, to which we now turn.

The purposes, features, and semantic range of ὑπομνήματα in Greco-Roman antiquity

The term ὑπομνήματα and its near equivalent, ἀπομνημονεύματα, had a wide semantic range in the ancient world.[141] They could refer to a preliminary draft of a historical work.[142] Or they could designate a loose collection of sayings or chreiai.[143]

---

139. Ibid., 208.

140. Kelly, *Petitions*, 42–44.

141. George Kennedy notes that the former were usually considered slightly less literary than the latter. In this respect, ὑπομνήματα were meant for private use and ἀπομνημονεύματα were usually intended for publication ("Classical and Christian Source Criticism," in Walker, *Relationships Among the Gospels: An Interdisciplinary Dialogue*, 136–37).

142. Lucian (*Hist. cons.*, 48) testifies to this sense of ὑπομνήματα, calling it the body of work that is ἀκαλλὲς ἔτι καὶ ἀδιάφθρωτον ("as yet with no beauty or continuity" [trans. Kilburn, LCL]). Gert Avenarius and Alan Kirk each note that the ὑπομνήματα of historical treatises will usually have undergone further stylistic revision (Avenarius, *Lukians Schrift zur Geschichtsschreibung* [Meisenheim am Glam: Anto Hain, 1956], 85–86; Kirk, *Q in Matthew: Ancient Media, Memory, and Early Scribal Transmission of the Jesus Tradition*, LNTS 564 [London: Bloomsbury, 2016], 44–45).

143. This function of ὑπομνήματα is evidenced in Diogenes Laertius, *Lives* 8.2 Empedocles (53). It is discussed by Jens Eric Skydsgaard, *Varro the Scholar: Studies in the*

But their most important meaning for our purposes connoted oral transcriptions of teaching.[144] Alan Kirk suggests that, in one of its connotations, "ὑπομνήματα refers to writing taken virtually direct from an oral instructional situation, serving as a 'reminder' of the oral material."[145]

Three Greco-Roman writers attest to this meaning of ὑπομνήματα: the philosopher-physician Galen, the rhetorician Quintilian, and the historian Lucian. In the case of the first two, the written reminders reduced from an oral teaching resulted in various forms of piracy, accidental publication, and plagiarism. With the third, the reader is informed that ὑπομνήματα were unadorned creations that could be later "literaturized" by more skilled writers.

Galen had the problem of persons re-performing his lectures from ὑπομνήματα. In *De libris propriis* 9–11, he gives his judgment on why so many people have taken to performing his lectures as their own.[146] Somehow or other, imposters got a hold of notes (ὑπομνήματα) that had been transcribed from things heard (ὧν ἤκουσαν) in his oral lectures.[147] These were never intended for publication (πρὸς ἔκδοσιν) and were passed along without a proper title (ἐδίδοτο χωρὶς ἐπιγραφῆς). Taking the oral transcriptions (ὑπομνήματα), the charlatans began to perform them as their own (ἀνεγίγνωσκον ὡς ἴδια).

First Book of Varro's de Re Rustica, Analecta Romana Instituti Danici 4 (Copenhagen: Munksgaard, 1968), 110–15; Kirk, *Q in Matthew*, 46.

144. This connotation of ὑπομνήματα is noted by Loveday Alexander, "Ancient Book Production and the Circulation of the Gospels," in *The Gospels for All Christians: Rethinking the Gospel Audiences*, ed. Richard Bauckham (Grand Rapids: Eerdmans, 1998), 89–99; Boudon-Millot, "Oral et écrit chez Galien," in *Colloque la médicine grecque antique: actes*, ed. Jacques Jouanna and Jean Leclant (Paris: Académie des Inscriptions et Belles-Lettres, 2004), 207; William A. Johnson, *Readers and Reading Culture in the High Roman Empire: A Study of Elite Communities* (Oxford: Oxford University Press, 2010), 86–87; Kirk, *Q in Matthew*, 46–47.

145. Kirk, *Q in Matthew*, 46.

146. Greek text in Georg Helmreich, Johannes Marquardt, and Iwani Müller, *Claudii Galeni Pergameni scripta minora*, vol. 2, (Leipzig: Teubner, 1891; repr. Amsterdam: Hakkert, 1967), 91–124. The most accessible English translation is *My Own Books* in *Galen: Selected Works*, ed. and trans. P. N. Singer (Oxford: Oxford University Press, 1997), 3–22.

147. Matthew D. C. Larsen suggests four different reasons for which texts in antiquity were accidentally published: (1) Notes were given to a friend and went public against an author's will; (2) untitled notes were taken by students from their teacher's lecture and these notes were claimed by someone else in a different region; (3) multiple copies of a text that was in demand in a certain community were made and then disseminated to another group; (4) a charlatan stole a text ("Accidental Publication, Unfinished Texts and the Traditional Goals of New Testament Textual Criticism," *JSNT* 39 [2017]: 369). This account from Galen falls under Larsen's second reason for accidental publication. Larsen himself addresses this same account from Galen and notes that "accidental publication was especially prevalent in unfinished texts or notes, like ὑπομνήματα" (ibid., 370).

Galen tells of another occasion when one of his lectures was dictated for a friend, but upon the recipient's death was widely disseminated much to his chagrin:

ἐπεὶ δ' ἱκανῶς ὁ λόγος ηὐδοκίμησεν, ἐδεήθη μού τις φίλος ἐπαχθῶς ἔχων πρὸς αὐτὸν ὑπαγορεῦσαι τὰ ῥηθέντα τῷ πεμφθησομένῳ παρ' αὐτοῦ πρός με διὰ σημείων εἰς τάχος ἠσκημένῳ γράφειν ὅπως, ἂν ἐξορμήσῃ τῆς πόλεως οἴκαδε, δύναιτο λέγειν αὐτὰ πρὸς τὸν Μαρτιάλιον ἐν ταῖς τῶν νοσούντων ἐπισκέψεσιν ... ὅτε τὸ δεύτερον ἧκον εἰς Ῥώμην ... τὸ βιβλίον δ' εἶχον οὐκ ὀλίγοι ... ἐξ ἐκείνου δ' ὥρισα μήτε διδάσκειν ἔτι δημοσίᾳ μήτ' ἐπιδείκνυσθαι. (*libr. propr.* 14–15)	Well, this speech got a very good response; and a friend of mine who was hostile to Martialius begged me to dictate what I had said to a person he would send to me who was trained in a form of shorthand writing, so that, if he suddenly had to leave Rome for his home city, he would be able to use it against Martialius during examinations of patients. When I subsequently returned to Rome on my second visit ... the book ... was now in the possession of a large number of people. From that moment I decided to give no more public lectures or demonstrations.[148]

Galen is understandably perturbed about this piracy. And this last incident, he tells his reader, was the straw that broke the camel's back. The risk that oral transcripts of his lectures would get leaked and be plagiarized had become too high for him to bear. And so he decided "to give no more public lectures or demonstrations."[149]

A few things are noteworthy about Galen's accounts. First, most if not all of these ὑπομνήματα were oral transcriptions (ὑπαγορευθέντων [*libr. propr.* 11]) of his lectures. Transcribing oral discourse for friends or students was a common practice for Galen, as it will have been for his contemporaries.[150] Second, the discourses were reappropriated by others because they were not intended for publication (πρὸς ἔκδοσιν) as literary texts.[151] Apparently this fact, along with their lack of a title, made them more susceptible to emendation. Third, the physician explicitly tells his readers that it is important that they know under what circumstances each text was produced, as this affects the form, purpose, and style of each work.[152] The purpose of *De libris propriis* is to elucidate these circumstances and inform his readers which of Galen's discourses initially existed as ὑπομνήματα and which did not.[153] Fourth, Galen's ὑπομνήματα were spuriously manipulated for reoralization.

148. *Galen: Selected Works*, trans. P. N. Singer, The World's Classics (Oxford: Oxford University Press, 1997), 6.

149. Ibid.

150. Loveday Alexander, *The Preface to Luke's Gospel: Literary Convention and Social Context in Luke 1:1–4 and Acts 1:1*, SNTSMS 78 (Cambridge: Cambridge University Press, 1993), 62–63; Johnson, *Readers*, 86.

151. For more on accidental publication in antiquity, see Larsen, "Accidental Publication," 369–72. He discusses multiple texts that attest to the phenomenon in antiquity, including Plato's *Parmenides*, Galen's *On my Own Books*, Arrian's writing up Epictetus's *Discourses*, *4 Ezra*, and Augustine's *De Trinitate*.

152. *libr. propr.* 23.

153. *libr. propr.* 9–10.

But they were also reworked for the book trade. Galen's counterfeiters were not only rereading and performing oral lectures from his ὑπομνήματα, they were also trying to pass off the written versions as their own.[154] These notes apparently existed at the borderland of orality and textuality and were manipulated for both modalities. Galen's aforementioned friend, in a less malicious manner, wanted a textualized account of Galen's oral speech with which he could defend himself at a public, oral examination of patients. The latter episode demonstrates that the reappropriation of an oral discourse by employing ὑπομνήματα was not always a disreputable act.

An account from Quintilian also implies that lecture notes could be employed with the best of intentions. In the preface to *Institutio oratoria* (1.0.7–8), Quintilian tells of a situation that will have been familiar to Galen. Quintilian informs Marcus Vitorius, to whom *Institutio oratoria* is dedicated, that two other books on rhetoric are already circulating in his name. Quintilian published neither, nor were they meant for such a purpose (*editi a me neque in hoc comparati*). Rather, they were discourses taken down in shorthand (*notando*) from lectures on two different occasions. Some fervent students of Quintilian rashly circulated the notes. Quintilian concedes that, for this reason, some of the content in *Institutio oratoria* will be familiar, but many things will be changed, added, and the whole text will be better written (*erunt eadem aliqua, multa mutata, plurima adiecta, omnia vero compositiora et quantum nos poterimus elaborare*).

As with the ὑπομνήματα made for Galen's friend, this is a case where the reappropriation of lecture notes was not done with the intent to deceive. Quintilian's students simply wanted to honor him. It is also noteworthy that Quintilian implies that these transcriptive notes are less polished than their published counterparts, presumably because they exhibit an oral register. For this reason, and probably others, Quintilian acquired the lecture notes and eventually reworked them into a more publishable literary form.[155]

In *Quomodo historia conscribenda sit* 16, Lucian gives further evidence that ὑπομνήματα were unadorned literary creations close to the vernacular and could be reworked by subsequent tradents. He observes the work of a certain historian who "compiled a bare record of the events and set it down on paper, completely prosaic and ordinary" (ὑπόμνημα τῶν γεγονότων γυμνὸν συναγαγὼν ἐν γραφῇ κομιδῇ πεζὸν καὶ χαμαιπετές).[156] Lucian does not think the amateur (ἰδιώτης) should be critiqued too harshly for this product. His ὑπόμνημα has cleared the way for

---

154. Galen reports that his friends found numerous copies of his ὑπομνήματα and that there were many discrepancies (διαφωνοῦντα) between them (*libr. propr.* 10). He begins *De libris propriis* with an anecdote about a man finding a text spuriously attributed to him in Rome's bookseller district (*libr. propr.* 8–9).

155. Galen states that he did the same. He writes about how, on a trip to Rome, he collected all the spurious ὑπομνήματα of various lectures, corrected them, gave them titles, and published them (*libr. propr.* 12–13).

156. Text and translation: Kilburn, LCL.

another historian with more literary taste and ability to handle (μεταχειρίσασθαι) the writing. While Lucian does not testify directly to the transcriptive nature of ὑπομνήματα here, he confirms that they were stylistically unadorned and could be reworked by someone other than their original author.[157]

From Galen, Quintilian, and Lucian we thus learn that a text might be identified as a ὑπόμνημα if (1) it is explicitly called a ὑπόμνημα; (2) it exhibits elements of an oral register; (3) its content has been altered or expanded; (4) it has been stylistically transformed into something more suitable for publication; (5) it does not have a title or author; and (6) it was not originally intended for publication. We also learn from them that ὑπομνήματα is a meta-generic category. Galen, Quintilian, and Lucian are representatives of diverse literary fields of Greco-Roman antiquity. Their testimony confirms that ὑπομνήματα is a versatile media form employed for a variety of purposes and literary genres.[158]

In the following chapters, I shall argue that many of these features of ὑπομνήματα apply to *Joseph and Aseneth* and Mark. Both narratives are residually oral, were expanded by later authors, were edited literarily, and are anonymous. They can be placed within the broad range of ὑπομνήματα. Lest it be objected that these narratives are too literary for this category, we should remember that a large portion of Galen's output, which was certainly literary, was, or at least began life as, ὑπομνήματα.[159]

Significantly, Mark is explicitly called a ὑπόμνημα in some of the earliest ecclesiastical testimony. In other testimonies, the narrative is not directly labeled as such, but the composition scenario presented echoes what we know about ὑπομνήματα from Galen, Quintilian, and Lucian. In what follows, I shall present some of the early testimony to the composition of Mark. Whether these texts accurately portray who was involved in the production of the gospel, namely, Mark and Peter, is of only subsidiary interest here. What is significant is that the ecclesiastical testimony presents a model of composition for Mark that passes for verisimilitude. The scenario consistently outlined is that two people were involved in the production of Mark, one as speaker and one as transcriber, indicating that the gospel began life as an oral transcription of a spoken account.

---

157. Lucian, *Hist. cons.* 48.

158. Larsen similarly offers "an odd assortment of examples [of accidental publication] from a wide variety of times, places, contexts and genres" ("Accidental Publication," 372). His intent is to demonstrate that textual fluidity and the phenomenon of accidental publication were widespread in antiquity (ibid.). My contention is similar here and provides another cause for the pervasiveness of accidental publication. The use of ὑπομνήματα was common across times, places, contexts, and genres. The prevalence of accidental publication stemmed in part from the ubiquitous employment of ὑπομνήματα as a medium of communication.

159. Johnson lists all of Galen's texts that began life as ὑπομνήματα (*Readers*, 87 n. 33).

Ecclesiastical testimony to Mark's composition

Clement, as reproduced in Eusebius's *HE* 2.15.1-2, calls Mark a ὑπόμνημα διδασκαλίας ("memoir of teaching"). The passage is replete with ancient media terms that suggest the gospel is a mixed product of orality and writing:

τοσοῦτον δ' ἐπέλαμψεν ταῖς τῶν ἀκροατῶν τοῦ Πέτρου διανοίαις εὐσεβείας φέγγος, ὡς μὴ τῇ εἰς ἅπαξ ἱκανῶς ἔχειν ἀρκεῖσθαι ἀκοῇ μηδὲ τῇ ἀγράφῳ τοῦ θείου κηρύγματος διδασκαλίᾳ, παρακλήσεσιν δὲ παντοίαις Μάρκον, οὗ τὸ εὐαγγέλιον φέρεται, ἀκόλουθον ὄντα Πέτρου, λιπαρῆσαι ὡς ἂν καὶ διὰ γραφῆς ὑπόμνημα τῆς διὰ λόγου παραδοθείσης αὐτοῖς καταλείψοι διδασκαλίας, μὴ πρότερόν τε ἀνεῖναι ἢ κατεργάσασθαι τὸν ἄνδρα, καὶ ταύτῃ αἰτίους γενέσθαι τῆς τοῦ λεγομένου κατὰ Μάρκον εὐαγγελίου γραφῆς. γνόντα δὲ τὸ πραχθέν φασὶ τὸν ἀπόστολον ἀποκαλύψαντος αὐτῷ τοῦ πνεύματος, ἡσθῆναι τῇ τῶν ἀνδρῶν προθυμίᾳ κυρῶσαί τε τὴν γραφὴν εἰς ἔντευξιν ταῖς ἐκκλησίαις· Κλήμης ἐν ἕκτῳ τῶν Ὑποτυπώσεων παρατέθειται τὴν ἱστορίαν, συνεπιμαρτυρεῖ δὲ αὐτῷ καὶ ὁ Ἱεραπολίτης ἐπίσκοπος ὀνόματι Παπίας.	But a great light of religion shone on the minds of the hearers of Peter, so that they were not satisfied with a single hearing or with the unwritten teaching of the divine proclamation, but with every kind of exhortation besought Mark, whose Gospel is extant, seeing that he was Peter's follower, to leave them a written statement of the teaching given them verbally, nor did they cease until they had persuaded him, and so became the cause of the Scripture called the Gospel according to Mark. And they say that the Apostle, knowing by the revelation of the spirit to him what had been done, was pleased at their zeal, and ratified the scripture for study in the churches. Clement quotes the story in the sixth book of the Hypotyposes, and the bishop of Hierapolis, named Papias, confirms him.[160]

Clement claims that the production of the gospel makes it a *tertium quid* between orality and textuality, an oral message transferred into the written medium. The implication of Peter's hearers not being satisfied with a single telling of the oral proclamation and Mark's leaving behind a "memoir of teaching" is that the teaching would be proclaimed again, presumably by a reader or performer reoralizing the ὑπόμνημα. Given that spuriously employing ὑπομνήματα could be considered a disreputable act, Peter might have found such reoralization problematic. This is apparently not the case. Clement assures his audience that Peter was "pleased" (ἡσθῆναι) at the prospect, and even sanctioned the ὑπόμνημα for employment in the churches.[161] In the next chapter, *HE* 2.16, Eusebius writes that Mark was sent

---

160. Text and translation: Lake, LCL.
161. In *HE* 6.14.6–7, Eusebius reproduces another testimony from Clement about the circumstances of Mark's production *apropos* of the discussion about ὑπομνήματα. After stating that Mark "writes up the things said" (ἀναγράψαι τὰ εἰρημένα) by Peter, Clement reports that the distribution (μεταδοῦναι) of the writing was not prohibited (κωλῦσαι) by Peter. Clement presumably includes this comment because the distribution of the gospel might have been perceived as mendacious in ancient media culture.

to Egypt with the text he had transcribed (συνεγράψατο) to establish churches.¹⁶² Lexemes for writing and preaching are paired directly: στειλάμενον, τὸ Εὐαγγέλιον ὃ δὴ καὶ συνεγράψατο, κηρῦξαι ("[Mark was] sent to preach the gospel which he transcribed"). Eusebius states that Mark employed his written text as a tool for preaching.

Clement is not the only early Christian writer who testifies to the transcriptive nature of Mark's Gospel, nor is he the first. Papias gives a similar account to the production of Mark, which he himself received from "the Elder" (ὁ πρεσβύτερος). According to *HE* 3.39.15, Mark was Peter's transcriber (ἑρμηνευτής) who wrote down accurately, though not in polished form (ἀκριβῶς ἔγραψεν, οὐ μέντοι τάξει), the words and deeds of Jesus which he had heard (ἤκουσε) in Peter's teaching.¹⁶³ Papias does not specify what purpose Mark's writing was to serve, but there are hints that he considers it to be in the range of ὑπομνήματα. These hints are found in the comment about Mark not writing stylistically (τάξει) and Peter not intending to create a σύνταξιν τῶν κυριακῶν ... λογίων ("an orderly composition of the Lord's words"). The fact that the writing comes out of Peter's oral teaching in a manner akin to Galen's disappearing lecture notes lends this further credence.

Following Papias, the tradition of Mark as Peter's transcriber is pervasive in the ecclesiastical testimony.¹⁶⁴ Marshaling and interpreting all the primary source evidence to it would only belabor the point. What I wish to impress here is the

---

162. It is noteworthy that συνεγράψατο is in the middle here, as it indicates something more transcriptive in this voice than in the active, wherein it connotes creatively composing prose or history. It most commonly often is used of drawing up treatises, contracts, and bonds in the middle (LSJ, s.v. "συγγράφω"; Isocrates, *Panath.* 12.158; P.Cair.Zen.199.5; P.Oxy. 729.17).

163. My translation here is dependent on considerations from Josef Kürzinger, who argues that ἑρμηνευτής and ἡρμήνευσεν, for Papias, do not indicate that Mark is Peter's interpreter in the sense that he translates words from one language into another ("Das Papiaszeugnis und die Erstgestalt des Matthäusevangeliums," *BZ* 4 [1960]: 26). Rather, these are technical terms connoting literary intermediaries or middlemen (ibid.). He similarly contends that τάξει and σύνταξιν do not refer to chronological order in this passage, but to lack of literary artistry ("Die Aussage des Papias von Hierapolis zur literarischen Form des Markusevangeliums," *BZ* 21 [1977]: 252–53). Larsen comes to the same conclusion about τάξει and σύνταξιν (*Gospels before the Book*, 92–93, 106–7). This is especially illuminating when compared to Papias's testimony about Matthew in *HE* 3.39.16, where he writes that Matthew "writes with literary artistry" (συνετάξατο). C. Clifton Black comes to a similar conclusion as Kürzinger, proposing that the Papian testimony about Mark is concerned with literary style and compositional norms (*Mark: Images of an Apostolic Interpreter*, Studies on Personalities of the New Testament [Columbia: University of South Carolina Press, 1994], 91).

164. It is also in Irenaeus, *Adv. Haer.*, 3.1.1; the Markan prologue of Hippolytus (Black, *Mark*, 119); Clement's *adumbrationes* on 1 Pet. 5:13; Clement *apud* Eusebius's *HE* 6.14.6–7; Origen, *De vir.* 8; Jerome, *Comm. on Matt.*, Pref.; Tertullian, *Adv. Marc.* 4.1.1, 2.1–2, 3.4, 5.3–4 (Black, *Mark*, 125–26).

plausibility of the composition scenario.[165] It is striking that, without exception, an interplay between orality and writing is reported in these early accounts about the production and reception of the Gospel of Mark.[166] The patristic writers found it plausible that an account was dictated to a scribe who either handed over the transcriptive record immediately or subsequently reworked it into a more literary form. In both cases, Mark lands within the flexible range of ὑπομνήματα and is closer to the transcriptive end of the oral-literal continuum than the compositional end. The ecclesiastical testimony presents a plausible model for the oral composition of Mark in Greco-Roman antiquity. I suggest that the composition scenario presented for Mark is credible, and even likely, for *Joseph and Aseneth* as well.

Conclusion

In this chapter I have pursued multiple tasks. I have advocated a theoretical mixed-media approach to orality's influence on textuality. This method maintains that the

---

165. Mark's dependence on Peter as testified in these sources need not be accepted as strictly historical to maintain that two people were involved in the production of Mark, one as speaker and one as writer. Following Martin Hengel, I find it as likely as not that Peter had a hand, or rather a mouth, in the earliest stages of the production of Mark (*Studies in the Gospel of Mark* [Philadelphia: Fortress, 1985], 50). The association with Peter accounts for Justin Martyr's reference to the "recollections of Peter" when he addresses Mk 3:16, the prominent role Peter plays in Mark, and what Hengel calls the "unexceptional quality" of Mark's Greek (ibid., 50–51). More recently, Richard Bauckham has argued that Peter's eyewitness testimony was the principal source behind Mark's Gospel (*Jesus and the Eyewitnesses: The Gospels as Eyewitness Testimony* [Grand Rapids: Eerdmans, 2013], 124–27, 155–80). His argument is fourfold. First, references to Peter in Mk 3:16 and 16:7 form an *inclusio* that "place Peter prominently at the end of the story as at the beginning" and suggest that Peter's testimony is contained within this *inclusio* (ibid., 125). Bauckham finds similar literary devices in the Gospel of John, Luke, Lucian's *Alexander the False Prophet*, and Porphyry's *Life of Plotinus*, which by his count establishes the structure as a literary convention (ibid., 127–47) Second, there is a phenomenon in Mark first noted by C. H. Turner that Bauckham names the "plural-to-singular narrative device" (Turner, "Marcan Usage: Critical and Exegetical on the Second Gospel V. The Movements of Jesus and His Disciples and the Crowd," *JTS* 26 [1925], 225–40; Bauckham, *Jesus and the Eyewitnesses*, 157–64). This device is "Mark's way of deliberately reproducing in his narrative the first-person perspective—the 'we' perspective"—from which Peter naturally told his stories" (Bauckham, *Jesus and the Eyewitnesses*, 164). Third, Peter's prominent role in Mark is a holdover from the eyewitness testimony from which the gospel was composed (ibid., 165–72). And fourth, that the audience is invited to identify with Peter is a holdover from the perspective presented by the gospel's primary eyewitness (ibid., 172–79).

166. Black notices a pattern in the patristic testimony wherein Mark is consistently involved in the shift "from oral tradition to written Gospel" (*Mark*, 142).

two modalities are neither separate nor competing. Rather, orality and textuality participate with one another in a variety of ways. I have evoked Foley's theory of verbal art as a theoretical starting point for investigating this interface in the early Jewish and Christian narratives *Joseph and Aseneth* and Mark. But I have contended that we can move beyond Foley's category "Voices from the Past" and be more specific about how orality has left its imprint on the textuality of these narratives. I have reviewed sociolinguistic research to establish that telling a story orally results in different syntax than writing a story.

From these sociolinguistic studies I have distilled three linguistic criteria for considering the probability that a narrative was composed by dictation in Greco-Roman antiquity, and I have reviewed how and why texts were composed in this manner. To show the utility of my proposed criteria I applied them to two texts from the papyri that were most likely composed by dictation. To the three linguistic criteria I added two metalinguistic criteria informed by orality theory. Collectively, these five criteria are an apparatus by which we can better explore the complex relationship between orality and textuality, especially when approaching the production of Koine Greek narratives. Finally, I identified one category from Greco-Roman media culture, ὑπομνήματα, to which Mark and *Joseph and Aseneth* are likely related. I argued that this was the category in which patristic writers placed the Gospel of Mark.

In the next two chapters, the criteria proposed here will be applied to *Joseph and Aseneth* and Mark. Chapter 3 considers the narratives' linguistic features and Chapter 4 their metalinguistic characteristics. I shall argue that Mark and *Joseph and Aseneth*, despite their theological and generic differences, exhibit remarkable similarities. These similarities result from their medium and mode of production. Both are textualized oral narratives that were initially committed to the written medium via dictation.

Chapter 3

LINGUISTIC ORAL RESIDUES

In this chapter, I will survey *Joseph and Aseneth* and Mark with the three linguistic criteria proposed in the previous chapter and argue that both narratives are residually oral. But before I do this, there are two significant subjects of prolegomena that must be addressed. The first is the textual reconstruction of *Joseph and Aseneth* I prioritize. Because there has long been a split among *Joseph and Aseneth* scholars about which reconstruction is most "original" and because it is now questionable whether using a single reconstruction of the narrative is the most appropriate way to approach the text, it is necessary to address my use of Philonenko's text. The second issue is bilingual influence on Mark and *Joseph and Aseneth*. While the consensus is that both texts were written in Greek, there are lingering questions about how Aramaic or Hebrew might have affected their style.

Textual traditions, recensions, and reconstructions of Joseph and Aseneth

Joseph and Aseneth is a well-preserved pseudepigraphon, existing in ninety-one different manuscripts in seven different languages.[1] These manuscripts have been categorized into four text groups: *a, b, c,* and *d*.[2] There is agreement that text families *a* and *c* are later revisions of earlier witnesses.[3] Group *a* improves

---

1. Standhartinger, "Recent Scholarship," 354.
2. These groups are named for their affinities with the four manuscripts, A, B, C, and D, that Batiffol used in his 1889–1890 *editio princeps* ("Le livre," 1–115). Paul Riessler translated Batiffol's edition into German (*Altjüdisches Schriftum ausserhalb der Bibel* [Augsburg: Filser, 1928], 497–538). Bernard Pick translated the same edition into English ("Joseph and Asenath," *Open Court* 27 [1913]: 467–96), as did Ernest W. Brooks (*Joseph and Asenath: The Confession of Asenath, Daughter of Pentephres the Priest* [London: Society for Promoting Christian Knowledge, 1918]). Since Batiffol, the manuscripts have retained their capital letter designations; lists; and descriptions of the manuscripts in Burchard, "New Translation," 178.
3. Standhartinger, "Recent Scholarship," 355.

upon its predecessors stylistically and literarily.[4] Group *c* demonstrates a similar style, but is based on an incomplete version of the narrative that was later given a Modern Greek ending.[5] The debate about which text group is eldest has centered on groups *b* and *d*. In 1968, Marc Philonenko published the first critical edition of *Joseph and Aseneth* relying on a manuscript from the shorter *d*-text group.[6] He argued that this text family was the basis of the later-expanded *b*-group.[7] Philonenko's reconstruction is 8,320 words. In contrast to Philonenko, over the course of his career Christoph Burchard has argued for the priority of the longer text family.[8] In 2003, Burchard published a critical edition based on a collation of Syriac, Armenian, Greek, and Latin manuscripts of the longer version of the narrative.[9] His reconstruction is about 5,000 words longer than Philonenko's at 13,401 words.[10]

Burchard's early arguments for the priority of the longer version were generally accepted. The consensus in the 1970s and 1980s was that the longer manuscripts

---

4. I address the phenomenon of stylistic improvement and its similarity to Synoptic redaction in Chapter 5. Manuscript A also explicitly identifies the angel in *Joseph and Aseneth* 14–17 with Michael. In the other text groups, the identity of this angel is ambiguous.

5. The text ends at 16:7 in Burchard's enumeration, and the Modern Greek text supplements down to 21:9 (Burchard, "New Translation," 178). Burchard translates the Modern Greek ending in "Joseph und Aseneth neugriechisch," *NTS* 24 (1978): 80–83.

6. Philonenko, *Joseph et Aséneth*.

7. Ibid., 16–26.

8. This group was formerly family *b*, but was later expanded and now includes family *f*, Syr, Arm, L2, and family *a*. Burchard argues for the priority of the longer versions in *Gesammelte Studien zu Joseph und Aseneth*, SVTP 13 (Leiden: Brill, 1996); idem, ed., *Joseph und Aseneth*, PVTG 5 (Leiden: Brill, 2003), 41–46; idem, "The Text of Joseph and Aseneth Reconsidered," *JSP* 14 (2005): 83–96.

9. More specifically, Burchard's critical edition, *Joseph und Aseneth*, relies heavily on family *f*, which contains three subsets of Greek, Romanian, and Latin manuscripts, two Syriac manuscripts, which he labels Syr, fifty Armenian manuscripts, labeled Arm, a group he labels L2, which contains manuscript 436 and another group of five manuscripts (435&), and family *a*, which comprises six other Greek manuscripts (A, CR, O, PQ). The texts for Burchard's reconstruction are commonly referred to as *f*, Syr, Arm, L2, *a*. In 2008, Burchard's student Uta Fink improved his text, addressing problems he had outlined in the "Verbesserungsvorschläge und Problemanzeigen zum Text des Ausgabe" section (pp. 369–84) of his critical edition (*Joseph und Aseneth: Revision des griechischen Textes und Edition der zweiten lateinischen Übersetzung*, Fontes et Subsidia ad Bibliam Pertinentes 5 [Berlin: de Gruyter, 2008]). Unfortunately, Fink's text is not a critical edition, making it cumbersome to compare the various readings in *Joseph and Aseneth* when using her reconstruction. To make textual comparisons of *Joseph and Aseneth* more manageable, Standhartinger suggests the publication of a synopsis edition of the texts, which would include actual readings of the manuscripts themselves (*Frauenbild*, 224; eadem, "Recent Scholarship," 363).

10. Word count in Standhartinger, "Recent Scholarship," 361.

best represent the "original" form of *Joseph and Aseneth*.¹¹ Edith M. Humphrey offers two reasons why this position became the consensus.¹² First, Philonenko did not actively engage Burchard in debate about the priority of the longer or shorter version.¹³ Second, Burchard's translation was included in Charlesworth's *Old Testament Pseudepigrapha*, effectively enshrining it as the scholarly reconstruction of choice.¹⁴ Additionally, Burchard's numerous publications defending the longer version meant that anyone arguing against the priority of these manuscripts would have to fight an uphill battle.

In the early 1990s, Ross Kraemer and Angela Standhartinger each engaged in this campaign.¹⁵ In her early publications on the narrative, Kraemer argues that text-critical considerations are not the only criteria for evaluating the different texts of *Joseph and Aseneth*.¹⁶ She traces the construction of gender in the two versions and finds that Philonenko's reconstruction represents a feminine perspective, while Burchard's a more patriarchal one.¹⁷ Comparing the feminine and masculine postures of the respective reconstructions, Kraemer does not draw any strong conclusions about the priority of either in her early publications.¹⁸ This

---

11. A summary of the early critiques of Philonenko's position are in Randall D. Chesnutt, *From Death to Life: Conversion in Joseph and Aseneth*, JSPSup 16 (Sheffield: Sheffield Academic, 1995), 65–69.

12. Humphrey, *Joseph and Aseneth*, Guides to Apocrypha and Pseudepigrapha (Sheffield: Sheffield Academic, 2000), 18–19.

13. Ibid., 19.

14. Ibid., 18–19.

15. Standhartinger, *Frauenbild*. Her own English summaries are in eadem, "From Fictional Text to Socio-Historical Context: Some Considerations from a Text-Critical Perspective on Joseph and Aseneth," *SBLSP* 35 (1996): 303–18; eadem, "Joseph and Aseneth: Perfect Bride of Heavenly Prophetess," in *Feminist Biblical Interpretation: A Compendium of Critical Commentary on the Books of the Bible and Related Literature*, ed. Luise Schottroff and Marie-Theres Wacker (Grand Rapids: Eerdmans, 2012), 578–85. Kraemer argues her case in "Women's Authorship of Jewish and Christian Literature in the Greco-Roman Period," in *"Women Like This": New Perspectives on Jewish Women in the Greco-Roman World*, ed. Amy-Jill Levine, EJL 1 (Atlanta: Scholars Press, 1991), 221–42; eadem, *Her Share of the Blessings: Women's Religions among Pagans, Jews, and Christians in the Greco-Roman World* (New York: Oxford, 1992); eadem, *Aseneth*, 50–80.

16. Kraemer, "Women's Authorship," 234–35.

17. Ibid., 235. In 1992, Kraemer expanded her argument that the longer version was more "androcentric and sexualized," laying out some of the differences between the two reconstructions (*Her Share*, 110–12).

18. This is likely a result of Kraemer's evaluation of the quest for the earliest, most original text of *Joseph and Aseneth*. She has repeatedly sounded the refrain that this is a misguided pursuit that only distracts interpreters from understanding the contextual issues inherent to each version ("Women's Authorship," 234–35; eadem, *Her Share*, 112; eadem, *Aseneth*, 305).

changed in 1998, when she made the case for the priority of the *d*-text family, citing numerous instances where Burchard's version contains words and phrases not present in Philonenko's text.[19] She argues that these were subtle editorial additions meant to elucidate ambiguities and make biblical allusions explicit.[20]

Standhartinger takes an approach similar to Kraemer's. She attempts to demonstrate that the versions are two independent narratives that each present a unique image of women in general and Aseneth in particular.[21] The two renditions are not "accidental products of textual growth or textual slippage, but rather two different versions of the same story."[22] She further argues that the unique image of women, the *Frauenbild*, presented in the shorter text of *Joseph and Aseneth* is most likely a unique contribution by that author. It would have been difficult, if not impossible, to create this *Frauenbild* out of textual revision of the longer version.[23] For these reasons, she concludes that "the short text [D] certainly cannot be an epitome of the long text [B]."[24] Standhartinger determines that the short text was created in the first century BCE, while the long text was a product of the first century CE.[25]

This debate over textual priority reveals that what was once a consensus is no more so.[26] The question concerning the priority of the longer or shorter version is still open. And it is now disputed whether "priority" is even the most important issue concerning the different versions of the narrative. In 2005 Patricia Ahearne-Kroll advocated a new approach for understanding the transmission of *Joseph and Aseneth*.[27] Looking at the two primary reconstructions of the narrative by Burchard and Philonenko, she found that the relationships between the various text families that they worked from were even more complex than was initially suggested.[28] Because of this complexity, Ahearne-Kroll ultimately concludes that there likely *was* one original and initial manuscript of *Joseph and Aseneth*, but that the possibility of ever discovering or reconstructing this original is extremely unlikely if not completely unrealistic.[29] Moreover, she determines that comparing

---

19. Kraemer, *Aseneth*, 50–88.
20. Ibid., 50.
21. Standhartinger, *Frauenbild*.
22. Standhartinger, "Fictional Text," 304.
23. Standhartinger, *Frauenbild*, 220–25.
24. Ibid., 220.
25. Ibid., 225.
26. Burchard responded to his critics in 2005, defending the priority of the longer reconstruction against the arguments made by Standhartinger and Kraemer and providing additional arguments for this priority ("Text"). The debate continues today. Standhartinger reviews the most recent publications related to it in "Recent Scholarship," 353–406.
27. Ahearne-Kroll, "Jewish Identity," 61–87.
28. Ibid., 20–61.
29. Ibid., 60.

the two reconstructions, especially to "discern the ideologies of redactors," is a misguided and problematic endeavor.[30]

Rather than argue for the priority of a single reconstruction of *Joseph and Aseneth* and work from that reconstruction, Ahearne-Kroll opts to utilize a methodology employed by Christine M. Thomas with respect to the Acts of Peter.[31] In place of a single reconstruction, Ahearne-Kroll constructs a "well-defined fabula" that the various textual instantiations of *Joseph and Aseneth* both attest to and themselves construct.[32] She suggests that we do better to consider these various textual versions as multiple textual "performances" of the *Joseph and Aseneth* tradition, and not as more or less original versions of the tradition.

Ahearne-Kroll's perspective on the textual traditions of *Joseph and Aseneth* has been well received and is quickly becoming the textual modus operandi for Aseneth studies.[33] With both Ahearne-Kroll and Kraemer, I believe the quest for the original text to be a misguided endeavor.[34] I also find compelling Ahearne-Kroll's argument that the most profitable way to handle the textual transmission of *Joseph and Aseneth* is to compare the various instantiations as equally original and contemporaneous traditions. Deviating from Ahearne-Kroll, however, I contend that *Joseph and Aseneth* did likely exist as an oral tradition before it was transferred into the written medium, and this helps to explain why a performance attitude was taken toward the tradition's textual transmission.[35] I also deviate from the textual modus operandi she has established in what follows. This is not because I find the perspective deficient or wanting in any respect or because I consider Philonenko's reconstruction to be the "original" version of *Joseph and Aseneth*; it is simply because of the nature of my particular project. Ahearne-Kroll's method is especially profitable for assessing the ideologies of various textual versions of *Joseph and Aseneth*. But it is particularly cumbersome to apply when assessing the language and style of the narrative since many of the manuscripts of *Joseph and Aseneth* aren't readily available for scrutiny. The following chapters investigate linguistic and stylistic features and patterns of *Joseph and Aseneth* throughout the entirety of the narrative. Working from a consistent reconstruction that is based

---

30. Ibid.
31. Thomas, *Acts of Peter*, 78; Ahearne-Kroll, "Jewish Identity," 71–74.
32. Ahearne-Kroll, "Jewish Identity," 81–83.
33. Most recently Jill Hicks-Keeton (*Arguing with Aseneth: Gentile Access to Israel's Living God in Jewish Antiquity* [Oxford: Oxford University Press, 2018]) has successfully employed Ahearne-Kroll's method in a systematic manner.
34. Ahearne-Kroll, "Jewish Identity," 61, 72; Kraemer, "Women's Authorship," 234–35; eadem, *Her Share*, 112; eadem, *Aseneth*, 305.
35. Ahearne-Kroll rejects the notion that *Joseph and Aseneth* began life as an oral tradition, though it is not entirely clear why she rejects the possibility ("Jewish Identity," 78–79). How *Joseph and Aseneth*'s existence as an oral tradition helps to explain the performance attitude take toward the narrative's manuscript transmission is addressed at greater length in Chapter 4.

on the eldest manuscript traditions is most profitable *for this particular endeavor*. Because this is the case, in what follows I have chosen to rely primarily on Philonenko's critical text. Using the shorter reconstruction, I will make reference to Burchard's longer version and various instantiations of the manuscript tradition when they are relevant.[36]

Bilingual influence

The scholarly consensuses are that *Joseph and Aseneth* and Mark were originally composed in Greek.[37] But the "Semitic flavor" of each is frequently noted, as well.[38] In *Joseph and Aseneth* this flavor is perceived in phrases such as καὶ ἰδού, εἰς τὸν αἰῶνα χρόνον, ὁ παράδεισος τῆς τρυφῆς, ἐχάρη χαρὰν μεγάλαν, ἐφοβήθη φόβον μέγαν, and ἀγρὸς τῆς κληρονομίας ἡμῶν.[39] In Mark it is likewise encountered

---

36. In my earlier argument for the oral conception of *Joseph and Aseneth*, I gave precedence to Burchard's reconstruction (Elder, "On Transcription"). While I now find it more likely that Philonenko's shorter reconstruction is an older version of *Joseph and Aseneth* than Burchard's, I do not believe the reconstruction that Burchard offers has moved far beyond the original oral conception of the narrative. Both Philonenko's and Burchard's reconstructions exhibit dense residual orality and lean to the oral side of the oral-literary continuum. Not until the literary improvements made in the *a*-text family does *Joseph and Aseneth* exhibit features more characteristic of literarily conceived discourse. In Chapter 5 I will compare Burchard's and Philonenko's reconstructions with Batiffol's to substantiate this claim.

37. Not since 1922, when Paul Riessler argued that certain mistranslations suggest a Hebrew *Vorlage*, has there been a case made for the existence of an underlying Hebrew text for *Joseph and Aseneth* ("Joseph und Asenath: Eine altjüdische Erzählung," *TQ* 103 [1922]: 1–22, esp. 1–3). Riessler's supposed mistranslations have been shown to be inconclusive by both Burchard and Chesnutt (Burchard, *Untersuchungen*, 92; Chesnutt, *From Death to Life*, 69–71). The original Greek character of the narrative is beyond doubt and frequently noted in scholarship (Burchard, "New Translation," 181; Chesnutt, *From Death to Life*, 69–71; Christoph Burchard, "The Present State of Research on *Joseph and Aseneth*," in idem, *Gesammelte Studien*, 302; Humphrey, *Joseph and Aseneth*, 31; Ahearne-Kroll, "Jewish Identity," 145). As to Mark, the closest anyone gets to expressing doubts about the original Greek character of the gospel is Maurice Casey. He argues that specific pericopes (Mk 9:11-13; 2:23–3:6; 10:35-45; 14:12-26) reflect Aramaic substrata (*Aramaic Sources of Mark's Gospel*, SNTSMS 102 [Cambridge: Cambridge University Press, 1998], 111–252).

38. "Semitic flavor" is a phrase used by Chesnutt (*From Death to Life*, 70).

39. Hebraic characteristics of *Joseph and Aseneth* are noted by Philonenko, *Joseph et Aséneth*, 30–31; Chesnutt, *From Death to Life*, 70. Similarities to the LXX have also been recognized (Philonenko, *Joseph et Aséneth*, 28–30; Humphrey, *Joseph and Aseneth*, 31–33; Ahearne-Kroll, "Joseph and Aseneth," 2526).

in the locutions εἰς τὸν αἰῶνα and ἐφοβήθησαν φόβον μέγαν, as well as several syntactical constructions.[40]

Why these narratives exhibit this Semitic flavor is a matter of debate, and the nature of Hebraic or Aramaic influence on early Jewish and Christian Greek texts, especially the New Testament, has a long history, the contours of which can only be broadly outlined here.[41]

It was once supposed that the register of the NT was a unique Jewish-Greek dialect.[42] At the turn of the twentieth century, this view became the object of sharp criticism by Adolf Deissmann, who argued that texts from the NT were remarkably similar to the nonliterary papyri and that both were products of the Greek vernacular.[43] Albert Thumb expanded Deissmann's theory, claiming that there was a common written and spoken Greek that extended throughout the Mediterranean world from about 300 BCE to 500 CE.[44] It was in this Koine language that the NT texts were written. This position quickly became influential and thus James H. Moulton would write in 1906, "The conclusion is that 'Biblical' Greek ... was simply the vernacular of daily life."[45] Hebraic and Aramaic influence were largely excluded from these early investigations of the Koine vernacular.

That perspective had a short lifespan. In the second volume of his grammar, Moulton admitted that many tenets of "Deissmannism" were applied too rigorously.[46] Moulton continued to work under the general premise that the NT was representative of the Greek vernacular, but he conceded that Aramaic and Hebrew

---

40. Aramaic or Hebraic characteristics of Mark are noted by Nigel Turner, *Style*, vol. 4 of *A Grammar of New Testament Greek* (Edinburgh: T&T Clark, 1976), 11–30; Elliott C. Maloney, *Semitic Interference in Marcan Syntax*, SBLDS 51 (Chico: Scholars Press, 1980); Casey, *Aramaic Sources*, 85–86; C. Leslie Reiter, *Writing in Greek but Thinking in Aramaic: A Study of Vestigial Verbal Coordination in the Gospels* (Lewiston: Mellen, 2013); Armin D. Baum, "Mark's Paratactic καί as a Secondary Syntactic Semitism," *NovT* 58 (2016): 1–26.

41. Maloney's review of scholarship surveys how debates about Semitic influence and the Greek vernacular developed from the turn of the twentieth century until just past its midway point (*Semitic Interference*, 7–25).

42. Linguistic studies in the pre-Deissmann period are reviewed in Constantine R. Campbell, *Advances in the Study of Greek: New Insights for Reading the New Testament* (Grand Rapids: Zondervan, 2015), 29–32.

43. Deissmann, *Bibelstudien* (Marburg: Elwert, 1895); idem, *Neue Biblestudien* (Marburg: Elwert, 1897); idem, *Bible Studies*, trans. Alexander Grieve (Edinburgh: T&T Clark, 1901); idem, *Light from the Ancient East*).

44. Thumb, *Die griechische Sprache im Zeitalter des Hellenismus* (Strassburg: Tübner, 1901).

45. Moulton, *Prolegomena*, vol. 1 of *A Grammar of New Testament Greek* (Edinburgh: T&T Clark, 1906), 4.

46. James H. Moulton and W. F. Howard, *Accidence and Word-Formation with an Appendix on Semitisms in the New Testament*, vol. 2 of *A Grammar of New Testament Greek* (Edinburgh: T&T Clark, 1929), 14.

affected these texts to a greater extent than was previously recognized.⁴⁷ Following Moulton's second volume, the mid-twentieth century saw many different theories about how Aramaic and Hebrew influenced the language of texts from the New Testament to varying degrees.⁴⁸

At present, bilingualism is the most common explanation for the presence of Aramaisms and Hebraisms in Greek texts. Studies on bilingualism show that a polyglot's first and second languages "interfere" with one another.⁴⁹ If our authors' first or second languages were Aramaic, then syntactical patterns characteristic of Aramaic will have affected their Greek.⁵⁰ It is from this perspective that Maloney argues for Semitic interference concerning the general style and syntax of Mark, as well as to five different parts of speech.⁵¹ C. Leslie Reiter similarly claims that the verbal coordination peculiar to the canonical gospels results from Semitic interference.⁵² And Maurice Casey briefly addresses Aramaic interference at the syntactical level, noting that a strong dose of parataxis, verb placement toward the beginning of a clause, and certain adverbial phrases likely stem from Semitic interference in certain Markan episodes.⁵³ These studies suggest that Mark was produced in a bilingual environment.⁵⁴ The gospel exhibits Semitic interference

---

47. Ibid., 14–34.

48. Maloney, *Semitic Interference*, 11–25.

49. Ibid., 11. Casey reviews the phenomenon of bilingual interference in *Aramaic Sources*, 93–95.

50. Joseph A. Fitzmyer addresses the linguistic situation of the first century, particularly in Palestine. He argues that Aramaic was a lingua franca, but that Greek would have been spoken by most, if not all, people ("The Study of the Aramaic Background of the New Testament," in *A Wandering Aramean: Collected Aramaic Essays*, ed. idem [Grand Rapids: Eerdmans, 1997], 6–10; idem, "The Language of Palestine in the First Century A.D." in ibid., 29–56 esp. 38–43). Rodney J. Decker asserts that Aramaic was the author of Mark's first language ("Markan Idiolect in the Study of the Greek of the New Testament," in *The Language of the New Testament: Context, History, and Development*, ed. Andrew W. Pitts and Stanley E. Porter, Linguistic Biblical Studies 6 [Leiden: Brill, 2013], 48). See also Hengel, *Studies*, 46.

51. Stylistic and syntactical interference is addressed in Maloney, *Semitic Interference*, 51–104, and interference with respect to various parts of speech in ibid., 104–96.

52. Reiter, *Writing in Greek*.

53. Casey, *Aramaic Sources*, 85–86.

54. Perhaps even a trilingual environment, if one considers the Latinisms in Mark to affect the gospel's style. The presence of Latinisms at the lexical level is undeniable. Words in Mark such as δηνάριον (*denarius*, "denarius;" Mk 6:37; 12:15; 14:5), μόδιος (*modius*; "measure"; Mk 4:21), ξέστης (*sextarius*; "quart"; Mk 7:4), σπεκουλάτωρ (*speculator*; "executioner," Mk 6:27), λεγιών (*legion*; "legion"; Mk 5:9, 15), κεντυρίων (*centurion*; "centurion"; Mk 15:39, 44, 45), κοδράντης (*quadrans*; "coin"; Mk 12:42) are of Latin, not Greek, origin (Brian J. Incigneri, *The Gospel to the Romans: The Setting and Rhetoric of Mark's Gospel*, BibInt 65 [Leiden: Brill, 2003], 101), though it is a matter of debate whether these lexical Latinisms suggest Mark was produced in a locale where Latin was widely

as to its vocabulary and syntactical style.⁵⁵ It is possible that the same kind of interference has affected the language of *Joseph and Aseneth*, though the topic has not yet been extensively examined. By investigating the residual orality of these narratives, I do not mean to imply that they are unaffected by other linguistic factors. I find it likely that both individuals were bilingual. But Aramaic or Hebraic interference does not preclude oral composition, or vice versa.⁵⁶ The former cannot account for all the unique similarities that *Joseph and Aseneth* and Mark share.

There is one characteristic of the narratives to which both Semitic interference and oral composition contribute, namely, their paratactic structures. As Casey puts it, "Increased frequency of καί is to be expected in people who are accustomed to saying ו."⁵⁷ Casey himself recognizes that parataxis is not unique to Semitic languages.⁵⁸ And neither is a Hebrew or Aramaic narrative paratactically structured by necessity. Frank H. Polak has shown that narratives from the Hebrew Bible exhibit varying degrees of syntactical complexity.⁵⁹ While Semitic interference might increase the degree to which a narrative is paratactically structured, it alone cannot account for a prominence of parataxis. Rather, as noted in Chapter 2, parataxis is a common device for structuring spoken narrative in most languages. When it occurs in a narrative, other features of oral composition often accompany it. This is what we find with both *Joseph and Aseneth* and Mark.

Residually oral linguistic characteristics

In what follows, I shall apply the three linguistic criteria for assessing residual orality to *Joseph and Aseneth* and Mark. The two narratives are most similar linguistically

spoken, such as Rome, or whether they are technical terms related to the political, military, and administrative life of the empire that were integrated into the vernacular of the Greek-speaking world. The former position is advocated by Incigneri (ibid., 100–3), and the latter by Kelber (*Kingdom in Mark: A New Place and a New Time* [Philadelphia: Fortress, 1974], 129) and Herman C. Waetjen (*A Reordering of Power: A Socio-Political Reading of Mark's Gospel* [Minneapolis: Fortress, 1989], 13).

55. Many find Semitic interference most clearly exhibited in Mark's paratactic structure (Baum, "Mark's Paratactic," 1–26; Decker, "Markan Idiolect," 47–49; Maloney, *Semitic Interference*, 66–67).

56. Kelber (*Oral and Written Gospel*, 66) argues similarly. Casey also notes that parataxis is not an exclusive feature of Semitic syntax and must have been prevalent in the vernacular because of its ubiquity in the Greek papyri (*Aramaic Sources*, 19–20).

57. Casey, *Aramaic Sources*, 95.

58. Ibid., 19–20.

59. Polak, "The Oral and the Written: Syntax, Stylistics, and the Development of Biblical Prose Narrative," *JANESCU* 26 (1998): 59–105. Susan Niditch likewise claims that there are various "textures" of Hebrew biblical literature ("Hebrew Bible and Oral Literature: Misconceptions and New Directions," in Weissenrieder and Coote, *Interface*, 6–14).

in their paratactic structures, employment of the idea unit, and repetitions. While they exhibit some resemblances in their verbal features, the ubiquity and function of the historical present in Mark is a denser residual oral characteristic than any of the verbal characteristics in *Joseph and Aseneth*.

Criterion #1: Parataxis, apposition, and the idea unit

Parataxis, Apposition, and the Idea Unit in Joseph and Aseneth *Joseph and Aseneth* is paratactically structured. Scholars have persistently noted this feature of the narrative, often deploring it as a sign of stylistic unsophistication.[60] The conjunction καί occurs 1,034 times out of a total 8,230 words in *Joseph and Aseneth*. This is 12.6% of its total words or once for every 7.96 words.[61] Most of the chapters in Philonenko's reconstruction begin with καί.[62] Dewey observes that oral literature is paratactic with respect not only to its individual clauses but also to entire episodes.[63] Only fourteen of the forty-two pericopes in *Joseph and Aseneth* do not start with καί, and eleven of these fourteen are in Aseneth's prayer in chaps. 12–13. When the story is in direct narration, 90% of the pericopes begin with "and" (καί). Few sentences in the narrative begin with a word other than καί.[64] Only six sentences in the entire text do not contain the connective.[65] This is to be expected given sociolinguistic research, which finds that the simple coordinating conjunction appears far more frequently—nearly twice as often—in oral narrative than in written narrative.[66]

Not only is the volume of καί in *Joseph and Aseneth* indicative of its oral conception, but the number of times the connective strings multiple clauses together in single sentences is also residually oral. In literarily conceived discourse, it is extremely rare for more than three or four coordinate clauses to be used consecutively.[67] In contrast, speakers will string six or seven clauses together by

---

60. Burchard, "New Translation," 186; Philonenko, *Joseph et Aséneth*, 30; Graham Anderson, *Fairytale in the Ancient World* (New York: Routledge, 2000), 37.

61. Burchard's reconstruction does not differ significantly. There, καί occurs 1,651 times out of a total 13,400 words. That is 12.3% of its total words or 1 in every 8.12 words.

62. This is the case in every chapter except for 1, 10, and 13. *Joseph and Aseneth* 1 begins with ἐγένετο, *Joseph and Aseneth* 10 with τότε, and *Joseph and Aseneth* 13 with ἐπίσκεψαι. Similarly, in Burchard's reconstruction, there are only two paragraphs that do not begin with καί. These paragraphs begin at *Jos. Asen.* 21:10 and 23:6 in his versification.

63. Dewey, "Oral Methods," 37.

64. Of the total 312 sentences, there are 58 that do not begin with καί: *Jos. Asen.* 1:4, 13, 14; 2:16; 4:5, 10, 12, 13, 14, 15, 16; 6:5, 6, 7; 7:2, 3, 6, 7; 8:6, 7; 10:1; 12:5, 6, 7, 9, 10, 11, 12; 13:1, 2, 3, 4, 5, 6, 7; 13:9, 11, 12; 15:3, 4, 5, 7, 10, 11, 14; 16:15; 23:6, 7, 12; 24:7, 8, 14; 25:6; 27:6; 28:5, 6, 13; 29:4. The majority of these are in direct discourse, specifically, monologues.

65. *Joseph and Aseneth* 1:1; 4:15; 7:7; 13:1; 16:15; 23:12.

66. Beaman, "Coordination and Subordination," 61.

67. Beaman notes that no writer coordinated more than seven clauses with *and* in her case studies (ibid., 58).

coordination.⁶⁸ This happens frequently in *Joseph and Aseneth*, and two examples illustrate the phenomenon well. The first occurs in *Jos. Asen.* 3:9, which narrates Aseneth dressing herself before she goes to meet her mother and father:

καὶ ἔσπευσεν Ἀσενὲθ	And Aseneth hastened
καὶ ἐνεδύσατο στολὴν βυσσίνην ἐξ ὑακίνθου χρυσοϋφῆ	And she put on her fine linen robe of blue interwoven with gold
καὶ ἐζώσατο ζώνην χρυσῆν	And she belted a golden belt
καὶ περιέθετο ψέλια περὶ τὰς χεῖρας καὶ τοὺς πόδας αὐτῆς	And she placed bracelets around her hands and her feet
καὶ περιεβάλετο ἀναξυρίδας χρυσᾶς	And she put on golden trousers
καὶ περὶ τὸν τράχηλον αὐτῆς περιέθετο κόσμον.	And around her neck she placed a necklace.⁶⁹

Here, six clauses are connected by the coordinating conjunction καί in a single sentence.⁷⁰ At 5.8 words each, the idea units fall into the four-to-seven-word range of these units in oral narrative.⁷¹ Another example shows that καί links multiple clauses together in a manner characteristic of oral narrative and uncharacteristic of written discourse. *Joseph and Aseneth* 10:4-5 details Aseneth's preparations for her lament:

καὶ ἔσπευσεν Ἀσενὲθ	And Aseneth hastened
καὶ καθεῖλεν ἐκ τῆς θύρας τὴν δέρριν τοῦ καταπετάσματος	And she took down the leather curtain from the door
καὶ ἔπλησεν αὐτὴν τέφρας	And she filled it with ashes
καὶ ἀνήνεγκεν εἰς τὸ ὑπερῷον	And she brought it into the upper room
καὶ ἀπέθετο αὐτὴν εἰς τὸ ἔδαφος	And she put it on the ground
καὶ ἔκλεισε τὴν θύραν ἀσφαλῶς	And she locked the door securely
καὶ τὸν μοχλὸν τὸν σιδηροῦν ἐπέθηκεν αὐτῇ ἐκ πλαγίων	And she placed the iron bar on it sideways
καὶ ἐστέναξε στεναγμῷ μεγάλῳ καὶ κλαυθμῷ.	And she groaned with great groaning and weeping.

---

68. While coordination of six or seven clauses is more common, Beaman finds that speakers can coordinate up to thirteen clauses with the simple conjunction (ibid.).

69. The versification and Greek text of *Joseph and Aseneth* is most frequently from Philonenko, *Joseph et Aséneth*. I have opted to translate Philonenko's reconstruction myself on most occasions, because in my estimation there is no adequate stand-alone English translation of Philonenko's text. When other reconstructions, versifications, and translations are referred to, this will be noted. English translations of the longer version of *Joseph and Aseneth* are most frequently Ahearne-Kroll's ("Joseph and Aseneth").

70. I limit the sentence to v. 9 following Chafe's conception of what a sentence consists of in spoken discourse. According to him, sentences in this mode are limited by a "single center of interest" (Wallace Chafe, "The Deployment of Consciousness in the Production of a Narrative," in *The Pear Stories*, 26). The next center of interest, which begins in v. 10, is connected by καί, but begins a new sentence because it shifts focus to a different topic.

71. Bakker, "How Oral?" 39.

In this case, Philonenko has chosen to punctuate vv. 4 and 5 as separate sentences. In my estimation, the two verses are better understood as one sentence, continuing the same idea. At the beginning of v. 4 Aseneth is explicitly stated as the subject of all the following verbs, indicating that this is one stream of thought centered on a single interest.[72] In this sentence eight clauses are coordinated using καί, before the subject changes in *Jos. Asen.* 10:6 and the next sentence is related to the previous one, again with the simple connective. The average length of the idea units, at 5.9 words per unit, is nearly identical to the last example. These two cases are not exceptions. There are several places in *Joseph and Aseneth* where more than five clauses are successively coordinated with καί.[73] This structural style is more common to orally conceived than literarily conceived narrative.[74]

Apposition, copulative constructions, and the "hitching post"

As stated in the previous chapter, extensive use of parataxis partitions oral narrative into idea units, which are typically four to seven words long.[75] Though that is the case, the idea unit is not produced by parataxis alone. There are other linguistic implements speakers use to separate their narrative into these units. Apposition and the copula commonly form idea units in *Joseph and Aseneth*.[76] In oral narrative, new descriptive information is not likely to reside in the subject of a clause but is more typically contained in its predicate.[77] Chafe offers the hitching post as a metaphor for this syntactical phenomenon.[78] The subject is the post to which new information is hitched. This allows hearers to relate the information to

---

72. *Joseph and Aseneth* 10:3 might also be included in this single sentence, which would further increase the number of clauses coordinated by καί in this sentence by three. I have chosen not to include v. 3 because Aseneth is restated as the subject of the aorist verbs in *Jos. Asen.* 10:4.

73. *Joseph and Aseneth* 1:4, 9; 2:5-6; 4:8-9; 5:6; 10:11-13, 13-17; 14:15-16; 16:4-5, 9-11; 18:3-6; 24:16-18; 27:3; 29:5-6 all contain six or more clauses connected by καί consecutively. A few of these contain ten clauses connected in this manner, and 10:13-17 and 18:3-6 contain thirteen and twelve clauses connected with καί in a single sentence, respectively.

74. Beaman finds that no writer coordinates more than seven clauses with *and*. But speakers coordinate up to thirteen clauses with the conjunction ("Coordination and Subordination," 58).

75. Chafe, *Discourse*, 53–70; idem, "Linguistic Differences," 106–11; Bakker, "How Oral?" 39.

76. Albert B. Lord argues that frequent apposition is a characteristic of oral literature ("Characteristics of Orality," *Oral Tradition* 2 [1987]: 55–56). On the syntax of copulas as predicate adjectives, see Smyth, *Greek Grammar*, §§917–18.

77. Chafe, *Discourse*, 108.

78. Wallace Chafe, "Givenness, Contrastiveness, Definiteness, Subjects, Topics, and Point of View," in *Subject and Topic*, ed. Charles N. Li (New York: Academic Press, 1976), 25–55, esp. 43–45.

its subject more easily. It is to this end that *Joseph and Aseneth* employs apposition and the verb ἦν as a copula.

This third-person singular form of εἰμί occurs fifty-four times in *Joseph and Aseneth*, nearly always in a predicate relationship with a nominative as both its subject and object, rather than with an adverb or prepositional phrase as its object. It is found commonly in descriptions of characters, as in those of Pentephres and Aseneth in *Jos. Asen.* 1:3-5, and of settings.[79] The description of Aseneth's house and room, which takes up the entirety of the narrative's second chapter, illustrates the copulative use of ἦν, along with the prominence of apposition. In this description ἦν occurs seventeen times, along with seven instances of the third-person plural form, ἦσαν. Indicative verbs that are not ἦν or ἦσαν appear only fourteen times in the chapter. Moreover, apposition is frequent in this description, employed on seventeen occasions, serving the same purpose as ἦν or ἦσαν, but with more economy. As a result, nominative forms far exceed all others in this chapter.[80] These two syntactical features illustrate how the grammar of descriptions in *Joseph and Aseneth* follows a pattern characteristic of oral narrative. Descriptive information is simply tacked onto a subject. In literarily conceived narrative, this mode of description is considered repetitive and unsophisticated. But in oral narrative, this is an effective and economical way to describe characters and settings.

Absence of literarily conceived syntax

While parataxis and the idea unit positively establish *Joseph and Aseneth*'s residual orality, there are three syntactical features absent from the narrative that are characteristic of written, literarily conceived discourse. These help to make an apophatic argument for the narrative's oral conception. First, relative pronouns are sparse in *Joseph and Aseneth*. Relative clauses often provide nuance and complexity to sentences in literarily conceived narrative. Nonuse of them is indicative of the syntactical simplicity of oral narrative.[81] It is telling that there are only thirty relative pronouns in *Joseph and Aseneth*. Second, conjunctions that are not καί rarely appear in the narrative. There are twenty-eight different conjunctions in *Joseph and Aseneth*. Those that are not καί appear only 196 times.[82] This is indicative of the narrative's paratactic structuring, but it also signifies that there are far fewer subordinate and complex clauses than coordinate clauses in the text.

---

79. I more thoroughly address ἦν and apposition in *Jos. Asen.* 1:3-5 in Elder, "On Transcription," 125–27.

80. Nominative forms occur forty-four times, genitive forms twenty-one times, dative forms thirteen times, and accusative forms fifteen times.

81. Chafe, "Linguistic Differences," 110; idem, "Integration and Involvement," 44–45.

82. διότι (56x), ὅτι (31x), ἀλλά (21x), ὡς (17x), γάρ (11x), δέ (10x), ἵνα (9x), εἰ (8x), οὔτε (4x), μήποτε (3x), ἐάν (2x), εἴτε (2x), καθά (2x), καθότι (2x), καθώς (2x), μηδέ (2x), οὐδέ (2x), πλήν (2x), ποτέ (2x), ἐπειδή (1x), ὅθεν (1x), ὅπως (1x), ὅτε (1x), οὖν (1x), πρίν (1x), τέ (1x), τοίνυν (1x).

In sum, *Joseph and Aseneth*'s heavy doses of parataxis, apposition, and copulative constructions, along with its nonuse of relative clauses, subordinating conjunctions, and attributive adjectives, are all features of the narrative's oral register. Mark resembles *Joseph and Aseneth* in its paratactic structure and employment of the idea unit.

Parataxis, apposition, and the idea unit in Mark

Frequency and location of καί in Mark In Mark, καί occurs 1,100 out of a total 11,312 words. This is 9.6% of the total words in the gospel or once for every 10.28 words. This is slightly less frequently than in *Joseph and Aseneth*, where καί appears once for every 7.96 words. Its frequency in Mark is also similar to the two papyrological narratives examined in Chapter 2. In BGU I.26, καί appears once for every 12.29 words in the letter as a whole and once for every 12.00 words in the narrative portion of the letter. In P.Oxy. 903, καί occurs 36 times out of a total 395 words, or once in every 10.97 words.

In both BGU I.26 and P.Oxy. 903, καί begins about half of the narrative clauses and sentences. It appears even more frequently at the beginning of sentences in *Joseph and Aseneth*. According to Philonenko's punctuation, the connective begins 254 of the narrative's 312 sentences, 81.4%. Mark statistically falls between the papyrological narratives and *Joseph and Aseneth* in this respect. According to Paul Ellingworth, καί begins 64.5% of the sentences in Mark.[83] And at the clausal level, Elliott Maloney finds that καί coordinates independent clauses 591 times in the gospel.[84] Finally, Mark is also similar to *Joseph and Aseneth* with respect to the number of paragraphs that begin with καί. The conjunction begins 114 of the 145 paragraphs in Mark, which is 92%.[85] This is comparable to *Joseph and Aseneth*, wherein 66.6%, twenty-eight out of forty-two, of the total pericopes begin with καί. If Aseneth's prayer in chaps. 12–13 is excluded, twenty-nine of the thirty-two in Philonenko's division of the text begin with καί. This is 90.6%.

It is instructive to compare the volume of καί in Mark and *Joseph and Aseneth* to other texts contemporaneous with them. In the NT, only Revelation has a higher frequency of καί than Mark. At 11.4% of the total words in the apocalypse, it is slightly below *Joseph and Aseneth*'s volume.[86] Excluding Mark, καί appears 8,061

---

83. Paul Ellingworth, "The Dog in the Night: A Note on Mark's Non-Use of KAI," *BT* 46 (1995): 125. This is 376 of the 583 sentences in the gospel.

84. Maloney, *Semitic Interference*, 66.

85. This is based on the punctuation in NA27. Baum finds that the percentage is nearly identical in Westcott-Hort's punctuation, wherein καί begins eighty of Mark's eighty-eight pericopes ("Mark's Paratactic," 20). Wire offers statistics for the number of times καί begins a new pericope in the various Greek editions of Mark (*Case*, 83).

86. In Revelation, καί appears 1,128 times of 9,856 total words. This is once for every 8.64 words. The volume of καί in Revelation might be significant for genre and compositional studies of that text, as well as for the reference to the reader (ὁ ἀναγινώσκων) and the hearers

times out of 126,846 total words in the NT. That is, 6.4% of the total words or once for every 15.34 words. Paul's letter to the Romans is a stark counter-example to our narratives. It is a text that was literarily conceived and will have gone through multiple rounds of literary revisions.[87] In the epistle, καί occurs 279 times out of 7,114 words. This is a mere 3.9% of its total words or 1 in every 25.50 words. In Chapter 5, I shall more thoroughly compare parataxis in Mark with Matthew and Luke. But it is worth foregrounding Mark's differences from the later Synoptics here. Καί appears 45% less frequently in Matthew and 33% less frequently in Luke than in Mark.[88]

The volume of καί in Mark and *Joseph and Aseneth* is closer to some texts from the LXX and other pseudepigraphical literature than it is to the NT. Narratives such as Ruth, Jonah, Judith, *1 Enoch*, and Tobit fall between Mark and *Joseph and Aseneth* in their volume of καί.[89] From the LXX, only 1 Chronicles and 1 Samuel exceed the volume of καί in both Mark and *Joseph and Aseneth*.[90] Many other early Jewish narratives, from the LXX or otherwise, show a much lower frequency of καί than Mark and *Joseph and Aseneth*. In Philo's *De Vita Mosis*, for example, καί appears about half as frequently as it does in *Joseph and Aseneth*.[91] The *Letter of*

(οἱ ἀκούοντες) in Rev. 1:3. David E. Aune writes that Revelation was "explicitly intended for oral performance" (*Revelation*, WBC 52A; [Dallas: Word, 1997], 21). Kristina Dronsch also addresses the aurality of Revelation in "Transmissions from Scripturality to Orality: Hearing the Voice of Jesus in Mark 4:1-34," in Weissenrieder and Coote, *Interface*, 121.

87. Robert Jewett argues that the elegance, rhetoric, and structure of Romans all suggest that it was carefully planned and took weeks to write (*Romans: A Commentary*, ed. Eldon Jay Epp, Hermeneia [Minneapolis: Fortress, 2006], 22–23). The fact that Romans is not a narrative certainly affects the frequency of the conjunction in the text, but it is nonetheless striking that καί appears about two and a half times more frequently in Mark than Romans. It is also of interest that Romans was dictated to Tertius (Rom. 16:21). This confirms that orality and writing were simultaneously at work in the composition of texts in the first century CE and that an educated writer could speak their composition literarily. This, along with the thorough editing process it underwent, accounts for why Romans reads as it does.

88. In Matthew there are 1,194 instances of καί out of a total 18,363 words, or 1 in every 15.38 words. In Luke there are 1,483 instances of καί out of a total 19,495 words, or 1 in every 13.14.

89. A total of 11.2% of the total words in Ruth LXX are καί, 11.9% of Jonah LXX, 10.7% of Judith, 11.1% of *1 Enoch*, and 10.5% of Tobit. The percentages for these texts were calculated with Accordance Bible Software's morphologically tagged version of Rahlfs.

90. A total of 13.7% of the words in 1 Chronicles LXX are καί. It is noteworthy that a large portion of these are in genealogies and not direct narration. 12.8% of the words in 1 Samuel are καί, which is nearly identical to *Joseph and Aseneth*'s 12.6%.

91. A total of 6.1% of the total words in the text. The volume of καί is nearly identical in Philo's *Legatio ad Gaium* and *De Abrahamo*, at 6.5% and 6.4%, respectively. These percentages have been calculated using Accordance Bible Software. The Greek Philonic

Aristeas and *3 Maccabees* also have a much lower volume of καί than Mark and *Joseph and Aseneth* do.

I note these other texts to suggest that there is a range of how paratactically structured narratives from antiquity are. The evidence from early Judaism and Christianity shows that the volume of καί can range anywhere from 4–5% of a narrative's total words on the lower end to 13–14% on the upper end. Where narratives fall on this range will depend on several factors, including their author's style, whether he or she was bilingual, their genre, whether they were written *sua manu* or dictated, how many times they were revised, and if they are translations from Hebrew or Aramaic. Of course, each text would need to be investigated in its own right to determine how residually oral it is. But if a given text possesses a higher volume of καί, it is more likely to exhibit other characteristics of an orally composed narrative, especially short, simple idea units.

Idea units in Mark Idea units can be connected by means other than parataxis. Chafe finds that speakers most frequently connect clauses with *and*, as Mark and *Joseph and Aseneth* do, but this does not preclude linkage with other connectives or grammatical constructions.[92] A preponderance of the simple connective will make it likely that a discourse is characterized by idea units, but to confirm as much we must determine whether the language of that discourse is marked by other characteristic features of idea units. According to Bakker, idea units are typically four to seven words in length, can be independent clauses that stand on their own, which is often the case in *Joseph and Aseneth*, or can be a unit that needs to be complemented to make syntactical sense, which is more frequently the case in Mark.[93] Idea units are usually marked by intentional boundaries.[94] Chafe adds that they have only one center of interest each.[95]

Antoinette Wire elucidates idea units in the gospel by translating Mk 1:1-15 and dividing the text into its respective units.[96] But she does not state what features of Markan syntax establish idea units. Following Wire's modus operandi, we see that two examples from the gospel demonstrate that, alongside coordination

texts for Accordance were prepared and morphologically tagged by The Norwegian Philo Concordance Project and later revised by Rex A. Koivisto and Marco V. Fabbri.

92. Wallace L. Chafe, "Linking Intonation Units in Spoken English," in *Clause Combining in Grammar and Discourse*, ed. Sandra Thompson and John Haiman, Typological Studies in Language 18 (Philadelphia: John Benjamins, 1988), 6–23. Linking with *and* is addressed in ibid., 10–12.

93. Bakker, "How Oral?" 39.

94. Ibid.

95. Chafe, *Discourse*, 140–41.

96. Wire, *Case*, 79. She does so following Bakker, who does the same for Homer ("How Oral?" 40).

with καί, simple finite verbs with an embedded subject, participial phrases, and prepositional phrases characterize idea units in Mark.

Mark 1:21-28 narrates Jesus's first encounter with an unclean spirit in the gospel. Dividing the text into idea units is revealing:

καὶ εἰσπορεύονται εἰς Καφαρναούμ	And they went into Capernaum
καὶ εὐθὺς τοῖς σάββασιν	And immediately on the Sabbath
εἰσελθὼν εἰς τὴν συναγωγὴν	He entered he synagogue,
ἐδίδασκεν.	And taught.
καὶ ἐξεπλήσσοντο ἐπὶ τῇ διδαχῇ αὐτοῦ·	And they were astonished at his teaching,
ἦν γὰρ διδάσκων αὐτοὺς ὡς ἐξουσίαν ἔχων	For he taught them as one who had authority,
καὶ οὐχ ὡς οἱ γραμματεῖς.	And not as the scribes.
καὶ εὐθὺς ἦν ἐν τῇ συναγωγῇ αὐτῶν ἄνθρωπος ἐν πνεύματι ἀκαθάρτῳ	And immediately there was in their synagogue a man with an unclean spirit;
καὶ ἀνέκραξεν λέγων·	And he cried out,
τί ἡμῖν καὶ σοί,	"What have you to do with us,
Ἰησοῦ Ναζαρηνέ;	Jesus of Nazareth?
ἦλθες ἀπολέσαι ἡμᾶς;	Have you come to destroy us?
οἶδά σε τίς εἶ,	I know who you are,
ὁ ἅγιος τοῦ θεοῦ.	The Holy One of God."
καὶ ἐπετίμησεν αὐτῷ ὁ Ἰησοῦς λέγων·	But Jesus rebuked him, saying,
φιμώθητι	"Be silent,
καὶ ἔξελθε ἐξ αὐτοῦ.	And come out of him!"
καὶ σπαράξαν αὐτὸν τὸ πνεῦμα τὸ ἀκάθαρτον	And the unclean spirit, convulsing him
καὶ φωνῆσαν φωνῇ μεγάλῃ ἐξῆλθεν ἐξ αὐτοῦ.	And crying with a loud voice, Came out of him.
καὶ ἐθαμβήθησαν ἅπαντες	And they were all amazed
ὥστε συζητεῖν πρὸς ἑαυτοὺς λέγοντας	So that they questioned among themselves, saying,
τί ἐστιν τοῦτο;	"What is this?
διδαχὴ καινὴ κατ' ἐξουσίαν	A new teaching! With authority
καὶ τοῖς πνεύμασι τοῖς ἀκαθάρτοις ἐπιτάσσει,	He commands even the unclean spirits,
καὶ ὑπακούουσιν αὐτῷ.	And they obey him."
καὶ ἐξῆλθεν ἡ ἀκοὴ αὐτοῦ εὐθὺς πανταχοῦ	And at once his fame spread everywhere,
εἰς ὅλην τὴν περίχωρον τῆς Γαλιλαίας.	Throughout all the surrounding region of Galilee. (RSV)

When the pericope is arranged this way, exactly half of its idea units are coordinated with paratactic καί. This is precisely what should be expected in light of Chafe's research.[97] The other idea units are connected by different means, such as

---

97. Chafe, "Linking Intonation Units," 10–12. In Chapter 2, we have seen that exactly half of the units in the two narratives addressed from the papyri were coordinated with καί.

apposition, prepositional and participial phrases, and direct discourse. Finite verbs are more common than any of these. They begin idea units on six occasions.[98] This is also not surprising, as spoken narrative is characterized by simple, indicative verbal clauses more than written narrative is.[99] The average length of the pericope's idea units is 4.43 words, on the lower end of the four-to-seven-word average Bakker finds for idea units in spoken narrative.[100]

Dividing Mk 5:25-29, the first half of the pericope of the hemorrhaging woman, into idea units is also instructive. It shows that a heavy dose of participial phrases is another characteristic of Mark's idea units.[101]

καὶ γυνὴ οὖσα ἐν ῥύσει αἵματος δώδεκα ἔτη	And there was a woman who had a flow of blood for twelve years
καὶ πολλὰ παθοῦσα ὑπὸ πολλῶν ἰατρῶν	And who had suffered much under many physicians,
καὶ δαπανήσασα τὰ παρ' αὐτῆς πάντα	And had spent all that she had,
καὶ μηδὲν ὠφεληθεῖσα	And was no better
ἀλλὰ μᾶλλον εἰς τὸ χεῖρον ἐλθοῦσα,	But rather grew worse.
ἀκούσασα περὶ τοῦ Ἰησοῦ,	She had heard the reports about Jesus,
ἐλθοῦσα ἐν τῷ ὄχλῳ ὄπισθεν	And came up behind him in the crowd
ἥψατο τοῦ ἱματίου αὐτοῦ·	And touched his garment.
ἔλεγεν γὰρ ὅτι	For she said,
ἐὰν ἅψωμαι κἂν τῶν ἱματίων αὐτοῦ	"If I touch even his garments,
σωθήσομαι.	I shall be made well."
καὶ εὐθὺς ἐξηράνθη ἡ πηγὴ τοῦ αἵματος αὐτῆς	And immediately the hemorrhage ceased;
καὶ ἔγνω τῷ σώματι ὅτι	And she felt in her body that
ἴαται ἀπὸ τῆς μάστιγος.	She was healed from her disease. (RSV)

Once again, καί occurs at the beginning of roughly half of these idea units. At 4.86 words, the average length of each unit is close to what we found in Mk 1:21-28. Noteworthy in this text is the frequency of participial phrases in vv. 25-27. There are seven participles before the finite verb ἥψατο in v. 27. Are these participial phrases best understood as hypotactic, subordinate clauses? R. T. France, Mark Strauss, and Christopher D. Marshall argue that this is the case. According to them, the evangelist employed hypotaxis to engender pathos for the hemorrhaging woman.[102] The compounding of participles might be out of Mark's compositional

---

98. One of these is ἦν in the periphrastic phrase ἦν γὰρ διδάσκων found in Mk 1:22.
99. Beaman, "Coordination and Subordination," 54–60.
100. Bakker, "How Oral?" 39.
101. For brevity I have included only the first half of the pericope. The entire pericope extends from Mk 5:25-34. The second half contains other characteristic features of Mark's idea units. Especially noteworthy is that καί followed by an indicative verb occurs frequently there.
102. R. T. France, *The Gospel of Mark*, New International Greek Testament Commentary (Grand Rapids: Eerdmans, 2002), 236; Mark Strauss, *Mark*, Zondervan Exegetical Commentary on the New Testament (Grand Rapids: Zondervan, 2014), 230; Christopher

character, but rather than an intentional use of hypotaxis, the participles are better interpreted as a verbal pattern of characterization typical of oral narrative.

In *Joseph and Aseneth* characters and settings are typically described with copulative constructions. I argued that Chafe's "hitching post" metaphor explicates the syntax in the narrative's descriptions. In spoken discourse new subjects initially "carry a light information load, as is appropriate for starting points."[103] That is, the subject is an anchor for new information. Chafe observes, "Clauses do not express a random collection of independent events or states, floating in the air like so many disconnected bubbles. Rather, each has a point of departure, a referent from which it moves on to provide its new contribution."[104] This phenomenon makes sense of Mk 5:25-27. "Woman" (γυνή) is the point of departure, the starting point or hitching post, for the seven following nominative participles that all provide new information about her. While the syntax of the woman's description is not identical to what we find in *Joseph and Aseneth*'s descriptions, which are characterized by ἦν or ἦσαν, the overall linguistic structure is familiar.[105] Both have an initial nominative form to which new information is attached with repetitive syntax.

Mark 1:21-28 and 5:25-29 are representatives of Mark's characteristic use of short idea units that are usually connected with the simple conjunction καί. At 4.43 and 4.86 words per idea unit, respectively, they fit within the average length sociolinguists have found for idea units. Throughout the entire gospel, the average length of idea units is consistent with what is found in these two pericopes and sociolinguistic studies. James A. Kleist has divided the entirety of Mark into Greek idea units.[106] The average length of his sense lines is 4.69 words per line.[107]

Other connectives in Mark The average length of idea units is not the only telling feature of whether a narrative is the product of spoken or written discourse. How a narrative connects idea units together is also indicative of its composition. As Steven A. Runge notes, "Connectives play the role of specifying what kind of relationship the writer [or speaker] intended. Each provides a unique constraint on how to process the discourse that follows."[108] Written narrative more explicitly

---

D. Marshall, *Faith as a Theme in Mark's Narrative*, SNTSMS 64 (Cambridge: Cambridge University Press, 1995), 104.

103. Chafe, *Discourse*, 85.

104. Ibid., 83.

105. Though ἦν and ἦσαν appear frequently in Mark compared to the other gospels. The auxiliary verb occurs with a nominative participle on twenty-four occasions (Turner, "Marcan Usage," 90–92).

106. James A. Kleist, *The Gospel of Saint Mark Presented in Greek Thought-Units and Sense-Lines with a Commentary* (New York: Bruce Publishing Company, 1936), 3–87.

107. Tabulations and calculations of the sense lines in his text are my own.

108. Steven A. Runge, *Discourse Grammar of the Greek New Testament: A Practical Introduction for Teaching and Exegesis* (Peabody: Hendrickson, 2010), 19.

relates each segment of discourse with its predecessors and successors. Greek possessed a more sophisticated system for placing clauses in levels of relation than English does. A. T. Robertson wrote, "The Greeks, especially in the literary style, felt the propriety of indicating the inner relation of the various independent sentences that composed a paragraph. This was not merely an artistic device, but a logical expression of coherence of thought."[109] He goes on to note that connectives serve this purpose.[110] Given Greek's capacity to create complex syntactical relationships with a host of different connectives, it is striking that Mark connects clauses with καί nearly twice as often as all other conjunctions combined.[111] In contrast to the 1,100 instances of καί, there are a combined 649 occasions of the twenty-four other conjunctions in the gospel. The most common is δέ, occurring 163 times followed by ὅτι at 102.[112] All other conjunctions in Mark occur less than 100 times.[113]

In short, Mark, like *Joseph and Aseneth*, is paratactically structured at the episodic, conjunctive, and sentential levels. There is a high volume of καί and a limited number of other connectives in both narratives. In a manner characteristic of spoken narrative, they both employ short idea units that are only loosely connected to one another syntactically.

Criterion #2: Repetition of syntactical patterns, words, phrases, and ideas

Repetition of syntactical patterns, words, phrases, and ideas in Joseph and Aseneth
Joseph and Aseneth is repetitive in all three aspects characteristic of oral narrative: individual and groups of lexemes, syntactical structuring, and episodes and concepts. On the level of lexemes, the recurrence of καί is most obvious. The discussion of parataxis in this chapter has confirmed the repetition of this connective. Numerous other words and phrases are also repeated consistently throughout the narrative. Five examples are illustrative. First, the prepositional phrase καὶ μετὰ ταῦτα occurs six times, serving to advance the narrative.[114] Second,

---

109. A. T. Robertson, *A Grammar of the Greek New Testament in the Light of Historical Research* (New York: Hodder and Stoughton, 1919), 443. Philo likewise recognized this aspect of his native tongue (*Moses* 2.38).

110. Robertson, *Grammar*, 443.

111. καί represents 62.9% of all the conjunctions in Mark. It is noteworthy that Chafe found that 50% of the explicit connectives in spoken discourse are "and" ("Linking Intonation Units," 10).

112. Chafe finds that "but" occurs one-fifth as often as "and" in spoken discourse ("Linking Intonation Units," 12). It is instructive, then, that ἀλλά and δέ appear a combined 202 times in Mark to the 1,100 occurrences of καί.

113. γάρ (66x), ἵνα (64x), ἀλλά (45x), ἐάν (36x), εἰ (35x), ὡς (22x), ὅταν (21x), ὅπου (15x), ἕως (15x), ὥστε (13x), ὅτε (12x), οὐδέ (10x), καθώς (8x), οὖν (6x), μηδέ (6x), μή (twice as a conjunction; seventy-five times as a particle), οὔτε (2x), ἄρα (2x) μήποτε (2x), πρίν (2x), ἐπεί (1x), ὅπως (1x).

114. The phrase occurs in *Jos. Asen.* 10:15; 22:1; 22:6; 24:19; 28:15; 29:12.

there is repetition of μόνος in *Jos. Asen.* 2:16 to emphasize that only Aseneth sat on a certain couch. Third, Joseph is consistently described as a powerful (δυνατός) man.[115] Fourth, the verb σπεύδω appears three times in the description of Aseneth's preparations for Joseph's initial visit.[116] Lastly, there is a sixfold repetition of χαρ- root lexemes in *Jos. Asen.* 3:4–4:4.

Joseph and Aseneth is also repetitive at the thematic level. Two examples illuminate this phenomenon. First, bravery is a persistent theme throughout *Joseph and Aseneth*. It is often expressed with imperative forms of the verb θαρσέω followed by a command not to fear.[117] Second, there is a precise verbal pattern, a form of ἀποδίδωμι with the prepositional phrase κακὸν ἀντὶ κακοῦ, repeated in *Joseph and Aseneth* 28 that propagates a non-retaliatory ethic. Other motifs recur without lexical repetition. This is the case with Aseneth's idol worship. The topic is first presented in the description of her room in *Jos. Asen.* 2:3-5, which tells the audience that the first chamber of Aseneth's tower was littered with golden and silver Egyptian gods that she worshiped and to which she sacrificed.[118] The subject is evoked again when the audience is subtly informed that the names of the Egyptian gods are engraved on Aseneth's jewelry in *Jos. Asen.* 3:10. It is reiterated in *Jos. Asen.* 8:5. Joseph refuses Aseneth's kiss because it is not right for a God-fearing man to kiss a woman who "blesses dead and dumb idols with her mouth and eats bread of strangulation from their table and drinks treachery from their cup of libation and is anointed with the balm of destruction." These words disgrace Aseneth and ultimately lead to her repentant idol-smashing bout in *Joseph and Aseneth* 10. There, the not-so-subtle and repetitive notes about Aseneth's idolatry are brought to their crescendo. Aseneth puts on her mourning tunic, throws her exotic garments and sacrificial foodstuffs from her window, and fasts in sackcloth and ashes for seven days. By repetitively echoing Aseneth's idolatry up to this point in the narrative, the speaker has primed the audience for her dramatic repentance.

---

115. Joseph is described as δυνατός in *Jos. Asen.* 3:6; 4:8, 9; 13:11; 18:1, 2. On four occasions the phrase Ἰωσὴφ ὁ δυνατὸς τοῦ θεοῦ recurs. It is likely a result of oral literature's preference for "heavy" characters whose deeds and epithets are memorable (Ong, *Orality and Literacy*, 69). This also accounts for the lengthy descriptions of Pentephres and Aseneth in *Jos. Asen.* 1:4-8, why Aseneth is repeatedly labeled a παρθένος (*Jos. Asen.* 1:6, 8; 4:9; 7:8, 10; 8:1; 8:10; 15:1; 19:2), and the adjectival epithet θεοσεβής applied to the story's various protagonists in *Jos. Asen.* 4:9; 8:5, 6; 20:8; 22:8; 23:9, 10; 28:4; 29:3.

116. *Joseph and Aseneth* 3:6, 9; 4:1.

117. In each instance the command not to fear is either μή with a subjunctive or imperative form of φοβέω (*Jos. Asen.* 14:11; 15:2, 3, 5; 23:15; 26:2. 28:4, 6).

118. According to Ahearne-Kroll, the statues and Aseneth's religious practices imply that her bedroom resembles a temple chamber and that the description makes it clear to the audience that Aseneth's living situation is odd ("Joseph and Aseneth," 2531). The description of this shared sacrificial-dwelling space further heightens Aseneth's devotion to her Egyptian idols and makes the idol-smashing scene in *Joseph and Aseneth* 10 climactic.

Intercalations These thematic and lexical repetitions in *Joseph and Aseneth* are oral residues and resemble the redundancies found in Mark that will be examined below. But there is also a similarity between how *Joseph and Aseneth* and Mark structure some of their episodes. Intercalations, or "sandwiches," are a well-studied literary device in the gospel. On at least six occasions in Mark, episodes are relayed in this A^1-B-A^2 pattern.[119] It is usually thought that the purpose of this structure is mutually to enrich the meaning of all the episodes contained within it.[120] Pericopes following this structure are meant to be heard and interpreted in light of one another. But this format may serve another purpose as well.

Writing, in contrast to speaking, significantly slows down a person's train of thought. This results in the analytic structure that characterizes the literary medium. Ong argues that linear and analytic thought and speech are "artificial creations," impossible without the technology of writing.[121] Oral literature, rather than being characterized by linear structure, is repetitive and concentric.[122] The oral mind employs various methods to aid recollection of stories.[123] Chief among these, as Eric A. Havelock notes, is framing and forecasting.[124] He writes, "All oral narrative is in structure continually both prophetic and retrospective."[125] It is within this framework that Mark's intercalations can be understood as a mnemonic structuring device that aid oral performance and reception.[126] They are tools that

---

119. Mark 3:20-35; 5:21-43; 6:6-30; 11:12-25; 14:1-11; 14:53-72 are the six typically identified (Frans Neirynck, *Duality in Mark: Contributions to the Study of the Markan Redaction*, revised ed. with supplementary notes, BETL 31 [Leuven: Peeters, 1988], 133; Tom Shepherd, "The Narrative Function of Markan Intercalation," *NTS* 41 [1995]: 522; John R. Donahue and Daniel J. Harrington, *The Gospel of Mark*, SP 2 [Collegeville: Liturgical Press, 2002], 18; Geoffrey David Miller, "An Intercalation Revisited: Christology, Discipleship, and Dramatic Irony in Mark 6.6b–30," *JSNT* 35 [2012]: 177). Others have found even more intercalations in Mark. Howard Clark Kee, for instance, identifies eight and James R. Edwards nine (Kee, *Community of the New Age: Studies in Mark's Gospel* [Philadelphia: Westminster, 1977], 54; Edwards, "Markan Sandwiches: The Significance of Interpolations in Markan Narratives," *NovT* 31 [1989]: 197–98).

120. Sandwiches are combined by theme, comparison, or contrast (Rhoads, Dewey, and Michie, *Mark as Story*, 51).

121. Ong, *Orality and Literacy*, 40.

122. Ibid., 39–41.

123. Ibid., 34.

124. Eric A. Havelock, "Oral Composition in the Oedipus Tyrannus of Sophocles," *New Literary History* 16 (1984): 183.

125. Ibid.

126. Dewey similarly argues that Markan sandwiches are "acoustic responses" characteristic of oral composition ("Oral Methods," 39), and Adela Yarbro Collins claims that interpolations likely served as aural aids (*Mark: A Commentary*, Hermeneia [Minneapolis: Fortress, 2007], 524).

stabilize utterances for future pronunciation.[127] When episodes are clustered, the speaker does not need to remember three separate narrative events, but only the one group that joins multiple episodes by comparison, contrast, or theme.

There are occasions where *Joseph and Aseneth* also follows this "prophetic and retrospective" structure characteristic of Mark and oral narrative. The clearest example is in *Joseph and Aseneth* 27–29. Here, Pharaoh's son has enacted his plan to kill Joseph and kidnap Aseneth. When Aseneth is face to face with the antagonist and fifty of his men in *Jos. Asen.* 26:8–27:1, Benjamin comes into the story for the first time. In a scene that echoes David's battle with Goliath, he hurls stones and slays Pharaoh's son's fifty men.[128] He also strikes Pharaoh's son with a stone, leaving him mortally wounded. The narrator abruptly shifts the scene away from Benjamin and Pharaoh's son and to the sons of Bilhah and Zilpah, Dan and Gad, who decide to abandon the plan to kidnap Aseneth and instead kill her and flee to the thicket of reeds (τὴν ὕλην τοῦ καλάμου). A "battle" between Dan and Gad and Aseneth is then narrated. But, unlike Benjamin, Aseneth wields no weapon. As her aggressors move toward her with their swords, she prays to her newfound God for protection and their blades crumble to dust. Having seen the miracle, Dan and Gad beg Aseneth for forgiveness and protection from their brothers, Simeon and Levi, who they suppose will surely avenge their attempt on Aseneth's life. Aseneth responds, assuring them that their brothers are God-fearing men (ἄνδρες θεοσεβεῖς) who do not repay evil for evil to any person (μὴ ἀποδιδόντες κακὸν ἀντὶ κακοῦ τινι ἀνθρώπῳ). In *Jos. Asen.* 28:5, she commands Dan and Gad to go hide in the thicket of reeds (εἰς τὴν ὕλην τοῦ καλάμου), which recalls their own plan laid out in *Jos. Asen.* 27:7, while she pacifies Simeon and Levi. After Aseneth does so, convincing them not to repay evil for evil (μηδαμῶς, ἀδελφέ, ἀποδώσεις κακὸν ἀντὶ κακοῦ τῷ πλησίον σου), the narrator returns to the conflict between Benjamin and Pharaoh's son in *Jos. Asen.* 29:1. Benjamin is about to lop off the antagonist's head when Levi steps in and convinces him that it is not fitting for a God-fearing man to repay evil for evil.[129] Instead, the two bandage the son of Pharaoh and return him to his father on horseback.

---

127. Jan Assmann argues that any formalized utterance, whether by rhythm, alliteration, parallelism, or some other such is a "text." According to him, writing is just as much a "secondary formalization" as the mnemonic devices found in spoken discourse. The primary difference is that writing is not as dependent on other mnemonic structuring devices since it is itself one ("Form as a Mnemonic Device: Cultural Texts and Cultural Memory," in Horsley, *Performing the Gospel*, 72–76).

128. The intertextual function of 1 Samuel 17 in *Joseph and Aseneth* 27–29 will be addressed in Chapter 4.

129. Levi's words in *Jos. Asen.* 29:3 are reminiscent of Aseneth's in 28:14. Levi tells Benjamin, "By no means should you do this deed, brother! Because we are God-fearing men and it is not fitting for a God-fearing man to repay evil for evil nor to trample a fallen man, nor to crush his enemy to death" (μηδαμῶς, ἀδελφέ, ποιήσῃς τὸ ἔργον τοῦτο, διότι ἡμεῖς ἄνδρες θεοσεβεῖς ἐσμεν, καὶ οὐ προσήκει ἀνδρὶ θεοσεβεῖ ἀποδοῦναι κακὸν ἀντὶ κακοῦ οὐδὲ πεπτωκότα καταπατῆσαι οὐδὲ ἐκθλίψαι τὸν ἐχθρὸν ἕως θανάτου).

Thus the episodes are prospective and retrospective in the form of an A¹-B¹-B²-A² intercalation. This "sandwich" can be visualized as follows:

A¹: Benjamin's battle with Pharaoh's son. (*Jos. Asen.* 27:1-5)
B¹: Aseneth's "battle" with the sons of Bilhah and Zilpah. (*Jos. Asen.* 27:6–28:3)
B²: Aseneth's non-retaliatory response to her opponents. (*Jos. Asen.* 28:4-16)
A²: Benjamin's non-retaliatory response to his opponent. (*Jos. Asen.* 29:1-7)

Not only is the intercalation reminiscent of the prophetic and retrospective structure of episodes in oral narrative, but recognizing it accentuates the purpose of these chapters in *Joseph and Aseneth*. At the center of the intercalation is a propagation of how a God-fearing person ought to respond to his or her enemy. This response is characterized by leaving vengeance and justice to the Lord and not repaying evil for evil. The latter idea is repeated four times in these chapters.[130] By separating Benjamin's battle with Pharaoh's son in *Jos. Asen.* 27:1-5 from his response to him in 29:1-7, the narrator has created didactic space for instructing the audience about what is, and what is not, fitting action for God-fearing people to take. Aseneth, who has only recently become a God-fearer herself, exemplifies the proper ethic and even becomes the teacher of those who have been God-fearers their entire lives, Simeon, Levi, and Benjamin.[131]

The intercalation in *Joseph and Aseneth* 27–29 is perhaps the clearest in the narrative. There are, however, a few other noteworthy passages that are structured in this prophetic-retrospective manner. Sometimes this is in the A-B-A "sandwich form," and other times in A-B-A-B, double-intercalation form. The former is represented by *Jos. Asen.* 1:1–3:6:

A¹: Joseph is introduced and comes into Heliopolis on the eighteenth day of the fourth month of the first year of plenty. (*Jos. Asen.* 1:1-3)
B: Aseneth is introduced. (*Jos. Asen.* 1:4–2:20)
A²: Joseph comes to Heliopolis in the fourth month of the first year of plenty. (*Jos. Asen.* 3:1-6)

The latter pattern appears in *Jos. Asen.* 4:11–7:11:

A¹: Aseneth spurns Joseph to her Pentephres. (*Jos. Asen.* 4:11-15)
B¹: Aseneth changes her mind about Joseph. (*Jos. Asen.* 5:1–6:8)
A²: Joseph spurns Aseneth to Pentephres. (*Jos. Asen.* 7:1-7)
B²: Joseph changes his mind about Aseneth. (*Jos. Asen.* 7:10-11)

---

130. *Joseph and Aseneth* 28:4, 10, 13; 29:3. The idea is also forecasted in *Jos. Asen.* 23:9, where Levi convinces Simeon not to act against Pharaoh's son when he proposes his machination to them.

131. Ahearne-Kroll notes that Aseneth has caused Levi to change his perspective on retaliatory violence, since in *Jos. Asen.* 27:6 he was involved in the six-man campaign that killed 2,000 of Pharaoh's son's Egyptian soldiers ("Joseph and Aseneth," 2581).

And it can also be detected in 23:1–24:19:

A¹: Pharaoh's son offers his plan to Simeon and Levi. (*Jos. Asen.* 23:1-6)
B¹: Simeon and Levi respond to Pharaoh's plan. (*Jos. Asen.* 23:7-16)
A²: Pharaoh's son offers his plan to Dan and Gad. (*Jos. Asen.* 24:1-11)
B²: Dan and Gad respond to Pharaoh's plan. (*Jos. Asen.* 24:12-19)

These intercalations are structural instantiations of residual orality in Aseneth that resemble the numerous intercalations in Mark.

Repetition of syntactical patterns, words, phrases, and ideas in Mark
Intercalation in Mark 11:12-21 There is one intercalation in the gospel that particularly resembles the Benjamin-Aseneth-Benjamin intercalation in *Joseph and Aseneth* 27–29. This is the fig tree-temple-fig tree sandwich in Mk 11:12-21. Here, Jesus and his disciples are on their way into Jerusalem when Jesus spots a fig tree from a distance. Walking up to it, he finds no figs, utters a curse on the tree, which his disciples overhear, and continues on his way to Jerusalem. Upon their arrival in the city, Jesus and his followers promptly enter the temple, wherein he scatters the merchants and teaches, provoking the ire of the chief priests and scribes. Having caused a commotion, the group leaves the city when evening comes. During their next day's travels, they spot the cursed fig tree which has now begun to wither at its roots. The intercalation is thus structured as follows:

A¹: Jesus curses the fig tree. (Mk 11:12-14)
B: Jesus enters and clears the temple. (Mk 11:15-19)
A²: The fig tree withers. (Mk 11:20-21)

Like A¹ in *Jos. Asen.* 27:1-5, Mk 11:12-14 is left unresolved. The demise of Aseneth's antagonist and the demise of the fig tree are both delayed by an intervening episode. For Mark, this structure punctuates the critique of the temple and its functionaries.[132] The fig tree symbolizes the temple.[133] Both the location of Jesus's

---

132. France detects a double intercalation here, further stressing the fig tree's symbolic relationship to the temple. In his reading, Mk 11:1, Jesus's first visit to the temple is the subject of A¹, the cursing of the fig tree in 11:12-14 that of B¹, Jesus's action in the temple in 11:15-19 is A², the withering of the fig tree in 11:20-25 is B², and Jesus's return to the temple in 11:27 is A³ (*Gospel of Mark*, 436).

133. This symbolic relationship has been proposed on several occasions (William Telford, *The Barren Temple and the Withered Tree: A Redaction-Critical Analysis of the Cursing of the Fig-Tree Pericope in Mark's Gospel and Its Relation to the Cleansing of the Temple Tradition*, JSNTSup 1 [Sheffield: JSOT Press, 1980], 238; N. T. Wright, *Jesus and the Victory of God*, Christian Origins and the Question of God 2 [Minneapolis: Fortress, 1996], 421–22; Craig A. Evans, *Mark 8:27–16:20*, WBC 34B (Nashville: Thomas Nelson, 2001), 160; Marcus, *Mark*, 2:790; J. R. Daniel Kirk, "Time for Figs, Temple Destruction, and

temple actions at the center of the intercalation and how the account of the cursing and withering of the fig tree is interweaved with aspects of the temple critique that permeates Mark 11–15 reveal that this is the case.[134] In Mark, the cursing and withering of the tree only makes sense in light of Jesus's temple actions in Mk 11:15-19. The resolution to the fig-tree account is directly informed by the center of the intercalation, just as the resolution to Benjamin's battle with Pharaoh's son is informed by Aseneth's action in the center of that intercalation.

Lexical and phraseological repetitions in Mark While Markan sandwiches are structural evidence for the gospel's residual orality, the repetitive nature of Mark is even more apparent at the lexical and phraseological levels. Pleonasms and redundancies abound. Robert H. Stein claims that there are 213 instances of grammatical redundancy in the gospel, though he offers neither a list of them nor their locations.[135] Frans Neirynck underscores hundreds of occasions of repetition in Mark's text and also instances of thirty different categories of dualities in the gospel.[136] John C. Hawkins provides an abbreviated inventory of over 100 examples of Markan redundancies.[137] He offers another thirty-nine instances

---

Houses of Prayer in Mark 11:12-25," *CBQ* 74 [2012]: 511–13). See also Telford's review of the history of research on the fig tree (*Barren Temple*, 1–38). In Chapter 5, I shall argue that Matthew's disruption of the intercalation mutes the temple critique found here.

134. The two are intertwined on at least three counts. First, the fig-tree episodes are set toward the beginning of five chapters (Mark 11–15) that prominently feature a critique of the temple and its authorities (Evans, *Mark 8:27–16:20*, 138). Second, there is parallelism between the fig tree and the temple with respect to the language of seeing. When Jesus first enters the temple in Mk 11:11 he "looks around at all the things" (περιβλεψάμενος πάντας). Similarly, Jesus "sees the fig tree" (ἰδὼν συκῆν) in 11:13 and the whole group of disciples "saw the fig tree" (εἶδον τὴν συκῆν) in 11:20 (Marcus, *Mark*, 2:790). Third, Mk 13:2, where Jesus addresses the impending destruction of the temple, parallels 11:21. In each text a disciple addresses Jesus with a vocative form of "teacher" (ῥαββί in Mk 11:21 and διδάσκαλε in Mk 13:2) followed by the imperative, ἰδέ ("look"). In Mk 13:2, Jesus is instructed to look at the soon-to-be-destroyed temple precincts and in Mk 11:21 the fig tree that withered because of his curse (Ched Myers, *Binding the Strong Man: A Political Reading of Mark's Story of Jesus* [Maryknoll: Orbis Books, 1988], 304).

135. Robert H. Stein, "Synoptic Gospels," in *Dictionary of Jesus and the Gospels*, ed. Joel B. Green, Scot McKnight, and I. Howard Marshall (Downers Grove: InterVarsity Press, 1992), 788.

136. Underscore of repetitions in Neirynck, "Mark in Greek," *ETL* 47 (1971): 144–98; lists in idem, "Duality in Mark," *ETL* 47 (1971): 394–463.

137. John C. Hawkins, *Horae Synopticae: Contributions to the Study of the Synoptic Problem* (Oxford: Clarendon, 1909), 125–26. He notes that these are not all the redundancies that appear in the gospel.

where pleonasms in Mark have been altered in Matthean and Lukan redaction.[138] The first item in Hawkins list, Mk 1:32, characterizes Mark's pleonastic manner of speaking:

ὀψίας δὲ γενομένης, ὅτε ἔδυ ὁ ἥλιος...	When evening came, when the sun had set...

This example is of interest not only because it shows the grammatical and lexical redundancy that exemplifies Mark, but also because the indicative phrase ἔδυ ὁ ἥλιος ("the sun set") is unique to Mark in the NT and appears twice in *Joseph and Aseneth* in a nearly identical construction.[139] In its redaction of the Markan verse, Mt. 8:16 eliminates the indicative phrase altogether, retaining only the genitive absolute, ὀψίας δὲ γενομένης ("when evening came"). Luke 4:40 has combined the two Markan constructions, removing the information about it becoming evening, and making Mark's indicative phrase into the genitive absolute, δύοντος δὲ τοῦ ἡλίου ("when the sun had set"). The participial form in Luke is the only other occasion of the verb δύνω in the NT or LXX. Since both Matthew and Luke avoid using the verbal form ἔδυ and several manuscripts of Mark alter it, the phrase might be a colloquialism considered inappropriate for the literary medium.[140] If so, it is a residually oral feature of Mark not only as a redundancy, but also as a unique, colloquial phrase.

Numerous other redundancies and repetitions in Mark's Gospel could be offered as evidence of its residual orality.[141] These are a result of the *copia* that characterize oral discourse. But there is one particular lexeme that sociolinguistic research and the argument of composition by dictation has significant explanatory power over, εὐθύς ("immediately"). This word is used forty-one times in Mark and only ten times elsewhere in the NT. It is often thought to give the gospel a sense of rapidity or "urgency."[142] Commentators note this effect of εὐθύς, but they do not usually clarify why it is ubiquitous in and relatively unique to Mark. My contention is that εὐθύς is what sociolinguists call a "discourse marker." This designation makes sense of its functions and frequency in the narrative, as well as its minimal presence in other NT texts.

---

138. Ibid., 139–42.

139. ἕως οὗ ἔδυ ὁ ἥλιος ("until the sun set") appears in *Jos. Asen.* 10:2 and 19. This is yet another example of verbal repetition in that narrative. The verbal phrase, ἔδυ ὁ ἥλιος ("the sun set") is identical to Mk 1:32, but it is also worth noting that the indicative verb is preceded by a temporal preposition on all three occasions.

140. ἔδυ is altered to ἔδυσεν by B D 28. 1424. 2427.

141. For example, Mk 1:35; 4:2, 39; 5:15, 19; 6:26; 7:33; 12:44; 14:61.

142. Donahue and Harrington, *Gospel of Mark*, 17. Marcus claims that the term offers "vividness" (*Mark*, 1:159).

εὐθύς *as a discourse marker in Mark* Discourse markers are notoriously difficult to define, primarily because they have widely variegated roles.¹⁴³ In English, words like *anyway, next, look, listen, then, however, now, oh, and, but, so, because, you know* can serve as discourse markers.¹⁴⁴ These words may or may not significantly affect the meaning of an utterance or a sentence and they primarily serve to move the discourse along sequentially. Explicating four characteristics of discourse markers clarifies their operations in spoken discourse and parallels the functions of εὐθύς in Mark.

First, discourse markers "generally belong to the word class of adverbs," and often serve as adverbs or in a manner similar to them.¹⁴⁵ They also typically have identical or nearly identical words that have a different syntactical role. Heine writes, "A characteristic of many discourse markers is that they have homophonous (or nearly homophonous) counterparts that are not discourse markers."¹⁴⁶ Often these corresponding words are adverbs. Whether identical or merely similar, these counterparts are not technically considered discourse markers themselves. Hansen gives the following English example, wherein *a* is not a discourse marker and *b* is:¹⁴⁷

a. She asked him to rewrite it *in other words*.
b. *In other words*, you must rewrite the whole essay.

---

143. Deborah Schiffrin's is the classic definition of discourse markers: "sequentially dependent elements which bracket units of talk" (*Discourse Markers*, Studies in Interactional Sociolinguistics 5 [Cambridge: Cambridge University Press, 1987], 31).

144. Much of the theoretical work on discourse markers is in English and focuses on English discourse markers. This does not imply that discourse markers do not operate similarly in other languages. José Luis Blas Arroyo notes that "interest in the study of discourse markers has spread to a number of different languages, as can be seen in recent work on English, Hebrew, German, Catalan and ... Spanish" ("From Politeness to Discourse Marking: The Process of Pragmaticalization of Muy Bien in Vernacular Spanish," *Journal of Pragmatics* 43 [2011]: 855).

145. Miriam Urgelles-Coll, *The Syntax and Semantics of Discourse Markers*, Continuum Studies in Theoretical Linguistics (London: Continuum, 2010), 1, 7–41. See also Elizabeth Closs Traugott and Richard B. Dasher who classify discourse markers as "a subclass of adverbials" or "connecting adverbs" (*Regularity in Semantic Change*, Cambridge Studies in Linguistics [Cambridge: Cambridge University Press, 2002], 152–53). Not all linguists categorize discourse markers as adverbs. Some maintain that discourse markers "are elusive to conventional categories of grammar and must be understood and described in their own right, and this position tends to be reflected in the use of separate categories and terms [to describe them]" (Bernd Heine, "On Discourse Markers: Grammaticalization, Pragmaticalization, or Something Else?" *Linguistics* 51 [2013]: 1207).

146. Ibid., 1208.

147. Maj-Britt Mosegaard Hansen, "The Semantic Status of Discourse Markers," *Lingua* 104 (1998): 236.

In the second sentence, *in other words* is an unessential phrase that helps the hearer process the discourse, whereas in the first sentence the prepositional phrase is critical to the sentence's meaning.

In Mark εὐθύς sometimes, though not always, operates adverbially meaning "immediately." This is the case in Mk 1:42, where the word connotes the swiftness by which the leper was healed: καὶ εὐθύς ἀπῆλθεν ἀπ' αὐτοῦ ἡ λέπρα καὶ ἐκαθαρίσθη ("and immediately the leprosy left him and he was healed"). Comparing εὐθύς in Mark with εὐθύς and εὐθέως in Matthew, Harold Riley concludes that, "When the word εὐθύς [in Mark] corresponds to an equivalent word in Matthew and/or Luke, it requires the sense of 'immediately.' When there is no corresponding word, the more natural translation is in almost every instance 'then.'"[148] These cases in Mark where εὐθύς is a true adverb represent the homophonous, adverbial counterpart to the word's more frequent role as a discourse marker. But εὐθύς also has a nearly homophonous, adverbial counterpart in εὐθέως. This adverb occurs on only one occasion in the gospel, Mk 7:35, though even in this instance several manuscripts omit the adverb or replace it with εὐθύς.[149] In contrast, εὐθέως occurs far more frequently in Matthew and Luke. This will be addressed in Chapter 5. The point is that the discourse marker εὐθύς has both a homophonous and a nearly homophonous counterpart in εὐθύς and εὐθέως, respectively.

Second, discourse markers are multifunctional.[150] This is because they serve a procedural rather than propositional role. One of their primary operations is to "signal a sequential relationship between the current utterance and the prior discourse."[151] Discourse markers "indicate how the listener is to relate the upcoming discourse to the previous discourse."[152] While εὐθύς acts adverbially in Mk 1:42, there are several occasions where this translation of the word is strained and it is better understood as sequencing the discourse.

Riley argues that εὐθύς often does not connote expediency in Mark, but, instead, discourse sequencing. He suggests the translation "then," "next," or "also," for these instances.[153] As an example of its discourse-sequencing function, he presents a cluster of occurrences of the word from Mark 1.[154] By contrasting the

---

148. Riley, *The Making of Mark: An Exploration* (Macon: Mercer University Press, 1989), 217.

149. ℵ B D L Δ 0131. 0274. 33. 579. 892 pc it sa[mss] bo all omit εὐθέως ("immediately"), while ℵ Δ L 0274. 892 replace it with εὐθύς ("immediately," "and then").

150. Schiffrin, *Discourse Markers*, 64; Arroyo, "From Politeness," 855–56; Laurel J. Brinton, *Pragmatic Markers in English: Grammaticalization and Discourse Functions*, Topics in English Linguistics 19 (Berlin: de Gruyter, 1996), 35.

151. Heine, "Discourse Markers," 1213.

152. Paul J. Hopper and Elizabeth Closs Traugott, *Grammaticalization* (Cambridge: Cambridge University Press, 2003), 129.

153. Riley, *Making of Mark*, 215. Riley claims that Mark writes in a "colloquial style," though he never develops what this means or how it is indicated in the gospel.

154. Ibid., 216–17.

Greek εὐθύς with an English translation, he exposes the problem of translating the term "immediately" on these occasions. His illustrative examples are:

Mark 1:21: and εὐθύς on the Sabbath Jesus entered into the synagogue and taught.

Mark 1:23: and εὐθύς there was a man in the synagogue.

Mark 1:28: and εὐθύς his fame spread abroad throughout the region of Galilee.

Riley concludes that "the three examples ... only bear the meaning 'then.'"[155] There are other Markan instances where "then," "also," or "next" are more adequate translations of εὐθύς than "immediately."[156] Mark 8:10 is one. Here Jesus has just released the four thousand, and Mark provides a transitory detail: καὶ εὐθὺς ἐμβὰς εἰς τὸ πλοῖον μετὰ τῶν μαθητῶν αὐτοῦ ἦλθεν εἰς τὰ μέρη Δαλμανουθά ("And then, when he had gotten into the boat with his disciples, he went to the region of Dalmanutha"). In this case, the sense of immediacy is by no means intrinsic to the sentence, and εὐθύς can just as well carry the temporal sense "next" or "then." Even if εὐθύς were omitted entirely the sentence would make just as much sense.[157] This is further evidence for εὐθύς's role as a discourse marker in Mark, since discourse markers are typically optional and do not add propositional content to a sentence's meaning.[158]

The discourse marker is especially superfluous when it precedes a participial or prepositional phrase in Mark, which happens frequently.[159] This is the case in Mk 14:43, where εὐθύς precedes a genitive absolute: καὶ εὐθὺς ἔτι αὐτοῦ λαλοῦντος παραγίνεται Ἰούδας ("And so, while he is still talking, Judas arrives").[160] If Mark intends εὐθύς to express a sense of immediacy here, the genitive absolute quickly

---

155. Ibid., 217.

156. G. D. Kilpatrick supposes that every time εὐθύς appears at the beginning of a clause in Mark, "we are not dealing with an adverb of time but with a connecting particle" ("Some Notes on Markan Usage," in Elliott, *Language and Style*, 168).

157. This is precisely the route Mt. 15:39 takes in its redaction of Mk 8:10: καὶ ἀπολύσας τοὺς ὄχλους ἐνέβη εἰς τὸ πλοῖον καὶ ἦλθεν εἰς τὰ ὅρια Μαγαδάν ("and having released the crowds, he got into the boat and went into the region of Magadan"). Matthew does this on several other occasions. Finding the term in Mark otiose, he removes εὐθύς altogether. I will address these in Chapter 5.

158. Schiffrin, *Discourse Markers*, 64; Peter Auer and Susanne Günther, "Die Entstehung von Diskursmarkern im Deutschen: Ein Fall von Gramatikalisierung?" in *Grammatikalisierung im Deutschen*, ed. Torsten Leuschner, Tanha Mortelmans, and Sarah De Groodt, Linguistik Impulse & Tendenzen 9 (Berlin: de Gruyter, 2005), 334; Heine, "Discourse Markers," 1210–11; Traugott and Dasher, *Regularity*, 155.

159. Mark 1:21, 28, 29; 2:8; 3:6; 5:30; 6:25, 27, 54; 7:25, 8:10; 9:24; 11:2; 14:43, 45; 15:1.

160. εὐθύς is paired with a historical present tense verb here, though it does not directly precede the verb.

curbs it. It is more likely that εὐθύς focuses the audience's attention, since this is a dramatic point in the narrative.¹⁶¹

One last example shows that Mark does not only use εὐθύς to carry a sense of immediacy and that the word has multiple operations in the gospel. We have seen, from Riley's example above, that Mk 1:23 juxtaposes εὐθύς with ἦν: καὶ εὐθὺς ἦν ἐν τῇ συναγωγῇ αὐτῶν ἄνθρωπος ἐν πνεύματι ἀκαθάρτῳ ("and then there was a man with an unclean spirit in their synagogue").¹⁶² Here, perhaps more clearly than anywhere else in Mark εὐθύς means something other than "immediately." The co-occurrence of εὐθύς with ἦν makes little syntactical sense from a literary perspective. Sociolinguistic research on discourse markers helps provide a way forward. Schiffrin shows that discourse markers are often sequentially dependent.¹⁶³ That is, they do *not* depend on other lexemes in a sentence to create meaning. Instead, they primarily rely on the discourse's sequence for it.¹⁶⁴ For this reason, discourse markers can contradict other elements within a sentence or utterance, such as tense and time. Schiffrin calls this "co-occurrence" and gives an example of a discourse marker with a past tense verb that is pertinent to Mk 1:23: "*Now* these boys were Irish. They lived different."¹⁶⁵ She writes, "*Now* is a temporal adverb which marks the reference time of a proposition as coterminous with the speaking time. Thus, we would not expect *now* to co-occur with indicators of a reference time prior to speaking, e.g. the preterit."¹⁶⁶ This may seem to be a grammatical violation, but is not because *now* is a sequentially dependent discourse marker.¹⁶⁷ If we consider εὐθύς in this manner in Mk 1:23, it becomes more appropriate to translate it not as "immediately," but with a different English discourse marker that implies sequencing. The force of εὐθύς does not adverbially press upon ἦν, but signals that a new discourse sequence is beginning.

Third, discourse markers typically occur toward the beginning of an utterance.¹⁶⁸ In Mark, εὐθύς almost always appears at the beginning of a clause and often in the

---

161. Matthew's redaction supports this hypothesis. Matthew retains most of the clause, changing only the finite verb and altering εὐθύς to ἰδού in Mt. 26:47.

162. Not surprisingly, there are textual witnesses that omit εὐθύς here (A C D W Θ ƒ13 M latt sy), finding it awkward.

163. By this Schiffrin means that "markers are devices that work on a discourse level: they are not dependent on the smaller units of talk of which discourse is composed" (*Discourse Markers*, 37).

164. Ibid., 37–40.

165. Ibid., 38; emphasis original.

166. Ibid.

167. Ibid. Marcus comments that Mark frequently employs εὐθύς in ungrammatical fashion (*Mark*, 1:159).

168. Brinton, *Pragmatic Markers*, 34.

stock phrase καὶ εὐθύς.[169] According to Decker, it precedes the verb that it modifies on thirty-eight occasions and follows it on only two.[170]

Finally, discourse markers are "predominantly a feature of oral rather than of written discourse."[171] Some linguists consider them a smoking gun for an oral register.[172] Because of their oral nature, they are negatively evaluated when they appear in formal, literary texts.[173] This accounts for the ubiquity of εὐθύς in Mark compared to its nonuse in other narratives. In Chapter 5, I will show that Matthew and Luke alter εὐθύς to its adverbial counterpart or they omit it altogether because they did not find it suitable for a literary composition.

In sum, εὐθύς is not just another repetitive lexeme in Mark. It is a discourse marker that serves numerous functions beyond providing the gospel with a sense of rapidity. A wider semantic range for translation of the word is in order. The discourse marker can be rendered temporally, conjunctively, adverbially, or as prompting attention. Above all, that εὐθύς is a discourse marker in Mark is further evidence for Mark's dense residual orality and my contention that the gospel is a textualized oral narrative.

Criterion #3: Verb employment

Residually oral verbal features in Joseph and Aseneth Joseph and Aseneth's tendencies with respect to verbal mood and voice and its penchant for direct discourse are two demonstrable features of its residual orality. The minimal use of the historical present, in contrast, does not constitute what might be expected of oral conception.

Concerning mood, the narrative relies on the indicative. Of the total verbal forms in *Joseph and Aseneth*, 76.3% are in the indicative.[174] The result is that other verbal moods rarely occur. Two observations about the non-indicative moods in *Joseph and Aseneth* are noteworthy. First, the infinitive and subjunctive moods

---

169. εὐθύς occurs at the beginning of a clause in Mk 1:10, 12, 20, 21, 23, 29, 42; 2:8; 4:29; 5:29, 30, 42; 6:27, 45, 50; 5:25; 8:10; 9:15, 24; 10:52; 11:2; 14:43, 45, 72; 15:1.

170. Rodney J. Decker, "The Use of Εὐθύς ('immediately') in Mark," *Journal of Ministry and Theology* 1 (1997): 93.

171. Brinton, *Pragmatic Markers*, 33.

172. Jan-Ola Östman, "The Symbiotic Relationship Between Pragmatic Particles and Impromptu Speech," in *Impromptu Speech: A Symposium; Papers of a Symposium Held in Åbo, Nov. 20–22, 1981*, ed. Nils Erik Enkvist (Åbo: Åbo Akademi, 1982), 170; Richard J. Watts, "Taking the Pitcher to the 'Well': Native Speakers' Perception of Their Use of Discourse Markers in Conversation," *Journal of Pragmatics: An Interdisciplinary Monthly of Language Studies* 13 (1989): 208.

173. Brinton, *Pragmatic Markers*, 33. In this vein, BDF §102.2 notes, "Mk always uses the vulgar εὐθύς (42 times) for 'immediately'."

174. 1,037 indicative verbs out of 1,357 total verbal forms.

combined make up only about 5% of the total verbal forms in the narrative.[175] This is a feature of the fragmentation of oral narrative as opposed to the integration of written narrative. Literarily conceived discourse has a higher proportion of dependent, complex, and complement clauses to integrate idea units into cohesive sentences in a manner that oral narrative does not.[176] Second, participles make up only 11.3% of the total verbal forms in *Joseph and Aseneth*.[177] Significantly, these are rarely circumstantial participles. Instead, supplementary participles in a copulative construction with εἰμί are most common in *Joseph and Aseneth*. Akin to the narratives in the papyri, *Joseph and Aseneth* typically avoids syntactically hypotactic relationships with a participle. The conjunction καί followed by an indicative verb is far more common.[178] In most of these instances, the indicative verb could have been rendered in participial form, creating more cohesive and integrated syntax. In texts conceived literarily, this would be expected.[179] But in oral narrative integrated syntax is rare.

It is well documented that passive verbs appear more frequently in written narrative than oral.[180] In *Joseph and Aseneth*, active indicative verbs occur almost ten times more frequently than passive indicatives.[181] When the purview is expanded to all the verbal moods, the active voice occurs over ten times more frequently than the passive.[182]

Regarding the historical present, *Joseph and Aseneth* does not exhibit features that are necessarily characteristic of oral narrative, nor does it demonstrate features that contradict oral conception. Unlike the Gospel of Mark, the historical present is not prominent in the narrative. In Chapter 2, I've argued that the historical present makes a speaker's represented consciousness more immediate and vivid to his or her audience. But speakers do not always aim for this vividness. In fact, in oral narrative the displaced or distal mode often dominates, and the immediate mode can be, but is not necessarily, evoked at climactic moments in the discourse.[183] The

---

175. 38 infinitives (3.8% of all verbal forms) and 24 subjunctives (1.8% of all verbal forms) occur in *Joseph and Aseneth*.

176. Chafe finds that complement clauses with infinitives are about three times more frequent in written discourse than spoken discourse ("Integration and Involvement," 44).

177. 153 participles out of 1,357 total verbal forms.

178. Mandilaras argues that καί with an indicative verb, rather than a participial phrase, is a feature of the Koine Greek vernacular (*Verb*, 366).

179. Philonenko details eight instances where καί with an indicative verb is rendered with a participial construction in the *a* MS family's redaction of *d*, producing a more elegant literary style (*Joseph et Aséneth*, 6). I provide other examples in Chapter 5.

180. Chafe, "Integration and Involvement," 45; Bennett, "Extended View," 45–48; Ochs, "Planned and Unplanned Discourse," 69–70.

181. There are 662 active indicative verbs compared to 67 passive indicative verbs.

182. When all verbal forms are considered, *Joseph and Aseneth* has 870 active forms compared to 82 passive forms.

183. Chafe, *Discourse*, 198–211.

displaced mode utilizes consciousness that is extroverted and does not depend on the immediate environment for its representation.[184] The distal mode represents the speaker's view at the point of time of the original event, whether it is real or imagined, and the past tense accomplishes this.[185] *Joseph and Aseneth* tends to remain in the distal mode, and infrequently enters the immediate mode.

The distal mode in *Joseph and Aseneth* is particularly demonstrated by the narrative's proportion of aorist verbs, even with forms of λέγω. It has been observed that attributions of direct speech and the historical present go hand in hand.[186] This is true of both written and oral discourse. A verb of saying in the present tense will often introduce quoted material. *Joseph and Aseneth* does not follow this pattern. Instead, aorist tense forms of λέγω abound. There are ninety-nine instances of aorist tense forms of this verb in the narrative, and only nineteen instances of present tense forms. This is significantly different from Mark and Matthew's narratives, where present forms of λέγω are more common than aorist forms. This is at a ratio of 1.83:1 and 1.40:1, respectively.[187] The fact that Matthew is more literarily conceived than Mark helps account for his greater frequency of the aorist tense, which I shall argue in Chapter 5. However, aorist tense forms of λέγω in *Joseph and Aseneth* result from the distal mode of speaking during its composition. This being the case, the historical present in *Joseph and Aseneth* is not a telltale sign of its oral conception, as it is in the Gospel of Mark. But the distal mode of speaking clarifies *Joseph and Aseneth*'s preference for the aorist tense.

Finally, the frequency of direct discourse in *Joseph and Aseneth* is a verbal indicator of its oral conception. Oral discourse tends to contain direct speech more often than written discourse.[188] Indirect discourse occurs less frequently than direct discourse.[189] There are 115 occasions of direct discourse in *Joseph and Aseneth*. It frequently appears in dialogue, as in *Jos. Asen.* 4:5-8, where a conversation between Aseneth and Pentephres contains six occurrences of εἶπεν. Elsewhere, direct discourse is evoked and a single character offers an extended monologue, as in *Jos. Asen.* 12:1-14:2 and *Jos. Asen.* 15:2-12. Indirect discourse, in contrast, is present on only one occasion, *Jos. Asen.* 13:10.[190]

---

184. Ibid., 198.
185. Ibid., 207-11.
186. Schiffrin, "Tense Variation," 58.
187. Mark has 154 present forms of λέγω compared with 84 aorist forms. Matthew has 282 present forms compared with 202 aorist forms. Luke is more similar to *Joseph and Aseneth*. There are more aorist forms of λέγω (295) than present forms (195) in his gospel, but present forms are not as minimal as in *Joseph and Aseneth*.
188. Chafe, "Integration and Involvement," 48.
189. Schiffrin, "Tense Variation," 58.
190. Even this occasion could be indicating direct discourse. Here, Aseneth is regretting that she believed those who told her Joseph was the son of a shepherd from Canaan. The text reads, εἶπόν μοι οἱ ἄνθρωποι ὅτι Ἰωσὴφ τοῦ ποιμένος ὁ υἱός ἐστι ἐκ γῆς Χαναάν. The

Residually oral verbal features in Mark

The historical present in Mark The most obvious verbal feature of Mark's residual orality is its preponderance of the historical present. This tense in Mark is best accounted as an oral residue, since it is not typically considered an Aramaism.[191] Conversational narratologists, sociolinguists, and literary critics have addressed the historical present in conversational narrative, oral narrative, and diverse types of literature, respectively. While it serves several distinct purposes in various media, settings, and genres, there have been some consistent conclusions drawn about this unique role of the present tense. Four aspects of these findings are especially germane to the historical present in Mark.

First, the historical present is a performative feature characteristic of oral narratives.[192] Nessa Wolfson writes, "The more fully a story is performed, the more likely it will contain [the historical present]."[193] At the same time, it is an optional aspect of oral narrative.[194] Not every oral narrative will feature the historical present.[195] Also, no oral narrative will exclusively appear in this tense. Narratives might eschew the historical present altogether, but it will never be the only tense found in a story.[196] That historical presents are characteristic of oral storytelling

ὅτι could indicate either direct or indirect discourse. For ὅτι introducing direct discourse in prose, see Smyth, *Greek Grammar*, §2590a; with indirect discourse, ibid., §§2576–2578.

191. Matthew Black writes that "there is nothing especially Semitic" about either the historical present or the imperfect and periphrastic, all of which are frequent in Mark and will be addressed below (*An Aramaic Approach to the Gospels and Acts*, 2nd ed. [Oxford: Oxford University Press, 1954], 130). The same point about the non-Semitic nature of the historical present is made by Moulton and Howard (*Accidence*, 456–57); E. P. Sanders (*The Tendencies of the Synoptic Tradition*, SNTSMS 9 [London: Cambridge University Press, 1969], 253); Carroll D. Osburn ("The Historical Present in Mark as a Text-Critical Criterion," *Biblica* 64 [1983]: 486).

192. Nessa Wolfson, "A Feature of Performed Narrative: The Conversational Historical Present," *Language in Society* 7 (1978): 215–37; eadem, *CHP: The Conversational Historical Present in American English Narrative*, Topics in Sociolinguistics (Dordrecht: Foris, 1982), 29; Monika Fludernik, "The Historical Present Tense in English Literature: An Oral Pattern and Its Literary Adaptation," *Language and Literature* 17 (1992): 78; Fleischman, *Tense and Narrativity*, 79.

193. Wolfson, *CHP*, 29.

194. Monika Fludernik, "The Historical Present Tense Yet Again: Tense Switching and Narrative Dynamics in Oral and Quasi-Oral Storytelling," *Text: An Interdisciplinary Journal for the Study of Discourse* 11 (1991): 387.

195. In one study, Wolfson finds that half of the oral narratives she collected switch between the past tense and the historical present ("Feature," 223). In another study, she finds that every narrative contains switching between the tenses (*CHP*, 29). Fleischman also addresses the optional nature of the historical present in oral narrative (*Tense and Narrativity*, 76).

196. Wolfson, *CHP*, 35.

does not preclude their presence in literary narratives. But their occurrence in literary narratives is usually considered a holdover from spoken discourse.[197]

Second, because the historical present always appears in conjunction with past tense verbs, how a narrative switches in and out of the tense is significant. Sociolinguists and narratologists find that speakers tend to shift into the historical present at predictable junctures in a discourse. This is predicated on the fact that the constituent episodes of oral narrative follow regular structural patterns.[198] Schiffrin and Fludernik argue that the historical present will never occur at the conclusion or resolution of a spoken episode.[199] Schiffrin finds that the majority of historical presents occur in "complicating action clauses."[200] According to her, it will not be found in clauses providing a reference time or orientation for the narrative, which usually begin an episode.[201] Fludernik finds that the historical present is most commonly used at "turns" in the narrative.[202] A turn can be at the beginning of an episode, its incipit, which she distinguishes from Schiffrin's concept "orientation."[203] If there is no orientation clause, a speaker's oral episode may begin with a historical present. Fludernik agrees with Schiffrin that the historical present will also be expected at major incidences in the narrative, that is, at "surprising, remarkable, or emotionally memorable" moments.[204] But she also finds that it appears at "incipit points of new story-internal episodes."[205] Fludernik calls these "incidence turns" and "incipit turns," phrases that I will employ here.[206]

Fludernik's and Schiffrin's research suggests that historical presents can be expected at three predictable points in an oral narrative: (1) the beginning of an episode; (2) when a new character or setting is introduced; and (3) at a surprising or climactic moment. Per their findings, a historical present will never appear as the last verb in an episode.

Third, the historical present frequently co-occurs with verbs of speaking. This was briefly addressed in Chapter 2. Schiffrin argues that this happens because both direct discourse and the historical present increase immediacy.[207] While this

---

197. Fleischman notes various studies that situate the origins of the historical present in speech in French, Italian, Latin, Old Icelandic, and English (*Tense and Narrativity*, 79).

198. Schiffrin argues that oral narratives have various types of clauses, including abstract, orientation, embedded orientation, complicating action, evaluation, and coda ("Tense Variation," 48).

199. Ibid., 51; Fludernik, "Historical Present Tense," 86; eadem, "Historical Present Tense Yet Again," 375–76.

200. Schiffrin, "Tense Variation," 51.

201. Ibid., 51–52.

202. Fludernik, "Historical Present Tense," 86.

203. Ibid., 81.

204. Ibid., 85.

205. Fludernik, "Historical Present Tense Yet Again," 375.

206. Ibid.

207. Schiffrin, "Tense Variation," 58. Similarly, Chafe, *Discourse*, 223.

may account for the development of the co-occurrence of the two phenomena, I am inclined to agree with Wolfson, who argues that the distinction between a historical present and a nonhistorical present of a verb of speaking is minimal because of the ubiquity of verbs related to *say*.[208] Because these verbs are the most common in any narrative, any significance between the tenses is negligible.

Fourth, both Wolfson and John R. Frey find that tense switching often co-occurs with adverbs expressing immediacy. Specifically, Frey found that the German adverb "plötzlich" frequently appears with the present tense. He writes, "Sooner or later the word 'plötzlich' bobs up so that it appears as if the part preceding the word 'plötzlich' had merely been the prelude to the sudden development in the story that calls for the present."[209] Wolfson similarly finds that the adverb "suddenly" and the phrase "all of a sudden" frequently co-occur with a shift in tense in American English.[210] She observes that no adverb demands a switch to the historical present, but that certain time expressions "constitute very favorable environments for the switch between the past tense and the [historical present.]"[211] This is consistent with Schiffrin's and Fludernik's findings about where a shift into or out of the historical present can be expected in oral narrative.

These features of the historical present cohere with its presence in the Gospel of Mark. First, the historical present is more frequent in Mark than any other text in the NT, occurring 150 times.[212] The Gospel of John has 162 instances of the historical present, but significantly more indicative verbs than Mark.[213] The historical present makes up 9.9% of the verbs in Mark's Gospel and 6.3% of those in John.[214] Since the historical present is more common in oral, performed narrative than it is in written literature, its frequency in Mark is not surprising. Further, the historical present was characteristic of the Koine Greek vernacular.[215] These factors account for its presence in Mark.

208. Wolfson, *CHP*, 50–52.

209. Frey, "The Historical Present in Narrative Literature, Particularly in Modern German Fiction," *The Journal of English and Germanic Philology* 45 (1946): 64.

210. Wolfson, *CHP*, 41.

211. Ibid., 40.

212. Frans Neirynck in collaboration with Theo Hansen and Frans van Segbroeck, eds., *The Minor Agreements of Matthew and Luke against Mark: With a Cumulative List*, BETL 37 (Leuven: Peeters, 1974), 224–27. Neirynck follows Hawkins here, removing only one instance, Mk 6:45, from Hawkins's list (*Horae Synopticae*, 114–18).

213. Hawkins, *Horae Synopticae*, 143.

214. 150/1520 in Mark and 162/2556 in John. Of course, the frequency of the historical present in John may be indicative of its media conception or form. It is noteworthy that historical presents are concentrated in certain sections of John's Gospel, whereas they are consistent throughout Mark's (ibid., 144). This may suggest a mixture of media conception within the Gospel of John itself.

215. George D. Kilpatrick, "Historic Present in the Gospels and Acts," *ZNW* 68 (1977): 258.

Second, the location of historical presents in Markan pericopes conforms to what should be expected given the research reviewed here. A historical present is never the last verb in an episode in Mark. Rather, historical presents typically appear at turns within pericopes, namely, when new action is initiated by a new character or the narrative moves into a new setting.[216] Their role in Mark is not exclusively to provide "vividness," as is sometimes proposed.[217] Rather, vividness is occasionally an effect of the switch into the historical present.[218] It is a result of the narrator moving into this tense at a turn that happens to be climactic. This is the case with the first historical present in Mark, ἐκβάλλει ("throws"), at an incidence turn in Mk 1:12:

| καὶ εὐθὺς τὸ πνεῦμα αὐτὸν ἐκβάλλει εἰς τὴν ἔρημον. καὶ ἦν ἐν τῇ ἐρήμῳ τεσσεράκοντα ἡμέρας πειραζόμενος ὑπὸ τοῦ σατανᾶ, καὶ ἦν μετὰ τῶν θηρίων, καὶ οἱ ἄγγελοι διηκόνουν αὐτῷ. | And then the spirit throws him into the desert. And he was in the desert forty days being tempted by Satan, and he was with the wild animals, and the angels were serving him.[219] |

While the verb is vivid and the action climactic, this is only part of the reason that the historical present appears. It is also the result of narrating a new series of events in a new setting. The verbs that follow ἐκβάλλει are unsurprisingly in the imperfect tense because they signal the resolution of this short episode.[220]

There are also several occasions in Mark's Gospel where the historical present does not make the episode more vivid. This is usually the case when a historical

---

216. Setting aside λέγει and λέγουσιν because the distinction between the present and past tenses has largely been lost, historical presents are used at the outset of a new episode in Mk 1:21; 3:13, 20; 6:30; 7:1; 8:22; 9:2; 10:1, 35 46; 11:1, 15, 27; 12:13, 18; 14:17, 32, 33, 66; 15:20 16:2. Over half of these occasions are forms of ἔρχεται. The sociolinguistic research on the historical present lines up well with what Buist Fanning has observed of its presence in the NT: "[It marks] a clear pattern of discourse-structuring functions, such as to highlight the beginning of a paragraph, to introduce new participants into an existing paragraph, to show participants moving to new locations" (*Verbal Aspect in the New Testament* [Oxford: Clarendon, 1990], 232). Moreover, Hyeon Woo Shin argues that most historical presents in Mark either introduce a new pericope, which happens on sixty-six occasions, or introduce a new event, which happens on thirty-six occasions ("The Historic Present as a Discourse Marker and Textual Criticism in Mark," *BT* 63 [2012]: 50).

217. BDF §321; Lane, *Gospel of Mark*, 26. In contrast, Shin argues that the historical present provides vivid description on three occasions ("Historic Present," 50).

218. Wolfson, Fludernik, Schiffrin, and Fleischmann all agree that creating vividness is not necessarily a function of the historical present (Wolfson, *CHP,* 34; Fludernik, "Historical Present Tense," 84; Schiffrin, "Tense Variation," 57; Fleischmann, *Tense and Narrativity,* 78).

219. I have opted to translate the text myself here because most English translations convert both the historical present and imperfect verbs to the simple past tense.

220. Fludernik, "Historical Present Tense," 84.

present occurs at an incipit turn.[221] For example, in Mk 8:22 the narrative moves to its new setting in Bethsaida, using a historical present:

καὶ ἔρχονται εἰς Βηθσαϊδάν. καὶ φέρουσιν αὐτῷ τυφλὸν καὶ παρακαλοῦσιν αὐτὸν ἵνα αὐτοῦ ἅψηται.	And they come into Bethsaida. And they bring to him a blind man and they beg him to touch him.[222]

Here, the first historical present appears at a turn to a new setting and new action, and it certainly does not to make the narrative vivid. The following two historical presents, φέρουσιν ("bring") and παρακαλοῦσιν ("beg"), follow a verbal pattern in Mark. After an initial historical present at a turn in the narrative, the speaker often continues to employ the tense for the next verb or two.[223] This is because there is a tendency for historical present tense verbs to cluster together in oral narrative.[224]

Third, verbs of speaking freely switch between the imperfect, aorist, and present tenses in Mark. Of the 150 historical presents, 73 are λέγει or λέγουσιν. When all the verbal moods are considered, there are 154 total present forms of λέγω to 84 aorists, 50 imperfects, and 2 futures. When the purview is limited to indicative forms, there are 106 presents, 70 aorists, 50 imperfects, and 2 futures. Mark freely employs both past and present tense forms of λέγω and there does not appear to be a significant reason for this variation. This lost distinction is most likely a result of the commonality of the verb in both oral and written narrative.

Fourth, it is striking that adverbs and phrases indicating immediacy often co-occur with the historical present in oral narratives. Both the historical present and the word εὐθύς are distinctive stylistic features of Mark's Gospel. Given the regularity of both in Mark and their frequent co-occurrence in oral narratives, we might expect εὐθύς to work in direct conjunction with historical present tense verbs. But this is not the case. There are only four occasions in the gospel where εὐθύς co-occurs with a historical present.[225] The word more consistently appears with aorist participles and indicatives.[226] This divergence from sociolinguistic expectation might result from the role of εὐθύς ("immediately") as a discourse marker. Be that as it may, it is telling that two linguistic phenomena peculiar to Mark's Gospel are also characteristic of oral narrative generally.

---

221. Forms of ἔρχομαι are the most common historical present to begin a new episode in Mark (Mk 3:20; 8:22; 10:1, 46; 11:15, 27; 12:18; 14:17, 32, 66; 16:2), though various other verbs do so as well (Mk 1:21; 3:13; 6:30; 7:1; 9:2; 10:35; 11:1; 12:13; 14:33, 43; 15:20).

222. As with Mk 1:12 above, the translation is my own here.

223. Mark 3:13; 5:15, 23, 40; 6:1; 7:32; 8:22; 9:2; 10:1; 11:1, 7, 27; 14:37; 15:17, 24.

224. Schiffrin, "Tense Variation," 51.

225. Mark 1:12; 30; 14:43; 45.

226. εὐθύς co-occurs with aorist participles on sixteen occasions (Mk 1:18, 21, 29; 2:8, 12; 3:6; 5:30; 6:25, 27, 54; 7:25; 8:10; 9:15, 24; 14:45; 15:1) and with aorist indicatives on fourteen occasions (Mk 1:20, 28, 42, 43; 4:5; 5:2, 29, 42 [x2]; 6:45, 50; 9:20; 10:52; 14:72).

Verbal mood, tense, and voice in Mark Just as the ubiquity of the historical present in Mark coheres with spoken norms, Mark's verbs conform to what is expected of oral narrative in terms of mood, tense, and voice. The indicative mood occurs far more frequently than any other in the gospel, though participles are more frequent in Mark than *Joseph and Aseneth*.[227] As for tense, there is a relatively even distribution of aorist, imperfect, and present tense verbs. Particularly notable is the high percentage of imperfect verbs.[228] These make up 19.2% of all indicative verbal forms in Mark.[229] Lastly, active forms occur far more frequently than passive forms. In the indicative mood, 1,003 verbs are in the active voice compared to 160 in the passive. When all moods are considered, there are 1,843 actives to 299 passives.

Direct discourse in Mark Finally, the frequency of direct discourse in Mark is evidence of its composition by dictation. This is primarily indicated by ὅτι *recitativum*, which is more frequent in Mark than any other NT text. Blass, Debrunner, and Funk state that this function of ὅτι is nearly identical to quotation marks.[230] In Mark, ὅτι signals direct discourse following a verb of speaking on forty-two occasions.[231] Several of these might be considered indirect discourse if ὅτι was not present.[232] Significantly, Matthew has omitted ὅτι on all but five of these, and Luke on all but three.[233]

In sum, the frequency of the historical present and its syntactical location in Mark are the most indicative verbal features of the gospel's composition by dictation. The historical present appears more frequently in Mark than any other text in the NT, and its location at turns in an episode is consistent with sociolinguistic research. On the subjects of mood, tense, and voice, Mark's residual orality is on display in the frequency of the indicative over all other moods, the

---

227. Indicative verbs make up 57.6% of the verbal forms in Mark, compared to 21.3% for participles, 7.6% for infinitives, and 7.9% for subjunctives. Participles make up only 11.3% of the total verbal forms of *Joseph and Aseneth*. In Mark, many, though certainly not all, of the participles are in "orientation" clauses, as would be expected of participles in oral narrative (Labov, *Language*, 388). That is, these participles suggest that "one event is occurring simultaneously with another" (ibid.). To this end, it is significant that 257 present tense participles occur in Mark.

228. As noted above, the imperfect tense is not considered an Aramaism (Black, *Aramaic Approach*, 94). It is, however, more characteristic of oral narrative than written (Schiffrin, "Tense Variation," 59).

229. Compared with 6.3% and 14.9% in Matthew and Luke, respectively. I will further address the imperfect in Matthew and Luke in Chapter 5.

230. BDF §470.

231. Turner, "Marcan Usage," 68–74.

232. Turner suggests that this is the case with Mk 3:21, 22; 6:4, 14–15; 7:6, 20; 9:31; 12:28-29, 32; 14:69 (ibid., 74).

233. Ibid.

active over all other voices, and the present and imperfect over the aorist, perfect, and pluperfect tenses.

Conclusion

In this chapter I have argued that both Mark and *Joseph and Aseneth* linguistically exhibit residual orality. They do so with respect to their paratactic structures, repetitions, and verbal features. Some of these similarities overlap in remarkable ways. This is the case with their volumes of καί, the number of times that connective begins paragraphs, sentences, and clauses, their intercalations, and their general preference for active indicative verbal forms. There are also ways in which each narrative is more residually oral than the other. Mark's employment of the discourse marker εὐθύς and the historical present are residually oral features that have no equivalent in *Joseph and Aseneth*. But the way *Joseph and Aseneth* strings five or more idea units together with καί is a denser residual orality than Mark exhibits when it comes to parataxis.

In the next chapter I will argue that there are metalinguistic indications that both *Joseph and Aseneth* and Mark are textualized oral narratives. Both are representatives of a pluriform tradition and a "performance attitude" was taken toward their early written versions. They also evoke intertexts in similarly imprecise ways that are characteristic of oral composition.

Chapter 4

METALINGUISTIC ORAL RESIDUES

In the previous chapter I argued that *Joseph and Aseneth* and Mark exhibit similarities with respect to their language and style. The first three criteria proposed in Chapter 2 served as a linguistic lens to view their resemblances. In this chapter we move toward metalinguistic characteristics of the texts by investigating them with the fourth and fifth criteria previously offered. These metalinguistic features will further the case that both Mark and *Joseph and Aseneth* are textualized oral narratives and were composed by dictation. First, I shall address the multiformity of both traditions. We shall see that *Joseph and Aseneth* exhibits a greater level of *mouvance* than Mark. But the latter is nonetheless more pluriform than the other Synoptic Gospels. Second, I shall argue that Mark and *Joseph and Aseneth* recall other traditions similarly. Both tend to evoke cultural texts mnemonically and are characterized by echoic intertextuality rather than lexical precision.

Criterion #4: Multiform traditions

The multiform tradition of Joseph and Aseneth

As noted earlier, *Joseph and Aseneth* is one of the best-attested pseudepigrapha, existing in ninety-one known manuscripts. Uta Fink provides a stemma of the witnesses and argues that they all go back to a single archetype.[1] Her stemma communicates the complexity of the textual tradition of *Joseph and Aseneth*. Burchard's apparatus to his critical edition also reveals the multiformity of the narrative's textual tradition.[2] On any given page, his apparatus is approximately four times longer than the reconstruction itself.[3] Ahearne-Kroll shows that the relationship between these textual witnesses is highly complex and argues that

---

1. Fink, *Joseph und Aseneth*, 17.
2. Burchard, *Joseph und Aseneth*.
3. Burchard's modus operandi was to include "all bits of material that are attested by at least one family, conforms in style to the undisputed passages, and fits smoothly into the 'narrative integrity' of the story" ("Text," 88).

there do not seem to be distinguishable patterns of redaction.[4] That is, the witnesses to *Joseph and Aseneth* were not edited in discernible stages and the tradition is so complicated that it is impossible to reconstruct, or even detect, an original text.[5]

Because she finds it impossible to reconstruct an original text, Ahearne-Kroll adopts a different method. Advancing Thomas's argument that a "performance attitude" was taken to *Joseph and Aseneth*, she considers the fixed-yet-fluid nature of the narrative's textual transmission.[6] In lieu of an original textual reconstruction, she outlines *Joseph and Aseneth*'s "well-defined fabula."[7] This fabula consists of a chronological sequence of thirty-one events and uniformity of location, situation, and characters in the story across the earliest, divergent textual witnesses.[8] Scribes adapted this fixed storyline and did not often reproduce the text verbatim.[9]

The fixed storyline was supplemented with fluid elements.[10] Portions of the narrative were frequently moved, removed, or altered. This was at the level not just of words and phrases but entire episodes. For example, manuscripts B and D omit most of the pericope about Pharaoh marrying Joseph and Aseneth, G omits 2:13–10:1, L1 omits 18:2–19:1, and several manuscripts end at different verses in ch. 16.[11]. Aseneth's psalm in *Jos. Asen.* 21:10-21 of Burchard's reconstruction also shows how mutable the tradition was. The psalm is fragmentary in many texts, nonexistent in others, and introduced in a variety of ways.[12]

Ahearne-Kroll's emphasis on the fixed-yet-fluid nature of *Joseph and Aseneth* has quickly taken root in scholarship.[13] Many now agree that the "original text" of this narrative is a red herring.[14] It is either a theoretical construct that never existed in actuality or it is irrecoverable. Despite these considerations, little attention has

---

4. Ahearne-Kroll, "Jewish Identity," 34. Burchard similarly observes that, especially in the *b* text family, the different versions vary significantly both in wording and in total length ("New Translation," 180).

5. Ahearne-Kroll, "Jewish Identity," 71.

6. Thomas, *Acts of Peter*, 78; Ahearne-Kroll, "Jewish Identity," 71–74.

7. Ahearne-Kroll, "Jewish Identity," 81–83.

8. Ibid.

9. Ibid., 87.

10. Ibid., 78–79.

11. Burchard, "New Translation," 178–79; Ahearne-Kroll, "Jewish Identity," 79.

12. Burchard, *Untersuchungen*, 76–90; idem, "New Translation," 236; idem, *Joseph und Aseneth*, 264–69.

13. Ahearne-Kroll's methodology is praised by both Standhartinger ("Recent Research," 362) and Jill Hicks-Keeton ("Rewritten Gentiles: Conversion to Israel's 'Living God' and Jewish Identity in Antiquity" [PhD diss., Duke University, 2014], 110–11).

14. Kraemer, *Aseneth*, 305; Thomas, *Acts of Peter*, 78; Tim Whitmarsh, "Joseph et Aséneth: Erotisme et Religion," in *Les hommes et les dieux dans l'ancien roman: Actes du colloque des Tours, 22–24 octobre 2009*, ed. Cécile Bost-Pouderon and Bernard Pouderon (Lyon: Maison de l'Orient et de la Méditerranée—Jean Pouilloux, 2012), 239; Standhartinger, "Recent Research," 362–63; Elder, "On Transcription," 133–35; Hicks-Keeton, "Rewritten Gentiles," 110–11.

been paid to *why Joseph and Aseneth* is fixed-yet-fluid and multiform in its textual instantiations. While Ahearne-Kroll sees that the narrative exhibits these qualities, she denies that it is because *Joseph and Aseneth* began at the oral level or was influenced by an oral tradition.[15] She follows Thomas's argument about a performance attitude being taken toward *Joseph and Aseneth* in its textual recensions on analogy with the *Actus Vercellenses*. But she excludes the stimulus that Thomas provides for this attitude, namely, that the tradition is influenced by the oral lifeworld.[16] In contrast, I contend that the narrative's existence as an oral tradition textualized via dictation best accounts for the performance attitude taken toward it.

Oral traditions are equiprimordial and exhibit *mouvance*. Every instantiation of the tradition, whether in text, voice, or ritual, is a "freshly autonomous event."[17] And thus pluriformity is a distinguishing mark of oral literature.[18] While the tradition will be contiguous with its past, it will also change in its new contexts. This mirrors the fixed-yet-fluid character of *Joseph and Aseneth*. This perspective also aids interpreters in examining each version of the narrative in its own setting. Folklorists and students of oral tradition are less concerned with Ur-forms and more with the purpose of each instantiation of the tradition.[19] This media-sensitive hermeneutic provides the impetus for viewing "the multiplicity of texts [of *Joseph and Aseneth*] as testimony to the multiplicity of people's lives, experiences, and self-understanding in antiquity" that Kraemer encourages.[20] But it also offers the reason that a performance attitude was taken to the textual versions of the narrative. This attitude was not applied secondarily. It is not as though *Joseph and Aseneth* was written and was only later considered pluriform. Rather, as an oral tradition the performance attitude toward *Joseph and Aseneth* persisted when it was transferred into its new modality via dictation. This perspective still affirms that *Joseph and Aseneth* is a written text. Once the narrative entered the textual medium, it could be redacted textually and literarily. Later tradents worked with the narrative in the textual mode. The different versions of the narrative, from this perspective, are not different oral tellings of it that are independent of its textual forms.[21] Rather, orality and textuality mutually affected *Joseph and Aseneth*'s multiformity.

15. Ahearne-Kroll, "Jewish Identity," 78–79. Burchard similarly excludes the possibility, writing, "The book is an author's work, not a folk tale which has no progenitor ("New Translation," 180).

16. Thomas, *Acts of Peter*, 82–86.

17. Kelber, "Works of Memory," 238.

18. Alan Dundes, *Holy Writ as Oral Lit: The Bible as Folklore* (Lanham: Rowman & Littlefield, 1999), 2.

19. Susan Niditch, *A Prelude to Biblical Folklore: Underdogs and Tricksters* (Urbana: University of Illinois Press, 2000), 13.

20. Kraemer, *Aseneth*, 305.

21. Each textual version of *Joseph and Aseneth* should not, in my estimation, be viewed as a "separate performance," as Thomas suggests (*Acts of Peter*, 85). This perspective does not appreciate how the narrative's new textual medium affects its transmission and reception.

The multiform tradition of Mark

Mark's textual attestation does not display the same "performance attitude" taken toward, nor the *mouvance* that characterizes, *Joseph and Aseneth*. The gospel is not textually fluid and multiform to the extent that *Joseph and Aseneth* and the *Actus Vercellenses* are.[22] In these textual traditions, material is frequently rearranged, lengthened, and shortened. Mark, in contrast, is characterized by, what Michael W. Holmes calls, "macro-level stability."[23]

While the overarching structure and episodes of Mark are mostly stable, many details of the gospel, especially its language, are fluid in its witnesses.[24] This is what Holmes labels "microlevel fluidity."[25] Especially compared to the other canonical gospels, Mark exhibits fluidity at the micro level. This is primarily indicated by the number of textual variants in the gospel. Mark has more variants than the other canonical gospels.[26] In addition, Mark has the least number of variant-free verses

---

22. The situation will be different if Morton Smith's Secret Gospel of Mark ever proves to be authentic (*Clement of Alexandria and a Secret Gospel of Mark* [Cambridge: Harvard University Press, 1973). The two additions to canonical Mark, if genuine, would be evidence of the narrative's multiformity. Be that as it may, there is nothing close to a consensus about whether the Secret Gospel and the *Letter to Theodore* that contains it are forgeries or authentic. It initially appeared that Stephen C. Carlson had delivered a devastating blow to the case for the letter's authenticity (*The Gospel Hoax: Morton Smith's Invention of Secret Mark* [Waco: Baylor University Press], 2005). But Scott G. Brown and Allan J. Pantuck have disputed Carlson's evidence that Smith forged the text and playfully left behind clues for the astute interpreter to recognize that it is a hoax (Brown, "Factualizing the Folklore: Stephen Carlson's Case against Morton Smith," *HTR* 99 [2006]: 291–327; idem, "The Letter to Theodore: Stephen Carlson's Case against Clement's Authorship," *JECS* 16 [2008]: 535–72; Brown and Pantuck, "Morton Smith as M. Madiotes: Stephen Carlson's Attribution of *Secret Mark* to a Bald Swindler," *Journal for the Study of the Historical Jesus* 6 (2008): 106–25; Pantuck, "A Question of Ability: What Did He Know and When Did He Know It? Further Excavations from the Morton Smith Archives," in *Ancient Gospel or Modern Forgery? The Secret Gospel of Mark in Debate: Proceedings from the 2011 York University Christian Apocrypha Symposium*, ed. Tony Burke [Eugene: Wipf & Stock, 2013], 184–211). Burke's edited volume, *Ancient Gospel or Modern Forgery?*, which contains ten essays that represent various positions, reveals how divergent the views on the origins of Secret Mark and the *Letter to Theodore* currently are. Since the debate is still so contentious, it seems to me that any claims made about canonical Mark on the basis of the Secret Gospel of Mark are precarious.

23. Holmes, "From 'Original Text' to 'Initial Text,'" in *The Text of the New Testament in Contemporary Research: Essays on the Status Quaestionis*, ed. Bart D. Ehrman and Michael W. Holmes, 2nd ed., NTTS 42 (Leiden: Brill, 2013), 674.

24. Wire, *Case*, 35–38; Collins, *Mark*, 125–26.

25. Holmes, "From 'Original Text,'" 674. Collins likewise notes that "many details of the text of Mark were remarkably fluid" (*Mark*, 125).

26. Joanna Dewey, "The Survival of Mark's Gospel: A Good Story?" *JBL* 123 (2004): 505; Burnett Hillman Streeter, *The Four Gospels: A Study of Origins* (London: Macmillan,

of the gospels and the highest number of variants per page in the Nestle-Aland reconstruction.[27]

The frequency of microlevel variants in Mark might hint at its oral transmission, but this evidence should be taken with a grain of salt, as early textual attestation to Mark is sparse. P^{45} is the sole witness to the gospel prior to the fourth century. While both Dewey and Wire take the scarcity of early textual witnesses to Mark as evidence for the gospel's oral transmission, the argument from silence is not conclusive in and of itself.[28] A better case can be made for *mouvance* in the textual tradition of Mark from the gospel's endings.[29] These do exhibit multiformity and are the strongest argument for a "performance attitude" taken to the gospel.

The endings are commonly referred to as the "Original Ending," concluding at 16:8, the "Shorter Ending," which also concludes at v. 8 but adds two additional sentences, and the "Longer Ending," consisting of Mk 16:9-20. The division of the endings into only three groups simplifies a more complex text-critical situation. There are certainly more than just three endings. Holmes argues that there are at least nine different conclusions to Mark's Gospel.[30] D. C. Parker finds six.[31] No matter how many there are, the same conclusion is to be drawn: The final chapter of Mark is textually multiform and probably was so as early as the second century.[32] This likely results from both a performance attitude taken to the textual tradition of Mark in the first few centuries CE and also from the fact that the abrupt ending

---

1924), 307; George D. Kilpatrick, *The Principles and Practice of New Testament Textual Criticism: Collected Essays*, ed. J. K. Elliott (Leuven: Leuven University Press, 1990), 7–8.

27. Dewey, citing Kurt and Barbara Aland, notes that 45.1% of Mark's verses are variant free, compared with 62.9% for the NT as a whole and over 60% for both Matthew and Luke ("Survival," 505; Aland and Aland, *The Text of the New Testament: An Introduction to the Critical Editions and to the Theory and Practice of Modern Textual Criticism*, trans. Erroll F. Rhodes [Grand Rapids: Eerdmans, 1989], 27–30). She takes this as one of three textual data points for the influence of oral transmission on Mark. Wire similarly takes the higher number of variants in Mark as evidence for the gospel's composition in performance (*Case*, 32).

28. Dewey, "Survival," 506; Wire, *Case*, 33–35.

29. Though not taken up here, an argument could also be made for Mark's *mouvance* given its subsummation into Matthew and Luke. One might argue that Mark was subject to rewriting precisely because it was not connected to individual authorship, nor was it considered anyone's intellectual property, as Kelber has suggested ("The History of the Closure of Biblical Texts," in Weissenrieder and Coote, *Interface*, 81–82).

30. Michael W. Holmes, "To Be Continued ... The Many Endings of the Gospel of Mark," *BR* 17 (2001): 12–23.

31. Parker, *The Living Text of the Gospels* (Cambridge: Cambridge University Press, 1997), 124–28.

32. Citing patristic references to the longer and shorter endings, Parker concludes that "verses 9–20 had come into existence by the end of the second century" (ibid., 133). David W. Hester provides a comprehensive review of the early testimony to the longer ending (*Does Mark 16:9–20 Belong in the New Testament?* [Eugene: Wipf & Stock, 2015], 114–24).

at Mk 16:8 seemed unsatisfying, especially in light of the endings of the other Synoptics.

Mark's near contemporary, Galen, will have been familiar with the manner in which the gospel was amended. In *De libris propriis* 9 he writes about how his texts were "shortened, lengthened, and altered" (μετὰ τοῦ τὰ μὲν ἀφαιρεῖν, τὰ δὲ προσ τιθέναι, τὰ δὲ ὑπαλλάττειν) by persons trying to pass off his work as their own. There was another form of intellectual property theft that Galen experienced. On at least one occasion someone attempted to turn a profit by affixing Galen's name to a text. The philosopher-physician begins *De libris propriis* with an anecdote about this latter kind of plagiarism. While in the bookseller district of Rome, Galen witnessed someone buying a book roll entitled *Galen the Doctor* (Γαληνὸς ἰατρός).[33] A bystander trained in letters (ἀνὴρ τῶν φιλολόγων) was struck by what was apparently an odd title and asked to look at the text. After reading only two lines, he declared it a farce and ripped off the inscription, claiming, "This is not Galen's style" (οὐκ ἔστι λέξις αὕτη Γαληνοῦ).[34] Galen does not tell his reader whether this spuriously titled work was based on any of his oral teachings that were transcribed into ὑπομνήματα, though this seems likely since this was the most common kind of intellectual theft Galen experienced, as we witnessed in Chapter 2. Moreover, immediately following the anecdote, Galen tells his reader that others have read and published his books under their names. He claims they were able to do so because these texts were ὑπομνήματα transcribed from oral lectures that were not intended for publication.[35]

The longer and shorter endings of Mark Mark's added endings correspond to Galen's experiences. If the gospel is an oral transcription and within the generic range of ὑπομνήματα, it is not surprising that a later tradent would amend the text in such a manner. Just as the text falsely attributed to Galen was not written in his style, the Longer Ending of Mark is not written in Mark's style. The sociolinguistic criteria I have proposed related to parataxis and verbal features expose an important difference between the Original Ending and the Longer Ending.[36] The

---

33. *libr. propr.* 9.
34. *libr. propr.* 8–9.
35. *libr. propr.* 10.
36. Other syntactical and grammatical comparisons of the long ending with the rest of Mark have considered words or phrases and overall grammatical structure. This is the case with William R. Farmer, *The Last Twelve Verses of Mark*, SNTSMS 25 (Cambridge: Cambridge University Press, 1974), 83–103; Hester, *Does Mark?* 141–42. Farmer concludes that only Mk 16:10 contains preponderant evidence for non-Markan authorship, that Mk 16:12, 14, 16, 17, 18, and 19 intimate neither Markan nor non-Markan authorship, and that Mk 16:9, 11, 13, 15, and 20 contain thoroughly Markan words and phrases (*Last Twelve Verses*, 103). Farmer compares only words and phrases from Mk 16.9-20 with their occurrences in the rest of the gospel, and is unconcerned with overarching syntactical patterns, such as parataxis and verbal tense, voice, and mood.

former coheres with the syntax of oral composition that characterizes the rest of the gospel, while the latter exhibits literary syntax. In other words, Mk 16:9-20 was not likely composed orally. Comparing the paratactic and verbal tendencies of Mk 1:1–16:8 with those of Mk 16:9-20 reveals that the Longer Ending does not exhibit dense residual orality.[37]

Linguistic characteristics of Mark's longer ending

Regarding parataxis, in the Longer Ending καί appears less frequently than Mk 1:1–16:8 and the syntactical locations of the copula differ in the two sections of text. Moreover, the Longer Ending employs δέ more frequently than the rest of Mark. In Mk 16:9-20, καί appears 13 times out of 174 total words, once for every 13.38.[38] This is about 30% less frequently than in the rest of Mark, which is close to Matthew's and Luke's reductions, which will be explored in the next chapter. More telling than the volume of καί in the Longer Ending is its syntactical locations and grammatical operations. The connective begins a new sentence on only one occasion, Mk 16:15. Unlike Mk 1:1–16:8, καί rarely begins a new clause in the Longer Ending. This only happens with the contracted forms κἄν in Mk 16:18 and κἀκεῖνοι in Mk 16:11 and Mk 16:13. On every other occasion καί serves as a copulative connecting individual words, not entire clauses or sentences. It is also instructive that the Longer Ending has a higher frequency of δέ than the rest of Mark. The conjunction appears six times, or once for every 29 words. This is once for every 2.17 times καί occurs. These proportions are much closer to the other two Synoptics than they are to Mk 1:1–16:8, where δέ occurs once for every 70.94 words and once for every 6.92 times καί occurs.[39]

Regarding verbs in the Longer Ending of Mark, the differences from Mk 1:1–16:8 in tense and voice are telling of each text's compositional mode. The Longer Ending of Mark does not contain any historical presents. As discussed in Chapter 3, historical presents are frequent in the rest of the gospel and evidence of its residual orality. Additionally, there is only one present indicative verb in Mk 16:9-20 and no imperfect verbs at all. As noted in Chapter 2, oral narrative heavily relies on the present and imperfect tenses, while written narrative is more dependent on the simple past tense.[40] It is significant, then, that aorist indicative verbs occur fourteen times in the Longer Ending compared to the

---

37. Here I employ the reconstruction of the long ending from NA28 and not any one specific long ending from the MS tradition.

38. Three of these instances are in the contracted forms κἀκεῖνοι and κἄν. Elsewhere in the Gospel, contracted forms with καί appear only six times in total.

39. In Matthew δέ occurs once for every 2.41 instances of καί and once for every 37.17 total words. In Luke δέ occurs once for every 2.74 instances of καί and once for every 35.97 total words.

40. Nearly half of the indicative verbs in Mk 1:1–16:8 are either in the present or in the imperfect.

one occasion of the present and the total absence of the imperfect. Regarding voice, the more frequent employment of the passive in the Longer Ending is also indicative of its literary conception. In Mk 16:9-20, 29.2% of the indicative verbs and 22.4% of the total verbal forms are in the passive, compared with 10.2% and 11.1%, respectively, in Mk 1:1–16:8. This also coheres well with sociolinguistic research that finds that the passive is more frequent in written than in spoken narrative.[41]

To summarize thus far, the endings of Mark are the best evidence that the gospel is textually fluid and multiform. While it is possible that the oral, and perhaps even the textual tradition of Mark was multiform before the third century when consistent manuscript attestation to it begins, this cannot be proven from the extant witnesses. Besides the *mouvance* of the ending of the gospel, textual multiformity does not necessarily witness to Mark's oral conception. Nonetheless, linguistic considerations shed light on the endings and suggest that the Longer Ending was composed in a manner different from the rest of the gospel. This is primarily evidenced by its lack of parataxis and its verbal features. Neither of these conforms to what is found in Mk 1:1–16:8.

This all supports the general scholarly consensus that Mk 16:9-20 is not "original" to the gospel. Sociolinguistic research further endorses the "originality" of the ending at Mk 16:8, since oral narratives often exhibit grammar that is considered unacceptable in the written medium.[42] Mk 16:8 infamously ends on the pregnant note ἐφοβοῦντο γάρ ("for they were afraid"). It is especially rare for sentences in narratives, and even more rare for entire narratives, to end with the conjunction γάρ ("for").[43] Yet this ending is not as unexpected when one recognizes that speakers employ syntax that is considered ungrammatical in literary registers. It is even more telling that one of the "ungrammatical" devices found in spoken narratives is a clause-final preposition.[44] It is surely significant then, and perhaps not so surprising, that, as N. Clayton Croy notes, Greek works that possess an oral style contain a sentence-ending γάρ far more frequently than those that exhibit a literary style.[45]

This, combined with the better textual attestation to the Original Ending, leads to the conclusion that Mk 16:8 is the oldest textual ending to the gospel. If the goal is to reconstruct the eldest textual form of Mark, then Mk 16:8 ought to be considered the end of the narrative. But, as I have argued, each instantiation of a tradition should be considered equiprimordially. Every manuscript of Mark is itself the tradition, not merely a witness to it. Thus, in those manuscripts in which Mk 16:9-20 is included, the Longer Ending is indeed "original," or, better,

---

41. Chafe, "Integration and Involvement," 45; Bennett, "Extended View," 69–70.
42. Chafe, "Linguistic Differences," 114–16.
43. N. Clayton Croy, *The Mutilation of Mark's Gospel* (Nashville: Abingdon, 2003), 49; Kelly R. Iverson, "A Further Word on Final Γάρ (Mark 16:8)," *CBQ* 68 (2006): 87.
44. Chafe, "Linguistic Differences," 115.
45. Croy, *Mutilation*, 48.

"traditional." It is no less primary or significant to the story's meaning in those textual instantiations. The dissimilar endings of Mark are in this way the direct result of manuscript *mouvance*. Alan Kirk writes, "The principle of *mouvance* means that manuscript texts would come to bear in their receptive materiality the marks of the social and cultural contexts that they traversed in the course of transmission."[46] In this case, the mark of the gospel's social and cultural contexts is anxiety over an abrupt ending.

With both *Joseph and Aseneth* and Mark, therefore, we see that new communicative contexts affect the written versions of the narrative. Later editors altered the texts and added to them at their volition. While no text, ancient or modern, is perfectly protected from emendation, texts that exist at the borderland between orality and textuality are less protected than those that are conceived as literary products. Because the latter are viewed as the intellectual property of single authors rather than anonymous and open traditions, they are less likely to be altered the way that *Joseph and Aseneth* and Mark were.

In this respect, the later Synoptic Gospels might also be considered evidence of Mark's pluriform tradition. If gospel tradents had no qualms about adding new endings to Mark because of its media form, perhaps the authors of Matthew and Luke also utilized the raw Markan textual material for the same reason. Matthew D. C. Larsen has suggested that this is precisely the case.[47] Taking Mark to be a ὑπόμνημα, he claims, "It would be anachronistic to categorize Matthew as creating a separate piece of literature from Mark, especially since Matthew's alterations of Mark, from the point of view of ancient writing practices, are fairly minor."[48] Rather, Matthew is simply part of "the same mushrooming textual tradition of the gospel."[49] If we were not so conditioned by the fixity of texts occasioned by our print culture and we possessed unlabeled versions of Mark and Matthew, would we likely consider them different traditions? The answer for Larsen is "no." This is because gospels are not books, but rather "fluid constellations of texts."[50] Thus the reuse of Markan material by the later Synoptic authors is, like Mark's multiple endings, evidence for the pluriformity of the tradition.

Criterion #5: Intertextuality

As is the case with the pluriformity of their traditions, *Joseph and Aseneth* and Mark are similar in the way that they evoke antecedent texts. Both exhibit an echoic

---

46. Kirk, "Manuscript Tradition as a *Tertium Quid*: Orality and Memory in Scribal Practices," in Thatcher, *Jesus, the Voice, and the Text*, 226.
47. Larsen, "Accidental Publication," 376–78.
48. Ibid., 377.
49. Ibid.
50. Ibid., 379.

mode of intertextual recall of the LXX. Texts from the Jewish Scriptures inform *Joseph and Aseneth* and Mark, but these are not typically reproduced verbatim in either narrative. They are recalled as cultural texts.

Also akin to the pluriformity of their traditions, *Joseph and Aseneth* and Mark differ in some of the ways that they relate to other textual traditions. There are a few instances in Mark where the intertextuality is best characterized as "imprecise." *Joseph and Aseneth* has no analogy to this. And both narratives intertextually evoke corpora that the other does not. *Joseph and Aseneth* exhibits an echoic intertextual relationship with the Greek romance novels, and Mark a similar relationship with the Book of the Watchers in *1 Enoch*. In the case of both narratives, their intertextuality is best described as echoic. This echoic intertextuality, I shall argue, results from their mode of composition.

Intertextuality in Joseph and Aseneth

Joseph and Aseneth never directly quotes another text. This does not suggest that textual traditions do not influence the narrative. To apply Hays's taxonomy, allusions and echoes abound.[51] In my estimation, verbatim reproduction of the LXX and other literature does not occur in *Joseph and Aseneth* because quotation is a phenomenon more characteristic of textuality than it is of orality. In place of quotations, *Joseph and Aseneth* evokes texts, traditions, and literary genres in an allusive manner. Key lexemes and thematic parallels register intertexts from the LXX and the novels in a manner characteristic of oral literature.

Intertextuality with the LXX in Joseph and Aseneth Two recent studies contend that the LXX, and the Joseph narrative in particular, is integral to *Joseph and Aseneth*.[52] The text's affinities with the LXX have been noticed in previous scholarship, but these similarities have usually been deemed incidental rather than essential.[53] In contrast, Kraemer argues that *Joseph and Aseneth* is constructed directly on the basis of materials from Jewish-Greek Scripture.[54] Susan Docherty claims that the narrative is an example of rewritten Bible and

---

51. Hays, *Echoes of Scripture in the Letters of Paul*, 29; idem, *Conversion*, 34–35.

52. Kraemer, *Aseneth*, 19–42; Susan Docherty, "Joseph and Aseneth: Rewritten Bible or Narrative Expansion?" *JSJ* 35 (2004): 27–48. These studies directly contradict Gruen's contention that *Joseph and Aseneth* is hardly related to or concerned with the biblical Joseph narrative in Genesis (*Heritage*, 99).

53. Victor Aptowitzer, "Asenath, the Wife of Joseph: A Haggadic Literary-Historical Study," *HUCA* 1 (1924): 239–306; Philonenko, *Joseph et Aséneth*, 27–32, and throughout the notes in the critical edition (pp. 128–221); Humphrey, *Joseph and Aseneth*, 31–33; Chesnutt, *From Death to Life*, 69–71; Burchard, "New Translation," 184–85.

54. Kraemer, *Aseneth*, 21–22.

is composed from the elements of the Joseph tale in Genesis.[55] Both offer a host of intertextual resonances between *Joseph and Aseneth* and the LXX to support their claims. Yet neither is precise in her intertextual terminology. They do not specify what kind of intertextual evocation *Joseph and Aseneth* makes, whether it is a citation, allusion, echo, or some other such. Critical scrutiny of the narrative's intertextual resonances reveals that *Joseph and Aseneth* is indeed indebted to the LXX, but does not offer citations from it. Three illustrative examples reveal this to be the case.

Joseph and Aseneth 1:3 and Gen. 41:46-49

Joseph and Aseneth begins by recalling Joseph's Egyptian grain-gathering expedition narrated in Gen. 41:46-49 LXX.[56] *Joseph and Aseneth* 1:3 verbally resonates with Gen. 41:49 LXX, and Docherty claims that this resonance grounds it in the biblical Joseph story.[57] This parallel is one of the clearest between *Joseph and Aseneth* and the Septuagintal version of the Joseph cycle:

καὶ ἦν συνάγων τὸν σῖτον τῆς χώρας ἐκείνης ὡς τὴν ἄμμον τῆς θαλάσσης.	And he was gathering the grain of that land like the sand of the sea. (*Jos. Asen.* 1:3)
καὶ συνήγαγεν Ιωσηφ σῖτον ὡσεὶ τὴν ἄμμον τῆς θαλάσσης πολὺν σφόδρα, ἕως οὐκ ἠδύναντο ἀριθμῆσαι, οὐ γὰρ ἦν ἀριθμός.	And Joseph gathered up very much grain— like the sand of the sea—until they were unable to count, for there was no counting. (Gen. 41:49 LXX, NETS)

Even in this obvious parallel the intertextuality is inexact. To be sure, five lexemes overlap. These are all in the phrase σῖτον ὡσ(εὶ) τὴν ἄμμον τῆς θαλάσσης.[58] Beyond this, the overlap is not verbatim. The other shared term is the verb συνάγω, which is in a different mood in the two texts. In addition, the particles ὡς and ὡσεί, while closely related, are different: *Joseph and Aseneth* makes σῖτος definite, and Gen. 41:49 emphasizes the amount of grain Joseph gathered with additional clauses. The inexact pairing of the verb συνάγω with the genitive phrase τὴν ἄμμον τῆς

---

55. Docherty, "Joseph and Aseneth," 27–48.

56. It is important to recognize, as Ahearne-Kroll does, that *Joseph and Aseneth* inverts the order of events given in Genesis 41. There, Joseph marries Aseneth before he goes out to gather Egyptian grain ("Joseph and Aseneth," 2529).

57. Docherty, "Joseph and Aseneth," 34.

58. The genitive phrase ἄμμος τῆς θαλλάσης appears to be stock, as it occurs several times in the LXX to indicate large numbers. See LXX Gen 32:13; 41:49; Josh. 11:4; Hos. 2:1; Isa. 10:22; Jer. 15:8. It also occurs in Rev. 20:8, which is its only appearance in the NT. Moreover, ἄμμος is often associated with θαλάσσα in other syntactical constructions in the LXX to indicate a large number. See LXX Gen 22:17; Judg. 7:12; 1 Sam. 13:5; 2 Sam. 17:11; 1 Kgs 2:35; 1 Kgs 2:46; 1 Kgs 5:9; 1 Macc. 11:1; Ps. 77:27; Odes Sol. 7:36; Sir. 1:2; Dan 3:36.

θαλάσσης recall Gen. 41:49 not as a quotation, but as a loud echo.[59] The Joseph story from Genesis is recalled here without a full excerpt.[60]

Joseph and Aseneth 4:9 and Gen. 41:38

Joseph and Aseneth 4:9 echoes an element of Joseph's character from the Genesis narrative. Pentephres tells Aseneth, "The spirit of God is upon [Joseph]" (πνεῦμα θεοῦ ἐστιν ὑπ' αὐτῷ). Contrary to Docherty's claim that the statement "is taken straight from Pharaoh's similar recognition in Genesis 41:38," the parallel is not a verbatim quotation from Genesis.[61] Rather, it is an ideological echo registered by the catchphrase πνεῦμα θεοῦ ("spirit of God"). The phrase occurs in Genesis 41:38 LXX when Pharaoh asks his servants if they will find another man like Joseph "who has the spirit of God in him" (ὃς ἔχει πνεῦμα θεοῦ ἐν αὐτῷ). The differences are obvious. First, in Genesis, the subject of the verb is Joseph while in *Joseph and Aseneth* it is the spirit of God. Second, the texts have different prepositions, ὑπό in *Joseph and Aseneth* and ἐν in Genesis. And third, *Joseph and Aseneth* makes its claim about Joseph with a finite clause, while Genesis uses a relative one.

Joseph and Aseneth 27–29 and 1 Samuel 17

Joseph and Aseneth 27–29 is an intercalation that recalls David's battle with Goliath in 1 Samuel 17.[62] The two outer layers of the intercalation, *Jos. Asen.* 27:1-5 and 29:1-7, narrate Benjamin's battle with Pharaoh's son, likening him to the valorous king.[63] At this point in the story, Joseph and Aseneth have already been married and are parting ways for a limited time. Joseph is off to act as savior of Egypt, distributing grain in the cities. And Aseneth plans to travel to the field of their

---

59. Hays offers suggestions for determining the volume of an echo (Hays, *Echoes of Scripture in the Letters of Paul*, 30; idem, *Conversion*, 34–37). Philonenko concludes that *Joseph and Aseneth* was "inspired" by Gen 41:49 LXX (*Joseph et Aséneth*, 9).

60. *Joseph and Aseneth* 1:1; 4:13-14; 20:7; 21:8; 22:1-6 all similarly assume or re-narrate elements from Genesis without directly quoting the text.

61. Docherty, "Joseph and Aseneth," 39.

62. The form of the intercalation is addressed in Chapter 3. It consists of A[1]: Benjamin's battle with Pharaoh's son (27:1-5); B[1]: Aseneth's "battle" with the sons of Bilhah and Zilpah (27:6–28:3); B[2]: Aseneth's non-retaliatory response to her opponents (28:4-16); A[2]: Benjamin's non-retaliatory response to his opponent (29:1-7).

63. Others have recognized that the episode is modeled after 1 Samuel 17 (Gerhard Delling, "Einwirkungen der Sprache der Septuaginta in 'Joseph und Asenath,'" *JSJ* 9 [1978]: 187; Burchard, "New Translation," 185; Gordon M. Zerbe, *Non-Retaliation in Early Jewish and New Testament Texts: Ethical Themes in Social Contexts*, JSPSup 13 [Sheffield: Sheffield Academic, 1993], 78; Ahearne-Kroll, "Joseph and Aseneth," 2578; Angela Standhartinger, "Humour in Joseph and Aseneth," *JSP* 24 [2015]: 253–56).

inheritance to await Joseph's return. On her way she runs into an ambush by Pharaoh's son, who has contrived a plan to murder Joseph, kidnap Aseneth, and take her as his wife. Up against Pharaoh's son and fifty of his soldiers, all hope looks lost for the heroine until Benjamin, Joseph's brother, steps in and fights Davidically. *Joseph and Aseneth* 27:1-5 reads:

| καὶ ἦν Βενιαμὴν καθεζόμενος μετ' αὐτῆς ἐπὶ τοῦ ὀχήματος. καὶ ἦν Βενιαμὴν παιδάριον ἰσχυρὸν ὡς ἐτῶν δέκα καὶ ὀκτώ, καὶ ἦν ὑπ' αὐτῷ κάλλος ἄρρητον καὶ δύναμις ὡς σκύμνου λέοντος, καὶ ἦν φοβούμενος τὸν θεόν. καὶ κατεπήδησε Βενιαμὴν ἐκ τοῦ ὀχήματος καὶ ἔλαβε λίθον ἐκ τοῦ χειμάρρου στρογγύλον καὶ ἐπλήρωσε τὴν χεῖρα αὐτοῦ καὶ ἠκόντισε κατὰ τοῦ υἱοῦ Φαραὼ καὶ ἐπάταξε τὸν κρόταφον αὐτοῦ τὸν εὐώνυμον καὶ ἐτραυμάτισεν αὐτὸν τραύματι μεγάλῳ καὶ βαρεῖ, καὶ ἔπεσεν ἐκ τοῦ ἵππου αὐτοῦ [ἡμιθανὴς τυγχάνων]. καὶ ἀνέδραμε Βενιαμὴν ἐπὶ πέτρας καὶ εἶπε τῷ ἡνιόχῳ τῆς Ἀσενέθ· δὸς δή μοι λίθους ἐκ τοῦ χειμάρρου πεντήκοντα. καὶ ἔδωκεν αὐτῷ [λίθους πεντήκοντα]. καὶ ἠκόντισε τοὺς λίθους Βενιαμὴν καὶ ἀπέκτεινε τοὺς πεντήκοντα ἄνδρας τοὺς ὄντας μετὰ τοῦ υἱοῦ Φαραὼ καὶ ἔδυσαν οἱ λίθοι ἐπὶ τοὺς κροτάφους ἑνὸς ἑκάστου αὐτῶν. | And Benjamin was seated with her [Aseneth] on the chariot. And Benjamin was a strong young man, eighteen years old, and he was very good-looking and as powerful as a young lion and he feared God. And Benjamin leapt down from the chariot and he took a round stone from the brook and he filled his hand and he threw it at the son of Pharaoh and he struck his left temple and wounded him severely and he fell off his horse nearly dead. And Benjamin ran onto a rock and said to Aseneth's chariot driver, "Bring me fifty stones from the river!" And he gave him the fifty stones, and Benjamin threw the stones and killed the fifty men that were with Pharaoh's son, and the stones sank into the foreheads of each one of them. |

The content of the narrative recalls David's battle with the giant. There are reminiscences of 1 Samuel 17 throughout this episode. 1 Samuel 17:49 LXX has the densest verbal resonance with *Jos. Asen.* 27:

| καὶ ἐξέτεινεν Δαυιδ τὴν χεῖρα αὐτοῦ εἰς τὸ κάδιον καὶ ἔλαβεν ἐκεῖθεν λίθον ἕνα καὶ ἐσφενδόνησεν καὶ ἐπάταξεν τὸν ἀλλόφυλον ἐπὶ τὸ μέτωπον αὐτοῦ, καὶ διέδυ ὁ λίθος διὰ τῆς περικεφαλαίας εἰς τὸ μέτωπον αὐτοῦ, καὶ ἔπεσεν ἐπὶ πρόσωπον αὐτοῦ ἐπὶ τὴν γῆν. | And David stretched out his hand into the bag and took out from there one stone and slung it and struck the allophyle on his forehead, and the stone penetrated through the helmet into his forehead, and he fell on his face on the ground. (NETS) |

Certain lexemes make it certain that the story from the LXX is being recalled. Both Benjamin and David are described as a "young man" (παιδάριον) and "good-looking" (κάλλος).[64] Both take stones (λίθους) from a stream (ἐκ τοῦ χειμάρρου) in denominations of five and use them as their missiles of choice.[65] These subsequently strike (ἐπάταξε[ν]) an area of their enemy's head.[66] But the intertextuality is inexact. Different words for forehead (*Jos. Asen.* 27:3: κρόταφον;

---

64. παιδάριον in *Jos. Asen.* 27:1; 1 Sam. 17:33, 42 LXX; κάλλος in *Jos. Asen.* 27:2; 1 Sam. 17:42 LXX.

65. *Joseph and Aseneth* 27:4; 1 Sam. 17:40 LXX.

66. *Joseph and Aseneth* 27:3: κρόταφον; 1 Sam. 17:49 LXX: μέτωπον.

1 Sam. 17:49 LXX: μέτωπον), to sling (*Jos. Asen.* 27:3: ἠκόντισε; 1 Sam. 17:49 LXX: ἐσφενδόνησεν), to sink (*Jos. Asen.* 27:5: ἔδυσαν; 1 Sam. 17:49 LXX: διέδυ), and round (*Jos. Asen.* 27:3: στρογγύλον; 1 Sam. 17:40 LXX: λεῖος) appear in each account. David takes five stones, Benjamin fifty.

And most importantly, the way that each narrative describes the antagonist's demise differs. This is because *Joseph and Aseneth* 27–29 recalls 1 Samuel 17 only to upend it.[67] David claims that the Lord will be with him as he fights the giant (1 Sam. 17:37 LXX). Aseneth also insists that the Lord takes action in battle (*Jos. Asen.* 28:11), but it is for this very reason that a human should not seek justice by means of physical force. Instead, she advocates a non-retaliatory ethic.[68] A God-fearing person will not do his or her enemy harm but will leave judgment and vengeance to the Lord (*Jos. Asen.* 28:6, 14).

Joseph and Aseneth 27–29's subversion of 1 Samuel 17 is illustrated in the different responses of David and Benjamin to their foes. Standing before Goliath, David announces the giant's fate to him in 1 Sam. 17:45-46:

καὶ εἶπεν Δαυιδ πρὸς τὸν ἀλλόφυλον σὺ ἔρχῃ πρός με ἐν ῥομφαίᾳ καὶ ἐν δόρατι καὶ ἐν ἀσπίδι, κἀγὼ πορεύομαι πρὸς σὲ ἐν ὀνόματι κυρίου σαβαωθ θεοῦ παρατάξεως Ισραηλ, ἣν ὠνείδισας σήμερον· καὶ ἀποκλείσει σε κύριος σήμερον εἰς τὴν χεῖρά μου, καὶ ἀποκτενῶ σε καὶ ἀφελῶ τὴν κεφαλήν σου ἀπὸ σοῦ καὶ δώσω τὰ κῶλά σου καὶ τὰ κῶλα παρεμβολῆς ἀλλοφύλων ἐν ταύτῃ τῇ ἡμέρᾳ τοῖς πετεινοῖς τοῦ οὐρανοῦ καὶ τοῖς θηρίοις τῆς γῆς, καὶ γνώσεται πᾶσα ἡ γῆ ὅτι ἔστιν θεὸς ἐν Ισραηλ.	And David said to the allophyle, "You come to me with sword and with spear and with shield, and I am coming to you in the name of the Lord Sabaoth, the God of the ranks of Israel, which you have reproached today. And today the Lord will shut you up into my hand, and I will kill you and remove your head from you, and I will give your limbs and the limbs of the camp of the allophyles on this day to the birds of the air and to the wild animals of the earth, and all the earth will know that there is a God in Israel." (NETS)

---

67. Zerbe claims that *Joseph and Aseneth* 27–29 is rewriting both the scriptural tradition and its implicit morality (*Non-Retaliation*, 79). Christopher Brenna argues that there is a similar reversal of the Samson narrative from Judges in *Joseph and Aseneth* ("The Lion, the Honey, and the New Timnite Woman: Joseph and Aseneth and the Samson Cycle," *JSP* 26 [2017]: 144–63). He notes lexical parallels between Judges 14 LXX and Aseneth's encounter with the angel who resembles Joseph (ibid., 158). As with *Joseph and Aseneth* 27–29, the intertextuality with Judges is thematic and echoic and serves to reimagine the actions of a protagonist from Jewish Scripture.

68. Zerbe notes similar non-retaliatory ethics in Second Temple Judaism (*Non-Retaliation*, 34–165). He argues that *Joseph and Aseneth*'s ethic is reflective of its Jewish provenance and biblical influences (ibid., 93–97). Nir comes to the opposite conclusion about *Joseph and Aseneth* on the basis of the non-retaliatory ethic, claiming that it results from the narrative's Christian provenance (*Joseph and Aseneth*, 160–66).

The contrast with Levi's words to Benjamin, which emulate Aseneth's ethic, is stark. Just as Benjamin is about to behead Pharaoh's son in *Jos. Asen.* 29:3-4, Levi grabs him and says:

μηδαμῶς, ἀδελφέ, ποιήσῃς τὸ ἔργον τοῦτο, διότι ἡμεῖς ἄνδρες θεοσεβεῖς ἐσμεν, καὶ οὐ προσήκει ἀνδρὶ θεοσεβεῖ ἀποδοῦναι κακὸν ἀντὶ κακοῦ οὐδὲ πεπτωκότα καταπατῆσαι οὐδὲ ἐκθλίψαι τὸν ἐχθρὸν ἕως θανάτου. ἀλλὰ δεῦρο καὶ θεραπεύσωμεν αὐτὸν ἀπὸ τοῦ τραύματος αὐτοῦ καὶ ἐὰν ζήσῃ ἔσται ἡμῶν φίλος καὶ ὁ πατὴρ αὐτοῦ φαραὼ ἔσται πατὴρ ἡμῶν.	By no means should you do this deed, brother, because we are God-fearing men, and it is not fitting for a God-fearing man to repay evil for evil, nor to trample one who has fallen, nor to afflict an enemy to death. But come and let us bandage up his wound and if he lives he will be our friend and his father, Pharaoh, will be our father.

Unlike 1 Samuel and Mark, there are thus no beheadings in *Joseph and Aseneth*.[69] Benjamin and Levi are not so Davidic as to the final actions they take against the antagonist. Rather than decapitating their enemy, they wash and bandage him, attempting to make amends and restore their severed relationship. These actions are informed by Aseneth's "battle" with Dan in Gad and her propitiation of their brothers in the center of the intercalation, and they undermine David's deed in 1 Sam. 17:48-51.

The motivation for subverting 1 Samuel 17 is twofold. First, *Joseph and Aseneth* promotes a non-retaliatory ethic. This is indicated by the repetition of a precise formula in *Joseph and Aseneth* 28. This formula consists of a verbal form of ἀποδίδωμι with the prepositional phrase κακὸν ἀντὶ κακοῦ.[70] Second, 1 Samuel 17 accentuates Goliath's foreignness, promulgating an implicit morality that *Joseph and Aseneth* rejects. Throughout 1 Samuel nominal forms of פְּלִשְׁתִּי ("Philistine") are not translated φυλιστίμ ("Philistine") and their equivalents, as elsewhere in the LXX, but ἀλλόφυλος ("allophyle," "foreigner") and its equivalents. The latter occurs twenty-three times in 1 Samuel 17, fifteen of which refer to Goliath. Goliath's foreignness is further accentuated in 1 Sam. 17:36-37, wherein David twice jeeringly calls him an "uncircumcised foreigner" (ὁ ἀλλόφυλος ὁ ἀπερίτμητος). The attitude toward the Other exhibited in 1 Samuel 17 runs counter to the outlook presented throughout *Joseph and Aseneth*.

In sum, Benjamin's stone-slinging account in *Joseph and Aseneth* 27-29 resembles David's battle with Goliath, but it also differs. Key lexemes and themes make it certain that the text is being recalled, but it is never quoted. The longest verbatim overlap between the texts is five words: καὶ ἔλαβε τὴν ῥομφαίαν αὐτοῦ ("And he took his sword").[71] The intertextuality between *Joseph and Aseneth* and the Septuagint in this case, as with those addressed above, is echoic.

---

69. 1 Samuel 17:51; Mk 6:17-20.

70. Zerbe suggests that the maxim behind this formula is μὴ ἀποδιδόναι κακὸν ἀντὶ κακοῦ and is also attested by Rom. 12:19; 1 Thess. 5:15; 1QS 10.17; *2 En.* 50:4 (*Non-Retaliation*, 87).

71. 1 Samuel 17:51 LXX; *Jos. Asen.* 29:2.

These examples of echoic intertextuality between *Joseph and Aseneth* and the LXX reveal that the former is familiar with the latter at the lexical level, but that no text is quoted verbatim. The tales from the LXX are recalled as cultural texts and not embedded in *Joseph and Aseneth* as literary artifacts.[72] The intertextual phenomenon found here is an example of how the medium shapes, and indeed *is*, the message.[73] Marshall McLuhan famously offered the truism that any medium is a technological extension of the human person and necessarily becomes inextricably bound with the message that it contains.[74] This being the case, writing structures thinking and serves as an external memory aid.[75] Texts store memories that are reactivated by authors, speakers, and audiences. This is done in at least two different ways. First, texts can be reproduced and embedded in other discourses, oral or written. This reproduction depends heavily on the technology of writing as a memory aid and less on pure memory itself. In this mode, either the text is read verbatim in oral reappropriation or it is copied verbatim in written replication. Exact reproduction is a hallmark of this method of recall. In the second mode, authors and speakers become familiar with texts through their experience of them, whether by hearing or by reading them. These texts then enter into the author's or speaker's memory and can be reactivated without directly consulting the writing itself. This method is dependent on the text, but only insofar as it has been assimilated into the author's or speaker's cultural repertoire. Recall in this mode is less exact than in the former mode. The intertextuality in *Joseph and Aseneth* represents this second model of textuality as an external memory aid. The Joseph story in Genesis and David's battle with Goliath in 1 Samuel 17 are indeed evoked, perhaps even from their textual versions. The textual recall is filtered mnemonically and culturally, though. This accounts for *Joseph and Aseneth*'s echoic intertextuality with the LXX.

Joseph and Aseneth *and the Greek romance novels* Joseph and Aseneth's intertextuality with the Greek romance novels resembles its intertextuality with the LXX. There is a significant difference, however. Whereas *Joseph and Aseneth* will often echo a specific Septuagintal text with key lexemes, the narrative *does not* echo particular novelistic texts. Rather, *Joseph and Aseneth* evokes tropes from this literary genre, which results in thematic and lexical resonances between the two

---

72. This proposal contrasts with Burchard's tentative suggestion that *Joseph and Aseneth*'s echoic intertextuality with the Joseph novella is the result of "a different form or forms of text" from the LXX ("New Translation," 185 n. 37).

73. McLuhan, *Understanding Media: The Extensions of Man* (Cambridge: MIT Press, 1994), 1–18.

74. Ibid., 4–8.

75. Jan Assmann calls this phenomenon "exteriorization" ("Remembering in Order to Belong: Writing, Memory, and Identity," 85).

textual traditions.[76] I will offer two examples that show that *Joseph and Aseneth*'s intertextuality with the novels is not verbatim but lexically echoic, as is the case with the LXX. This suggests that *Joseph and Aseneth* recalls tropes from the novels, but it does not imply that *Joseph and Aseneth* directly reproduces, or is literarily dependent on, any of the novels.[77]

The description of Aseneth's beauty in *Jos. Asen.* 1:6-8 thematically echoes those of the female protagonists in the novels, particularly Callirhoe in Chariton's *Chaereas and Callirhoe* and Anthia in Xenophon's *Anthia and Habrocomes*.[78]

---

76. Many scholars have recognized the similarities between *Joseph and Aseneth* and the novels. See especially Philonenko, *Joseph et Aséneth*, 43–48; Stefanie West, "Joseph and Asenath: A Neglected Greek Romance," *ClQ* 24 (1974): 70–81; Burchard, *Der dreizehnte Zeuge: Traditions- und kompositionsgeschichtliche Untersuchungen zu Lukas' Darstellung der Frühzeit des Paulus*, FRLANT 103 (Göttingen: Vandenhoeck & Ruprecht, 1970), 59–86; idem, "Joseph et Aséneth: Questions actuelles," in *Littérature juive entre Tenach et Mischna: Quelques problèmes*, ed. W. C. van Unnik (Leiden: Brill, 1974), 230–42; idem, "New Translation," 183–87. The standard inference drawn from these similarities is that *Joseph and Aseneth* is an atypical novel of some sort (Richard I. Pervo, "Joseph and Asenath and the Greek Novel," *SBLSP* 10 [1976]: 174; Chesnutt, *From Death to Life*, 88–92; Lawrence M. Wills, *The Jewish Novel in the Ancient World* (Ithaca: Cornell University Press, 1995),184; Gruen, *Heritage*, 93–94; Humphrey, *Joseph and Aseneth*, 44–46; Sara Raup Johnson, *Historical Fictions and Hellenistic Jewish Identity: Third Maccabees in Its Cultural Context* [Berkeley: University of California Press, 2005], 120; Ahearne-Kroll, "Jewish Identity," 137). I agree that *Joseph and Aseneth* exhibits a generic relationship to the Greco-Roman novels. But there are significant differences between the novels and *Joseph and Aseneth*. Standhartinger and I have both noted these (Standhartinger, "Recent Scholarship," 376; Elder, "On Transcription," 136–40). Many of them can be best elucidated by differences in media tradition.

77. I primarily note similarities with the two extant pre-Sophistic novels, Chariton's *Chaereas and Callirhoe* and Xenophon's *Anthia and Habrocomes*. These two novels are chronologically nearer to *Joseph and Aseneth* than the Sophistic novels. Per Ronald F. Hock and Tomas Hägg, *Chaereas and Callirhoe* was likely written in the first century BCE or the first century CE and *Anthia and Habrocomes* was likely written in the first or second century CE (Hock, "The Greek Novel," in *Greco-Roman Literature and the New Testament*, ed. David E. Aune [Atlanta: Scholars Press, 1988], 128; Hägg, *The Novel in Antiquity* [Berkeley: University of California Press, 1983], 34).

78. West, Nina V. Braginskaya, and Brenna all note the similar appearance of Aseneth and the novels' heroines (West, "Joseph and Asenath," 71–72; Braginskaya, "Joseph and Aseneth in Greek Literary History: The Case of the 'First Novel,'" in *The Ancient Novel and Early Christian and Jewish Narrative: Fictional Intersections*, ed. Marília P. Futre Pinheiro, Judith Perkins, and Richard I. Pervo, Ancient Narrative Supplementum 16 [Groningen: Barkhuis, 2012], 98–100; Brenna, "Lion," 152–53). Characterization of the heroes and heroines in *Chaereas and Callirhoe* and *Joseph and Aseneth* are addressed by Ahearne-Kroll ("Jewish Identity," 111–19).

All three narratives state that their heroines are excessively comely παρθένοι ("virgins") whose allure surpasses that of their fellow countrywomen.[79] Callirhoe and Anthia are described as goddess-like in appearance.[80] *Joseph and Aseneth*, whose audience worshiped an aniconic God, compares Aseneth to the Israelite damsels of old, Rebecca, Sarah, and Rachel, rather than to a goddess. Finally, in both *Joseph and Aseneth* and *Chaereas and Callirhoe*, the rumor (ἡ φήμη) of the respective maiden's pulchritude is spread far and wide, generating strife among many love-stricken potentates.[81] While the three narratives never directly cite one another, there are several persistent lexemes that recall the familiar trope of the protagonist's incomparable beauty in each of the texts: μεγάλη, ὡραία, εὐπρεπής, κάλλος, παρθένος, φήμη, θέαμα, θυγάτηρ, θαυμάσια, and θαυμάζω.

The thematic allure of the protagonists runs into another trope shared between the novels and *Joseph and Aseneth*: love at first sight that results in physical illness.[82] After the beauty of the lovers is described in the novels, the two lock eyes and become immediately enamored. Following their initial infatuation, one or more of the lovers mentally and physically grieve until they are eventually joined in matrimony. Examples from *Chaereas and Callirhoe* and *Anthia and Habrocomes* illustrate this theme.[83]

Chaereas and Callirhoe's auspicious meeting is described in 1.1.6. Tyche herself contrives a chance encounter that ensures the two see each other (ἑκάτερος τῷ ἑτέρῳ ὀφθῇ) as Chaereas is on his way home from the gymnasium. The two fall in love at first sight (ταχέως οὖν πάθος ἐρωτικὸν ἀντέδωκαν ἀλλήλοις). Chaereas is so smitten that he no longer can stand (στῆναι δὲ μὴ δυνάμενος). Callirhoe

---

79. *Joseph and Aseneth* 1:6 relates the following about Aseneth's appearance: παρθένος μεγάλη καὶ ὡραία καὶ εὐπρεπὴς τῷ κάλλει σφόδρα ὑπὲρ πᾶσαν παρθένον ἐπὶ τὴν γῆν. *Chaereas and Callirhoe* 1.1.1–3 describes Callirhoe's beauty similarly: Καλλιρόην τοὔνομα, θαυμαστόν τι χρῆμα παρθένου καὶ ἄγαλμα τῆς ὅλης Σικελίας. ἦν γὰρ τὸ κάλλος οὐκ ἀνθρώπινον ἀλλὰ θεῖον, οὐδὲ Νηρηΐδος ἢ Νύμφης τῶν ὀρειῶν ἀλλ' αὐτῆς Ἀφροδίτης [παρθένου]. Finally, *Anthia and Habrocomes* 1.2.5 has similar language to describe its protagonist: ἦν δὲ τὸ κάλλος τῆς Ἀνθίας οἷον θαυμάσαι καὶ πολὺ τὰς ἄλλας ὑπερεβάλετο παρθένους. *Anthia and Habrocomes* 1.2.6 goes on to describe Anthia's physical features in detail.

80. Callirhoe is also mistaken for a goddess throughout the novel. See especially *Chaer*. 1.14.1–2; 2.3.8; 3.3.5; 3.9.1.

81. *Joseph and Aseneth* 1:9-11 reports that Aseneth's beauty spread throughout the land of Egypt. *Chaereas* 1.1.2–3 similarly reports that Callirhoe's beauty spread throughout all of Italy, as her suitors poured in from the entire continent.

82. Braginskaya notes the shared themes of love at first sight and lovesickness in *Callirhoe* and *Joseph and Aseneth* ("Joseph and Aseneth," 96–97). She concludes that the narratives were independent of each other or that *Joseph and Aseneth* influenced *Callirhoe*. She recognizes that lovesickness is a "novelistic topos" but does not note the similar lexemes in the narratives (ibid., 97).

83. Though, see also Achilles Tatius's *Leuc. Clit.* 1.4.4–5 and Apuleius's *Metam.* 5.22.

likewise falls (προσέπεσε) at the feet of Aphrodite. The meeting brings physical and mental torment (δεινή) to them both. Chaereas ceases his exercise routine, much to the chagrin of his compatriots, who themselves abandon the gymnasium on account of his absence.[84] Thus his lovesickness endangers his own well-being as well as that of his friends. Callirhoe, much like Aseneth, agonizes on her bed. During her weeping, she receives the report that she is to be married, but she knows not to whom. Presuming her betrothal is not to Chaereas, "her knees collapsed and her heart within her" (τῆς δ' αὐτοῦ λύτο γούνατα καὶ φίλον ἦτορ).[85] The parallel with *Jos. Asen.* 6:1 is striking: "Her heart was broken and her knees were paralyzed" (συνεκλάσθη τὰ σπλάγχνα αὐτῆς καὶ τὰ γόνατα αὐτῆς παρελύθησαν). The protagonists' physical and mental despair is finally assuaged when they are married at the end of *Chaer.* 1.1.

Similarly, in *Anthia and Habrocomes* 1.3.1, upon seeing the other (ὁρῶσιν ἀλλήλους) each falls into a deep love-trance and cannot look away from the other's gaze. Upon their separation, both are lovelorn and emotionally disheveled. Each offers passion-laments, Habrocomes in 1.4.1 and Anthia in 1.4.6–7.[86] The narrative then reports in 1.5.5 that Habrocomes's body and mind begin to wither away (τὸ σῶμα πᾶν ἠφάνιστο καὶ ἡ ψυχὴ καταπεπτώκει). Anthia fares no better.[87] Both are so lovesick that "they were expected to die at any moment" (ὅσον οὐδέπω τεθνήξεσθαι προσδοκώμενοι).[88] Like Chaereas and Callirhoe, Anthia and Habrocomes's conditions only improve when they get word of their betrothal in 1.7.4.

Joseph and Aseneth 6:1-8 takes up these same tropes about the physical and mental state of the story's protagonists. But it applies them to only one of the lovers, namely, Aseneth. When Aseneth sees (εἶδεν) Joseph for the first time, "her soul was strongly stabbed, her affections were shattered, her knees failed, her whole body shook, and she feared greatly" (κατενύγη ἰσχυρῶς τῇ ψυχῇ καὶ συνεκλάσθη τὰ σπλάγχνα αὐτῆς καὶ τὰ γόνατα αὐτῆς παρελύθησαν καὶ συνετρόμαξεν ὅλον τὸ σῶμα αὐτῆς καὶ ἐφοβήθη φόβον μέγαν). Aseneth laments in *Jos. Asen.* 6:2-8. Features of her lament resemble Habrocomes's and Anthia's.[89]

---

84. *Chaereas* 1.1.10: ἐπόθει δὲ τὸ γυμνάσιον Χαιρέαν καὶ ὥσπερ ἔρημον ἦν. ἐφίλει γὰρ αὐτὸν ἡ νεολαία.

85. *Chaer.* 1.1.14. Trans. Goold, LCL. The phrase is directly quoted from *Odyssey* 4.703 and also occurs in *Chaer.* 3.6.3 and 4.5.9.

86. The narrative explicitly states in 1.5.1 that "each of them spent the entire night lamenting these things" (ταῦτα ἑκάτερος αὐτῶν δι' ὅλης νυκτὸς ὠδύρετο).

87. Anthia's condition is summarized in *Anthia and Habrocomes* 1.4.6. The audience is told that "Anthia too was in a bad way" and that she "hurt in ways strange and inappropriate" (Henderson, LCL).

88. Trans. Henderson, LCL.

89. This is because there are certain features characteristic of the Greek laments. These are (1) a hesitant beginning with an initial question; (2) questions, sporadic or successive, that carry the lament along; (3) a series of hypotheses, differentiated from reality that are proposed and rejected; (4) a contrast between past, present, and future time, resulting

All three pose several questions.⁹⁰ Both Aseneth and Habrocomes apply self-deprecating terms to themselves with ἐγώ.⁹¹ Anthia speaks the pronoun similarly, but with an adjective that is not necessarily deprecating.⁹² Along with a superfluity of the personal pronoun ἐγώ, all three have an abundance of first-person verbal forms.⁹³ Both Aseneth and Habrocomes consign themselves to slavery, Aseneth in *Jos. Asen.* 6:8 and Habrocomes in *Anthia and Habrocomes* 1.4.1. Finally, both Aseneth and Habrocomes utter an invocational νῦν on multiple occasions.⁹⁴ These similarities are best accounted for by their generic connection. They are the result of lament topoi, not direct literary influence one way or the other.⁹⁵

Once again, the lexical affinities between the laments in the novels and Aseneth's lament in *Joseph and Aseneth* are inexact. Neither directly quotes, or even alludes to, the other. Rather, they are similar in syntax and resonate with each other verbally because they belong to a common literary genre that possesses recurring verbal tropes. Since the limits of what constitute intertextuality are methodologically wide, it is appropriate to deem these narratives intertextually related.⁹⁶ To be more precise, the relationship might be called intergeneric.

in a variety of verbal tenses; (5) a prominence of the invocational now (νῦν); and (6) an abundance of first-person pronouns and verbal forms. I have synthesized these elements of Greek laments from Margaret Alexiou, *The Ritual Lament in Greek Tradition* (Lanham: Rowman & Littlefield, 2002), 161–68; Casey Dué, *The Captive Woman's Lament in Greek Tragedy* (Austin: University of Texas Press, 2006), 12–15, 53–55; R. L. Fowler, "The Rhetoric of Desperation," *Harvard Studies in Classical Philology* 91 (1987): 6. Edgar Wright Smith explicitly addresses questions in laments ("Form and Religious Background of Romans 7:24–25a," *NovT* 13 [1971]: 130–31).

90. Aseneth asks six questions in her lament, Habrocomes four, Anthia five.

91. In *Anthia and Habrocomes* 1.4.2, Habrocomes states ὦ πάντα ἄνανδρος ἐγὼ καὶ πονηρός. Aseneth predicates the adjectives ταλαίπωρος, ἄφρων, and θρασεῖα to ἐγώ in her lament.

92. *Anthia and Habrocomes* 1.4.6: παρθένος ἐγὼ φρουρουμένη.

93. Aseneth speaks thirteen first-person verbal forms, Habrocomes nine, Anthia seven.

94. *Joseph and Aseneth* 6:4, 5, 8; *Anthia and Habrocomes* 1.4.1, 2 (x2).

95. There are laments in the other Greek romance novels that also feature these topoi. See especially *Chaer.* 7.6. My conclusion about literary influence is contra Braginskaya, who argues that the similarities between the novels and *Joseph and Aseneth* are the result of the latter's direct literary influence on the former ("Joseph and Aseneth," 102).

96. Hays provides a concise overview of the different methodological applications of the term intertextuality in the foreword to the English edition of *Reading the Bible Intertextually*, ed. idem, Stefan Alkier, and Leroy A. Huizenga (Waco: Baylor University Press, 2009), xi–xv. In the same volume, Stefan Alkier offers a thorough history of the development of intertextuality in literary theory and biblical scholarship ("Intertextuality and the Semiotics of Biblical Texts," 3–21).

In conclusion, the intertextuality between *Joseph and Aseneth* and the LXX is echoic. I have argued that the narrative does evoke specific texts in the LXX, but it does not directly quote or embed those texts. This echoic intertextuality is more characteristic of oral narratives than it is of literarily conceived narrative. Concerning the Greco-Roman novels, *Joseph and Aseneth* contains themes and tropes that appear in those novels, but never evokes any one novel in particular. It is more accurate to call the textual relationship between the novels and *Joseph and Aseneth* intergeneric.

Intertextuality in Mark

The Gospel of Mark is certainly influenced by antecedent Jewish writings. Nominal forms of the word γραφή ("writing") appear in Mk 12:10, 24; 14:49. Verbal forms of γράφω ("to write") occur in Mk 1:2; 7:6; 9:12, 13; 10:4, 5; 11:17; 12:19; 14:21, 27, often in the perfect tense form, γέγραπται ("it has been written").[97] The evangelist considers written Scriptures authoritative and employs references to writings for rhetorical leverage. Along with these conscious evocations of written Scripture, the gospel, and especially the passion narrative, is peppered with echoes of the LXX.[98] There can be no doubt that Mark is familiar with both the LXX and other

---

97. γέγραπται occurs in Mk 1:2; 7:6; 9:12, 13; 11:17; 14:21, 27. It is reminiscent of the formula καθὼς γέγραπται and its Hebrew equivalent, כאשר כתוב, which frequently introduce authoritative antecedent texts in early Jewish and Christian writings (2 Kgs 14:6; 2 Chr 25:4; Lk. 2:23; Acts 7:42; Rom. 1:17, 3:4, 10; 8:36; 9:13, 33; 10:15; 11:8, 26; 15:3, 9, 21; 1 Cor. 1:31; 2:9; 2 Cor. 8:15; 9:9; 1QS V, 17; VIII, 14; CD VII, 19; 1 Clem. 48:2). Yet this precise formula introduces quoted material in only Mk 1:2. The other time καθὼς γέγραπται appears in the gospel is Mk 14:21, where no particular text is quoted but a body of authoritative writings are alluded to.

98. Rudolf Bultmann influentially argued that the passion narrative was constructed out of the kerygma of the early church that was enriched with allusive elements from Scripture (*The History of the Synoptic Tradition*, trans. John Marsh [New York: Harper & Row, 1968], 275–84). Dibelius similarly reasoned that the kerygmatic passion narrative congealed out of the reading of discrete biblical texts that then made their way into the written account by way of allusion rather than citation (*Tradition*, 184–85). He calls special attention to allusions in the dividing of Jesus's garments, the vinegar offered to him, the passersby mocking him, and his maltreatment after his trial (ibid., 186–88). That the passion narrative developed out of the early church's kerygma is no longer taken as axiomatic, though most agree that it was heavily influenced by Scripture. Interpreters vary on the number of allusions and echoes that are found therein. Howard Clark Kee detects hundreds ("The Function of Scriptural Quotations and Allusions in Mark 11–16," in *Jesus und Paulus: Festschrift für Werner Georg Kümmel*, ed. E. Earle Ellis and Erich Grässer [Göttingen: Vandenhoeck & Ruprecht, 1975], 167–71). Kelli S. O'brien finds that scholars have proposed over 270 different allusions or echoes to the OT in the passion narrative (*The Use of Scripture in the Markan Passion Narrative*, LNTS 384 [London: T&T Clark, 2010], 17). She critiques the

traditions and evokes them in the gospel more often than *Joseph and Aseneth*, which does not appear to contain a single quotation from Scripture.

Nonetheless, in this section I shall argue that Mark's intertextuality is both echoic and imprecise. The gospel rarely quotes extended texts from the LXX verbatim.[99] Christopher Bryan finds that there are only two precise quotations in the entire gospel, Mk 7:6b-7, where two lines from Isa. 29:13 LXX are reproduced, and Mk 12:10-11, where four lines from Ps. 117:22-24 LXX are quoted.[100] While this truncated manner of drawing upon Scripture reveals that Mark's intertextuality is echoic, other characteristics indicate its mode of intertextual evocation is imprecise. The gospel "miscites" and "misquotes" Scripture and appeals are made to "writings" when no explicit text seems to be in mind.[101]

The conclusion to be drawn is that the evangelist does not regularly rely directly on written texts of Jewish Scripture while composing the gospel. Rather, the speaker recalls texts and traditions primarily from memory.[102] We should not imagine multiple scrolls laid out and their words copied directly into the gospel.[103] Instead, we should think of the speaker evoking texts that he or she has

---

maximalist approach as methodologically unsound and after testing the proposed allusions concludes there are only sixteen instances that have sufficient verbal or thematic overlap to be designated as such (ibid., 112).

99. Christopher Bryan notes that very few of the intertexts recalled in Mark are quotations, and those that are quotations are never of much length (*A Preface to Mark: Notes on the Gospel in Its Literary and Cultural Settings* [New York: Oxford University Press, 1993], 146).

100. Ibid., 148–49. He argues that both texts were easy to memorize because of their parallelism and that there is no evidence that the evangelist read any Scripture (ibid., 149). I find it more likely than not that Mark was semi-literate, having some capacity to read the LXX, but it does not appear as though he is consistently making eye contact with scrolls as he composes the gospel.

101. I do not mean to imply that the evangelist's mode of intertextual recall is in any way malicious or dishonest. Conditioned by the norms of print culture, we think of miscitation and misquotations as academically mendacious. In the case of oral literature, however, mnemonic recall is simply another mode of evoking a tradition.

102. Eve argues that memorial recall ought to be scholars' default assumption when it comes to the gospel writers' source materials (*Writing the Gospels*, xii, 39–51). He does not imagine that the evangelists worked entirely from memory but that during the composition process they rarely consulted texts directly (ibid., 50). In my estimation, Eve's position holds true for the Gospel of Mark. But, as we shall see in this chapter and the next, Matthew and Luke are more precise with their intertextuality. It is more likely that they had more eye contact with various texts during the composition process than the Markan evangelist did.

103. Contra Burton Mack, who imagines that Mark "was composed at a desk" with written sources, including the Wisdom of Solomon, Samaritan texts, and Maccabean

internalized, either by memorization or by familiarity through reading them or hearing them read.[104]

Before showing how this mnemonic mode of recall is realized in Mark, there are three potential objections to be addressed. First, it could be argued that Mark's imprecise intertextuality is a result of theological intentionality. That is, the author has advertently changed the wording of Scripture for theological purposes. While I don't believe this argument can be sustained for the divergent varieties of intertextual imprecision in Mark, it is certainly possible that the evangelist has kneaded traditions to fit his or her theological mold. In fact, this would be easier to do with oral literature than written literature, since direct comparison of texts is a hallmark of the literary mode of production and reception and not the oral mode.[105] Second, it might be objected that if the evangelist is a Greek-Aramaic bilingual, he or she is recalling Aramaic versions of Scripture and translating them on an ad hoc basis. There is no way to prove that this is not the case for some intertextual evocations in Mark. But it is clear on other occasions, such as Mk 7:6b-7 and 12:10-11, that the Septuagint, and not a translated Aramaic text, is quoted.[106] If the evangelist were producing a literary text in Greek, we would expect he or she would make the effort to consult the Greek version of Scripture whenever authoritative traditions are evoked, not just sporadically. And third, claiming that the evangelist evokes Scripture mnemonically is not to minimize its importance in Mark. It is simply to observe that the medium affects the message. Mnemonic evocation is more appropriate to the oral mode of composition than the literary mode.

In what follows, I shall first review those ways in which Mark's echoic intertextuality differs from *Joseph and Aseneth*'s. The latter's echoic intertextuality manifests itself in its evocation of themes from the Greco-Roman romances and its recollection of the Septuagint by key lexemes, as we have seen above. There are occasions when Mark evokes intertexts similarly, but there are also instances when the gospel's intertextuality manifests itself differently. We shall look to examples of the latter first, in the form of "miscitations," "misquotations," and inexplicit

---

literature, strewn about (*A Myth of Innocence: Mark and Christian Origins* [Philadelphia: Fortress, 1988], 322–23).

104. William A. Graham (*Beyond the Written Word: Oral Aspects of Scripture in the History of Religion* [Cambridge: Cambridge University Press, 1987], 161) and Horsley ("Oral and Written Aspects of the Emergence of the Gospel of Mark as Scripture," 98) similarly argue that the evangelist has "internalized" Scripture and does not work from written texts during the composition process.

105. Kirk notes, "It is the written medium, with its visual, material properties, that makes variation evident" (*Q in Matthew*, 6).

106. As W. D. Davies and Dale C. Allison note, we have no indication from the gospel that Mark was familiar with any other text of Scripture than the LXX (*A Critical and Exegetical Commentary on the Gospel according to Saint Matthew*, 3 vols., ICC [Edinburgh: T&T Clark, 2004], 1:45).

references to writings, which I have called "imprecise intertextuality," before considering two instances of the former.[107]

Misciting and misquoting scripture in Mark Mark's first miscitation occurs in the opening lines of the gospel, immediately following its incipit. Mark 1:2-3 ostensibly quotes Isaiah, introducing the text with the phrase καθὼς γέγραπται ἐν τῷ Ἡσαΐᾳ τῷ προφήτῃ ("as it is written in Isaiah the Prophet"). But the quotation is not from Isaiah alone. It is a composite. The first two lines recall Exod. 23:20 LXX and Mal. 3:1 LXX:

Mark 1:2:	Exod. 23:20:	Mal. 3:1:
ἰδοὺ ἀποστέλλω τὸν ἄγγελόν μου πρὸ προσώπου σου, ὃς κατασκευάσει τὴν ὁδόν σου.	καὶ ἰδοὺ ἐγὼ ἀποστέλλω τὸν ἄγγελόν μου πρὸ προσώπου σου, ἵνα φυλάξῃ σε ἐν τῇ ὁδῷ.	ἰδοὺ ἐγὼ ἐξαποστέλλω τὸν ἄγγελόν μου, καὶ ἐπιβλέψεται ὁδὸν πρὸ προσώπου μου.
Behold, I send my messenger before thy face, who shall prepare thy way. (RSV)	And look, I am sending my angel in front of you, in order to guard you on the way. (NETS)	Behold, I am sending my messenger, and he will oversee the way before me. (NETS)

The text in Mark does not exactly reproduce either Exod. 23:20 or Mal. 3:1.[108] The same is true of the next verse, Mk 1:3, which recalls Isa. 40:3:

Mark 1:3:	Isa. 40:3:
φωνὴ βοῶντος ἐν τῇ ἐρήμῳ· ἑτοιμάσατε τὴν ὁδὸν κυρίου, εὐθείας ποιεῖτε τὰς τρίβους αὐτοῦ.	φωνὴ βοῶντος ἐν τῇ ἐρήμῳ ἑτοιμάσατε τὴν ὁδὸν κυρίου, εὐθείας ποιεῖτε τὰς τρίβους τοῦ θεοῦ ἡμῶν.
The voice of one crying in the wilderness: Prepare the way of the Lord, make his paths straight. (RSV)	A voice of one crying out in the wilderness, "Prepare the way of the Lord, make straight the paths of our God." (NETS)

Here, the intertextuality is more precise than in the preceding verse, but it is still not completely exact. The final genitive nouns differ between the two texts.

---

107. Imprecise intertextuality differs from an echo. The latter refers to a subtle intertextual reference (Hays, *Echoes of Scripture in the Letters of Paul*, 29). Imprecise intertextuality refers to a textual evocation wherein the second text differs from or misrepresents the content of the antecedent text. Imprecise intertextuality is not in the same category as citation, allusion, and echo. Thus an echo can be imprecise or precise, as can an allusion or citation.

108. For this reason interpreters differ on which text is being recalled. Collins argues that Mal. 3:1 better fits Mark's intention and thus is the primary text evoked (*Mark*, 136). In contrast, Richard B. Hays makes a case that the wording of Exod. 23:23 and its surrounding literary context make it the more likely intertext. According to him, by evoking this text at the beginning of the gospel, Mark metaleptically recalls themes of restoration and judgment from Exodus 20 that will be consistently echoed in Mark (*Echoes of Scripture in the Gospels* [Waco: Baylor University Press, 2016], 22–23).

Several reasons have been offered for the composite quotation that begins the gospel and why it is attributed to Isaiah.¹⁰⁹ Guelich, Marcus, and Hays argue that there is theological intention behind the Isaian attribution and that it metaleptically recalls the entire context of Isaiah 40, which is an "announcement of a revelation of the divine advent."¹¹⁰ Marcus argues that Mark himself has formed the composite quotation, stringing the texts together because he knows that Mal. 3:1 and Isa. 40:3 are related by the Hebrew phrase פנה דרך, despite the fact that the phrase has been translated ἐπιβλέψεται and ἑτοιμάσατε in Malachi LXX and Isaiah LXX, respectively.¹¹¹ If Mark has created the composite citation, he does not bother to be textually precise about where all of it comes from. If he was literarily sophisticated enough to create a composite citation based on the Hebrew catchphrase פנה דרך, it is surprising that he has included the prepositional phrase ἐν τῷ Ἠσαΐᾳ τῷ προφήτῃ ("in Isaiah the Prophet"), which he could easily have rendered ἐν τοῖς προφήταις ("in the prophets"), ἐν ταῖς γραφαῖς ("in the writings"), or some other such, instead. Perhaps the imprecision is theologically intentional, its aim being to carry more Isaian freight. Or perhaps the evangelist mnemonically conflated texts and attributed them all to Isaiah. Whatever the case may be, Matthew and Luke found this imprecision problematic, as they retain the attribution to Isaiah but omit the words that are not from the prophet (Mt. 3:3; Lk. 3:5-6).

Mark 2:23-28 and 1 Sam. 21:2-10

Mark 2:23-28 is another instance where Matthew and Luke emend a textual referent because of Mark's imprecision. In Mk 2:25-26, Jesus responds to the Pharisees' challenge about his disciples having picked heads of grain on the Sabbath. Jesus asks if the Pharisees have read the account of David and his compatriots eating the bread of the presence when Abiathar was high priest. The notorious problem is that Jesus gets the High Priest's name wrong. In the account he is referring to, 1 Sam. 21:2-10, Ahimelech, Abiathar's father, is the high priest who gives David the bread.¹¹² This is not technically a case of miscitation or misquotation

---

109. Collins reviews three possibilities that have been entertained: (1) The citation is from a collection; (2) Mark created the composite citation himself and attributed it to Isaiah because of its popularity; and (3) Mark attributed the conflation to Isaiah for theological reasons (*Mark*, 136).

110. Quotation from Joel Marcus, *The Way of the Lord: Christological Exegesis of the Old Testament in the Gospel of Mark* (Edinburgh: T&T Clark, 1993), 19. See also Robert A. Guelich, "'The Beginning of the Gospel': Mark 1:1–15," *BR* 27 (1982): 5–15; Hays, *Echoes of Scripture in the Gospels*, 20–21.

111. Marcus, *Way of the Lord*, 17–19.

112. Horsley argues that Mark is referring to a popular, folkloristic version of the tale from 1 Samuel, not the text itself (*Hearing*, 164–65). To him, this accounts for many of the peculiar aspects of Jesus's version of the story, including the misnaming in Mk 2:26.

because a text is neither directly cited nor quoted. It might better be called a false recollection. Collins notes that Abiathar is a better-known associate of David than Ahimelech.[113] It is likely that the discrepancy in Mark results from a memory of Abiathar's connection with David. Even though he was not the high priest at the time, Abiathar was recalled because of his connection with David. This inaccuracy, while understandable from an oral-memorial perspective, was unacceptable in the literary mode. It is a significant enough blunder that some manuscripts of Mark omit the phrase ἐπὶ Ἀβιαθὰρ ἀρχιερέως ("when Abiathar was High Priest") in 2:26, as do Matthew (12:4) and Luke (6:4).[114] This is to be expected of literary compositions, which are characterized by intertextual exactitude more than oral narratives are. The change thus exhibits the "precision of verbalization" that typifies writing on account of its editability.[115]

Mark 14:27 and Zech. 13:7

Mark 14:27 is the last explicit citation in the gospel that uses the introductory phrase καθὼς γέγραπται ("as it written"). Mark's intertext is clearly Zech. 13:7, but his quotation differs from any known Hebrew or Septuagintal version of it.[116] The quotation from Mk 14:27 compared with Zech. 13:7b in Rahlfs edition of the LXX reads:

Mark 14:27: πατάξω τὸν ποιμένα, καὶ τὰ πρόβατα διασκορπισθήσονται.	Zech. 13:7b: πατάξατε τοὺς ποιμένας καὶ ἐκσπάσατε τὰ πρόβατα, καὶ ἐπάξω τὴν χεῖρά μου ἐπὶ τοὺς ποιμένας.
I will strike the shepherd, and the sheep will be scattered. (RSV)	Smite the shepherds, and remove the sheep, and I will bring my hand against the shepherds. (NETS)

There are two differences. First, in Mark the sheep (τὰ πρόβατα) are the subject of the passive verb διασκορπισθήσονται, rather that the object of the imperative verb

---

113. Collins, *Mark*, 203 n. 130. Marcus also argues that a better-known figure can replace a lesser-known figure in the development of a tradition, and so the replacement of Ahimelech with Abiathar may simply be a mistake (*Mark*, 1:241).

114. B, D, 2427, r¹, and t, all omit the phrase. Hays notes that Matthew's omission "is one of many editorial nuances that show how carefully Matthew was reading his sources. He does not merely take over scriptural references from Mark; he cross-checks them, either directly against the Old Testament text or against his comprehensive knowledge of that text" (*Echoes of Scripture in the Gospels*, 398 n. 65). We might call Matthew's cross-checking "intertextual precision."

115. "Precision of verbalization" is a phrase used by Ong to characterize writing over against oral performance, which knows nothing of editability and this precision (*Orality and Literacy*, 103).

116. Ibid., 81.

ἐκσπάσατε.¹¹⁷ Second, the leading verb in Mark is the first-person future πατάξω with the Lord as its subject. This reading appears to begin with Mark.¹¹⁸ The LXX versions either have the second-person plural imperative, as in Rahlfs, following MSS B, ℵ*, and W, or the second-person singular imperative, πατάξον (A, Q, ℵᶜ, L, and C).¹¹⁹ It is possible that Mark has intentionally altered the tense and number of the verb πατάσσω in Zech. 13:7b to serve his purposes. Changes like this occur in the literary mode. Yet they are more common in oral narrative, because neither the speaker nor the hearer is cross-checking the tense and voice of the quoted text. The other differences between Mark's version and the LXX, including the change of number of the shepherds, the different placement of "the sheep" (τὰ πρόβατα) either before or after the verb, and the general abbreviation of the passage, evoke the referent mnemonically, not textually.¹²⁰ In this case, the discrepancies between the texts result from both an intentional change that makes the antecedent text fit the context of Mark better and from a mnemonic mode of recall.¹²¹ This is far more likely than the theory that Mark knew an earlier Greek version of the passage that is no longer extant.¹²²

Inexplicit references to writing Along with Mark's imprecise citations and quotations, there are three inexplicit references to writing, purportedly of Scripture, in Mark. In these instances, the gospel is not intertextually precise about what text is being recalled. The first case is Mk 9:12. Here, the disciples ask Jesus why the scribes claim Elijah must come first. Jesus responds and poses a question of his own, "And how is it written about the Son of Man that he must greatly suffer and be despised?" (καὶ πῶς γέγραπται ἐπὶ τὸν υἱὸν τοῦ ἀνθρώπου ἵνα πολλὰ πάθῃ καὶ ἐξουδενηθῇ;) As Marcus notes, there is precedent for using the introductory phrase "it is written" of conflations of biblical passages and even

---

117. There is one manuscript, LXX^Q, that witnesses to this reading. See the apparatus in Rahlfs; Hays, *Echoes of Scripture in the Gospels*, 81.

118. Hays, *Echoes of Scripture in the Gospels*, 387 n. 127. Matthew 26:31 also attests to πατάξω and some later LXX attestations (V, 538, 46, 86, 711, 106, 233, Arab, Arm, Cyr.) correct to the reading found in the gospels (Joseph Ziegler, ed., *Duodecim prophetae*, vol. XIII/2 of *Septuaginta: Vetus Testamentum Graecum Auctoritate Academiae Scientarum Gottingensis editum* [Göttingen: Vandenhoeck & Ruprecht, 1967], 322).

119. Hays, *Echoes of Scripture in the Gospels*, 387 n. 127. The singular reading corresponds to the singular imperative verb in the MT.

120. Moreover, Mark has not quoted the first half of the passage, ῥομφαία, ἐξεγέρθητι ἐπὶ τοὺς ποιμένας μου καὶ ἐπ' ἄνδρα πολίτην μου, λέγει κύριος παντοκράτωρ ("'Awake, O sword, against my shepherds and against his fellow citizen,' says the Lord Almighty" [NETS]).

121. James R. Edwards suggests that the change to the first-person singular future verb may have been a result of mnemonic recall facilitated by the first-person singular future verb, ἐπάξω ("I will bring upon"), in the second half of Zech. 13:7 (*The Gospel according to Mark*, The Pillar New Testament Commentary [Grand Rapids: Eerdmans, 2002], 428 n. 34).

122. As Collins tentatively suggests (*Mark*, 669).

exegetical conclusions drawn from specific texts.¹²³ In this case it is difficult to determine what specific texts or exegetical conclusions are being recalled, since "there is ... no discrete OT passage that describes the suffering and rejection of the Son of Man."¹²⁴ It could be that Mark is alluding to Isaiah's suffering servant, the Son of Man in Daniel 7, or the righteous sufferer of the Psalms.¹²⁵ Or, as Horsley argues, Mark might employ the introductory formula "it is written" (γέγραπται) as a general appeal to written authority without a specific textual referent.¹²⁶ This would be akin to the petitioner of P.Oxy. 903, examined in Chapter 2, who makes a general appeal to "the laws" (οἱ νόμοι).

The second and third cases of appeals to writing without an explicit citation or quotation occur in Mk 14:21 and 49. The former is again a reference to the Son of Man: "because the Son of Man goes as it is written about him." Collins and France argue that the reference to writing in v. 21 continues an allusion to Ps. 40:10 LXX that they find in Mk 14:18.¹²⁷ This might be so, but in neither v. 18 nor v. 21 is the citation or allusion explicit. In the final non-explicit appeal to writing, Jesus states that Judas and his cohort come at night with weapons to arrest him, even though he had been teaching daily in the synagogues. This happened in order that "the writings may be fulfilled" (ἵνα πληρωθῶσιν αἱ γραφαί). Again, there is debate as to whether "the writings" refers to a specific text.¹²⁸ If so, none is provided by citation or quotation. The intertextuality is imprecise.

In Mark's three instances of general appeals to writing discussed above, Matthew, Luke, or both emend their predecessor. Jesus's question in Mk 9:12 is removed altogether in Mt. 17:11-12. Luke does not have the pericope at all. Mark 14:21 is only lightly redacted in Mt. 26:24, and the reference to writing is retained. But in Luke it is not. Rather than "the Son of Man goes as it is written about him" (ὁ μὲν υἱὸς τοῦ ἀνθρώπου ὑπάγει καθὼς γέγραπται περὶ αὐτοῦ), Luke reads "the Son of Man goes as it has been determined" (ὁ υἱὸς μὲν τοῦ ἀνθρώπου κατὰ τὸ ὡρισμένον πορεύεται). Finally, Luke omits the reference to the writings being fulfilled in Mk 14:49 altogether, and Matthew specifies that the writings being fulfilled are the prophets (αἱ γραφαὶ τῶν προφητῶν). Just

---

123. Marcus cites Gal. 4:22; Jn 7:38; 4Q266 11.3–5; 4Q270 7 1.17–18 as examples (*Mark*, 2:645).

124. Ibid.

125. Marcus argues all three are possibilities (ibid.). Collins likewise reviews the various intertexts that have been proposed (*Mark*, 430–31).

126. Horsley, "Oral and Written Aspects," 98.

127. Collins, *Mark*, 652; France, *Gospel of Mark*, 567.

128. According to Collins, "the writings" alludes to Jeremiah 13:7b, already cited in Mk 14:27. Specifically, v. 49 fulfills the claim that the "sheep will be scattered" (*Mark*, 687). Alfred Suhl and Reinhold Liebers each argue that no specific text is being recalled (Suhl, *Die Funktion der Alttestamentlichen Zitate und Anspielungen im Markusevangelium* [Gütersloh: Mohn, 1965], 41–44; Liebers, *"Wie Geschrieben Steht:" Studien zu einer Besonderen Art Frühchristlichen Schriftbezuges* [Berlin: de Gruyter, 1993], 384–89).

as they found Mark's imprecise citations and quotations problematic, so also do Matthew and Luke find Mark's general appeals to writing without a specific referent inadequate.

Echoic intertextuality Mark's imprecise intertextuality explored thus far has not resembled the intertextuality exhibited in *Joseph and Aseneth*. Unlike Mark, there are no explicit appeals to Scripture or writings in the pseudepigraphon. There are also no quotations of Scripture, whether imprecise or exact. In fact, the verb γράφω occurs on only two occasions in *Joseph and Aseneth*, and the nominal form γραφή never appears.[129] This does not imply that *Joseph and Aseneth* has no relationship to Jewish Scriptures. As I have argued above, the narrative allusively evokes cultural texts with key lexemes and themes on several occasions. Mark likewise allusively recalls texts and traditions. In fact, this mode of evocation is far more common than citation and quotation. As Hays puts it, "Mark's way of drawing upon Scripture, like his narrative style more generally, is indirect and allusive."[130] According to him, Mark has intentionally hidden intertextual layers of meaning within the narrative for the discerning reader.[131] In contrast, I see this phenomenon as a result of Mark's mode of composition. Like *Joseph and Aseneth*, Mark frequently evokes texts and traditions with key lexemes and themes because the gospel is orally composed and texts are recalled mnemonically. Nowhere is this more noticeable than the sea-stilling narrative in Mk 4:35-41, which recalls Jon. 1:1-15 LXX and Ps. 106:23-32 LXX.

Mark 4:35-41, Jon. 1:1-15, and Psalm 106 LXX

Mark 4:35-41 recalls Jonah by mirroring the content and order of Jon. 1:1-15.[132] There are also several specific lexemes that are shared between the two texts that make it unmistakable that Jonah is behind the Markan pericope.[133] Four parallels are noteworthy.

---

129. *Joseph and Aseneth* 15:3; 22:9.

130. Hays, *Echoes of Scripture in the Gospels*, 98. He shows how ubiquitous allusive recall is throughout the Gospel in ibid., 15–103.

131. Hays argues that Mk 4:21-25 is a hermeneutical signification for the reader to be attentive to these hidden, allusive meanings (ibid., 101).

132. Marcus also notes Jesus's similarities to Jonah and the shared vocabulary between the texts. He argues that Mark's readers will have registered the similarities to the Jonah account, but he concludes Jesus acts more like the Lord than he does Jonah (*Mark*, 1:337–38). Robert H. Stein does not see as strong a connection between the texts. He concludes that "the analogies in wording ... are interesting," but that Mark makes "no intentional effort to tie these stories together" (*Mark*, Baker Exegetical Commentary on the New Testament [Grand Rapids: Baker Academic, 2008], 245).

133. It is also likely, as Strauss argues, that several texts from the Psalms that extol the Lord's power over the sea, such as Ps. 18:15; 104:7; 106:9; 107:23-29, intertextually inform the Markan pericope (*Mark*, 208).

First, the rising of the storm puts both Jonah's and Jesus's boat in danger:

Jonah 1:4:	Mark 4:37:
καὶ κύριος ἐξήγειρεν πνεῦμα εἰς τὴν θάλασσαν, καὶ ἐγένετο κλύδων μέγας ἐν τῇ θαλάσσῃ, καὶ τὸ πλοῖον ἐκινδύνευεν συντριβῆναι.	καὶ γίνεται λαῖλαψ μεγάλη ἀνέμου καὶ τὰ κύματα ἐπέβαλλεν εἰς τὸ πλοῖον, ὥστε ἤδη γεμίζεσθαι τὸ πλοῖον.
And the Lord aroused a wind in the sea, and a great surge came upon the sea, and the ship was in danger of breaking up. (NETS)	And a great storm of wind arose, and the waves beat into the boat, so that the boat was already filling. (RSV)

The similarity in narrative order is striking. Both texts report the rising of the storm, mention the waves, and then tell of the danger that the boat is in. Nonetheless, the only distinctive shared lexeme between Jon. 1:4 and Mk 4:37 is πλοῖον ("boat"). The storms, the waves, and the danger are all described with different words and phrases.

Second, in both accounts the minor characters are characterized by their fear. Jonah 1:5 first reports the sailors' fear with the verb ἐφοβήθησαν ("they were afraid"), which is then repeated in 1:10 with the phrase καὶ ἐφοβήθησαν οἱ ἄνδρες φόβον μέγαν ("and the men feared a great fear"). The second report of the sailors' fear comes after Jonah tells the men he worships the Lord God (τὸν κύριον θεόν). Similarly, the disciples fear in Mk 4:41 after Jesus calms the storm and asks them why they are cowards and do not yet believe. The same phrase, ἐφοβήθησαν φόβον μέγαν is used in both narratives.[134] These are the most distinctive words that the two pericopes have in common.

Third, in both narratives, the main character is sleeping below deck as the storm rises:

Jonah 1:5	Mark 4:38
Ιωνας δὲ κατέβη εἰς τὴν κοίλην τοῦ πλοίου καὶ ἐκάθευδεν καὶ ἔρρεγχεν.	καὶ αὐτὸς ἦν ἐν τῇ πρύμνῃ ἐπὶ τὸ προσκεφάλαιον καθεύδων.
But Jonah went down into the hold of the ship and was sleeping and snoring. (NETS)	But he was in the stern, asleep on the cushion. (RSV)

Once more, the content is nearly identical, but there is only one distinctive shared lexeme between the two texts, the imperfect verb ἐκάθευδεν ("he was sleeping") in Jonah and the participial form, καθεύδων ("sleeping"), in Mark.

---

134. Interestingly, both Matthew and Luke redact the verbal phrase ἐφοβήθησαν φόβον μέγαν. Matthew 8:27 replaces ἐφοβήθησαν ("they were afraid") with ἐθαύμασαν ("they marveled"). Luke 8:25 alters the indicative form of φοβέω ("to fear") to the participle, φοβηθέντες ("fearing"), which appears alongside the indicative form ἐθαύμασαν ("they marveled"). A nearly identical phrase, ἐφοβήθη φόβον μέγαν ("feared a great fear"), occurs in *Jos. Asen.* 6:1. Only the number of the verb has been changed. That Mark and *Joseph and Aseneth* have the phrase and Matthew and Luke redact it from the former may indicate that it is colloquial.

Fourth, and finally, the manner in which the sea is stilled is similar in both accounts. The captain of the ship approaches Jonah in 1:6, commanding him to rise up (ἀνάστα) and call upon his God so that all aboard are not destroyed (μὴ ἀπολώμεθα). Jonah then tells the sailors in Jon. 1:11-12 to pick him up and throw him into the sea, informing them that this will cause the storm to abate (κοπάσει ἡ θάλασσα ἀφ᾽ ὑμῶν). As soon as they do, the sea ceases from its surge (καὶ ἔστη ἡ θάλασσα ἐκ τοῦ σάλου αὐτῆς). In Mk 4:38, the disciples wake Jesus (ἐγείρουσιν αὐτόν) and ask him if he is concerned that they are being destroyed (οὐ μέλει σοι ὅτι ἀπολλύμεθα;). Jesus then rises up (διεγερθείς), rebukes the wind and sea, and as a result, "the storm ceased and there was a great calm" (καὶ ἐκόπασεν ὁ ἄνεμος καὶ ἐγένετο γαλήνη μεγάλη). Once more, the narrative order is similar and some of the central lexemes are related, but the intertextuality is inexact. Mark does not directly quote Jonah, though there can be no doubt that the narrative is behind the pericope.

Yet it is not just the Jonah narrative that resonates with Mk 4:35-41. There are several Psalms and other texts that tell of the Lord's power over the wind and sea that are evoked. Hays calls attention to Job 38:1-11, Ps. 89:9, 106:8-12, and Isa. 51:9-11.[135] More consequential than any of these is Ps. 107:23-32 (106:23-32 LXX):[136]

> Those who used to go down to the sea in ships,
> doing business on many waters—
> it was they who saw the deeds of the Lord
> and his wondrous works in the deep.
> He spoke (εἶπεν) and the tempest's blast stood (ἔστη),
> and its waves (τὰ κύματα) were raised on high.
> They mount up as far as the heavens,
> and they go down as far as the depths;
> their soul would melt away in calamity;
> they were troubled (ἐταράχθησαν); they staggered like the drunkard,
> and all their wisdom was gulped down.
> And they cried to the Lord when they were being afflicted,
> and out of their anguish he brought them,
> and he ordered the tempest (ἐπέταξεν τῇ καταιγίδι), and it subsided to a breeze,
> and its waves became silent (ἐσίγησαν).
> And they were glad, because they had quiet,
> and he guided them to a haven of their want.
> Let them acknowledge the Lord for his mercies
> and for his wonderful works to the sons of men.
> Let them exalt him in an assembly of people
> and in a session of elders praise him. (NETS)

---

135. Hays, *Echoes of Scripture in the Gospel*, 66–69.
136. Ibid., 67.

The content of the psalm resembles the Markan pericope.¹³⁷ In both, people in ships are troubled because of a great storm and they beseech an agent who speaks to the storm on their behalf, causing it to cease. As was the case with Jon. 1:1-15, the Markan narrative echoes Psalm 106:23-32 LXX thematically. There are a few key terms shared between the texts (τὰ κύματα, τὸ πλοῖον, ἡ θάλασσα), but many also differ. In fact, more terms are shared between Jonah and the Psalm than Mark and the Psalm. This is not to imply that Mark is not related to Psalm 106 LXX. Rather, it is likely that Jonah and the Psalm are intertextually related and Mark recalls both of them by mnemonically evoking central themes and words they have in common.¹³⁸

Mark 5:1-20 and the Book of the Watchers (1 En. 1–36)

Most investigations of Mark's intertextuality are concerned with the gospel's evocations of Jewish Scripture. Its intertextual relationship to other Jewish texts has not garnered as much attention. But there is at least one pericope in the gospel that recalls a noncanonical tradition. Mark 5:1-20, the pericope of the Gerasene Demoniac, evokes the Watchers tradition, a popular Second Temple myth textually attested to in *1 En.* 1–36, known as the Book of the Watchers.¹³⁹ Mark does not

---

137. Hays claims that they are so similar that "Mark 4:35-41 looks very much like a midrashic narrative based on the psalm" (*Echoes of Scripture in the Gospels*, 67).

138. It is probable that Greco-Roman sea-storm and storm-stilling accounts function as cultural intertexts in Mk 4:35-41 as well. Diogenes Laertius reports that Empedocles was called "wind-stayer" (κωλυσανέμας) because of his ability to catch winds that were damaging crops (*Lives* 8.2 Empedocles [60]). In *Lives* 1.5 Bias (86), he writes that Bias encountered a storm on a voyage with impious men who called to the gods for help. Bias rebuked the men, saying "Peace!" (σιγᾶτε), for fear that the gods would hear their voices. In this case the storm is not explicitly stilled, but the narrative content resembles Mk 4:35-41. Sea-storm accounts in the *Odyssey* (5.291–390; 10.28–55) and *Aeneid* (1.81–142) may also inform Mk 4:35-41. This further characterizes Mark's intertextuality as echoic in this pericope, as no specific Greco-Roman accounts appear to be alluded to.

139. The popularity of the Watchers tradition is indicated by retellings of the myth and allusions to it in early Jewish and Christian texts, including the dream visions of *1 Enoch* (*1 En.* 85–90); *2 Enoch*; *3 Enoch*; *Jubilees*; Philo, *De gigantibus*; Josephus, *A.J.* 1.3.1 §72–74; Bar. 3:26; Sir. 16:7; 2 Macc. 2:4-8; 1 Pet. 3:19-20; 2 Pet. 2:4; Jude 14–15, T. Reu. 5:6-7; Justin, *2 Apol.* 5; Athenagoras, *Leg.* 24–26; Iranaeus, *Haer.* 1.10; 1.15.6; the Pseudo-Clementine *Homilies* (8.12-18) and *Recognitions* (4.26); the *Kephalaia of the Teacher* (92.27-28; 93.24-28; 117:2; 171.1); Ap. John 19.16-20.11. Allusions to and echoes of the Watchers myth in early Jewish and Christian texts are noted by James C. VanderKam, "1 Enoch, Enochic Motifs, and Enoch in Early Christian Literature," in *The Jewish Apocalyptic Heritage in Early Christianity*, ed. idem and William Adler, CRINT III.4 (Assen: Van Gorcum, 1996), 33–101; Rick Strelan, "The Fallen Watchers and the Disciples in Mark," *JSP* 10 (1999): 73–92. I first argued that Mk 5:1-20 shares strong conceptual and verbal affinities with the Book of the

directly quote this text but alludes to it with themes and lexemes characteristic of that tradition.

First, the demoniac is not called a δαιμόνιον ("demon") when he is introduced in Mk 5:2. Instead, he is called an ἄνθρωπος ἐν πνεύματι ἀκαθάρτῳ ("man with an unclean spirit").[140] Mark knows the term δαιμόνιον, as there are participial forms of the verb δαιμονίζομαι ("to be demon possessed") in the second half of this pericope and the nominal form appears elsewhere in the gospel.[141] The best explanation for the demoniac's initial characterization as a "man with an unclean spirit" is a mnemonic reference to the Book of the Watchers. There, uncleanness is a characteristic trait of both the watchers and their progeny. The verb μιαίνω ("to make unclean") is repeated throughout *1 En.* 6–16.[142] It always appears in connection with the watchers' illicit sexual union with human women. Most relevant to Mk 5:1-20 is the verb's occurrence in *1 En.* 10:11, where it is used with the dative prepositional phrase ἐν ἀκαθαρσίᾳ ("in uncleanness").[143] In the Book of the Watchers, the fallen angels are indelibly marked by their uncleanness, as are their offspring, the giants. Because these giants are mixed creatures—half human, half angelic—they are considered unclean.[144] The actions of the giants are characterized by impurity (ἀκαθαρσία) in *1 En.* 10:11-22. In a telling passage, the Lord commands his angels to purify the earth from the giants' uncleanliness. Multiple verbal forms of καθαρίζω ("to cleanse") appear in *1 En.* 10:20-22. Like the watchers in *1 Enoch*, the spirits that inhabit the man in Mk 5:1-20 are characterized as unclean and must be destroyed to restore cleanliness.

Watchers in "Of Porcine and Polluted Spirits: Reading the Gerasene Demoniac (Mark 5:1-20) with the Book of Watchers (*1 Enoch* 1–36)," *CBQ* 78 (2016): 430–46. There, I avoided making any claim about how the gospel intertextually evokes the watchers tradition (ibid., 433 n. 9). It now seems to me that the broad interplay between Mk 5:1-20 and *1 En.* 1–36 is best understood as a mnemonic mode of recalling the cultural tradition about the watchers.

140. Mark 5:8, 13.

141. Nominal forms of δαιμόνιον occur in Mk 1:34, 39; 3:15, 22; 6:13; 7:26, 29; 9:38; [16:9, 17].

142. *1 Enoch* 7:1; 9:8; 10:8, 11; 12:4; 15:3, 4.

143. In *1 En.* 10:11, the Lord commands Michael, "Go and declare to Shemihaza and the rest of those with him who mixed with women to be defiled in their uncleanness." All translations of the Greek text of *1 Enoch* are my own from Matthew Black and Albert-Marie Denis, eds., *Apocalypsis Henochi Graece*, PVTG 3 (Leiden: Brill, 1970).

144. Clinton Wahlen writes that the giants are unclean in a manner analogous to creatures in the HB that are considered impure because they do not physically fit into established categories (*Jesus and the Impurity of Spirits in the Synoptic Gospels*, WUNT 2/185 [Tübingen: Mohr Siebeck, 2004], 32 n. 44). See also Archie T. Wright, "Evil Spirits in Second Temple Judaism: The Watcher Tradition as a Background to the Demonic Pericopes in the Gospels," *Henoch* 28 (2006): 145.

Second, Mk 5:1-20 alludes to the watchers tradition by giving details about the demoniac's dwelling and previous attempts to restrain him.[145] Mark 5:3-4 reports that the demoniac "had a dwelling in the tombs" (τὴν κατοίκησιν εἶχεν ἐν τοῖς μνήμασιν) and that "no one was able to restrain him with a chain any longer" (οὐδὲ ἁλύσει οὐκέτι οὐδεὶς ἐδύνατο αὐτὸν δῆσαι). "Dwelling" (κατοίκησις) is a NT *hapax legomenon*. Its presence here is best understood with reference to the four occasions of it in *1 En.* 15:7-10.[146] In that text, the Lord tells Enoch that the watchers' dwelling (ἡ κατοίκησις) will be in the earth (ἐν τῇ γῇ). Just like the watchers, the demoniac has a dwelling inside the earth. Furthermore, that the demoniac has a habit of cutting himself with rocks (κατακόπτων ἑαυτὸν λίθοις) in his lodging place is likely analogous to the detail given in *1 En.* 10:5 that Raphael places "rough and sharp rocks" (λίθους τραχεῖς καὶ ὀξεῖς) atop Asael's dwelling.[147]

The detail about the inability to bind the demoniac recalls the binding of the watchers in *1 En.* 10, wherein the Lord commands Michael to bind (δῆσον) Asael, Shemihaza, and the other watchers. This is to be their lot until they face final, eternal judgment. After *1 En.* 10, the watchers are always encountered in their bound form. Mark evokes this theme not only with the verb δέω ("to bind"), which appears twice in the Markan pericope and is found multiple times in the Book of the Watchers, always with reference to the fallen angels (*1 En.* 9:4; 10:4, 12, 14; 13:1; 14:5; 18:16; 21:3, 6; 22:11), but also by the lexemes ἅλυσις ("chain"), πέδη ("shackle"), διασπᾶν ("to tear"), and δαμάζειν ("to tame").

Third, the demoniac's request that Jesus not torment him recalls the oath the watchers take in *1 En.* 6. He states, "I implore (ὁρκίζω) you, don't torment me!" The verb evokes not only the place, Mount Hermon, where the watchers join in oath together, but also the dative nominal form ὅρκῳ ("with an oath") found in *1 En.* 6:4 and the threefold repetition of forms of the verb ὀμνύω ("to swear") in *1 En.* 6:4-6.

These similarities between Mark and the Book of the Watchers indicate that the gospel evokes this pseudepigraphical narrative in the pericope of the Gerasene demoniac. Like the recall of Jon. 1:1-15, the Book of the Watchers is never quoted. Rather, there are striking thematic and lexical similarities between the two texts. The evangelist evokes the watchers tradition this way presumably because he recalls it mnemonically as a cultural text. Given the popularity of the myth in

---

145. I more fully address the demoniac's dwelling and the theme of binding in "Porcine and Polluted," 439–45.

146. Others have offered terms in the near sematic range of κατοίκησις to interpret its presence here (Juan Mateos and Fernando Camacho, *El Evangelio de Marcos: Análisis lingüístico y comentario exegético*, 2 vols., En los origenes del Cristianismo 11 [Córdoba: Ediciones El Almendro, 2000], 1:434; Rudolf Pesch, *Das Markusevangelium*, 4th ed., Herders theologischer Kommentar zum Neuen Testament, 2 vols. [Freiburg: Herder, 1984], 1:286).

147. Many exegetes consider the demoniac's self-harm a characteristic of his madness (Collins, *Mark*, 267; Donahue and Harrington, *Gospel of Mark*, 164; Robert A. Guelich, *Mark 1–8:26*, WBC 34A [Waco: Word Books, 1989], 278).

the Second Temple period, he might even be recalling an oral tradition about the watchers and no particular textual version.

The geographical mistake in the setting of Mark 5:1-20

While the watchers tradition has often been overlooked as the formative demonological framework for Mk 5:1-20, the geographical "mistake" in Mk 5:1 has not been missed. The pericope's setting "in the region of the Gerasenes" (εἰς τὴν χώραν τῶν Γερασηνῶν) has brought many Markan interpreters face to face with a question presumably far afield from their area of expertise: the maximum distance a porcine herd can run at one stretch. Gerasa, modern Jerash, is situated thirty-seven miles from the Sea of Galilee, into which the 2,000 pigs plunge in Mk 5:13.[148] Interpreters frequently note this would be an impossible run for the herd.[149] Other details in the story further signify that the action takes place near the sea. In Mk 5:2, the demoniac meets Jesus after he exits the boat (καὶ ἐξελθόντος αὐτοῦ ἐκ τοῦ πλοίου εὐθὺς ὑπήντησεν αὐτῷ). Mark 5:14 then narrates that the pig herders announce what had happened "in the city" (εἰς τὴν πόλιν). By setting the pericope in Gerasa, Mark has created an implausible series of events when it comes to geographical concerns. Both the pigs and the herders will have had to travel a marathon and a half's distance, presumably within the span of a single day.

The difficulty of distance was recognized as early as Matthew's gospel, in which "the region of the Gerasenes" (τὴν χώραν τῶν Γερασηνῶν) is changed to "the region of the Gadarenes" (τὴν χώραν τῶν Γαδαρηνῶν).[150] This is an attempt to make the events more plausible, as Gadara is only five miles from the Sea of Galilee.[151] Several Markan MSS similarly change the location, either to the region of the Gadarenes (Γαδαρηνῶν) or the Gergasenes (Γεργεσηνῶν).[152] The latter is the most geographically and topographically plausible, as Gergasa is flanked by the sea on the West and has a steep embankment leading into it.[153] However, the region

---

148. John McRay, "Gerasenes," *ABD* 2:991.

149. The problem of distance between Gerasa and the Sea of Galilee is recognized as early as Origen (*Comm. Jo.* 6.24), and modern commentators frequently note it (Guelich, *Mark*, 1:275; McRay, "Gerasenes," 2:991; Marcus, *Mark*, 1:342; Donahue and Harrington, *Gospel of Mark*, 163; Edwards, *Gospel According to Mark*, 153; Collins, *Mark*, 267; Stein, *Mark*, 251).

150. Matthew 8:28. Luke retains Mark's reading, though there are significant textual variants, as there are in Mark and Matthew.

151. McRay, "Gerasenes," 2:991.

152. The region of the Gadarenes (Γαδαρηνῶν) is supported by A, C, f^{13}, 𝔐, sy^p, sy^h; the region of the Gergasenes (Γεργεσηνῶν) by ℵ, L, Δ, Θ, f^1, 28., 33., 565., 579., 700., 892., 1241., 1424., 2542, sy, bo, and others; and the region of the Gerasenes (Γερασηνῶν) by ℵ, B, D, 2427, latt, sa.

153. Guelich, *Mark*, 1:275; McRay, "Gerasenes," 2:991.

of the Gerasenes (Γερασηνῶν), as the *lectio difficilior* and with the best textual support, remains the preferred reading of Mk 5:1.

Changing the pericope's location is but one way that interpreters have dealt with the porcine problem. Others have taken the plasticity of the word "region" (χώρα) to mean "the general territory of the Decapolis on the eastern side of the lake."[154] In this view, Mark is not necessarily ignorant of the geography. He simply does not have the specific city of Gerasa in mind. Still others let the tension remain. They suggest that either Mark is unfamiliar with the geography of the region or that the location "is best held in abeyance due to the textual confusion."[155]

Dean W. Chapman presents the most theoretically informed argument about Mark's geographical "mistake."[156] According to him, it is no mistake at all. It is only considered such when viewed from a Euclidean, projective perspective of spatial geography, which is characterized by knowledge of the quantifiable distances between spaces and objects, such as cities and geographical landmarks.[157] Put simply, it is only an error if you've seen a modern map of the region. But Mark does not conceptualize space from this perspective. He works with a cosmographic map.[158] The evangelist is most familiar with the spaces that he regularly traffics in, which Chapman concludes is Jerusalem and its surrounding areas.[159] Gerasa is the borderland of his Galilean homeland and is "only nebulously positioned in Mark's mind."[160] Because it was the hinterland of Mark's geographical knowledge, "everything in the Decapolis was in the vicinity of the Sea of Galilee."[161] From a cosmographic conception of geography, places and spaces lack precision in scale.[162] Chapman is comfortable with the geographical imprecision, and he refuses to belittle the evangelist's mental capacities on its account. Mark's geographical outlook provokes his imprecision.

The gospel's compositional mode also helps sustain this geographical imprecision. It is prudent to acknowledge the mistaken geography in Mk 5:1. But it is also likely the case that the evangelist has little concern for being geographically precise. Oral narrative works with "heavy" characters and settings.[163] This is why in Mk 2:26, as argued above, Abiathar is mistakenly recalled as the High Priest when David ate the bread of the presence in 1 Sam. 21:2-10.

---

154. Strauss, *Mark*, 215. Similarly, Edwards, *Mark*, 153; France, *Gospel of Mark*, 227.

155. Stein, *Mark*, 250. Similarly, Pesch, *Markusevangelium*, 1:282; Donahue and Harrington, *Gospel of Mark*, 163; Marcus, *Mark*, 1:342.

156. Dean W. Chapman, "Locating the Gospel of Mark: A Model of Agrarian Biography," *BTB* 25 (1995): 24–36.

157. Ibid., 28.

158. Ibid., 31–33.

159. Ibid., 34.

160. Ibid., 35.

161. Ibid., 33.

162. Ibid., 30.

163. Ong, *Orality and Literacy*, 69.

Gerasa was a more memorable location than Gergasa or Gadara for two reasons. First, the Hebrew root גרשׁ means "to drive or cast out."[164] The city's name was thus appropriate for the events narrated there. Second, Vespasian's military actions in Gerasa in the years preceding 70 CE will have made the city culturally significant for Mark's audience. In J.W. 4.487–489, Josephus recounts that Vespasian sent Lucius Annius to Gerasa with a party of horsemen and many infantrymen. Lucius and his "legions" killed one thousand young men, took their families captive, plundered the city, and left it in flames. If Mk 5:1-20 carries the political and military critique that several interpreters find, then Gerasa was a convenient setting that will have resonated with the audience's recent cultural imagination of it.[165] Gerasa was politically freighted and thus appropriate for a politically charged story.

Mark may have known that the run from Gerasa to the Sea of Galilee was improbable for a herd of swine. Or he may have been unfamiliar with the geography of the Decapolis. In either case, it appears that the narrative is set in Gerasa for onomatological and cultural reasons. The city fit the narrative bill and was memorable because of its lexical and political connotations. Of course, a similar move could have been made in the written mode of composition. But it is more likely to occur in the oral-aural mode. Not only does oral narrative work with heavy characters and settings, but speakers and hearers are also not concerned with precision to the extent that writers and readers are. We have already seen Mark's imprecision illustrated on the lexical and intertextual levels. Here it manifests on the geographical.

In sum, Mark's mnemonic recall of traditions, as exhibited in Mk 4:35-41 and Mk 5:1-20, the gospel's appeal to writings without a specific citation or quotation, its lexical imprecision when writings are quoted, and its geographical imprecision regarding the setting of Mk 5:1, are all evidence of the oral-memorial mode of composition. The imprecision exhibited in Mark does not characterize the other Synoptic Gospels as it does their counterpart. Matthew and Luke frequently correct Mark's imprecision.

---

164. BDB, s.v. "גָּרַשׁ"; J. Duncan M. Derrett, "Spirit-Possession and the Gerasene Demoniac," Man 14 (1979): 286–93; Marcus, Mark, 1:287; Stephen D. Moore, "'My Name Is Legion, for We Are Many': Representing Empire in Mark," in Empire and Apocalypse: Postcolonialism and the New Testament, ed. idem, Bible in the Modern World 12 (Sheffield: Sheffield Phoenix, 2006), 28. See, for example, Gen 3:14; Exod. 2:17; 33:2; Num. 22:6; Josh. 24:18.

165. The pericope is interpreted as a critique of the Roman Empire or Roman military forces by Walter Wink, Unmasking the Powers: The Invisible Forces That Determine Human Existence (Philadelphia: Fortress, 1986), 43–48; Myers, Binding the Strong Man, 190–94; Richard A. Horsley, Hearing the Whole Story: The Politics of Plot in Mark's Gospel (Louisville: Westminster John Knox, 2001), 140–48; Moore, "My Name is Legion," 24–44; Hans Leander, Discourses of Empire: The Gospel of Mark from a Postcolonial Perspective (Atlanta: Society of Biblical Literature, 2013), 201–19; Warren Carter, "Cross-Gendered Romans and Mark's Jesus: Legion Enters the Pigs (Mark 5:1–20)," JBL 134 (2015): 139–55.

Conclusion

In this chapter I have argued that Mark and *Joseph and Aseneth* are similar in two metalinguistic aspects: their pluriformity and their mode of evoking intertexts. With respect to the former, tradents emended or added to the textual versions of the narratives. This is most likely because both were considered traditions characterized by equiprimordiality and *mouvance*. These are exhibited more clearly in the textual instantiations of *Joseph and Aseneth* than they are of Mark. Nonetheless, the microlevel fluidity of Mark and its multiple endings reveal that the tradition possesses some level of *mouvance*.

As to intertextuality, both narratives echoically recall cultural texts. *Joseph and Aseneth* never directly quotes a text from the LXX or the Greco-Roman novels but is related to these corpora intertextually. Mark more self-consciously evokes written texts, but in an echoic and sometimes imprecise manner. The way Mk 4:35-41 recalls Jonah and texts from the Psalms, as well as how Mk 5:1-20 recalls the watchers tradition, resembles *Joseph and Aseneth* 27–29's evocation of 1 Samuel 17. These similarities are rooted in a mnemonic mode of recall characteristic of oral literature.

In the next chapter we will look to how the linguistic characteristics that Mark and *Joseph and Aseneth* share were altered by subsequent editors and authors. I shall argue that their similarities, which result from a comparable mode of composition, were objectionable to later editors. Both narratives' residual orality is similarly altered to syntax characteristic of literary psychodynamics.

Chapter 5

LINGUISTIC TRAJECTORIES OF *JOSEPH AND ASENETH* AND MARK

Introduction

There has been a tendency among some orality and media critics to interpret every NT writing with the same oral hermeneutic, paying little regard to a given text's written form and literary features. In this line of thinking, orality swallows up textuality altogether. This is the case when Dunn suggests that Matthew and Luke are retelling Mark in an oral rather than a written mode.[1] The perspective also pervades a strain of performance criticism that considers all NT texts as something orally conceived and aurally received.[2] When Wire introduces her

---

1. Dunn, "Altering," 44.
2. For example, David Rhoads claims, "Simply put, the writings we have in the New Testament are examples of 'performance literature,' that is, literature that was meant for performance—like music or theater or ancient poetry" ("Performance Events in Early Christianity: New Testament Writings in an Oral Context," in Weissenrieder and Coote, *Interface*, 169). According to Rhoads, all the NT writings are of the same performative ilk. Similarly, Paul J. Achtemeier writes, "What has not been considered [in NT scholarship], I would urge, is the fact that both the writing and reading of this material [the NT writings] involved the oral performance of the words, and that therefore clues to the structure which the author provided were intended for the ear, not the eye" ("Omne Verbum Sonat: The New Testament and the Oral Environment of Late Western Antiquity," *JBL* 109 [1990]: 25). In his programmatic article on performance criticism, Larry W. Hurtado critiques this "zero-sum game" in which orality is featured at the expense of textuality ("Oral Fixation and New Testament Studies? 'Orality,' 'Performance' and Reading Texts in Early Christianity," *NTS* 60 [2014]: 232–24). I agree with Hurtado that *some* performance critics have played this zero-sum game. Yet it seems that as this discipline continues to develop, more performance critics are recognizing what Kelly R. Iverson calls in a response to Hurtado's critique "the symbiotic relationship between orality and literacy" ("Oral Fixation or Oral Corrective? A Response to Larry Hurtado," *NTS* 62 [2016]: 186). Iverson cites the following as evidence for the development in performance criticism: James A. Maxey, *From Orality to Orality: A New Paradigm for Contextual Translation of the Bible*, Biblical Performance Criticism Series

case that Mark is composed in performance, she asks, "But how were the gospels composed?" and answers, "They were composed, not by individual authors with pens in hand, but orally in performance; that is, they were shaped in the telling."[3] But Wire does not address the gospels; she addresses *a* gospel, Mark. Presumably because she concludes that Mark was composed in performance, Matthew, Luke, and John must have been as well. This overemphasis on orality in the NT and the gospels is another instantiation of the Great Divide approach. What is needed, and what I will argue for in this chapter, is a perspective that appreciates that the gospels are products of a mixed-media culture and that they interface with orality and textuality in various ways.

This claim can be substantiated by comparing Mark's linguistic features to Matthew's and Luke's. Matthew and Luke consistently alter many Markan traits that are characteristic of oral storytelling. They make changes in order to construct more literary texts. These are similar to alterations made by a later text group of *Joseph and Aseneth*. The *a*-manuscript family of *Joseph and Aseneth* reaches a higher literary standard than both the *d*-text family and Burchard's longer reconstruction based on L2, Syr, Arm, and *f*.

A comparison of *a*'s redaction of earlier witnesses of *Joseph and Aseneth* with Matthew's and Luke's redaction of Mark reveals that the process of literaturizing an orally composed Greek narrative involved making predictable linguistic changes. There were ways to mold an orally conceived text into a more literary form. The linguistic characteristics of Mark and *Joseph and Aseneth* that I have argued result from oral composition are the very features that Matthew, Luke, and the *a*-text family find disagreeable. I shall show that by altering their predecessor's paratactic structures and verbal features these tradents are scrubbing away residual orality. Just as Mark and *Joseph and Aseneth* were composed similarly, so also were they edited similarly.

This has consequences for both *Joseph and Aseneth* and the Synoptic Gospels. With respect to the former, it substantiates the claim that *a* literarily improves upon *d*. It also casts doubt on Burchard's and Fink's contention that the *d*-family that Philonenko based his critical edition on is a later abridgement of the *a*-text family.[4] The *a*-family's "precision of verbalization," a mark of the editability of

---

2 (Eugene: Cascade, 2009); Robert D. II Miller, *Oral Tradition in Ancient Israel*, Biblical Performance Criticism Series 4 (Eugene: Cascade, 2011); Pieter J. J. Botha, *Orality and Literacy in Early Christianity*, Biblical Performance Criticism Series 5 (Eugene: Cascade, 2012); J. A. Loubser, *Oral and Manuscript Culture in the Bible: Studies on the Media Texture of the New Testament—Explorative Hermeneutics*, Biblical Performance Criticism Series 7 (Eugene: Cascade, 2013). In any nascent field, nuance develops over time as scholars begin to paint with fine rather than broad strokes. Performance and orality criticism of the NT is no exception.

3. Wire, *Case*, 2.

4. Burchard, *Joseph und Aseneth*, 24–26; Fink, *Joseph und Aseneth*, 72–98, and the stemma on p. 17.

writing, was possible only after the oral tradition was transferred into its written medium.⁵ Concerning the Synoptics, it reveals that the gospels are not equal as to their media form. Matthew and Luke attempt to articulate the gospel tradition for a new, more literary medium of reception.⁶ While Matthew and Luke represent an interfacial relationship between orality and textuality, they appear to be linguistically affected by literary psychodynamics to a greater extent than Mark is. The Synoptic Gospels exemplify a mixed-media environment and this can be demonstrated linguistically. If Mark exists at the borderland between orality and textuality, Matthew's and Luke's narratives self-consciously move in a literary direction.

Redacting parataxis and simplicity of clauses

Redacting parataxis and simplicity of clauses in Joseph and Aseneth

Joseph and Aseneth, in Philonenko's reconstruction, exhibits paratactic structuring and simplicity of syntax. The volume of καί in this textual version, the frequency with which the connective strings five or more clauses together, the general nonuse of other conjunctions, and the recurrence of this conjunction and apposition are all oral residues. The situation is much the same in Burchard's reconstruction and Fink's improvements to his critical edition.⁷ The *a*-text family, however, differs from these witnesses.

The volume of καί in Burchard's preferred MSS and in the *d*-text group is reduced in the *a*-text group. Whereas in Philonenko's and Burchard's reconstructions καί occurs once for every 7.96 and 8.12 words, respectively, in Batiffol's reconstruction based on the *a* group the connective appears only once for every 11.56 words.⁸ Thus καί occurs about 30% more often in the less literary versions than in the more literary.⁹ The connective also appears less frequently in sentence-initial and paragraph-initial positions in Batiffol's reconstruction. With respect to the former,

---

5. Ong, *Orality and Literacy*, 103.

6. Here I echo Alan Kirk's media-sensitive definition of redaction: "the means by which written tradition is articulated for new or altered contexts of reception" ("Orality, Writing, and Phantom Sources: Appeals to Ancient Media in Some Recent Challenges to the Two Document Hypothesis," *NTS* 58 [2012]: 22).

7. I more thoroughly address parataxis as evidence of oral conception in Burchard's reconstruction in "On Transcription," 122–25.

8. 1,010 times of 13,400 total words. This is 8.63% of the total words in *a*, 12.6% of the total words in *d*, and 12.3% of the total words in Burchard's reconstruction.

9. This is nearly identical to Matthew's redaction of Mark. καί occurs 33% more often in Mark than in Matthew.

102 of 293 (34.8%) sentences begin with καί.[10] As for the latter, 15 of the 29 (51.7%) paragraphs begin with καί.[11] The *a*-text family links clauses together with the simple connective less frequently than the two other groups do. As a result, there are significantly more connectives that are not καί in Batiffol's reconstruction than Philonenko's. In orally conceived discourse, it is common for a storyteller to string along well over five clauses with a simple connective. In contrast, writers producing literary narratives do not usually join more than five clauses together with *and*.[12] It is instructive to compare directly the *d*-family witness with the *a*-family as to their different paratactic tendencies. Two examples reveal that *a* does not string clauses along in the same fashion that *d* does.

In *Joseph and Aseneth* 27, Pharaoh's venal toadies, the sons of Bilhah and Zilpah, go rogue, abandon Pharaoh's son's insidious machination, and resolve to murder Aseneth. As they approach her with their bloodied swords, she prays to the Lord for protection and the blades immediately crumble to dust. *Joseph and Aseneth* 28:1-2 narrates the pawns' response. In Philonenko's reconstruction, five clauses are coordinated consecutively with καί. Batiffol's *a*-text witness, in contrast, coordinates only two of the clauses with καί, and these two clauses are not successive. It is revealing to view the two side by side:

Joseph and Aseneth 28:1 (Philonenko):	*Joseph and Aseneth* 28:11-14 (Batiffol):
καὶ εἶδον οἱ υἱοὶ Βάλλας καὶ Ζέλφας τὸ θαῦμα τὸ γεγονὸς καὶ ἐφοβήθησαν καὶ εἶπον· κύριος πολεμεῖ καθ' ἡμῶν ὑπὲρ Ἀσενέθ. καὶ ἔπεσον ἐπὶ πρόσωπον ἐπὶ τὴν γῆν καὶ προσεκύνησαν τῇ Ἀσενὲθ λέγοντες ...	ἰδόντες δὲ οἱ υἱοὶ Βάλλας καὶ Ζέλφας τὸ γεγονὸς παράδοξον θαῦμα ἐφοβήθησαν καὶ εἶπον· κύριος πολεμεῖ καθ' ἡμῶν ὑπὲρ Ἀσενέθ. τότε πεσόντες ἐπὶ πρόσωπον ἐπὶ τὴν γῆν, προσεκύνησαν τῇ Ἀσενέθ, καὶ εἶπον ...
And the sons of Bilhah and Zilpah saw the miracle that had happened and they were afraid and said, "The Lord fights against us for Aseneth." And they fell on their faces on the ground and they bowed to Aseneth, saying ...	But having seen the strange wonder that had happened, the sons of Bilhah and Zilpah were afraid and said, "The Lord fights against us for Aseneth." Then, having fallen on their faces on the ground, they bowed to Aseneth, and said ...

The *a*-family recension removes καί before the indicative verbs ἐφοβήθησαν ("they were afraid") and προσεκύνησαν ("they bowed"). The redactor also substitutes the first καί ("and") in the passage with a postpositive δέ ("but") and has altered the indicative verb εἶδον ("they saw") to the participial form ἰδόντες ("saving seen"). He or she similarly changes the verbal mood of the verb ἔπεσον ("they fell") at the beginning of *Jos. Asen.* 28:2, correlating the next sentence to its predecessor with the adverb τότε ("then") instead of καί ("and"). These types of changes are common throughout the *a*-text family. Particularly significant

---

10. Compare with Philonenko's reconstruction, where καί begins 254 of 312 (81.4%) sentences.

11. Batiffol divides the narrative into lengthy paragraphs, as each chapter contains one paragraph.

12. Beaman, "Coordination and Subordination," 58.

in this case is the redactor's tendency to remove coordination and modify it to subordination.

Time adverbials are the most common type of subordinate clause in both spoken and written narrative but are 33% more frequent in written narratives.[13] They "clarify the sequence of events to the reader, whereas extra-linguistic factors are available to the speaker to provide this information" and provide written discourse with a higher level of cohesion.[14] The *a*-text family of *Joseph and Aseneth* displays this cohesive quality of written narrative. It employs several different time adverbials and conjunctions to establish cohesion between clauses.[15] None of the adverbs and conjunctions in this textual witness is more indicative of its literary conception than τότε ("then").

Beaman has found that the adverb "then" without a preceding coordinator is far more common in written narrative than in spoken.[16] "And then," in contrast, is more common in oral narrative.[17] The *a*-text family's frequent use of τότε ("then") is revealing in this respect. In Batiffol's version, τότε occurs forty-two times, never with καί directly preceding it.[18] In Philonenko's reconstruction there are only two instances of τότε.[19] Against both, Burchard's reconstruction omits the adverb altogether and simply has καί. The frequency of τότε in the *a*-family against its minimal use and nonuse in the *d* and *b* recensions, respectively, are emendations meant to make the text of a higher literary quality. The addition of various conjunctions and adverbs in the *a*-text family is best understood as editorial activity meant to make the narrative read more literarily.

Redacting parataxis and simplicity of clauses in Mark

Mark's paratactic structure is found in the overall frequency of καί and the number of times it appears in clause-, sentence-, and paragraph-initial positions. The preponderance of the connective in Mark is one demonstration of how the idea unit characterizes the narrative, indicating that it was composed orally. Matthew

---

13. Ibid., 76.

14. Ibid. Tannen also addresses establishing cohesion in written discourse, and experimentally compares it to spoken narrative. She found that sentences in the written versions of a narrative were more integrated and complex than their spoken counterparts ("Oral and Literate Strategies," 9–10).

15. δέ occurs 148 times in Batiffol's reconstruction compared to ten in Philonenko's reconstruction. λοιπόν appears ten times in Batiffol, compared to four in Philonenko. There are twenty-seven occurrences of οὖν in Batiffol and just one in Philonenko.

16. Beaman, "Coordination and Subordination," 76–77.

17. Ibid.; Chafe, "Linking Intonation Units," 16.

18. Moreover, εἶτα ("then"), which never appears in Philonenko's reconstruction, occurs twelve times in Batiffol's text.

19. *Joseph and Aseneth* 10:1; 27:6.

and Luke restrain Mark's parataxis in their redaction and their own unique materials are not marked by it to the extent that their predecessor is.[20]

The connective καί begins 64.5% of the sentences and 92% of the episodes in Mark.[21] It appears 1,100 times in the gospel and coordinates independent clauses on 591 occasions.[22] Matthew and Luke each drastically curb these numbers. Matthew employs καί 94 more times than Mark, but also contains 7,225 additional words. Thus καί occurs about 45% less frequently in Matthew compared to Mark.[23] The reduction is similar in Luke, where καί appears 33% less frequently.[24] These reductions are similar to Batiffol's reconstruction of *Joseph and Aseneth*. Just as significant is that they cohere with sociolinguistic research.[25] Turning to sentence- and paragraph-initial occasions of καί in Matthew, we find that the connective begins only 20.6% of the gospel's sentences and 20.7% of its paragraphs.[26] For Luke it is 30.4% and 32.1%, respectively.[27]

The decreased frequency of καί in Matthew and Luke is accompanied by an increase of other connectives. In spoken discourse, idea units, usually connected by "and" or asyndeton, are the norm. In written discourse, by contrast, the relationships between clauses are more overtly marked. Tannen names this phenomenon "the literate strategy of establishing cohesion by lexicalization."[28] Subordinating conjunctions are one of the principal tools writers employ to establish such cohesion.[29] As Chafe summarizes, "Spoken language consists typically of chains of relatively brief, relatively independent idea units. Written language not only has longer idea units, but places them in various relations

---

20. Matthew's and Luke's limitation of parataxis is noted in Sanders, *Tendencies*, 250–51; Joseph A. Fitzmyer, *The Gospel according to Luke*, 2 vols., AB 28–28A (New York: Doubleday, 1981), 1:108; Neirynck, *Minor Agreements*, 203–10; Davies and Allison, *A Critical and Exegetical Commentary on the Gospel according to Saint Matthew*, 1:74; François Bovon, *Luke*, 3 vols., trans. Christine M. Thomas, Hermeneia (Minneapolis: Fortress, 2002), 1:5.

21. See Chapter 3 and the table below.

22. Maloney, *Semitic Interference*, 66.

23. In Mark καί occurs 1,100 times out of 11,138 words. This is 9.9% of the total words in the gospel or once for every 10.12 words. In Matthew there are 1,194 instances of καί out of a total 18,363 words. This is 6.5% of the total words or once for every 15.38 words.

24. In Luke there are 1,483 instances of καί out of a total 19,495 words. This is 7.6% of the total words or once for every 13.14 words.

25. Especially Beaman, "Coordination and Subordination," 60–61; Chafe, "Linguistic Differences," 111.

26. According to the division and punctuation in NA27, καί begins 202 of the 979 total sentences in Matthew and 29 of 237 paragraphs.

27. 309 of 1,017 sentences and 77 of 240 paragraphs in NA27.

28. Tannen, "Oral and Literate Strategies," 7.

29. Ibid., 8; Chafe, "Linguistic Differences," 111–12; idem, "Linking Intonation Units," 23; Chafe and Danielwicz, "Properties," 104; Beaman, "Subordination and Coordination," 76.

of dependence."³⁰ In this respect, it is telling that Matthew and Luke have, in place of Mark's paratactic καί, a wider variety of differing conjunctions uniting clauses, sentences, and episodes, and they employ them at a greater frequency than Mark.³¹ Compared to the twenty-five different conjunctions in Mark, there are thirty-four and thirty-six in Matthew and Luke, respectively. In Matthew, there are 1,157 conjunctions that are not καί compared to 1,196 in Luke and only 593 in Mark.³²

Next to the variety and frequency of cohesion devices in the later Synoptics, the most significant observation to make is their location in a sentence or clause. In Mark, aside from καί, rarely is a cohesion device, whether it be a conjunction, sentence adverb, or participle, in a sentence-initial position. When such a word or phrase does appear toward the beginning of a sentence or clause, it is typically preceded by καί. This is common in spoken discourse.³³ The situation is different in writing, wherein connectives are treated as their own punctuation units and "the linkage itself is given full attention."³⁴ The weighted connective without "and" occurs about six times more frequently in written than spoken discourse.³⁵

It is no surprise, then, that in Matthew and Luke various connectives that are not καί occur more frequently in clause- and sentence-initial positions than in Mark.³⁶ The case of τότε is instructive in this respect, as it coheres with sociolinguistic findings and the differences between the text families of *Joseph and Aseneth* discussed above. Both Beaman and Chafe find that "then" is exceedingly rare as a connective that is not preceded by "and" in spoken discourse.³⁷ Nonetheless, it occurs relatively frequently without "and" in written discourse.³⁸ In Philonenko's and Burchard's less literary reconstructions of *Joseph and Aseneth*, τότε occurs twice and never, respectively. In Batiffol's reconstruction based on the witnesses that literaturize their predecessors, it appears forty-two times. In like manner, there are only six instances of τότε in Mark, five of which are directly preceded

---

30. Chafe, "Linguistic Differences," 112.
31. Neirynck has compiled a cumulative list of how paratactic καί and asyndeton in Mark are altered by Matthew and Luke (*Minor Agreements*, 203–13).
32. Thus 50.4% and 46.5% of the total conjunctions in Matthew and Luke, respectively, are not καί. This compared to the 36.0% in Mark.
33. Chafe, "Linking Intonation Units," 13–16.
34. Ibid., 22.
35. Ibid., 24.
36. ἤδη, οὕτως, πάλιν, and ὕστερον commonly begin sentences in Matthew, while ἐπειδήπερ, ἐπειδή, and πλήν all begin sentences in Luke.
37. Beaman, "Coordination and Subordination," 76–77; Chafe, "Linking Intonation Units," 13.
38. Beaman, "Coordination and Subordination," 76–77.

by καί.³⁹ In contrast, the adverb appears fifteen times in Luke, only thrice with καί directly preceding it and seven times in a sentence-initial position without καί. Even more telling is Matthew's ninety occasions of τότε.⁴⁰ Of these, only ten are directly preceded by καί, and seventy are in sentence-initial position without the coordinating conjunction.

Both Matthew and Luke prefer to make the relationships between clauses, sentences, and episodes more grammatically explicit than Mark does. This is because, for writers, the stream of consciousness is slowed in the process of composing. The constituent elements of a narrative are more explicitly considered in light of one another. For speakers, the consciousness continues to march forward, and clauses, sentences, and episodes are relayed in an additive manner.⁴¹ Breaking down the paratactic structure of an oral narrative to make it more hypotactic is precisely what is to be expected in the process of literaturization.⁴² The table below shows not only how this happens in Matthew, Luke, and Batiffol's reconstruction of *Joseph and Aseneth*, but also how they alter parataxis in their predecessors.

Redacting verbal mood, tense, and voice

Redacting verbal mood, tense, and voice in Joseph and Aseneth

Literaturization similarly makes sense of the verbal differences between the text groups of *Joseph and Aseneth* and Mark. In Chapter 2 I noted that subliterary narratives from the papyri prefer indicative verbs to participial forms. Mandilaras observes that the frequency of καί with an indicative verb, and thus a minimal presence of hypotactic participial phrases, is characteristic of verbal construction in both papyrological texts and the Koine Greek vernacular.⁴³ Chafe's sociolinguistic research confirms that a higher frequency of participles creating hypotactic constructions is a characteristic of written narrative.⁴⁴

The *a*-text family of *Joseph and Aseneth* predictably and consistently changes indicative verbs to participles.⁴⁵ Batiffol's reconstruction contains 342 participles,

---

39. Mark 2:20; 3:27; 13:21; 13:26, 27. Mark 13:14 is the only occasion where τότε is not directly preceded by καί.
40. Many of these replace a Markan καί (Neirynck, *Minor Agreements*, 205–7).
41. Ong, *Orality and Literacy*, 38; Chafe, *Discourse*, 53; Bakker, "How Oral?" 38.
42. Chafe, "Linguistic Differences," 112.
43. Mandilaras, *Verb*, 366.
44. Chafe, "Linguistic Differences," 112; idem, "Integration and Involvement," 40–41.
45. Burchard notes this tendency of the *a* witnesses, along with the use of various adverbs, conjunctions, and subordinate clauses. He does not, however, offer any figures for how often these changes are made, nor does he indicate why they are made (*Joseph und Aseneth*, 23).

Table 5.1 Parataxis in Mark, Matthew, Luke, and Joseph and Aseneth

	Mark	Matthew	Luke	Joseph and Aseneth (Philonenko)	Joseph and Aseneth (Batiffol)
Total volume of καί	1,100/11,138: 9.9% of total words or 1 in every 10.12 words	1,194/18,363: 6.5% of total words or 1 in every 15.38 words (45% less frequently than Mark)	1,483/19,494: 7.6% of total words or 1 in every 13.14 words (33% less frequently than Mark)	1,034/8,230: 12.6% of total words or 1 in every 7.96 words	1,010/13,400: 8.6% of total words or 1 in every 11.56 words (31% less frequently than Philonenko's reconstruction)
καί in sentence-initial location	376/583: 65%	202/979: 21%	309/1,017: 30%	254/312: 81%	102/293: 35%
καί in paragraph-initial location	114/145: 92%	29/237: 21%	77/240: 32%	28/42: 67% In direct narration: 28/31: 90%	15/29: 52%
Other connectives	593 total (καί 1.85x more common)	1,157 total (καί 1.03x more common)	1,196 total (καί 1.24x more common)	190 total (καί 5.44x more common)	553 total (καί 1.83x more common)

compared to 153 in Philonenko's text.[46] As a result, the former employs indicative verbs slightly less frequently than the latter. More significantly, Batiffol's text has 1 participle for every 3.59 indicative verbs, while Philonenko's has 1 for every 6.77. In Batiffol's witness, participles curb the ubiquitous presence of the idea unit found in Philonenko's orally conceived text. The *a*-text family is not as grammatically choppy as the *d*-text family and Burchard's based on Syr, L2, Arm, and *f*. This is particularly discernible when the differences between Burchard's reconstruction of *Jos. Asen.* 18:3 are compared with the same content in Batiffol's text:

Joseph and Aseneth 18:3 (Burchard):	*Joseph and Aseneth* 18:11-14 (Batiffol):
καὶ εἶδεν αὐτὴν ὁ τροφεὺς αὐτῆς καὶ ἰδοὺ ἦν τὸ πρόσωπον αὐτῆς συμπεπτωκὸς ἐκ τῆς θλίψεως καὶ τοῦ κλαυθμοῦ καὶ τῆς ἐνδείας τῶν ἑπτὰ ἡμερῶν καὶ ἐλυπήθη καὶ ἔκλαυσε καὶ ἔλαβε τὴν χεῖρα αὐτῆς τὴν δεξιὰν καὶ κατ εφίλησεν αὐτὴν καὶ εἶπεν ...	ἰδὼν δὲ αὐτὴν ὁ ἐπὶ τῆς οἰκίας (ἦν γὰρ τὸ πρόσωπον αὐτῆς συμπεπτωκὸς ἀπὸ τῆς θλίψεως καὶ τοῦ κλαυθμοῦ καὶ τῆς ἐνδείας τῶν ἑπτὰ ἡμερῶν) λυπηθεὶς ἔκλαυσεν, καὶ λαβὼν τὴν χεῖρα αυτῆς τὴν δεξιάν, καταφιλήσας αὐτὴν εἶπεν ...
And her attendant saw her and, behold, her face was downcast from the distress and the weeping and the seven days of privation and she grieved and wept and took her right hand and kissed it and said ...	But when the attendant over the household saw her (for her face was downcast from the distress and the weeping and the seven days of privation), grievously she wept, and, having taken her right hand and kissed it, she said ...

Burchard's version has seven indicative verbs and each clause is connected by καί. There are only three indicative verbs in Batiffol's text, the other four having been altered to participial forms. This allows the redactor to omit καί before ἐλυπήθη ("grieved"), ἔκλαυσεν ("wept"), and κατεφίλησεν ("kissed") and to emend the καί that preceded εἶδεν ("saw") to a postpositive δέ. He or she substitutes καί in the first line with γάρ ("for"), giving the clause a parenthetical and causal force that specifies the subject of the verbs ἐλυπήθη and ἔκλαυσεν, which are ambiguous in Burchard's version.

In the end, Batiffol's reconstruction coordinates clauses with καί on only one occasion, while Burchard's reconstruction, in a manner typical of orally conceived literature, coordinates seven clauses with the simple conjunction. The nonuse of participles in Burchard's reconstruction compared to the notable presence of them in Batiffol's is precisely what one would expect of orally and literarily conceived narrative, respectively.

One final example of participial constructions and redaction reveals the differences between the text families. A comparison of a passage that exists in the *d*-text family, the *a*-family, and Burchard's version exposes these differences and how the three versions are related to one another. In *Joseph and Aseneth* 14, the appearance of Aseneth's angelic visitor is described:

---

46. Participles make up 1.86% of the total words in Philonenko, occurring 1 in every 53.79 words. They make up 2.8% of the words in Batiffol, or 1 in every 35.66 words.

Joseph and Aseneth 14:8-10 (Philonenko)	Jos. Asen 14:9-10 (Burchard)	Joseph and Aseneth 14:13-21 (Batiffol)
καὶ ἦρε τοὺς ὀφθαλμοὺς αὐτῆς καὶ εἶδε, καὶ ἰδοὺ ἀνὴρ ὅμοιος κατὰ πάντα τῷ Ἰωσὴφ τῇ στολῇ καὶ τῷ στεφάνῳ καὶ τῇ ῥάβδῳ τῇ βασιλικῇ, πλὴν τὸ πρόσωπον αὐτοῦ ἦν ὡς ἀστραπὴ καὶ οἱ ὀφθαλμοὶ αὐτοῦ ὡς φέγγος ἡλίου καὶ αἱ τρίχες τῆς κεφαλῆς αὐτοῦ ὡς φλὸξ πυρὸς καὶ αἱ χεῖρες καὶ οἱ πόδες αὐτοῦ ὥσπερ σίδηρος ἐκ πυρός. καὶ εἶδεν Ἀσενὲθ καὶ ἔπεσεν ἐπὶ πρόσωπον ἐπὶ τοὺς πόδας αὐτοῦ ἐν φόβῳ μεγάλῳ καὶ τρόμῳ.	καὶ ἐπῆρε τὴν κεφαλὴν αὐτῆς Ἀσενὲθ καὶ εἶδε καὶ ἰδοὺ ἀνὴρ κατὰ πάντα ὅμοιος τῷ Ἰωσὴφ τῇ στολῇ καὶ στεφάνω καὶ τῇ ῥάβδῳ τῇ βασιλικῇ πλὴν τὸ πρόσωπον αὐτοῦ ἦν ὡς ἀστραπὴ καὶ οἱ ὀφθαλμοὶ αὐτοῦ ὡς φέγγος ἡλίου καὶ αἱ τρίχες τῆς κεφαλῆς αὐτοῦ ὡς φλὸξ πυρὸς ὑπολαμπάδος καιομένης καὶ αἱ χεῖρες καὶ οἱ πόδες αὐτοῦ ὥσπερ σίδηρος ἐκ πυρὸς ἀπολάμπων καὶ σπινθῆρες ἀπεπήδων ἀπό τε τῶν χειρῶν καὶ τῶν ποδῶν αὐτοῦ. καὶ εἶδεν Ἀσενὲθ καὶ ἔπεσεν ἐπὶ πρόσωπον αὐτῆς ἐπὶ τοὺς πόδας αὐτοῦ ἐπὶ τὴν γῆν. καὶ ἐφοβήθη Ἀσενὲθ φόβον μέγαν καὶ ἐτρόμαξε πάντα τὰ μέλη αὐτῆς.	ἡ δὲ ἐπάρασα τὸ πρόσωπον αὐτῆς εἶδε, καὶ ἰδοὺ ἀνὴρ ὅμοιος κατὰ πάντα τῷ Ἰωσὴφ τῇ τε στολῇ καὶ τῷ στεφάνῳ καὶ τῇ ῥάβδῳ τῇ βασιλικῇ, πλὴν τὸ πρόσωπον αὐτοῦ ἦν ὡς ἀστραπή, καὶ οἱ ὀφθαλμοὶ αὐτοῦ ὡς φέγγος ἡλίου, αἱ δὲ τρίχες τῆς κεφαλῆς αὐτοῦ ὡς φλὸξ πυρὸς ὑπὸ λαμπάδος καιομένης, καὶ αἱ χεῖρες αὐτοῦ καὶ οἱ πόδες ὥσπερ σίδηρος ἐκ πυρὸς ἀπολάμπων, ὥσπερ γὰρ σπινθῆρες ἀπέσπενδον ἀπό τε τῶν χειρῶν καὶ τῶν ποδῶν αὐτοῦ. ταῦτα τοίνυν ἰδοῦσα Ἀσενὲθ ἐφοβήθη καὶ ἔπεσεν ἐπὶ πρόσωπον μηδ' ὅλως δυνηθεῖσα στῆναι ἐπὶ τοὺς πόδας αὐτῆς, πάνυ γὰρ ἐφοβήθη καὶ ἐτρόμαξαν πάντα τὰ μέλη αὐτῆς.
And she lifted her eyes and saw and, behold, there was a man alike in every respect to Joseph with a robe and crown and royal staff, except his face was like a star and his eyes like the radiance of the sun and the hairs on his head like a flame of fire and his hands and feet just like iron from fire. And Aseneth saw and fell on her face at his feet in great fear and trembling.	And Aseneth lifted up her head and saw and, behold, there was a man alike in every respect to Joseph with a robe and crown and royal staff, except his face was like a star, and his eyes like the radiance of the sun, and the hairs on his head like a flame of fire burning in a window, and his hands and feet just like iron shining out of a fire and sparks were shooting from his hands and his feet. And Aseneth saw and fell on her face at his feet on the ground. And she was exceedingly afraid and all the parts of her body trembled.	But she, lifting up her face, saw, and, behold, there was a man alike in every respect to Joseph, with a robe and crown and royal staff, except his face was like a star, and his eyes like the radiance of the sun, and the hairs of his head like a flame of fire burning in a window, and his hands and feet just like iron shining out of a fire, for they were just like sparks pouring out from both his hands and feet. Moreover, having seen these things, Aseneth was afraid and fell on her face, completely unable to stand on her feet, for she was very afraid and all the parts of her body trembled.

Of the different versions, Batiffol's reconstruction is clearly the most literary. Despite being the longest of the three, καί occurs least often. Typical of this witness, indicative verbs are converted into participles on two occasions and καί is twice altered to a postpositive δέ. This version also employs the adverb πάνυ ("completely") and the conjunction γάρ ("for"), which are absent in both Burchard's and Philonenko's reconstructions. This is evidence of the more complex grammatical structure of the *a*-text group compared with the other witnesses.

The stylistic features of Burchard's and Philonenko's reconstructions are comparable. Both contain more indicative verbs, have less participial clauses, are heavily indebted to parataxis for their grammatical structure, and minimally employ other conjunctions and adverbs. More striking are some of the lexical similarities between Burchard's and Batiffol's reconstructions in this passage. The phrases ὑπὸ λαμπάδος καιομένης ("burning in a window") and σπινθῆρες ἀπέσπενδον ἀπὸ τε τῶν χειρῶν καὶ τῶν ποδῶν αὐτοῦ ("sparks were shooting from his hands and his feet") are in both texts but absent in Philonenko's reconstruction. The final clauses in Batiffol and Burchard, which is not contained in Philonenko, are identical, save for the number of the aorist verb τρομέω ("to tremble").[47] Finally, forms of the compound verb ἀπαίρω ("to lift up") are present at the beginning of the passage in both Burchard and Batiffol, while Philonenko has the non-compounded ἦρε ("lifted up").

Lexical overlap between Burchard's and Batiffol's reconstructions could support the text-critical contention that the *a*-text family and *f*, L2, Syr, Arm share a closer affinity than the *a* and *d* families do.[48] However, there are instances where *a* and *d* agree against Burchard's and Fink's preferred witnesses.[49] In *Joseph and Aseneth* 14 alone there are five cases of this sort of agreement.[50] Rather than draw conclusions about the proximity of *a* to either of the other text groups based on lexical resonances, the most judicious conclusion is that *a* is the youngest of all the groups and made use of texts from the other two families, literarily improving on each of them.[51] It is unlikely that the author of *a* considered a single witness from any text group more authoritative or original than other versions since, as I have already argued, *Joseph and Aseneth* was a pluriform tradition. Most consequential is that the *a*-family recension constructs a new, more literary textual version of *Joseph and Aseneth* that is stylistically dissimilar to all its predecessors. This discordance results from its higher literary ambitions.

---

47. Standhartinger notes other locations where Burchard's text and *a* correspond against *d*. She argues that these support the case for the priority of the *d*-family (*Frauenbild*, 39–40).

48. As is the case in ibid., 39–40.

49. Burchard argues that shared readings and especially the shared errors between *a* and *d* suggest that the two versions are of a common family (*Joseph und Aseneth*, 25–26; idem, "Zum Stand der Arbeit am Text von Joseph und Aseneth," in *Das Ende der Tage und die Gegenwart des Heils: Begegnungen mit dem Neuen Testament und seiner Umwelt: Festschrift für Heinz-Wolfgang Kuhn zum 65 Geburtstag*, ed. Michael Becker and Wolfgang Fenske [Leiden: Brill, 1999], 16–24).

50. Christoph Burchard, "Zum Text von 'Joseph und Aseneth,'" *JSJ* 1 (1970): 30–34; Ahearne-Kroll, "Jewish Identity," 37.

51. This is Ahearne-Kroll's evaluation of *a*'s relationship to *b* and *d* ("Jewish Identity," 36). She suggests *Jos. Asen.* 10:11 (*Jos. Asen.* 10:12 in Burchard's text) is an instance where *a* combines both *b* and *d*. She does not note the literary differences that *a* exhibits from both *d* and *b*.

Redacting verbal mood, tense, and voice in Mark

Introductory participial phrases in Mark, Matthew, and Luke Akin to the narratives from the papyri and the less literary witnesses to *Joseph and Aseneth*, Mark typically begins new narrative units and sentences with καί followed by an indicative verb. Also analogous to the redaction of *Joseph and Aseneth* in the later, more literary *a*-text versions, Matthew and Luke predictably replace the simple connective followed by an indicative verb with a participial phrase at the beginning of a sentence. According to Neirynck, this happens on fifty-three occasions in Matthew and forty-eight in Luke.[52] There are four and ten instances where this structure is changed to a genitive absolute in Matthew and Luke, respectively.[53] By replacing καί and an indicative verb with a participial phrase, Matthew and Luke have employed one of the three principal devices for integrating idea units into sentences in written narrative, whose elements are marked by more complex degrees of relation than in spoken narrative.[54] They have also changed a syntactical structure characteristic of both the Greek papyri and vernacular.[55] Whereas Mark exhibits a simple, paratactic structure characterized by short idea units, Matthew and Luke each strive to make their narrative read more literarily. They do so primarily by using a wider variety of subordinating conjunctions more frequently than their predecessor and by creating hypotactic clauses with an introductory participle.

The historical present in Mark, Matthew, and Luke In Chapter 3 I argued that the ubiquity, purpose, and location of historical present tense verbs in Mark is the gospel's densest oral residue when it comes to verbal features. The tense function makes up nearly 10% of all verbal forms in Mark, appearing 150 times, more than half of which are not in speech margins.[56] The historical present predictably occurs at incipit turns in the narrative or incidence turns within individual episodes, but never in the resolution of a pericope. Occasionally, switching into the historical present does make the narrative in Mark more vivid, but this is an effect of the switch, not necessarily its purpose.

Matthew and Luke less frequently employ the historical present and they do so in a manner that differs from Mark. In Luke, the historical present is almost completely absent, appearing thrice in nonspeech margins and eight times in

---

52. Neirynck, *Minor Agreements*, 207–10.
53. Ibid., 210–11.
54. Chafe, "Linguistic Differences," 111–12. The other two devices for creating the complexity that characterizes sentences in written narrative over against idea units in spoken that Chafe observes are subordinating conjunctions and appositives (ibid.).
55. Mandilaras, *Verb*, 366.
56. See Chapter 3; Neirynck, *Minor Agreements*, 224–27; Hawkins, *Horae Synopticae*, 114–18.

speech margins.⁵⁷ One of these cases, Lk. 8:49, is retained from Mark. But on eighty-nine other occasions, Luke alters a Markan historical present to another tense form, usually an aorist or imperfect.⁵⁸ Thus Luke is a representative of one stream of Hellenistic literary writers who deliberately avoid the historical present.⁵⁹ It was apparently too colloquial for his taste.⁶⁰

Matthew does not avoid the historical present as rigorously as Luke does, but neither does its frequency reach that of Mark. There are ninety-four occurrences of the historical present in Matthew.⁶¹ Matthew removes 130 instances of Mark's historical presents, retains 20 of them, and produces 74 of his own.⁶² As a result, 4.2% of Matthew's indicative verbs are historical presents compared to just over 10% of Mark's. Most cases, seventy-six of ninety-four or 80.8%, of Matthean historical presents are in speech margins. In Chapters 2 and 3, I argued that historical presents in speech margins carry little interpretive weight, as the present tense and verbs of speaking go hand in hand in both written and oral narrative.⁶³ Historical present tense verbs in speech margins "approach a stereotyped idiom."⁶⁴ This leaves the eighteen historical presents in nonspeech margins in Matthew as most noteworthy.

---

57. Nonspeech margins: ἔρχεται ("comes") in Lk. 8:49 (// Mk 5:35); βλέπει ("sees") in Lk. 24:12; ὁρᾷ ("sees") in Lk. 16:23. Speech margins: λέγει ("says") in Lk. 11:45; 13:8; 16:7, 29; 19:22; 24:36; φησίν ("says") in Lk. 7:40; ἐρωτᾷ ("asks") in Lk. 11:37. These are listed in Hawkins, *Horae Synopticae*, 149; Neirynck, *Minor Agreements*, 225–29. Kilpatrick argues that the number of historical presents in Luke might be even lower, as some cases of it may be scribal intrusions to avoid repetition of εἶπεν ("said"). He concludes that only two historical presents are certain and the remainder questionable ("Historic Present," 259–60). At most, historical presents make up 0.4% of the indicative verbs in Luke.

58. Bovon, *Luke*, 1:397 n. 12; Ulrich Busse, *Die Wunder des Propheten Jesus: Die Rezeption, Komposition, und Interpretation der Wundertradition im Evangelium des Lukas*, Forschung zur Bibel 24 (Stuttgart: Katholisches Bibelwerk, 1977), 222 n. 1; Neirynck et al., *Minor Agreements*, 224–29.

59. Kilpatrick, "Historic Present," 259.

60. Robertson, *Grammar*, 867; BDF §321; Turner, *Syntax*, 61 all indicate that the historical present is colloquial or vulgar and that it is on this basis that Luke avoids it.

61. I follow the list from Hawkins (*Horae Synopticae*, 148–49) and Neirynck (*Minor Agreements*, 224–29), but with Stephanie Black ("The Historic Present in Matthew: Beyond Speech Margins," in *Discourse Analysis and the New Testament*, ed. Stanley E. Porter and Jeffrey T. Reed [Sheffield: Sheffield Academic, 1999], 121) and S. M. B. Wilmshurst ("The Historic Present in Matthew's Gospel: A Survey and Analysis Focused on Matthew 13.44," *JSNT* 25 [2003]: 273–74) include λέγει ("says") from Mt. 26:25 as well.

62. Willoughby C. Allen, *A Critical and Exegetical Commentary on the Gospel according to St. Matthew*, 3rd ed., ICC 26 (Edinburgh: T&T Clark, 1912), xx.

63. Black and Wilmshurst also minimize the role of the historical present in speech margins (Black, "Historic Present," 126; Wilmshurst, "Historic Present," 275).

64. Black, "Historic Present," 126.

Matthew strategically employs these eighteen historical presents for rhetorical ends. Stephanie Black and S. M. B Wilmshurst have each argued that this is especially true in those pericopes where historical presents are clustered.[65] Black addresses the six in Mt. 4:1-11, wherein Jesus is tempted by the devil in the wilderness, arguing that they help escalate the pericope to a rhetorical climax in Mt. 4:8-10.[66] She divides the episode into four parts: vv. 1-4; vv. 5-7; vv. 8-10; v. 11. Each of these begins with a temporal adverb, consists of four total sentences (or three in the case of the last section), and connects two of its constituent sentences with καί and one with a different connective.[67] Black observes that Matthew has employed historical presents at increasing frequency in these sections. There are no present tense forms in vv. 1-4, two in vv. 5-7, three in the climax, that is, vv. 8-10, and one in the drop-off, v. 11.[68] In Black's reading, Matthew employs the historical present as a discourse-structuring device that builds the pericope to a staggered climax. The evangelist has consciously shaped the episode with this marked tense form to have a rhetorical effect on the reader. The historical presents, along with the upward movement from the desert to the summit of the temple to the exceedingly high mountain, make vv. 8-10 the focal point of the pericope and serve to heighten rhetorically Jesus's rebuke of the tempter.

Wilmshurst offers a similar interpretation of the cluster of three historical presents in Mt. 13:44, the parable of hidden treasure.[69] Following Jacques Dupont, he argues that this pericope is at the chiastic center of the collection of parables in Mt. 13:24-52.[70] Matthew weaves together three thematic threads that are of utmost importance to his gospel: revelation of what is hidden, eternal treasure, and overwhelming joy.[71] Given this thematic coalescence and its location, Wilmshurst proposes that the parable of the hidden treasure has a special role to play not only in this collection of parables, but in the gospel as a whole. The three historical presents that conclude the parable, ὑπάγει ("he goes"), πωλεῖ ("he sells"), ἀγοράζει

---

65. Ibid., 127–39; Wilmhurst, "Historic Present," 277–85.

66. Black, "Historic Present," 129–35. Davies and Allison make a similar argument, though not on syntactic grounds. They suggest that "the three temptations exhibit a spatial progression, from a low place to a high place," and that this spatial progression "corresponds to the dramatic tension which comes to a climax in the third temptation" (*Matthew*, 1:352).

67. Black, "Historic Present," 130–31.

68. There are noteworthy variants in Mt. 4:9 for the aorist verb εἶπεν. The historical present λέγει is supported by L W Θ 0233 f^1, and the aorist by ℵ B C D Z f 33. If the present is accepted, Black's argument is further strengthened, as there are then four historical presents in these verses and no aorists.

69. Wilmhurst, "Historic Present," 278–85.

70. Ibid., 278–79; Jacques Dupont, "Les paraboles du trésor et de la perle," *NTS* 14 (1968): 408–18.

71. Wilmhurst, "Historic Present," 284.

("he buys"), function, as Wilmshurst suggests, like a light switch that illuminates its significance for the reader.[72]

In both Mt. 4:1-11 and 13:44, then, the historical present is employed strategically and selectively to mark important events or themes. Black maintains that the cluster of historical presents in Mt. 26:36-46 works similarly.[73] These three texts account for eleven of the eighteen historical presents in nonspeech margins in Matthew. The remaining seven occur either at climactic points in the narrative or at the "seams," serving in a structuring capacity.[74]

According to these studies, literary design is what characterizes Matthew's employment of the historical present. Black writes, "[Matthew] intentionally juxtaposes present and aorist or imperfect tense-forms within these passages for dramatic effect."[75] Utilizing the historical present sparingly aids this. In writing, the past tense is the foundation on which the other tenses can be employed for artistic influence and rhetorical flourish.[76] Matthew falls in line with this pattern. In spoken narrative, the historical present is utilized more frequently, unconsciously, and at expected locations in an episode. In Chapter 3 I argued that Wolfson's claim that "the more fully a story is performed, the more likely it will contain [the historical present]" makes sense of the frequency of the historical present in Mark.[77] The converse is true of Matthew and Luke. Furthermore, the location of historical presents in Matthew differs from Mark. Mark employs historical presents at incipit and incidence turns and never in a coda or resolution clause. While historical presents sometimes appear at incipit turns in Matthew, primarily as a discourse-structuring device, they rarely appear at incidence turns in an episode.[78] More importantly, historical presents occur in resolution clauses on two occasions in the gospel: Mt. 3:15 and 13:44. This position of the historical present is foreign to both Mark and oral narrative.[79]

In sum, the historical present occurs far less frequently in Matthew and Luke than it does in Mark, and it follows the norms of written narrative more

---

72. Ibid.

73. Black, "Historic Present," 135–39.

74. Wilmshurst makes this very point for these seven remaining historical presents ("Historic Present," 286). Wolfgang Schenk argues that the primary function of historical presents in Matthew is to structure the discourse ("Das Präsens historicum als makrosyntaktisches Gliederungssignal im Matthäusevangelium," *NTS* 22 [1976]: 464–75).

75. Black, "Historic Present," 139.

76. Chafe, *Discourse*, 236.

77. Wolfson, *CHP*, 29.

78. Incipit turns begin a new episode in the historical present, whereas incidence turns are embedded in the body of the episode itself (Wolfson, "Historical Present Tense Yet Again," 375).

79. See Chapter 3; Schiffrin, "Tense Variation," 51; Fludernik, "Historical Present Tense," 86; eadem, "Historical Present Tense Yet Again," 375–76.

than spoken. What should be gathered from this is not only that the historical present is a dense oral residue in Mark that is largely altered in Matthean and Lukan redaction, but that being conscious of a given narrative's mode of composition when assessing the historical present, as it has operations peculiar to written and oral narratives, affects evaluation of it. The type of discourse being evaluated, its mode of composition, and its medium of reception all matter for interpretation.

The imperfect tense in Mark, Matthew, and Luke Schiffrin observes that a prominence of the historical present tense is often accompanied by a similar pervasiveness of the past progressive tense in oral narrative.[80] It is complemented by reports of direct speech as well.[81] This is because the memories of events reported, what Chafe calls the extroverted consciousness, play back in the speaker's mind not as singular events but as a continuous stream.[82] When these memories are reported in speech, the progressive tenses are most appropriate for depicting the events and portraying them as immediate to the hearer.[83] Direct discourse also aligns the speaker's consciousness with the hearer's by collapsing the distance between the former's recollection of the words and the latter's experience of them.[84] The speaker presents the direct discourse to the hearer as if he or she was hearing it him- or herself.

A lower frequency of the historical present, imperfect tense, and direct discourse in written narrative is a result of, what Chafe calls, "displaced immediacy."[85] Oral storytelling, on the one hand, brings the speaker's memory directly in line with the hearer's memory. Writing, on the other, obviates the necessity of copresence, and memories of events are not transferred in the same immediate sense as they are in spoken discourse. Consciousness is displaced onto another object, the written text. Because the flow of consciousness is slowed down and edited in the process of writing, events are commonly depicted in a more punctiliar manner in this mode.

It follows, then, that both the imperfect tense and direct discourse are less frequent in Matthew and Luke than in Mark. Imperfect verbs make up 19.6% of the indicative verbs in Mark, compared to 6.3% in Matthew and 14.8% in Luke.[86]

---

80. Schiffrin, "Tense Variation," 59.
81. Ibid., 58; Chafe, "Integration and Involvement," 48; idem, *Discourse*, 210.
82. Chafe, *Discourse*, 197–208.
83. Ibid., 195–223; Egbert J. Bakker, "Storytelling in the Future: Truth, Time, and Tense in Homeric Epic," in Bakker and Kahane (eds.), *Written Voices, Spoken Signs*, 15.
84. Chafe, *Discourse*, 215–19.
85. Ibid., 226–32.
86. In Mark this is 293 imperfects of 1,496 indicative forms, 142 of 2,245 in Matthew, and 363 of 2,445 in Luke. When total verbal forms are considered, Matthew and Luke's reduction is just as stark, with imperfects making up 3.5% of total verbal forms (142/4,000) in Matthew, 8.2% (363/4,449) in Luke, and 11.3% in Mark (293/2,586).

Matthew changes a Markan imperfect to an aorist on 41 occasions and removes another 187, by either deletion or paraphrase.[87] With respect to direct discourse, Matthew omits a Markan ὅτι *recitativum* on twenty-three occasions, while Luke does so on eighteen.[88]

The active and passive voice in Mark, Matthew, and Luke Finally, Matthew and Luke exhibit only a slightly higher frequency of passive verbs in their narratives than Mark does. Chafe, Bennett, and Ochs each found a higher preponderance of passive voice verbs in written narrative than spoken.[89] This is also the case in *Joseph and Aseneth*, wherein active verbs appear approximately ten times more frequently than passives.[90] It is somewhat unexpected that passive voice verbs make up 10.2% of the indicatives in Mark, compared to 13.1% in Matthew and 11.2% in Luke.[91] There are, however, sixteen occasions in Matthew and seventeen in Luke where a Markan active has been changed to a passive.[92] The inverse, a passive in Mark with an active in the redacted text, occurs only once for Matthew and never for Luke.[93]

In sum, just as the ubiquity, function, and location of the historical present is the densest oral residue of the verbal features in the Gospel of Mark, so also is the nonuse of it in Luke and the altered employment of it in Matthew evidence that these narratives are literarily conceived. Other verbal features, such as the curbed frequency of the imperfect and a substitution of a participial phrase for καί with an indicative, further support this contention. Differences in verbal voice in the Synoptics are not as strong indicators of each narrative's oral or literal conception as might have been expected.

Redacting repetitive syntactical patterns, words, phrases, and ideas in Mark

Both orality critics and sociolinguists note that repetition is a distinctive mark of oral communication.[94] I argued in Chapter 3 that repetition is ubiquitous in

87. Allen, *Matthew*, xx–xxi.
88. Neirynck, *Minor Agreements*, 213–16.
89. Chafe, "Integration and Involvement," 40–41; Bennett, "Extended View"; Ochs, "Planned and Unplanned Discourse," 69–70.
90. See Chapter 3.
91. 153/1,496 in Mark; 293/2,245 in Matthew; 275/2,445 in Luke. The case is similar when expanded to all verbal forms. Passives make up 11.1% (288/2,586) of the total verbal forms in Mark, 14.9% (595/4,000) in Matthew, and 13.3% (592/4,449) in Luke.
92. Neirynck, *Minor Agreements*, 251–52.
93. Ibid.
94. In orality studies this claim is made by Bennison Gray ("Repetition in Oral Literature," *Journal of American Folklore* 84 [1971]: 289–30), Ong (*Orality and Literacy*, 39–41), Zumthor (*Oral Poetry*, 111), Lord ("Characteristics of Orality," 57–62), and Foley (*Singer of Tales*, 90). Sociolinguists who argue that repetition is characteristic of oral

Mark and *Joseph and Aseneth*, occurring at the thematic, episodic, structural, grammatical, and lexical levels. While the *a*-text family of *Joseph and Aseneth* does alter some of the repetitions of its predecessors, especially their paratactic structures, it is not nearly as patent as Matthew's and Luke's redaction of this characteristic of their predecessor.

Hawkins and Neirynck have each compiled lists of Matthean and Lukan redaction of Markan redundancies, repetitions, and pleonasms at the clausal level.[95] While these are not without consequence, my interest here is in how the later tradents modify two of the Markan repetitions I called attention to in Chapter 3, namely, intercalations and the discourse marker εὐθύς ("immediately," "so then").

Intercalations in Mark, Matthew, and Luke

Matthew and Luke appear to have little concern for maintaining the integrity of Markan intercalations. In Chapter 3 I claimed, following Havelock and Dewey, that intercalations in Mark are an oral residue that serve, or at least formally served, a mnemonic purpose.[96] Of these six commonly identified "sandwiches" in Mark, only one is retained by both Matthew and Luke together. On three other occasions an intercalation is preserved in one gospel but not the other. And in two instances, both Matthew and Luke disrupt the intercalation by removing one or more of its constituent pericopes, combining episodes, or rearranging material.[97] Thus Matthean and Lukan redaction of Markan intercalations is as follows:

discourse include Tannen ("Oral and Literate Strategies," 7) and Ochs ("Planned and Unplanned Discourse," 70–72). Kelber (*Gospel*, 67), Achtemeier ("Omne Verbum Sonat," 21), Joanna Dewey ("Mark as Interwoven Tapestry: Forecasts and Echoes for a Listening Audience," *CBQ* 53 [1991]: 225), and Mournet (*Oral Tradition*, 174–79) are NT interpreters who also make the claim.

95. Hawkins lists thirty-nine Markan pleonasms that are altered in Matthew and Luke (*Horae Synopticae*, 139–42). He also provides a list of over one hundred "context-supplement" repetitions in Mark. Though he does not indicate which texts in the list are altered in Matthean and Lukan redaction, he does note that there are "certainly very few [repetitions] in comparison with those in Mark" (ibid., 125–26). Neirynck catalogs twenty-six "duplicate expressions" in Mark that are replaced by "simple expressions" in Matthew and Luke (*Minor Agreements*, 287).

96. Havelock, "Oral Composition," 183; Dewey, "Oral Methods," 39.

97. The pattern of redaction changes only slightly if one concludes that there are more than six intercalations in Mark. Edwards finds nine "sandwiches" in the gospel. He shows that Matthew and Luke agree in retaining two and disrupting two and that there are five places where only one or the other follows Mark. Thus, if there are nine intercalations instead of six, about half of them remain intact. Even on those occasions, however, "[Mark's] intention is often lost" ("Markan Sandwiches," 197–99).

Matthew and Luke disrupt intercalation:

Content	Mark 3:20-25	Matthew 12:22-30, 46-50	Luke 11:14-23; 8:19-21
A^1: Jesus's companions attempt to seize him	A^1: 3:20-21	A^1: N/A	A^1: N/A
B: Beelzebub controversy	B: 3:22-30,	B: 12:22-30 (vv. 31–45, intervening, unrelated material)	B: 11:14-23
A^2: Jesus's family seek him	A^2: 3:31-35,	A^2: 12:46-50	A^2: 8:19-21

Content	Mark 11:12-25	Matthew 21:18-22	Luke 13:6-9; 19:45-48
A^1: Cursing of the fig tree	A^1: 11:12-14	A^1: (21:18-22)	A^1: (13:6-9)
B: Jesus in the Temple	B: 11:15-19	B: 21:12-17	B: 19:45-48
A^2: Withered fig Tree	A^2: 11:20-21	A^2: 21:18-22	A^2: (13:6-9)

Matthew disrupts intercalation, but Luke retains it:

Content	Mark 6:6-30	Matthew 10:5-16; 14:1-14	Luke 9:1-11
A^1: Disciples sent out	A^1: 6:6-13	A^1: (10:5-16)	A^1: 9:1-6
B: Herod and John	B: 6:14-29	B: 14:1-12	B: 9:7-9
A^2: Disciples return	A^2: 6:30	A^2: 14:13-14	A^2: 9:10-11

Luke disrupts intercalation, but Matthew retains it:

Content	Mark 14:1-11	Matthew 26:3-16	Luke 22:1-3; 7:36-50
A^1: Jewish leaders conspire	A^1: 14:1-2	A^1: 26:3-5	A^1: 22:1-2
B: A woman anoints Jesus	B: 14:3-9	B: 26:6-13	B: (7:36-50)
A^2: Judas goes to Jewish leaders to conspire	A^2: 14:10-11	A^2: 26:14-16	A^2: 22:3

Content	Mark 14:53-72	Matthew 26:57-75	Luke 22:54-71
A^1: Peter warms himself by a fire	A^1: 14:53-54	A^1: 26:57-58	A^1: N/A
B: Jesus before the high priest	B: 14:55-65	B: 26:59-68	B: 22:63-71
A^2: Peter warms himself and denies Jesus	A^2: 14:66-72	A^2: 26:69-75	A^2: 22:54-62

Both Matthew and Luke retain intercalation:

Content	Mark 5:21-43	Matthew 9:18-26	Luke 8:40-42
A^1: Jairus's Daughter	A^1: 5:21-24	A^1: 9:18-19	A^1: 8:40-42
B: Woman with a flow of blood	B: 5:25-34	B: 9:20-22	B: 8:43-48
A^2: Jairus's daughter	A^2: 5:35-43	A^2: 9:23-26	A^2: 8:49-56

As seen here, Matthew and Luke do not avoid the Markan "sandwich" structure as ardently as they do the historical present or parataxis. But neither do they rely on it to structure their narratives as frequently as Mark. On some occasions, they retain the intercalations. On others, they alter them in order to strengthen the rhetoric or make a different rhetorical point altogether. The latter is the case with Matthew's alteration of the Fig Tree-Temple-Fig Tree intercalation from Mark 11.

In Mark, the fig-tree and temple episodes occur on two successive days and the structure of the pericopes accentuates Mark's temple critique.[98] Matthew removes the intercalation and does not spread the cursing and withering of the fig tree over multiple days. Instead, in Mt. 21:18-22 the withering follows immediately upon Jesus's curse. This heightens the miraculous nature of the episode and mutes the temple critique.[99] Brent Kinman writes, "It is less clear in Matthew (than in Mark) that the fig tree episode is meant to draw attention to the destruction of the Temple."[100] By dismantling the Markan intercalation Matthew has recast the episode from a critique of the temple and a symbol of its destruction to a miraculous tale that imports "open and indefinite" pronouncement of judgment on Israel.[101] Rather than serving a "prophetic and retrospective" role characteristic of oral narrative, the cursing of the fig tree in Matthew begins a pronouncement of condemnation that is sharpened as Jesus goes on to speak two botanic parables against the chief priests and elders in Mt. 21.[102]

εὐθύς *in Mark, Matthew, and Luke* Intercalations are a structural repetition in Mark that Matthew and Luke alter. But there is a lexical redundancy that is removed or modified even more in their redaction than intercalations. In Chapter 3 I argued that εὐθύς ("immediately," "so then") is best understood as a discourse marker in Mark. This is one of Mark's densest oral residues and one of the most prominent repetitions that Matthew and Luke consistently revise.

---

98. As argued in Chapter 3 and by Telford (*Barren Temple*, 238), Wright (*Jesus and the Victory of God*, 421–22), Evans (*Mark*, 2:160), Marcus (*Mark*, 2:790), and Kirk ("Time for Figs," 511–13).

99. Donald A. Hagner, *Matthew*, 2 vols., WBC 33A–33B (Dallas: Thomas Nelson, 1995), 2:606: Ulrich Luz, *Matthew*, 3 vols., trans. James E. Crouch, Hermeneia (Minneapolis: Fortress, 2005), 3:22.

100. Brent Kinman, "Lucan Eschatology and the Missing Fig Tree," *JBL* 113 (1994): 670.

101. Luz, *Matthew*, 3:23.

102. Luz argues that the pronouncement of judgment contained within Matthew's fig-tree episode primes the reader for the Parable of the Wicked Tenants in Mt. 21:33-44 (ibid.). However, his contention can be broadened to include Mt. 21:23-46. The Parable of the Man with Two Sons (Mt. 21:28-32) and the Parable of the Wicked Tenants (Mt. 21:33-41) are both set in a vineyard and themes of faith, fruit, and judgment are echoed throughout the section.

Discourse markers are a subclass of adverbs that appear with high frequency in oral narrative.[103] They have multiple discourse-sequencing capacities.[104] They typically play procedural rather than propositional roles in a narrative, are optional, occur toward the beginning of a sentence or utterance, and have homophonous or nearly homophonous adverbial counterparts.[105] In written narrative, discourse markers are commonly disparaged as subliterary.[106] Understanding these features of discourse markers helps to make sense of Matthean and Lukan redaction of εὐθύς in Mark. Matthew and Luke do one of three things with the discourse marker: (1) omit it altogether; (2) alter it to another adverb; or (3) retain it.

Because discourse markers are optional, appear with high frequency in oral narrative, and are informal, the later gospel writers take the first route most often. Finding εὐθύς otiose and inappropriate for the literary medium, they remove it altogether. This happens on eighteen occasions in Matthew and twenty-two in Luke.[107] The parallels to Mk 1:12 are a case in point in this respect:

Mark 1:12:	Matthew 4:1:	Luke 4:1:
καὶ εὐθὺς τὸ πνεῦμα αὐτὸν ἐκβάλλει εἰς τὴν ἔρημον.	τότε ὁ Ἰησοῦς ἀνήχθη εἰς τὴν ἔρημον ὑπὸ τοῦ πνεύματος, πειρασθῆναι ὑπὸ τοῦ διαβόλου.	Ἰησοῦς δὲ πλήρης πνεύματος ἁγίου ὑπέστρεψεν ἀπὸ τοῦ Ἰορδάνου, καὶ ἤγετο ἐν τῷ πνεύματι ἐν τῇ ἐρήμῳ.
And then the Spirit throws him into the wilderness.[108]	Then Jesus was led up by the Spirit into the wilderness to be tempted by the devil. (RSV)	And Jesus, full of the Holy Spirit, returned from the Jordan, and was led by the Spirit ... in the wilderness. (RSV)

Here, Mark's discourse marker does not connote immediacy, but discourse sequencing.[109] As they do many other times, both Matthew and Luke find this role objectionable and remove εὐθύς altogether.

---

103. The informality and oral nature of discourse markers are established in Östman, "Symbiotic Relationship," 169; Watts, "Taking the Pitcher," 208; Brinton, *Pragmatic Markers*, 33. Urgelles-Coll (*Syntax*, 1, 7–41), Traugott and Dasher (*Regularity*, 152–52), and Heine ("Discourse Markers," 1207) all classify them as adverbs.

104. Schiffrin (*Discourse Markers*, 64), Arroyo ("From Politeness," 855–56), and Brinton (*Pragmatic Markers*, 35) each argue that multifunctionality is a constituent feature of discourse markers.

105. Brinton addresses the location of discourse markers in a sentence or utterance (*Pragmatic Markers*, 34). Their adverbial counterparts are discussed by Hansen, "Semantic Status," 236; Heine, "Discourse Markers," 1208.

106. Brinton, *Pragmatic Markers*, 33.

107. Neirynck, *Minor Agreements*, 274–75.

108. Given the sequencing function of discourse markers discussed in Chapter 3, I have translated εὐθύς "then" here.

109. The discourse-sequencing function of εὐθύς in Mk 1:12 is confirmed by τότε and δέ in Mt. 4:1 and Lk. 4:1, respectively.

There are occasions when the force of εὐθύς in Mark is not totally removed from Matthean and Lukan redaction. The later Synoptic tradents frequently replace the word with one of two adverbial counterparts to εὐθύς. Matthew, on the one hand, changes seven instances of εὐθύς to the nearly homophonous adverb εὐθέως ("immediately").[110] Luke, on the other, prefers παραχρῆμα ("immediately"), replacing εὐθύς with this adverb six times and for εὐθέως ("immediately") once.[111] The adverbs appear in Matthew's and Luke's shared and unique materials as well. Altogether, there are a combined fifteen cases of εὐθέως ("immediately") and παραχρῆμα ("immediately") in Matthew and sixteen in Luke.

Rarely do Matthew and Luke retain the discourse marker εὐθύς from their predecessor. Luke never keeps it from his Markan source and Matthew does so only five times.[112] When εὐθύς does appear in the latter, it serves as an adverb rather than a discourse marker. "Immediately" seems to serve as the best translation in these cases.[113] For example, Mt. 13:20-21 preserves two instances of εὐθύς from Mk 4:16-17, presumably because its adverbial indication of haste is literarily unobjectionable. The translation "immediately" is entirely appropriate for both instances in Mt. 13:20-21:

ὁ δὲ ἐπὶ τὰ πετρώδη σπαρείς, οὗτός ἐστιν ὁ τὸν λόγον ἀκούων καὶ εὐθὺς μετὰ χαρᾶς λαμβάνων αὐτόν, οὐκ ἔχει δὲ ῥίζαν ἐν ἑαυτῷ ἀλλὰ πρόσκαιρός ἐστιν, γενομένης δὲ θλίψεως ἢ διωγμοῦ διὰ τὸν λόγον εὐθὺς σκανδαλίζεται.	As for what was sown on rocky ground, this is he who hears the word and immediately receives it with joy; yet he has no root in himself, but endures for a while, and when tribulation or persecution arises on account of the word, immediately he falls away. (RSV)

The correspondence between the adverbial use of εὐθύς and its synonyms εὐθέως ("immediately") and παραχρῆμα ("immediately") in Matthew, Luke, and Mark leads Riley to conclude, "When the word εὐθύς [in Mark] corresponds to an equivalent word in Matthew and/or Luke, it requires the sense of 'immediately.' When there is no corresponding word, the more natural translation [in Mark] is in almost every instance 'then.'"[114] Riley's point is similar to that which I made about the roles of εὐθύς in Chapter 3. The discourse marker is multifunctional in Mark. But his claim calls attention to another pattern in Synoptic redaction, namely, that

---

110. Matthew 4:20, 22; 8:3; 13:5; 14:22; 20:34; 26:49 (Neirynck, *Minor Agreements*, 274–75). With respect to the relationship between εὐθύς and εὐθέως, it is noteworthy that discourse markers are often a shortened or phonologically reduced form of their adverbial counterparts (Östman, "Symbiotic Relationship," 149; Schiffrin, *Discourse Markers*, 328).

111. Neirynck, *Minor Agreements*, 274–75.

112. There is one occurrence of εὐθύς in Lk. 6:49 that has no parallel in Mark. Matthew's five instances of a Markan εὐθύς are in Mt. 3:16; 13:20, 21; 14:27; 21:3.

113. This being the case, εὐθύς in Matthew and Luke is the homophonous adverbial counterpart to the discourse marker εὐθύς in Mark.

114. Riley, *Making of Mark*, 217.

Matthew and Luke do not object to the adverbial capacity of εὐθύς in Mark, but they do object to its discourse-sequencing role.

In conclusion, Matthew and Luke curb the repetition of εὐθύς in Mark. The word occurs far less frequently in the former two than the latter. More interestingly, though, Matthew's and Luke's patterns of redaction correspond to the unique functions of discourse markers in oral narrative. It is exactly those places where εὐθύς resembles oral patterns of discourse markers in Mark that Matthew and Luke remove the word. When it is employed in an adverbial sense, which is at home in both oral and written narrative, Matthew and Luke either retain εὐθύς or alter it to a more appropriate adverbial form, εὐθέως or παραχρῆμα.

This follows a pattern that we have seen emerging in Matthew's and Luke's editorial activity. The linguistic features that are most characteristic of oral storytelling found in Mark are not retained by the later Synoptic tradents. They make Mark's paratactic structure more complex, are less dependent on the imperfective aspect, modify or remove historical presents and the discourse marker εὐθύς, alter linguistic repetitions, and disrupt intercalations. By doing so, they write texts that read more literarily. Like the *a*-text family of *Joseph and Aseneth*, Matthew and Luke exhibit the "precision of verbalization" that is a mark of writing's editability.[115] They do so because they are products of different media and possess higher literary ambitions than Mark.

This is indicated not only by Matthew's and Luke's linguistic registers, but also by how each gospel begins. Texts frequently signal their generic affiliations and contents with their opening words. In the case of the Synoptics, we have three narratives that begin quite differently. In the following, I shall argue that Matthew and Luke declare that they are more "bookish" than Mark with their opening words. Just as the later Synoptics reveal their literary conception by their linguistic variance from Mark, so also do they suggest their differing media affiliations from their outset.

The media forms of the Synoptic Gospels

All three Synoptic Gospels contain what Gérard Genette has called *paratexts*.[116] Paratexts are the "thresholds" between discourse and audience that suggest how the former is to be received by the latter.[117] Under the wide umbrella of paratexts, Genette distinguishes between those that exist outside of the text itself, which he designates *epitexts*, and those that are around or within the text, which he calls *peritexts*.[118] It is Genette's latter concept that is applicable to the opening verses

---

115. Ong, *Orality and Literacy*, 103.
116. Genette, *Paratexts: Thresholds of Interpretation*, trans. J. E. Lewin; Lecture, Culture, Theory 20 (Cambridge: Cambridge University Press, 1997).
117. Ibid., 1–2.
118. Ibid., 4–5.

of the gospels. Peritexts are devices such as titles, prefaces, publisher's notes, dedications, and tables of contents that precede the body of the text itself.[119] They provide information about the text's production, content, and intended mode of reception. Aune employs Genette's theoretical concept in service of elucidating Matthew's and Mark's genre.[120] He argues that Mk 1:1 and Mt. 1:1 are "[para]textual clues that reflexively move the reader to apply a certain schema to their interpretation."[121] The schema, for Aune, is a generic one. On the basis of the gospels' peritexts and their content, he argues that Matthew is properly a Greco-Roman βίος ("biography") and Mark is a parody of the βίοι ("biographies").[122]

What is striking about the peritexts in all three Synoptic Gospels is that they divulge not only something about each narrative's generic affiliations, as Aune argues, but also their media affiliations. As to Mark and Matthew, neither a "gospel" (εὐαγγέλιον) nor a "book" (βίβλος) is a genre. These are media terms. The same can be said about Luke's first four verses, which serve as the narrative's preface. The mere presence of a preface in a discourse does not imply one genre or another.[123] But it does signify that a text is a literary product. Each Synoptic contains a peritext that hints at its media form. "Gospel" (εὐαγγέλιον) in Mark connotes something orally produced and proclaimed, while Matthew's opening titular sentence and Luke's preface suggest something more "bookish."

Mark's Gospel (εὐαγγέλιον)

Mark begins with the phrase ἀρχὴ τοῦ εὐαγγελίου Ἰησοῦ Χριστοῦ ("Beginning of the gospel of Jesus Christ"), which likely serves as a meta- or paratextual title for the entire narrative.[124] Four aspects of the incipit suggest that this is the case. First, ἀρχή ("beginning") is anatharous, making Mk 1:1 a nominative absolute.

---

119. Ibid., 16–343.
120. Aune, "Genre Theory," 145–75.
121. Ibid., 152.
122. Ibid., 166–73.
123. Rather, a discourse's genre affiliations are suggested by the *content* of the preface.
124. As Collins notes, "title" is somewhat of a misnomer, since the opening words of a document and its title proper may or may not be distinguished from one another (*Mark*, 87). By "title" I mean a textual indication that occurs at the beginning of the work suggesting what the text is and how it should be received. That Mk 1:1 serves as the title of Mark is the majority opinion in scholarship (Allen Wikgren, "ΑΡΧΗ ΤΟΥ ΕΥΑΓΓΕΛΙΟΥ," *JBL* 61 [1942]: 15–17; Pesch, *Markusevangelium*, 1:74–75; M. Eugene Boring, "Mark 1:1–15 and the Beginning of the Gospel," *Semeia* 52 [1990]: 50–51; John G. Cook, *The Structure and Persuasive Power of Mark: A Linguistic Approach*, SemeiaSt [Atlanta: Scholars Press, 1995], 138–40; Marcus, *Mark*, 1:143–46; France, *Gospel of Mark*, 50–51; Donahue and Harrington, *Gospel of Mark*, 60; M. Eugene Boring, *Mark: A Commentary*, NTL [Louisville: Westminster John Knox, 2006], 29; Collins, *Mark*, 130; Aune, "Genre Theory," 161–62).

Nominative absolutes frequently occur in introductory materials to texts.¹²⁵ Second, reminiscent of conventions for titles, the sentence is verbless.¹²⁶ Third, it was customary for Jewish texts to begin with an "independent titular sentence."¹²⁷ And fourth, Greek historians indicated what their subjects were by the opening words of their discourse.¹²⁸ By syntactical, medial, and generic counts, then, Mk 1:1 appears to be a peritextual title for the entire narrative.

If this is the case, Mark has employed the term εὐαγγέλιον to a written text in novel fashion. In the first century this word did not connote a literary genre as it would as soon as the second.¹²⁹ Nor did it designate something written at

---

125. Aune, following Wallace, claims that the phrase in Mk 1:1 is a nominative absolute (Aune, "Genre Theory," 162; Wallace, *Greek Grammar*, 49–51). From Wallace's perspective, the nominative absolute differs from the *casus pendens* insofar as the latter appears in a sentence and the former does not (*Greek Grammar*, 51). The nominative referent in the *casus pendens* is generally resumed later in the sentence in an oblique case (BDF §466). Moulton, following F. J. A. Hort, takes a similar perspective to Aune and Wallace, though he does not use the same nomenclature. He claims that sentences that serve as headings frequently have anatharous subjects, but he does not explicitly call Mk 1:1 a nominative absolute (*Prolegomena*, 82; Hort, *The Epistle of St. Peter 1:1–2:17* [London: Macmillan, 1898], 15). This is also J. K. Elliott's argument ("Mark 1.1–3—A Later Addition to the Gospel?" *NTS* 46 [2000]: 585). Whether or not nominative absolute is the most fitting label is less significant than the fact that anatharous nominative phrases often serve an independent, titular role. And so Marcus notes that the definite article is similarly absent in the titular constructions at the beginning of Hosea, Proverbs, the Songs of Solomon, Matthew, and Revelation (*Mark*, 1:141).

126. Boring, "Mark 1:1–15," 50–51; Eugene LaVerdiere, *The Beginning of the Gospel: Introducing the Gospel according to Mark*, vol. 1 (Collegeville: Liturgical Press, 1999), 4.

127. Davies and Allison, *Matthew*, 1:151. Ibid. (151–52) offers the following list of Jewish texts that begin with the titular convention: "Proverbs, Ecclesiastes, Canticales, Hosea, Amos, Joel, Nahum, Tobit, Baruch, the Community Rule, the War Rule, the *Testaments of the Twelve Patriarchs, Jubilees, 1 Enoch, 2 Enoch* (in some mss), the *Testament of Job*, and the *Apocalypse of Abraham*." To this list Collins adds Isaiah, Jeremiah, Obadiah, Habakkuk, Zephaniah, and Malachi (*Mark*, 132).

128. Alexander, *Preface*, 29.

129. How the term εὐαγγέλιον ("gospel") came to designate a literary genre is a subject of debate. Both Hans von Campenhausen and Helmut Koester argue that Marcion of Sinope is the innovator who first applied the label to a written text (von Campenhausen, *The Formation of the Christian Bible* [Philadelphia: Fortress, 1972], 157–60, 170–77; Koester, *Ancient Christian Gospels: Their History and Development* [Philadelphia: Trinity Press International, 1990], 35–36). According to them, Marcion mistook Paul's phrase "my gospel" (εὐαγγέλιόν μου) in Rom. 2:16 as a reference to Luke and began to use the literary designation in protest against the oral traditions that were authoritative for his contemporaries (Koester, *Ancient Christian Gospels*, 36). James A. Kelhoffer and Michael F. Bird have each critiqued this position, arguing that εὐαγγέλιον refers to a literary genre in texts that antedate Marcion (Kelhoffer, "'How Soon a Book' Revisited: EUANGELION

all. Gerhard Friedrich notes that the substantive derives from the term messenger (εὐάγγελος) and so εὐαγγέλιον is "that which is proper to an εὐάγγελος," namely orally proclaimed news, the reward given to a messenger for bringing news, or sacrifices made in celebration of an announcement.[130] In Greco-Roman literature, forms of εὐαγγέλιον and εὐαγγελίζομαι consistently refer to messages that are news themselves and to sacrifices performed in celebration of a message delivered.[131] Similarly, in the LXX the verbal form translates בשר ("to proclaim good news"), and the nominal form בשרה ("good news"), which has a semantic range similar to the Greco-Roman εὐαγγέλιον, indicating either news or a reward offered to the מבשר ("messenger") for bringing good news.[132] Philo and Josephus attest to these standard meanings of εὐαγγελ—root words in the Hellenistic period, as they always relate both the

---

as a Reference to 'Gospel' Materials in the First Half of the Second Century," *ZNW* 95 [2004]: 1–34; Bird, *The Gospel of the Lord: How the Early Church Wrote the Story of Jesus* [Grand Rapids: Eerdmans, 2014], 266–69). They both hypothesize that an earlier copyist or bookseller of Matthew misinterpreted Mark's incipit as a literary designation and applied it to Matthew (Kelhoffer, "How Soon?" 31; Bird, *Gospel*, 258–59). In my opinion, their primary source evidence against von Campenhausen's and Koester's case is strong, but their theory about how "gospel" became a generic appellation is unconvincing. It is more likely that when Mark transferred the oral gospel tradition into the written medium, he also widened the semantic range of the term. "Gospel," in Christian circles, came to designate the message about the life, death, and resurrection of Jesus in multiple media forms.

130. Friedrich, "εὐαγγελίζομαι, εὐαγγέλιον, προευαγγελίζομαι, εὐαγγελιστής," *TDNT* 2:721–22; John P. Dickson, "Gospel as News: Εὐαγγελ—from Aristophanes to the Apostle Paul," *NTS* 51 (2005): 212–13.

131. The latter is the case in Xenophon's *Hellenica* 1.6.36, wherein Eteonicus spuriously "sacrifices the good tidings" (ἔθυε τὰ εὐαγγέλια) at the Battle of Arginusae. Similarly, in Diodorus Siculus's *The Library of History* 15.74.2.3, an entrepreneurial εὐάγγελος hastily departs from Athens to Syracuse to be the first to offer Dionysius the good news that his tragedy had been victorious at Lenaea. Not only is the messenger rewarded, but Dionysius "was himself so overjoyed that he sacrificed to the gods for the good tidings [τοῖς θεοῖς εὐαγγέλια θύσας] and instituted a drinking bout and great feasts" (Sherman, LCL). In Plutarch's *Pompeius* 66.3, Pompey's allies prematurely declare to Cornelia the good news that the war had come to an end (εὐαγγελιζόμενοι πέρας ἔχειν τὸν πόλεμον). Dickson ("Gospel," 213) offers other examples of nominal and verbal forms of the εὐαγγελ—root that relate to military and imperial news, including Lycurgus, *Against Leocrates*, 1.18; Demosthenes, *On the Crown*, 18.323; Plutarch, *Sertorius*, 11.4; Plutarch, *Phocian*, 23.4; Plutarch, *Moralia*, 347.D; Chariton, *Callirhoe*, 8.2.5; Philostratus, *Life of Apollonius*, 8.27.2; Philostratus, *Lives of the Sophists*, 1.508.14. Further examples in Bird, *Gospel*, 6–7.

132. Bird, *Gospel*, 9–11. The nominal form εὐαγγελία appears in 2 Sam. 18:20, 22, 25, 27; 2 Kgs 7:9, and the verbal form occurs in 1 Sam. 31:9; 2 Sam. 1:20; 4:10; 18:19-20, 26, 31; 1 Kgs 1:42; 1 Chr 10:9; Ps. 39:10; 67:12; 95:2; Sol 11:1; Joel 3:5; Nah. 2:1; Isa. 40:9; 52:7; 60:6; 61:1; Jer. 20:15.

nominal and verbal forms to proclaimed news.[133] NT writers also follow this pattern.[134] As Friedrich puts it, "In the NT εὐαγγέλιον is oral preaching."[135] In short, εὐαγγέλιον ("gospel") was originally "something of a media term" concerned with orally proclaimed news in Greco-Roman literature, the LXX, Philo, Josephus, and the NT.[136] Mark 1:1 seems to diverge from this consistent pattern by designating a written text a εὐαγγέλιον.

But Mark's use of the term does not appear aberrant if, as I have argued, the narrative exists at the borderland between orality and textuality. The εὐαγγέλιον referenced in Mark's title is the orally proclaimed preaching about Jesus that has been committed to writing. Oral proclamation is thus the content of Mark's written medium.[137] Mark offers a glimpse into the beginning stages of the Jesus tradition's media transference from orally proclaimed message to written text. This is not to imply that Mark puts an end to oral traditions about Jesus.[138] Rather,

---

133. In Philo's *On the Life of Joseph* 245, Joseph encourages his brothers to return to their father to report the good news of his discovery (αὐτῷ τὰ περὶ τῆς ἐμῆς εὑρέσεως εὐαγγελίσασθαι). In *On Dreams* 2.281, Philo writes that the death of the Egyptians on the shores of the Red Sea "announces three beautiful things to the soul" (τρία δ᾽ εὐαγγελίζεται τῇ ψυχῇ τὰ κάλλιστα). Josephus shows a similar pattern. Dickson notes that all sixteen instances of εὐαγγελ—in Josephus similarly "connote the telling of news" ("Gospel," 216).

134. Friedrich, *TDNT* 2:727–35; Dickson, "Gospel," 220–23. The nominal form frequently appears with verbs of speaking and hearing. For instance, all four Matthean occurrences of the εὐαγγέλιον are the object of κηρύσσω (Mt. 4:23; 9:35; 24:14; 26:12), a verb that most often connotes public pronouncement (BDAG, s.v. "κηρύσσω"). In Acts 15:6 the nominal form is similarly in a genitive construction indicating the kind of word (λόγον) that was heard (ἀκοῦσαι). In the Pauline corpus, εὐαγέλλιον co-occurs with verbs of proclamation and hearing in 1 Cor. 9:14, 17; 15:1; 2 Cor. 11:7; Gal. 1:10; Eph. 1:13; Col. 1:5, 23; 1 Thess. 2:2, 9; 2 Thess. 1:8.

135. Friedrich, *TDNT* 2:735; Annette Yoshiko Reed, "Εὐαγγέλιον: Orality, Textuality, and the Christian Truth in Irenaeus' *Adversus Haereses*," *VC* 56 (2002): 15.

136. Dickson, "Gospel," 213. Similarly, Kristina Dronsch and Annette Weissenrieder write, "The etymology of εὐαγγέλιον indicates that it functions as a medium" ("A Theory of the Message for the New Testament Writings or Communicating the Words of Jesus: From Angelos to Euangelion," in Weissenrieder and Coote, *Interface*, 223).

137. McLuhan writes, "The 'content' of any medium is always another medium. The content of writing is speech, just as the written word is the content of print, and print is the content of the telegraph" (*Understanding Media*, 8). In the case of Mk 1:1, the peritextual title is self-conscious about this phenomenon.

138. Parker argues that oral Jesus traditions did not end when written ones began (*Living Text*, 210). He suggests that we should "think instead of an oral tradition extending unbroken from the lips and actions of Jesus [to the present], since people have never stopped talking about the things he said and did. Sometimes the oral tradition has been influenced by the written tradition, and sometimes the influence has been in the opposite

the gospel opens a new media vista by orally transferring these traditions into a different modality.¹³⁹ Mark is a written text insofar as the narrative exists in manuscript form. But the fact that this written narrative commends itself as an oral phenomenon in its title and remains residually oral throughout shows that it has not abandoned the oral lifeworld altogether. Mark is a link between orality and textuality, orally produced and aurally received when the writing is reactivated in performance.¹⁴⁰

Matthew's book (βίβλος)

Matthew similarly begins with an incipit that serves as a title for the entire narrative.¹⁴¹ But he employs a "more conventional literary term" than Mark, βίβλος ("book").¹⁴² This word and its Hebrew equivalent, ספר, frequently

---

direction. The written and oral tradition have accompanied, affected and followed one another" (ibid.).

139. As Keith puts it, "If Mark's gospel was anything in the ancient Christian media world, it was not the oral tradition's Grim Reaper but rather the catalyst for a new genre that harnessed the technology of writing and manuscripts in, at times, unprecedented ways" (Keith, "Prolegomena," 163).

140. This is similar to the perspective that both Dronsch and Weissenrieder and Keith adopt on the textualization of Mark. The former argue that the gospel (εὐαγγέλιον) is a message that connects the absent Jesus with the Christian community in the act of performance (Dronsch and Weissenrieder, "Theory," 222–28). Keith argues that Jan Assmann's *zerdehnte Situation* ("extended situation") is the most apt methodological framework for understanding Mark's textualization ("Prolegomena," 170–81). For Assmann, by creating an "extended situation," a written tradition escapes the confines of copresence inherent to oral tradition ("Form as Mnemonic Device," 77). By transferring the oral-performative tradition about Jesus into the written medium, Mark created a *zerdehnte Situation* that "extended the audience of his Gospel beyond the limits of interpersonal communication" (Keith, "Prolegomena," 178).

141. Those that argue that Mt. 1:1 is the title of the entire narrative include Davies and Allison, (*Matthew*, 1:149–55), Jack D. Kingsbury (*Matthew: Structure, Christology, Kingdom* [Philadelphia: Fortress, 1975], 10 n. 54), Boring ("Mark 1:1–15," 50–51), Dale C. Allison (*Studies in Matthew: Interpretation Past and Present* [Grand Rapids: Baker Academic, 2005], 157–62), Luz (*Matthew*, 1:69), and Aune ("Genre Theory," 171). The strongest arguments for this position are as follows: (1) it follows literary convention (Davies and Allison, *Matthew*, 1:151–52); (2) like Mk 1:1, the opening verse of Matthew is verbless and βίβλος anatharous; and (3) "book" or "papyrus" was the primary meaning of βίβλος in the NT and the patristic period (ibid., 151; Luz, *Matthew*, 1:69).

142. Aune, *New Testament*, 17. In its entirety Mt. 1:1 serves as the title and reads βίβλος γενέσεως Ἰησοῦ Χριστοῦ υἱοῦ Δαυὶδ υἱοῦ Ἀβραάμ ("The Book of the Genesis of Jesus Christ, Son of David, Son of Abraham").

introduce Jewish texts both antecedent to and contemporary with Matthew.[143] Moreover, Matthew's first two words, βίβλος γενέσεως ("book of the genealogy," RSV), mirror a phrase that appears in Gen. 2:4 and 5:1, likely associating the First Gospel with that text of Jewish Scripture.[144] By calling the narrative a βίβλος ("book"), Matthew has placed it into a category of written literature that has "biblical-like importance."[145]

Designating the narrative a book was not necessarily an obvious choice. Matthew has chosen to omit εὐαγγέλιον ("gospel") from his predecessor's incipit and newly describe his text. Genette states that authors chose peritextual labels to the exclusion of others.[146] The implication is that Matthew found βίβλος ("book") to be a more suitable designation than εὐαγγέλιον ("gospel"). The most likely reason is that the latter had not yet come to designate authoritative traditions about Jesus as it would in the second century.[147] Matthew understood Mark's peritextual title to connote orally proclaimed news, and he did not consider this an apposite designation for what he himself was writing.[148] Matthew might not have objected to gospel as a designation for Mark, but he found the incipit inapplicable for his own text because he was producing something for a different mode of reception.[149]

---

143. Davies and Allison (*Matthew*, 1:152) list Nah. 1:1; Tob. 1:1; Bar. 1:1; T. Job 1:1; Apoc. Ab.; 2 Esd 1:1-3; *Sepher Ha-Razim* 1 as examples of texts that begin with βίβλος or ספר.

144. The first book of Jewish Scripture had come to be known as Γένεσις ("Genesis") by the time Matthew wrote (Philo, *Abr.* 1; *Post.* 127; *Aet.* 19; Davies and Allison, *Matthew*, 1:151; Craig A. Evans, "'The Book of the Genesis of Jesus Christ': The Purpose of Matthew in Light of the Incipit," in *Biblical Interpretation in Early Christian Gospels*, ed. Thomas R. Hatina, vol. 2: *The Gospel of Matthew*, LNTS 310 [New York: T&T Clark, 2008], 66). Thus, "Matthew almost certainly intended to set up the story of Jesus as a counterpart to the story of Genesis" (Davies and Allison, *Matthew*, 1:151).

145. Luz, *Matthew*, 1:70. J. Andrew Doole similarly argues that by calling his text a βίβλος Matthew has evoked other βίβλοι, namely scripture, and attempts to set his narrative on par with them (*What Was Mark for Matthew? An Examination of Matthew's Relationship and Attitude to His Primary Source*, WUNT 2/344 [Tübingen: Mohr Siebeck, 2013], 182).

146. Genette, *Paratexts*, 12.

147. Aune, "Genre Theory," 172.

148. As Doole puts it, "Mark was written to be heard, and one can announce a εὐαγγέλιον ... while one cannot announce a βίβλος" (*What was Mark?*, 182).

149. Joanna Dewey suggests that Mark will have taken an hour and a half to two hours to read and that this was a customary duration for performances ("The Gospel of Mark as an Oral/Aural Event: Implications for Interpretation," in eadem, *Oral Ethos*, 95). Luz determines that Matthew takes four hours to read in its entirety and that this makes it unlikely that it was meant to be heard or read in one sitting (*Matthew*, 1:8). Instead, he proposes that the narrative would have been experienced in sections (ibid., 9). If Dewey and Luz are correct, then it appears that Mark and Matthew were experienced differently and even produced for unique purposes.

Luke's historical prologue

Luke similarly diverges from Mark's opening words, likely for the same reason as Matthew. Luke's Gospel signals its media affiliation not with an incipit, but a prologue. Prologues were conventions that began texts from a variety of Hellenistic literary genres, including historiography, scientific treatises, novels, and biographies.[150] Luke 1:1-4 shows an affinity with this literary trope in three ways. First, these verses are stylistically set off from the rest of the gospel. The prologue is, like its Hellenistic counterparts, written in an elevated style.[151] It consists of a single, well-balanced periodic sentence.[152] Second, Luke's introduction contains most of the elements that were standard in prefaces.[153] And third, these first four verses of the gospel teem with technical terms characteristic of literary prologues.[154]

By introducing the narrative in this way, the Gospel of Luke declares itself literature.[155] What kind of literature is debated. History and historiography are usually considered the most likely candidates.[156] In this vein, Luke's prologue is commonly compared with sections from Josephus's prefaces in *J.W.* 1.17 and *Ag.*

---

150. John Nolland, *Luke*, 3 vols., WBC 35A–35C (Dallas: Word Books, 1989), 1:4–5; Mikeal C. Parsons, *Luke*, Paideia Commentaries on the New Testament (Grand Rapids: Baker Academic, 2015), 25.

151. Fitzmyer, *Luke*, 1:288; Nolland, *Luke*, 1:4.

152. Three phrases constitute the protasis and each is paralleled by one of another three in the apodosis (Fitzmyer, *Luke*, 1:288).

153. Parsons (*Luke*, 25–26) argues that Lk. 1:1-4 contains six of the seven elements commonly found in Hellenistic literary prologues: (1) a statement about the author's predecessors; (2) an indication of the work's subject matter; (3) an inventory of the writer's qualifications; (4) a plan for the work's arrangement; (5) a statement of the writing's purpose; and (6) the addressee's name. The only characteristic of literary prefaces absent from Luke is the name of the author.

154. ἐπειδήπερ, ἀνατάσσομαι, διήγησις, and αὐτόπτης are all *hapax legomena* in the NT. Though not *hapax legomena*, ἐπεχειρέω, καθεξῆς, and κράτιστος appear in only Luke or Acts. These terms and others in Lk. 1:1-4 have been found to be characteristic of Hellenistic literary conventions of prologues by Fitzmyer (*Luke*, 1:290–301), I. J. Du Plessis ("Once More: The Purpose of Luke's Prologue [Lk 1:1-4]," *NovT* 16 [1974]: 259–71), Richard J. Dillon ("Previewing Luke's Project from His Prologue [Luke 1:1-4]," *CBQ* 43 [1981]: 205–27), and Alexander (*Preface*, 106–42).

155. von Campenhausen, *Formation*, 124; W. C. van Unnik, "Once More St. Luke's Prologue," *Neot* 7 (1973): 12; Klaus Wengst, *Pax Romana and the Peace of Jesus Christ*, trans. John Bowden (London: SCM, 1987), 101; Aune, *New Testament*, 116; Nolland, *Luke*, 1:5.

156. Many have followed the influential work of Henry J. Cadbury, who compared Luke-Acts to Hellenistic historiographical and biographical literature and found that it had more affinities with the former than the latter ("Commentary on the Preface of Luke," in *The Beginnings of Christianity: Part I, The Acts of the Apostles*, ed. F. J. Foakes-Jackson and Kirsopp Lake, 5 vols. [London: Macmillan, 1922], 2:489–510; idem, *The Making of Luke-Acts* [New York: Macmillan, 1927]).

Ap. 1.1–18.[157] The former is especially relevant, as it contains many of the technical terms found in Lk. 1:1-4.[158] But Loveday Alexander has contested the consensus that Luke belongs to a historical genre and that Josephus's prologues are the most relevant analogues to Luke's.[159] She acknowledges Lk. 1:1-4's relationship to the prologues in Josephus and other Jewish historians, but suggests that it is a "lateral relationship of siblings or cousins," rather than a maternal or paternal one.[160] There are many members in the Greek preface kinship-group, and Luke's closest ties are to "scientific literature" and "technical prose" (*Fachprosa*).[161] For this reason, the gospel is an "immediate link in to a large and neglected area of 'middlebrow' literature of the first century AD."[162] This middlebrow literature was varied in content but singular in function. It was employed with respect to a "living teaching tradition" that came in a variety of forms, some closer to oral lectures and others to written literature.[163] Luke recasts Mark's more oral Jesus tradition in a literary form, which is indicated as soon as the opening words of the prologue. The Third Gospel moves away from oral storytelling and toward written literature.

Thus both Matthew and Luke signify from their outset that they are something different from Mark. All three Synoptic Gospels provide their audiences with peritextual clues about their medium. Mark informs its readers that it is a εὐαγγέλιον, an "orally proclaimed message," about Jesus Christ. Matthew and Luke both eschew the oral implication of Mark's incipit. Matthew designates his work a βίβλος, a "book" about Jesus Christ the son of David, the Son of Abraham. Luke employs a literary convention to express the "bookishness" of his text. He writes (γράψαι) a narrative (διήγησιν) about events that have been fulfilled (περὶ τῶν πεπληροφορημένων ἐν ἡμῖν πραγμάτων).

What the later gospel tradents promise with their opening salvos, they fulfill in their texts. As we have seen, both Matthew and Luke consistently literaturized

---

157. Nolland, *Luke*, 1:4–5; Aune, *New Testament*, 121.

158. The words ἐπείδηπερ, πολύς, συνετάσσομαι, and μετ᾽ ἀκριβείας all appear in close proximity in Josephus's *J.W.* 1.17.

159. Alexander, *Preface*.

160. Ibid., 166–67. She addresses the similarities between Lk. 1:1-4 and prefaces in the likes of 2 Macc., Philo, Josephus, the *Letter of Aristeas*, and Ben Sira, concluding that these Hellenistic Jewish authors, as well as Luke, are influenced by Greek preface-writing conventions independently of each other (ibid., 147–67).

161. Loveday Alexander, "Luke's Preface in the Context of Greek Preface-Writing," *NovT* 28 (1986): 48–74; eadem, *Preface*, esp. 102–42. For Alexander, "scientific literature" does not connote science in opposition to the arts and humanities, but something akin to the German *wissenschaftlich* (*Preface*, 21).

162. Alexander, "Luke's Preface," 60.

163. Alexander, *Preface*, 204–10; eadem, "Luke's Preface," 69. By analogy to oral folk literature, she argues that Luke would be a "new performance" of the tradition that he has received (*Preface*, 209).

those stylistic features of Mark that are residually oral. By doing so, they take the oral gospel tradition that Mark first put into writing and make it better conform to literary norms. Εὐαγγέλιον, which had initially been a media term, came, by means of Matthew's and Luke's literaturization, to be about content. Within a few decades the word would be identified with the message about Jesus's life, death, ministry, and resurrection in a variety of media, both oral and written. The seeds for this semantic growth were sown in the Synoptic Gospels themselves.

CONCLUSION

In his influential monograph, *Readers and Reading Culture in the High Roman Empire*, William A. Johnson offers what he calls a simple proposition: "The reading of different types of texts makes for different types of reading events."[1] The proposition presumes the obvious, yet overlooked, fact that there are different types of texts in Greco-Roman antiquity. In the preceding chapters I have argued that Mark and *Joseph and Aseneth* are similar kinds of texts. They are textualized oral narratives. Both existed as oral traditions and were subsequently committed to the textual medium via dictation. The narratives represent one way that orality and textuality interface in early Judaism and Christianity.

I have made this case on the basis of the linguistic and metalinguistic characteristics that Mark and *Joseph and Aseneth* share with each other and with oral literature. Concerning their shared linguistic qualities, both narratives are paratactically structured by idea units connected with καί, minimally employ other connectives, are repetitive at the lexical, ideological, and thematic levels, and frequently use verbs that are imperfective in aspect and indicative in mood. Concerning their metalinguistic features, both Mark and *Joseph and Aseneth* were freely altered by later tradents. *Joseph and Aseneth* is characterized by macro-level fluidity and a performance attitude was taken toward the written versions of the narrative. Mark exhibits microlevel fluidity and was the object of emendation by later tradents who added new endings to the narrative or, in the case of Matthew and Luke, incorporated Mark's material into their new texts. Mark and *Joseph and Aseneth* are also similar as to their echoic intertextuality. They recall traditions by evoking key themes and lexemes, rather than embedding antecedent texts into their narrative verbatim.

By arguing that Mark and *Joseph and Aseneth* are textualized oral narratives, I have in many ways been more concerned with the process of these texts' creation than with the products themselves. This has not been a sustained study of specific exegetical issues in Mark or *Joseph and Aseneth*. By focusing on the process, I have been more invested in the medium than in the message. But if the medium is indeed the message, as McLuhan influentially claims, then freshly

---

1. Johnson, *Readers*, 11.

considering the process of composition will necessarily affect how one interprets the product.[2]

To that end, I wish to conclude by drawing out exegetical results that have been reached with respect to *Joseph and Aseneth* and Mark over the course of this investigation. I'd also like to extract interpretive effects that have not been fully developed here but might be fruitful areas of inquiry for subsequent media-critical work on these texts.

Results of reading Joseph and Aseneth *as a textualized oral narrative*

Recognizing that *Joseph and Aseneth* is an oral tradition textualized via dictation produces the following results. First, Aseneth's name change in *Jos. Asen.* 15:6 makes better sense if the narrative has a storied tradition behind it.[3] In this verse, the angel tells Aseneth that her name will no longer be Aseneth but "City of Refuge" (πόλις καταφυγῆς). The "problem" of the name change is that the pun is completely lost in the Greek version of the narrative and the protagonist is never called "City of Refuge" again in the text. In earlier interpretations of *Joseph and Aseneth*, the missing pun was taken as evidence for a lost Semitic *Vorlage*.[4] But presently the overwhelming consensus is that *Joseph and Aseneth* was first written in Greek. This begs a question: How does an Aramaic or Hebrew wordplay work itself into a Greek text? If the narrative is a textualized oral tradition, the answer is simple: The wordplay was a constituent element of the tradition not to be discarded when it was committed to the written, Greek medium. The tradition began in one language but was continued and given permanence via writing in another.[5]

Second, the long-standing debate over the priority of the long and short recensions of *Joseph and Aseneth* is reframed by the perspective I have outlined. Past debates about "originality" might be reconsidered and the quest for the narrative's Ur-text abandoned. This has already proved itself a trend in recent *Joseph and Aseneth* scholarship.[6] Considering the tradition as pluriform and

---

2. McLuhan, *Understanding Media*, 1–18.

3. I have addressed the name change at greater length in Elder, "On Transcription," 140–41.

4. Chesnutt lists the various Semitic reconstructions that have been proposed for the wordplay (*From Death to Life*, 70). He concludes that these illustrate how much uncertainty surrounds the pun and suggests a Jewish author exploited the etymological possibility of the wordplay in Aramaic or Hebrew but wrote *Joseph and Aseneth* in Greek (ibid.).

5. Wire notes that this commonly happens with oral traditions (*Case*, 61–62).

6. Kraemer concludes *Aseneth* by expressing her dissatisfaction with the search for the "original" text, as she believes that that endeavor obscures how each version of the tradition is significant in its own right (*Aseneth*, 305). As discussed in Chapter 4, Ahearne-Kroll concerns herself with the fixed-yet-fluid nature of *Joseph and Aseneth*

each instantiation of it as equiprimordial provides firmer theoretical ground to build upon. If *Joseph and Aseneth* was an oral narrative textualized via dictation then it is not so surprising that a performance attitude was taken toward the earliest textual distillations of the tradition. *Joseph and Aseneth*'s antecedent oral tradition provided the impetus for the attitude taken toward the written tradition.

Third, *Joseph and Aseneth*'s relationship to the novels is clarified by understanding it as a textualized oral tradition. In Chapter 4, I argued that the pseudepigraphon evokes tropes and themes from the romance novels. However, differences in length and style make it certain that *Joseph and Aseneth* is not properly a novel.[7] That is, the narrative was not conceived as the novels were. With his tongue firmly in his cheek, B. E. Perry famously claims, "The first romance was deliberately planned and written by an individual author, its inventor. He conceived it on a Tuesday afternoon in July, or some other day or month of the year."[8] According to Perry the novel was first created by a single literary genius and not by a slow and steady merging of genres. In this line of thinking, each subsequent novel was, in a manner similar to the first novel, composed by individual literary artists.[9] Each text had an original written version. This does not appear to be the case with the developmental and compositional processes of *Joseph and Aseneth*. Nonetheless, *Joseph and Aseneth* originated in a context where the novels were popular and so took on novelistic topoi. Because the narrative existed in a different medium and was orally conceived, it does not display the psychodynamics of writing to the extent the novels do nor does it approach them in length. Differing media generate these dissimilarities between *Joseph and Aseneth* and the ideal novels, despite their similarities in theme.

Fourth, *Joseph and Aseneth* shares a hitherto unnoticed structural similarity with Mark, namely, intercalations. In Markan scholarship, these "sandwiches"

and abandons the search for an original version of the narrative in favor of a "well-defined fabula" ("Jewish Identity," 81–83). This method has recently been praised by Standhartinger ("Recent Research," 362) and Hicks-Keeton ("Rewritten Gentiles," 110–11). The perspective I have taken here is indebted to both Kraemer's and Ahearne-Kroll's. It carries theirs forward by clarifying the media dynamics that are at work in the tradition.

7. *Joseph and Aseneth*, at 8,320 words in Philonenko's reconstruction, is about half the length of the shortest of the novels, *Ephesian Tale*, which is about 15,000 words (Wills, *Jewish Novel*, 27). Chariton's *Callirhoe*, which is the second shortest novel at about 35,000 words, is four times longer than *Joseph and Aseneth*, and the longest, Heliodorus's *Ethiopica*, is almost ten times longer at around 80,000 words (ibid.).

8. B. E. Perry, *The Ancient Romances: A Literary-Historical Account of Their Origins*, Sather Classical Lectures 37 (Berkeley: University of California Press, 1967), 175.

9. For example, Stefan Tilg writes that Xenophon's Ephesiaca "is too literary a text to regard as a direct outgrowth of oral folklore" (*Chariton of Aphrodisias and the Invention of the Greek Love Novel* [Oxford: Oxford University Press, 2010], 87).

have long been recognized and the form helps interpreters determine where the emphasis falls in a pericope. This is also the case with the A^1-B^1-B^2-A^2 intercalation in *Joseph and Aseneth* 27–29 examined in Chapter 3. A^1 and A^2, which narrate Benjamin's battle with and subsequent non-retaliatory action toward Pharaoh's son, flank and mirror Aseneth's battle with and pacifistic response to the sons of Bilhah and Zilpah in B^1 and B^2. Edwards notes that in Mark, "the middle story nearly always provides the key to the theological purpose of the sandwich" and "the insertion interprets the flanking halves."[10] This is precisely the case with the intercalation in *Joseph and Aseneth* 27–29. Benjamin's actions in the outer segments are directly informed by Aseneth's actions in the middle story, which serves to propagate *Joseph and Aseneth*'s non-retaliatory ideal. Benjamin's battle is meant to be heard in conjunction with Aseneth's.

Finally, there are a few ways in which treating *Joseph and Aseneth* as a textualized oral tradition might affect readings of the narrative that have not been explicitly addressed here. First, the perspective can contribute to gender studies of the narrative. Much recent scholarship has focused on the construction of gender in *Joseph and Aseneth*.[11] Kraemer has even entertained the idea that the feminine concerns found in *Joseph and Aseneth* imply female authorship.[12] Yet this argument is hampered by female literacy rates in antiquity.[13] Those investigating

10. Edwards, "Markan Sandwiches," 196.

11. Some studies claim that *Joseph and Aseneth* is conducive to feminist readings. For example, Susan Elizabeth Hogan Doty argues that Aseneth's actions and words subvert the "male word" that controls much of her life toward the beginning of the story ("From Ivory Tower to City of Refuge: The Role and Function of the Protagonist in 'Joseph and Aseneth' and Related Narratives" [PhD diss., The Iliff School of Theology and University of Denver, 1989], 197–98). Similarly, Pervo suggests that *Joseph and Aseneth* possesses feminist characteristics ("Aseneth and Her Sisters: Women in Jewish Narrative and in the Greek Novels," in Levine, *"Women Like This,"* 148–55). In another line of feminist interpretation of the narrative, Standhartinger and Kraemer have concerned themselves with how gender is constructed in the different versions of *Joseph and Aseneth*. Both argue that the longer version presents a more patriarchal perspective than the shorter one (Standhartinger, *Frauenbild*, 225–37; idem, "Fictional Text," 314–15; Kraemer, *Aseneth*, 206–10).

12. Kraemer, "Women's Authorship," 232–42. Though she later adopted a more agnostic approach about the author's gender (*Aseneth*, 216).

13. According to Harris, female literacy rates will have been lower than male literacy rates throughout most periods and locations in the Greco-Roman world (*Ancient Literacy*, 22–24). Kraemer names two other obstacles that female production and transmission of texts in antiquity will have faced. First, for a woman to compose a narrative, she would need to have had the education, financial resources, and leisure to do so. These were not as close at hand for women as they were for men (Kraemer,

either the construction of gender in the narrative or the gender of the author have assumed that *Joseph and Aseneth* is a literary text created by a single writer. But if the narrative is an oral tradition textualized by dictation, then this ought to recast questions about the production and transmission of the narrative regarding gender. There is ample evidence for female storytelling traditions in antiquity and at least one modern folkloristic study finds that male storytellers are far less likely than female storytellers to feature a female main character.[14] The textualized-oral-narrative perspective makes it more probable that a female voice or female voices influence *Joseph and Aseneth*.

The theory argued here also opens new avenues for reconsidering the purpose of *Joseph and Aseneth*. A distinction ought to be made between the intent for which the tradition first came into being and for which it was textualized. As to the former, no shortage of interpretations has been offered.[15] An oral hermeneutic does not necessarily support one proposed purpose over the others. Concerning the latter, Wire claims that there are at least three reasons an oral tradition is transferred to the written medium: (1) There is a power struggle in the community and that writing can validate a certain version of a tradition to serve one particular

---

"Women's Authorship," 239–42). Second, works authored by women, if they were identified as such, were less likely to be transmitted and copied by scribes steeped in ancient and medieval patriarchy (ibid., 241). Kraemer concludes that Jewish and Christian women probably did write texts in the Greco-Roman period, but that these were mostly lost or only preserved under the guises of pseudonymity or anonymity (ibid., 242).

14. Alex Scobie has collected a wealth of primary source evidence for storytelling and storytellers in Greco-Roman antiquity ("Storytellers, Storytelling, and the Novel in Graeco-Roman Antiquity," *Rheinisches Museum für Philologie* 122 [1979]: 229–59). And Virginia Burrus adduces primary source evidence to the ubiquity of female storytellers in this context (*Chastity as Autonomy: Women in the Stories of Apocryphal Acts*, Studies in Women and Religion 23 [Lewiston: Mellen, 1987], 70–72). With respect to female main characters in stories told by men and women, Margaret Mills's study found that only 11% of tales told by males had a female main character, whereas 49% of tales told by females had a female main character ("Sex Role Reversals, Sex Changes, and Transvestite Disguise in the Oral Tradition of a Conservative Muslim Community in Afghanistan," in *Women's Folklore, Women's Culture*, ed. Rosan A. Jordan and Susan J. Kalcik, Publications of the American Folklore Society 8 [Philadelphia: University of Pennsylvania Press, 1985], 187).

15. From rewritten Bible based on Gen. 41:45 (Docherty, "Joseph and Aseneth") to a typological foundation myth for the Oniad temple at Heliopolis (Bohak, *Joseph and Aseneth*) to a Christian allegorical interpretation of Jesus and the Church (Nir, *Joseph and Aseneth*), the purpose for which the narrative was written is one topic on which there is little consensus.

group's interest;[16] (2) an oral tradition might be textualized in response to some great crisis;[17] and (3) a tradition comes into contact with social circumstances where writing benefits it in one way or another.[18] The third reason seems most likely for *Joseph and Aseneth*.[19] Textualization afforded at least two advantages to the narrative: It acquired physical permanence as well as geographic and chronological portability. Audiences did not have to wait for a new telling of the story to experience it. They could read it themselves, if they possessed the skill, or they could have it read to or performed for them. And, second, the tale could be disseminated more widely.

Finally, the textualized-oral-narrative perspective might influence theories about *Joseph and Aseneth*'s Jewish or Christian authorship.[20] Recently, Robert A. Kraft has suggested that the "default position" for the composition of pseudepigraphical texts ought to be Christian, since nearly every pseudepigraphon was transmitted by Christians.[21] From this default position, interpreters can work backward toward a text's origins, whether they be Jewish or Christian.[22] In some cases, Jewish composition will be concluded upon further consideration. Even in these cases the texts are Christian insofar as they were transmitted and read by Christians.[23] In Kraft's words, "Sources transmitted by way of Christian communities are 'Christian,' whatever else they might be."[24] Even if *Joseph and Aseneth* was initially a Jewish tradition, it became a Christian one when transmitted by Christians. A media-sensitive approach that recognizes the tradition's equiprimordiality and multiformity can affirm that both Christianity *and* Judaism received and affected the narrative in its various forms. With Collins, I find the narrative's central concerns Jewish, suggesting

---

16. Ibid., 48. This is precisely Kelber's theory about the composition of Mark's gospel. The oral tradition was put into writing in order to silence the living voice of the gospel tradition (*Oral and the Written Gospel*, 90–131).

17. Wire, *Case*, 48.

18. Ibid., 48–49.

19. The first two are specifically concerned with traditions that are formative for social groups. It is difficult to imagine that our narrative was the central story that a social group constructed its identity around.

20. A number of studies extensively review the history and present state of research on the question of Jewish or Christian provenance: Chesnutt, *From Death to Life*, 23–64, 76–80; Nir, *Joseph and Aseneth*, 4–7; Standhartinger, "Recent Research," 367–71. These all reveal that the debate about Jewish and Christian authorship has been, until recently, dichotomous.

21. Robert A. Kraft, "The Pseudepigrapha and Christianity, Revisited: Setting the Stage and Framing some Central Questions," in idem, *Exploring the Scripturesque: Jewish Texts and Their Christian Contexts*, JSJSup 137 (Leiden: Brill, 2009), 36–37.

22. Ibid., 27–33.

23. Ibid., 36.

24. Ibid.

that this was its originating context.²⁵ All the same, there is much in the narrative that will have been amenable to Christian allegorical interpretation, such as titles attributed to Joseph in the narrative and the bread, cup, and ointment sequences in *Joseph and Aseneth* 8 and 15.²⁶ An oral hermeneutic supports the

---

25. According to Collins, the fact that intermarriage is a particularly Jewish concern in the Second Temple period is most telling of *Joseph and Aseneth*'s Jewish provenance ("Joseph and Aseneth," 102–7). Collin's argument dovetails with the methodological criteria that Kraft's student, James Davila, has developed for judging the Jewish or Christian provenance of pseudepigrapha (*The Provenance of the Pseudepigrapha: Jewish, Christian, or Other?*, JSJSup 105 [Leiden: Brill, 2005], 65–71). Davila's "internal criteria" are fivefold: (1) the amount of "substantial Jewish content" and "strong internal evidence that the narrative was composed in the pre-Christian era"; (2) evidence that the pseudepigraphon was translated from Hebrew; (3) demonstrable concern for Jewish rituals; (4) interest in Torah, Jewish law, and *halakah*; and (5) interest in Jewish ethnic and national issues (ibid., 65–66). Collins claims that "the issue of intermarriage is ubiquitous in ancient Jewish literature," but not in early Christian literature ("Joseph and Aseneth," 103). This is well in line with Davila's fifth criteria. As Hicks-Keeton puts it, "Hebrew ethnicity matters in this tale" ("Rewritten Gentiles," 167). Davila's first and second criteria are also informative of *Joseph and Aseneth*'s Jewish heritage. As to the first, *Joseph and Aseneth* exhibits "substantial Jewish content" with respect to the popularity of Joseph as a literary figure in Hellenistic Jewish texts, particularly in Egypt. Ahearne-Kroll shows that three Egyptian-Jewish authors, Philo, Artapanus, and the author of the Wisdom of Solomon, all ruminated on signature features of Joseph's character ("Jewish Identity," 180–86). In her estimation, *Joseph and Aseneth* takes a similar approach to the characterization of Joseph as a Jewish hero. All of these Jewish authors accentuate Joseph's stateliness and temperance (ibid., 187–89). As to Davila's second criteria, Aseneth's name change in *Jos. Asen.* 15:6 is relevant. Davila claims that if a text was translated from Hebrew it is most likely to be of Jewish origin (*Provenance*, 65). Of course, the scholarly consensus is that *Joseph and Aseneth* was not originally written in Hebrew (Humphrey, *Joseph and Aseneth*, 31; Burchard, "Present State," 302). I concur with the consensus as to the *writing* of *Joseph and Aseneth*. But, as I have argued above and elsewhere, the frequent Semitisms and the change of Aseneth's name hint at a bilingual context for oral tellings of the story ("On Transcription," 141). While the textual version of *Joseph and Aseneth* was not translated from Hebrew, the name change and the Semitisms are compelling evidence that the narrative did exist in a Hebrew or Aramaic form at some point, even though this form was not likely textual. Thus, at least three of Davila's five criteria support a Jewish originating context for *Joseph and Aseneth*.

26. With respect to titles for Joseph, he is called κύριος on five occasions in Philonenko's reconstruction (*Jos. Asen.* 7:8; 8:2; 9:4; 13:9; 20:1, 3). While κύριος likely possessed allegorical or typological resonances in Christian reception of *Joseph and Aseneth*, this is by no means a smoking gun for Christian composition. Other characters are addressed by this honorific throughout the narrative. It is applied to Pentephres (*Jos. Asen.* 4:5, 7, 12), Aseneth's angelic visitor (*Jos. Asen.* 16:2, 6; 17:1), and Pharaoh's son (*Jos. Asen.* 23:10; 24:4, 12). In these latter three cases, it's an honorific title for someone in a position of authority (BDAG, s.v.

distinction between production and reception and helps reframe the issue of the narrative's provenance. Because *Joseph and Aseneth*, as an oral tradition, was not the intellectual property of any one author, it was more conducive to reception in new contexts. As with so many other Jewish writings, *Joseph and Aseneth* was transmitted and perhaps even flourished in Christian contexts. It was Christianity's tendency to preserve various Jewish texts, including storytelling traditions, along with *Joseph and Aseneth*'s propensity to be interpreted allegorically that led to its copying in later Christian circles, though it never lost its Jewish roots.

Results of reading Mark as a textualized oral narrative

As with *Joseph and Aseneth*, there are exegetical results produced by understanding Mark as a textualized oral narrative. The following eight have been addressed.

The first two concern linguistic features characteristic of Mark. It has long been thought that εὐθύς provides the gospel with an air of rapidity. I have argued that this can be affirmed to some extent, but that the word serves multiple roles as a discourse marker. I showed in Chapter 3 that recent studies of discourse markers illuminate εὐθύς in Mark. The lexeme is an oral residue since discourse markers

"κύριος," 577). This is how Ahearne-Kroll accounts for it as a reference to Joseph ("Joseph and Aseneth," 2533–34). Joseph is called the son of God (ὁ υἱὸς τοῦ θεοῦ) on four occasions (*Jos. Asen.* 6:2, 6; 13:10; 21:3), beloved by God (ἀγαπητὸς τῷ θεῷ) on another (*Jos. Asen.* 23:10), and the chosen one (ὁ ἐκλεκτός) on one more (*Jos. Asen.* 13:10). Aseneth also calls Joseph "the sun from heaven" (ὁ ἥλιος ἐκ τοῦ οὐρανοῦ) in *Jos. Asen.* 6:5. Following Kraemer's claim that this title recalls the Greek god Helios and his Roman equivalent, Sol Invictus, Nir argues that Joseph's depiction as Helios and identification with the sun are Christian elements of the narrative (Kraemer, *Aseneth*, 156–66; Nir, *Joseph and Aseneth*, 116–24). The titles appended to Joseph by various characters in the narrative along with Aseneth's declaration that he is "the sun from heaven" will have resonated typologically in Christian reception, but they are not indicative of Christian composition or even redaction. The same can be argued of the bread, cup, and ointment sequences. There can be no doubt that these will have recalled the Lord's Supper and, to a lesser extent, baptism in Christian reception of *Joseph and Aseneth*. The allegorical potential of the sequence lies in the commonality of its elements. This is the very purpose of allegory—to take common elements and endow them with a higher symbolism. As Standhartinger's recent review shows, no shortage of interpreters has offered a variety of symbolic referents, whether Jewish or Christian, for the bread, cup, and ointment in *Joseph and Aseneth* ("Recent Research," 383–84). This is because common elements create allegorical space for a variety of interpretations. Christians no doubt will have seized the allegorical potential of these common elements. This does not suggest that Christians composed *Joseph and Aseneth* any more than it suggests that they composed Jewish scriptures that were interpreted eucharistically.

are more at home in oral discourse than in written. Moreover, understanding εὐθύς as a multifunctional discourse marker permits a wider translation of it. Similarly, I have argued that the historical present is held over from Mark's oral composition. Like the frequency of εὐθύς in the gospel, the notable recurrence of the historical present is often recognized by interpreters, but its raison d'être rarely hypothesized. The process of composition argued for here carries explanatory power in this respect. The historical present is not usually considered a Semitism but is characteristic of oral narrative.[27] Thus with both the historical present and with εὐθύς we have characteristically Markan linguistic features that are notably distinctive of oral narrative.

Third and fourth, the beginning and the ending of Mark both hint at and are illuminated by its oral genesis. The incipit in Mk 1:1, "Beginning of the gospel of Jesus Christ" (ἀρχὴ τοῦ εὐαγγελίου Ἰησοῦ Χριστοῦ), is normally taken to be the title for the narrative.[28] But at the time that Mark came into being, "gospel" (εὐαγγέλιον) did not yet signify something written, much less a literary genre. Rather, the term connoted orally proclaimed news.[29] If Mark, as a textualized oral narrative, exists at the borderland between orality and textuality, then this helps explain the novel application of "gospel" to something written. Gospel was a suitable title because the content of the written message was one instantiation of the oral tradition. This also clarifies how the term came to be a literary designation by the second century. The term gospel in Mark's title bridges the oral connotation of the word with the written connotation it would subsequently take on.

Three aspects of Mark's endings are elucidated when the gospel is understood as a textualized oral narrative. First, ending the text on γάρ ("for") in Mk 16:8 might be unexpected of written discourse, but it is not as aberrant in oral discourse.[30] Croy has shown that Greek texts with an oral style more frequently possess a sentence-ending γάρ, and Chafe has found that a clause-final preposition is one of the "ungrammatical" devices more common to spoken discourse than

---

27. Black, who finds significant Aramaic influence on Mark, acknowledges that the historical present is not a holdover from Hebrew or Aramaic (*Aramaic Approach*, 130). Similar claims are made by Moulton and Howard (*Accidence*, 456–57), Sanders (*Tendencies*, 253), and Osburn ("Historical Present," 486). The oral nature of the historical present is well documented in various linguistic fields (Wolfson, "Feature of Performed Narrative," 215–37; idem, *CHP*, 29; Fludernik, "Historical Present Tense," 78; Fleischman, *Tense and Narrativity*, 79).

28. Wikgren, "ΑΡΧΗ ΤΟΥ ΕΥΑΓΓΕΛΙΟΥ," 15–17; Pesch, *Markusevangelium*, 1:74–75; Boring, "Mark 1:1–15," 50–51; idem, *Mark*, 29; Cook, *Structure and Persuasive Power*, 138–40; Marcus, *Mark*, 1:143–46; France, *Gospel of Mark*, 50–51; Donahue and Harrington, *Gospel of Mark*, 60; Collins, *Mark*, 130; Aune, "Genre Theory," 161–62.

29. Friedrich, "εὐαγγελίζομαι, εὐαγγέλιον, προευαγγελίζομαι, εὐαγγελιστής," 721–22; Dickson, "Gospel as News," 212–13.

30. The rarity of ending a sentence or entire narrative with γάρ is catalogued by Croy (*Mutilation*, 49) and Iverson ("Further Word," 87).

written.³¹ Second, Galen offers an analogous case to Mark's added endings in *De libris propriis* 9. He states that his discourses that were taken down via dictation were "shortened, lengthened, and altered" (μετὰ τοῦ τὰ μὲν ἀφαιρεῖν, τὰ δὲ προστιθέναι, τὰ δὲ ὑπαλλάττειν), just as Mark was. And third, as argued in Chapter 4, the textualized-oral-narrative perspective accounts for why the Longer Ending (Mk 16:9-20) so drastically differs from the rest of the gospel syntactically. The former was conceived as a written text, while the latter was composed orally.

Fifth, just as Mark's endings could be amended because it was a textualized oral narrative, so also could the ὑπόμνημα be reappropriated by the later gospel tradents Matthew and Luke. Following Larsen, we have seen that it might be more productive to view Matthew and Luke as macro-level revisions of their predecessor.³² These authors could redeploy Markan literary materials precisely because of their media form.³³

Sixth, there are numerous occasions where Mark appears to miscite or misquote antecedent texts. Moreover, Mark's intertextuality is frequently echoic. Rarely are extended texts from the LXX quoted verbatim. In Chapter 4, I argued that this was a result of the mnemonic mode of recall that the author works from. He is not concerned with intertextual precision, as this is a hallmark of the literary, written medium and not the oral. Of course, once Mark was committed to writing, textual evocations could be made more precise. This happened frequently enough in Markan MSS. But on the whole, Mark's relationship with antecedent texts is allusive.

Seventh, there is a "problem" with geographical imprecision in Mk 5:1-20. In the story of the Gerasene demoniac, the setting in Gerasa requires the 2,000 pigs to sprint thirty-seven miles to reach the Sea of Galilee. While the location is problematic for anyone who has seen Gerasa's proximity (or lack thereof) to the Sea of Galilee on a map, the setting works in oral narrative, which prefers memorable characters and places. Gerasa was embedded in the first-century cultural memory for at least two reasons. Etymologically, it means "to drive

---

31. Croy notes that in Plato's dialogues γάρ is followed by a period 158 times and by a question mark 182 times (*Mutilation*, 48). Chafe lists clause-final prepositions as one of the ungrammatical devices found more frequently in oral than written discourse in "Linguistic Differences," 115.

32. Larsen, "Accidental Publication," 379.

33. This raises an interesting question about whether or not Matthew and Luke are the kinds of texts that will have been unprotected from reappropriation. The question has gone unanswered here. But if Matthew and Luke are indeed better protected because they are more literary than Mark, then this might inform debates about the Two-Source and Farrer-Goulder hypotheses that have been rejuvenated in recent scholarship (Mark S. Goodacre, *The Case against Q: Studies in Markan Priority and the Synoptic Problem* [Harrisburg: Trinity Press International, 2002]; John C. Poirier and Jeffrey Peterson, eds., *Markan Priority without Q: Explorations in the Farrer Hypothesis*, LNTS 455 [London: Bloomsbury T&T Clark, 2015]).

or cast out."³⁴ Its name fit the contents of the pericope. And it was also on the cultural radar of Mark's audience because Vespasian had recently taken military action there.³⁵ The anxiety about the pigs' improbable thirty-seven mile run that is betrayed in later MSS of Mark and in Matthew 8:28, which changes "the region of the Gerasenes" (τὴν χώραν τῶν Γερασηνῶν) to "the region of the Gadarenes" (τὴν χώραν τῶν Γαδαρηνῶν), is felt more acutely in reading the story than it is in hearing it.

Eighth, and finally, the early ecclesiastical testimony about Mark's composition supports the argument I have made throughout this book. The tradition that begins with Papias that claims Mark to be Peter's amanuensis perdured through multiple sources in antiquity. In all of these accounts the composition scenario is one in which both orality and textuality exert influence. Mark writes down Peter's oral testimony and this new writing is employed to reoralize the tradition. Recently Bauckham has made a spirited argument that this testimony is accurate and that Peter's witness truly stands behind the Gospel of Mark.³⁶ My interest is less in the identities of the persons involved and more in the composition scenario that passed verisimilitude for multiple persons in antiquity. This composition scenario makes best sense of Mark's multiple oral residues and how Mark is a written document birthed out of the oral lifeworld.

Results of reading antique textualized oral narratives

The similarities between *Joseph and Aseneth* and Mark outlined above as well as the realized and potential exegetical results of reading them as textualized oral narratives suggest that our interpretive endeavors ought to consider more seriously a text's medium and mode of composition. As is the case with other cultures that employ both the written and oral modality of communication, texts from early Judaism and Christianity are influenced by orality and textuality to varying degrees. Every narrative is affected by these influences differently. Mark and the early versions of *Joseph and Aseneth* are shaped by oral norms more than Matthew, Luke, and the *a*-family recension of *Joseph and Aseneth* are. It is likely the case that other early Jewish and Christian narratives share Mark and *Joseph and Aseneth*'s oral influence and might be categorized as textualized oral narratives. To confirm as much, the language, length, method of invoking intertexts, and pluriformity of the specific tradition would need to be thoroughly investigated. While this media type is not likely to be as well attested from Greco-Roman antiquity as the literary medium, determining how other early Jewish and Christian texts exhibit an

---

34. BDB, s.v. "גֶּרֶשׁ"; Derrett, "Spirit-Possession," 286–93; Marcus, *Mark*, 1:287; Moore, "My Name Is Legion," 28.

35. Josephus, *J.W.* 4.487–489.

36. Bauckham, *Jesus and the Eyewitnesses*, 155–80.

interface between orality and textuality similar or dissimilar to *Joseph and Aseneth* and Mark is likely to pay interpretive dividends.

These interpretive dividends might include the following: First, understanding a text's relationship to orality and textuality can help determine why certain documents survived or even flourished in antiquity. With Mark and *Joseph and Aseneth* we have seen that two "unpolished" texts might have survived because of their relationship to an antecedent oral tradition. There are any number of other reasons that texts survive. Sometimes, as in the case of amulets and other apotropaic devices, texts endure that were not meant to be read at all. They abide because of their symbolic value. In these cases, it is the textuality or writtenness of the document that carries weight. Thus, considering the oral and literate functions of a given text can help us understand its function and reasons for survival in antiquity. Second, considering how orality and textuality interface in a document can bring greater nuance to its genre, purpose, linguistic influences, and authorship. Where a text or tradition lands on the oral-literal continuum might affect whether these interpretive issues are influenced multilaterally or unilaterally. A text affected by the oral lifeworld is more likely to have multilateral influences and a more literary text is likely to be affected unilaterally. Third, considering the medium and mode of composition better facilitates the comparison of seemingly dissimilar texts. This has certainly proved true for *Joseph and Aseneth* and Mark. Fourth, and perhaps most importantly, approaching a text with a media-sensitive hesrmeneutic will necessarily alter the reader's experiential frame. Not all texts should be approached the same way. This harkens back to Johnson's simple proposition that different types of texts make for different types of reading events. To best understand a text, we must consider what type of text it is and what kind of reading event it will have made for in antiquity.

WORKS CITED

Abbott, H. P. (2009), "Narrativity," in P. Hühn (ed.), *Handbook of Narratology*, 309–28, Berlin: de Gruyter.
Achtemeier, P. J. (1990), "Omne Verbum Sonat: The New Testament and the Oral Environment of Late Western Antiquity." *JBL*, 109: 3–27.
Ahearne-Kroll, P. (2005), "*Joseph and Aseneth* and Jewish Identity in Greco-Roman Egypt," PhD diss., University of Chicago, Divinity School.
Ahearne-Kroll, P. (2013), "Joseph and Aseneth," in L. H. Feldman, J. L. Kugel, and L. H. Schiffman (eds.), *Outside the Bible: Ancient Jewish Writings Related to Scripture*, 2525–89, Vol. 3. Philadelphia: Jewish Publication Society.
Aland, K., and B. Aland (1989), *The Text of the New Testament: An Introduction to the Critical Editions and to the Theory and Practice of Modern Textual Criticism*, trans. E. F. Rhodes, Grand Rapids: Eerdmans.
Alexander, L. (1986), "Luke's Preface in the Context of Greek Preface-Writing." *NovT*, 28: 48–74.
Alexander, L. (1993), *The Preface to Luke's Gospel: Literary Convention and Social Context in Luke 1:1–4 and Acts 1:1*. SNTSMS 78, Cambridge: Cambridge University Press.
Alexander, L. (1998), "Ancient Book Production and the Circulation of the Gospels," in R. Bauckham (ed.), *The Gospels for All Christians: Rethinking the Gospel Audiences*, 71–111, Grand Rapids: Eerdmans.
Alexiou, M. (2002), *The Ritual Lament in Greek Tradition*, 2nd ed., Greek Studies. Lanham: Rowman & Littlefield.
Alkier, S. (2009), "Intertextuality and the Semiotics of Biblical Texts," in R. B. Hays, S. Alkier, and L. A. Huizenga (eds.), *Reading the Bible Intertextually*, 3–21, Waco: Baylor University Press.
Allen, W. C. (1912), *A Critical and Exegetical Commentary on the Gospel according to St. Matthew*, 3rd ed., ICC 26, Edinburgh: T&T Clark.
Allison, D. C. (2005), *Studies in Matthew: Interpretation Past and Present*, Grand Rapids: Baker Academic.
Alston, R. (2002), *The City in Roman and Byzantine Egypt*, London: Routledge.
Anderson, G. (2000), *Fairytale in the Ancient World*, New York: Routledge.
Aptowitzer, V. (1924), "Asenath, the Wife of Joseph: A Haggadic Literary-Historical Study." *HUCA*, 1: 239–306.
Arroyo, J. L. B. (2011), "From Politeness to Discourse Marking: The Process of Pragmaticalization of Muy Bien in Vernacular Spanish." *Journal of Pragmatics*, 43: 855–74.
Assmann, J. (1992), *Das Kulturelle Gedächtnis: Schrift, Erinnerung und Politische Identitiät in Frühen Hochkulturen*, 6th ed., Münich: Beck.
Assmann, J. (2006), "Cultural Texts Suspended Between Writing and Speech," in Jan Assmann (ed.), trans. R. Livingstone, *Religion and Cultural Memory: Ten Studies*, 101–21, Stanford: Stanford University Press.

Assmann, J. (2006), "Form as a Mnemonic Device: Cultural Texts and Cultural Memory," in R. A. Horsley, J. A. Draper, and J. M. Foley (eds.), *Performing the Gospel: Orality, Memory, and Mark*, 67–82, Minneapolis: Fortress.
Assmann, J. (2006), "Introduction: What Is Cultural Memory?" in J. Assmann (ed.), trans. R. Livingstone, *Religion and Cultural Memory: Ten Studies*, 1–30, Stanford: Stanford University Press.
Assmann, J. (2006), *Religion and Cultural Memory: Ten Studies*, trans. R. Livingstone, Stanford: Stanford University Press.
Assmann, J. (2006), "Remembering in Order to Belong: Writing, Memory, and Identity," in J. Assmann (ed.), trans. R. Livingstone, *Religion and Cultural Memory: Ten Studies*, 81–100, Stanford: Stanford University Press.
Auer, P., and S. Günther (2005), "Die Entstehung von Diskursmarkern im Deutschen: ein Fall von Gramatikalisierung?" in T. Leuschner, T. Mortelmans, and S. De Groodt (eds.), *Grammatikalisierung im Deutschen*, 335–62, Linguistik Impulse & Tendenzen 9. Berlin: de Gruyter.
Aune, D. E. (1987), *The New Testament in Its Literary Environment*, LEC 8, Philadelphia: Westminster.
Aune, D. E. (1997), *Revelation*, Word Biblical Commentary 52A, Dallas: Word Books.
Aune, D. E. (2011), "Genre Theory and the Genre-Function of Mark and Matthew," in E.-M. Becker and A. Runesson (eds.), *Mark and Matthew I*, 145–75, WUNT 271, Tübingen: Mohr Siebeck.
Avenarius, G. (1956), *Lukians Schrift zur Geschichtsschreibung*, Meisenheim am Glam: Anto Hain.
Bakker, E. J. (1997), "Storytelling in the Future: Truth, Time, and Tense in Homeric Epic," in E. J. Bakker and A. Kahane (eds.), *Written Voices, Spoken Signs: Tradition, Performance, and the Epic Text*, 11–36, Cambridge: Harvard University Press.
Bakker, E. J. (1999), "How Oral Is Oral Composition?" in A. E. Mackay (ed.), *Signs of Orality: The Oral Tradition and Its Influence in the Greek and Roman World*, 29–47, Leiden: Brill.
Bakker, E. J., and A. Kahane, eds. (1997), *Written Voices, Spoken Signs: Tradition, Performance, and the Epic Text*, Cambridge: Harvard University Press.
Bar-Ilan, M. (1998), "Writing in Ancient Israel and Early Judaism Part Two: Scribes and Books in the Late Commonwealth and Rabbinic Period," in M. J. Mulder (ed.), *Mikra: Text, Translation, Reading and Interpretation of the Hebrew Bible in Ancient Judaism and Early Christianity*, 21–38, Philadelphia: Fortress.
Batiffol, P. (1889), "Le Livre de La Prière d'Aseneth," in E. Leroux (ed.), *Studia Patristica: Études D'ancienne Littérature Chrétienne*, Vol. 1-2, 1–115, Paris: Leroux.
Bauckham, R. (2013), *Jesus and the Eyewitnesses: The Gospels as Eyewitness Testimony*, Grand Rapids: Eerdmans.
Baum, A. D. (2016), "Mark's Paratactic Καί as a Secondary Syntactic Semitism." *NovT*, 58: 1–26.
Beaman, K. (1984), "Coordination and Subordination Revisited: Syntactic Complexity in Spoken and Written Narrative," in D. Tannen (ed.), *Coherence in Spoken and Written Discourse*, 45–80, Advances in Discourse Processes 12, Norwood: Ablex.
Beavis, M. A. (1989), *Mark's Audience: The Literary and Social Setting of Mark 4:11–12*, JSNTSup 33, Sheffield: JSOT Press.
Bennett, T. (1977), "An Extended View of Verb Voice in Written and Spoken Personal Narratives," in E. O. Keenan (ed.), *Discourse Across Time and Space*, 43–49, Southern California Occasional Papers in Linguistics 5, Los Angeles: University of Southern California.

Best, E. (1989), "Mark's Narrative Technique," *JSNT*, 37: 43–58.
Bird, M. F. (2014), *The Gospel of the Lord: How the Early Church Wrote the Story of Jesus*, Grand Rapids: Eerdmans.
Black, C. C. (1994), *Mark: Images of an Apostolic Interpreter*, Studies on Personalities of the New Testament, Columbia: University of South Carolina Press.
Black, M. (1954), *An Aramaic Approach to the Gospels and Acts*, 2nd ed., Oxford: Oxford University Press.
Black, S. (1999), "The Historic Present in Matthew: Beyond Speech Margins," in S. E. Porter and J. T. Reed (eds.), *Discourse Analysis and the New Testament*, 120–39, Sheffield: Sheffield Academic.
Black, M., and A.-M. Denis, eds. (1970), *Apocalypsis Henochi Graece*, PVTG 3, Leiden: Brill.
Blumell, L. H., and T. A. Wayment, eds. (2015), *Christian Oxyrhynchus: Texts, Documents, and Sources*, Waco: Baylor University Press.
Bohak, G. (1996), *Joseph and Aseneth and the Jewish Temple in Heliopolis*, EJL 10, Atlanta: Scholars Press.
Boring, M. E. (1990), "Mark 1:1–15 and the Beginning of the Gospel," *Semeia*, 52: 43–81.
Boring, M. E. (2006), *Mark: A Commentary*, NTL, Louisville: Westminster John Knox.
Botha, P. J. J. (1991), "Mark's Story as Oral Traditional Literature: Rethinking the Transmission of Some Traditions about Jesus," *Hervormde Teologiese Studies*, 47: 304–31.
Botha, P. J. J. (2012), *Orality and Literacy in Early Christianity*, Biblical Performance Criticism Series 5, Eugene: Cascade.
Boudon-Millot, V. (2004), "Oral et écrit chez Galien," in J. Jouanna and J. Leclant (eds.), *Colloque la médicine grecque antique: actes*, 199–218, Paris: Académie des Inscriptions et Belles-Lettres.
Bovon, F. (2002), *Luke*, trans. Christine M. Thomas, 3 vols, Hermeneia. Minneapolis: Fortress.
Braginskaya, N. V. (2012), "*Joseph and Aseneth* in Greek Literary History: The Case of the 'First Novel,'" in M. P. Futre Pinheiro, J. Perkins, and R. I. Pervo (eds.), *The Ancient Novel and Early Christin and Jewish Narrative: Fictional Intersections*, 79–105, Ancient Narrative Supplementum 16, Groningen: Barkhuis.
Brenna, C. (2017), "The Lion, the Honey, and the New Timnite Woman: *Joseph and Aseneth* and the Samson Cycle," *JSP*, 26: 144–63.
Brinton, L. J. (1996), *Pragmatic Markers in English: Grammaticalization and Discourse Functions*, Topics in English Linguistics 19, Berlin: de Gruyter.
Brooks, E. W. (1918), *Joseph and Asenath: The Confession of Asenath, Daughter of Penephres the Priest*, London: Society for Promoting Christian Knowledge.
Brown, S. G. (2006), "Factualizing the Folklore: Stephen Carlson's Case Against Morton Smith," *HTR*, 99: 291–327.
Brown, S. G. (2008), "The Letter to Theodore: Stephen Carlson's Case Against Clement's Authorship," *JECS*, 16: 535–72.
Brown, S. G., and A. J. Pantuck (2008), "Morton Smith as M. Madiotes: Stephen Carlson's Attribution of *Secret Mark* to a Bald Swindler," *Journal for the Study of the Historical Jesus*, 6: 106–25.
Brown, F., S. R. Driver, and C. A. Briggs (1907), *A Hebrew and English Lexicon of the Old Testament: With an Appendix Containing the Biblical Aramaic*, Oxford: Clarendon Press.
Bryan, C. (1993), *A Preface to Mark: Notes on the Gospel in Its Literary and Cultural Settings*, New York: Oxford University Press.

Bultmann, R. (1968), *The History of the Synoptic Tradition*, trans. J. Marsh, New York: Harper & Row.
Burchard, C. (1961), "Ei nach einem Ausdruck des Wissens oder Nichtwissens Joh 9:25, Act 19:2, 1 Cor 1:16, 7:16." *ZNW*, 52: 73–82.
Burchard, C. (1965), *Untersuchungen zu Joseph und Aseneth: Überlieferung – Ortsbestimmung*, WUNT 8, Tübingen: Mohr Siebeck.
Burchard, C. (1970), *Der dreizehnte Zeuge: Traditions-und Kompositionsgeschichtliche Untersuchungen zu Lukas' Darstellung der Frühzeit des Paulus*, FRLANT 103, Göttingen: Vandenhoeck & Ruprecht.
Burchard, C. (1970), "Fußnoten Zum Neutestamentlichen Griechisch." *ZNW*, 61: 157–71.
Burchard, C. (1970), "Zum Text von Joseph und Aseneth." *JSJ*, 1: 3–34.
Burchard, C. (1974), "Joseph et Aséneth: Questions Actuelles," in W. C. Van Unnik (ed.), *Littérature Juive Entre Tenach et Mischna*, 77–100, Leiden: Brill.
Burchard, C. (1978), "Joseph und Aseneth Neugriechisch." *NTS*, 24: 68–84.
Burchard, C. (1985), "*Joseph and Aseneth*: A New Translation and Introduction," in J. H. Charlesworth (ed.), *The Old Testament Pseudepigrapha*, 177–247, Vol. 2, Garden City: Doubleday.
Burchard, C. (1987), "The Importance of *Joseph and Aseneth* for the Study of the New Testament: A General Survey and a Fresh Look at the Lord's Supper." *NTS*, 33: 102–34.
Burchard, C. (1996), *Gesammelte Studien zu Joseph und Aseneth*, SVTP 13, Leiden: Brill.
Burchard, C. (1996), "The Present State of Research on *Joseph and Aseneth*," in C. Burchard (ed.), *Gesammelte Studien zu Joseph und Aseneth*, 297–320, SVTP 13, Leiden: Brill.
Burchard, C. (1999), "Zum Stand der Arbeit am Text von Joseph und Aseneth," in M. Becker and W. Fenske (eds.), *Das Ende der Tage und die Gegenwart des Heils: Begegnungen mit dem Neuen Testament und seiner Umwelt: Festschrift für Heinz-Wolfgang Kuhn zum 65 Geburtstag*, 1–28, Leiden: Brill.
Burchard, C. (2005), "The Text of *Joseph and Aseneth* Reconsidered." *JSP*, 14: 83–96.
Burke, T., ed. (2013), *Ancient Gospel or Modern Forgery? The Secret Gospel of Mark in Debate: Proceedings from the 2011 York University Christian Apocrypha Symposium*, Eugene: Wipf & Stock.
Burridge, R. A. (1992), *What Are the Gospels? A Comparison with Graeco-Roman Biography*, SNTSMS 70, Cambridge: Cambridge University Press.
Burrus, V. (1987), *Chastity as Autonomy: Women in the Stories of Apocryphal Acts*, Studies in Women and Religion 23, Lewiston: Mellen.
Busse, U. (1977), *Die Wunder des Propheten Jesus: Die Rezeption, Komposition, und Interpretation der Wundertradition im Evangelium des Lukas*, Forschung zur Bibel 24, Stuttgart: Katholisches Bibelwerk.
Cadbury, H. J. (1922), "Commentary on the Preface of Luke," in F. J. Foakes-Jackson and K. Lake (eds.), *The Beginnings of Christianity: Part I, The Acts of the Apostles*, 489–510, Vol. 2, 5 vols, New York: Macmillan.
Cadbury, H. J. (1927), *The Making of Luke-Acts*, New York: Macmillan.
Campbell, C. R. (2015), *Advances in the Study of Greek: New Insights for Reading the New Testament*, Grand Rapids: Zondervan.
von Campenhausen, H. (1972), *The Formation of the Christian Bible*, Philadelphia: Fortress.
Carlson, S. C. (2005), *The Gospel Hoax: Morton Smith's Invention of Secret Mark*, Waco: Baylor University Press.

Carter, W. (2015), "Cross-Gendered Romans and Mark's Jesus: Legion Enters the Pigs (Mark 5:1–20)." *JBL*, 134: 139–55.
Casey, M. (1998), *Aramaic Sources of Mark's Gospel*, SNTSMS 102, Cambridge: Cambridge University Press.
Chafe, W. L. (1976), "Givenness, Contrastiveness, Definiteness, Subjects, Topics, and Point of View," in C. N. Li (ed.), *Subject and Topic*, 25–55, New York: Academic Press.
Chafe, W. L. (1980), "The Deployment of Consciousness in the Production of a Narrative," in W. L. Chafe (ed.), *The Pear Stories: Cognitive, Cultural, and Linguistic Aspects of Narrative Production*, 9–50, Advances in Discourse Processes 3, Norwood: Ablex.
Chafe, W. L., ed. (1980), *The Pear Stories: Cognitive, Cultural, and Linguistic Aspects of Narrative Production*, Norwood: Ablex.
Chafe, W. L. (1985), "Linguistic Differences Produced by Differences between Speaking and Writing," in D. R. Olson, N. Torrance, and A. Hildyard (eds.), *Literacy, Language, and Learning: The Nature and Consequences of Reading and Writing*, 105–23, Cambridge: Cambridge University Press.
Chafe, W. L. (1988), "Linking Intonation Units in Spoken English," in S. Thompson and J. Haiman (eds.), *Clause Combining in Grammar and Discourse*, 1–27, Typological Studies in Language 18, Philadelphia: John Benjamins.
Chafe, W. L. (1994), *Discourse, Consciousness, and Time: The Flow and Displacement of Conscious Experience in Speaking and Writing*, Chicago: University of Chicago Press.
Chafe, W., and J. Danielwicz (1987), "Properties of Spoken and Written Language," in R. Horowitz and S. Jay Samuels (eds.), *Comprehending Oral and Written Language*, 83–113, San Diego: Academic Press.
Chapman, D. W. (1993), *The Orphan Gospel: Mark's Perspective on Jesus*, The Biblical Seminar 16, Sheffield: JSOT Press.
Charles, R. H. (1913), *The Apocrypha and Pseudepigrapha of the Old Testament in English*, 2 vols, Oxford: Clarendon.
Chesnutt, R. D. (1995), *From Death to Life: Conversion in Joseph and Aseneth*, JSPSup 16, Sheffield: Sheffield Academic.
Collins, A. Y. (2007), *Mark: A Commentary*, Hermeneia, Minneapolis: Fortress.
Collins, J. J. (2005), "*Joseph and Aseneth*: Jewish or Christian?" *JSP*, 14: 97–112.
Cook, J. G. (1995), *The Structure and Persuasive Power of Mark: A Linguistic Approach*, Atlanta: Scholars Press.
Cribiore, R. (1996), *Writing, Teachers, and Students in Graeco-Roman Egypt*, American Studies in Papyrology 36, Atlanta: Scholars Press.
Croy, N. C. (2003), *The Mutilation of Mark's Gospel*, Nashville: Abingdon.
Danker, F. W., W. Bauer, W. F. Arndt, and F. W. Gingrich. (2000), *Greek-English Lexicon of the New Testament and Other Early Christian Literature*, 3rd ed., Chicago: University of Chicago Press.
Davies, W. D., and D. C. Allison (2004), *A Critical and Exegetical Commentary on the Gospel according to Saint Matthew*, 3 vols, ICC, Edinburgh: T&T Clark.
Davila, J. R. (2005), "The Old Testament Pseudepigrapha as Background to the New Testament." *Expository Times*, 117: 53–57.
Davila, J. R. (2005), *The Provenance of the Pseudepigrapha: Jewish, Christian, or Other?* Vol. JSJSup 105, Leiden: Brill.
Decker, R. J. (1997), "The Use of Εὐθύς ('immediately') in Mark." *Journal of Ministry and Theology*, 1: 90–120.

Decker, R. J. (2013), "Markan Idiolect in the Study of the Greek of the New Testament," in A. W. Pitts and S. E. Porter (eds.), *The Language of the New Testament: Context, History, and Development*, 43–66, Linguistic Biblical Studies 6, Leiden: Brill.
Deissmann, A. (1895), *Bibelstudien*, Marburg: Elwert.
Deissmann, A. (1897), *Neue Biblestudien*, Marburg: Elwert.
Deissmann, A. (1901), *Bible Studies*, trans. A. Grieve, Edinburgh: T&T Clark.
Deissmann, A. (1910), *Light from the Ancient East: The New Testament Illustrated by Recently Discovered Texts of the Graeco-Roman World*, trans. L. R. M. Strachan, London: Hodder & Stoughton.
Delling, G. (1978), "Einwirkungen der Sprache der Septuaginta in 'Joseph und Aseneth.'" *JSJ*, 9: 29–56.
Derrenbacker, R. A. (2005), *Ancient Compositional Practices and the Synoptic Problem*, BETL 186, Leuven: Leuven University Press.
Derrett, J. D. M. (1979), "Spirit-Possession and the Gerasene Demoniac." *Man*, 14: 286–93.
Derrida, J. (1982), "Signature Event Context," in *Margins of Philosophy*, 309–30, trans. A. Bass, Chicago: University of Chicago Press.
Dewey, J. (1989), "Oral Methods of Structuring Narrative in Mark." *Int*, 43: 32–44.
Dewey, J. (1991), "Mark as Interwoven Tapestry: Forecasts and Echoes for a Listening Audience." *CBQ*, 53: 221–36.
Dewey, J. (2004), "The Survival of Mark's Gospel: A Good Story?" *JBL*, 123: 495–507.
Dewey, J. (2008), "The Gospel of Mark as Oral Hermeneutic," in T. Thatcher (ed.), *Jesus, the Voice, and the Text: Beyond the Oral and the Written Gospel*, 71–87, Waco: Baylor University Press.
Dewey, J. (2013), "The Gospel of John in Its Oral-Written Media World," in J. Dewey (ed.), *The Oral Ethos of the Early Church: Speaking, Writing, and the Gospel of Mark*, 31–49, Biblical Performance Criticism Series 8, Eugene: Cascade.
Dewey, J. (2013), "The Gospel of Mark as an Oral/Aural Event: Implications for Interpretation," in J. Dewey (ed.), *The Oral Ethos of the Early Church: Speaking, Writing, and the Gospel of Mark*, 93–108, Biblical Performance Criticism Series 8, Eugene: Cascade.
Dibelius, M. (1965), *From Tradition to Gospel*, trans. B. L. Woolf, New York: Scribner, Translation of *Die Formgeschichte des Evangeliums*, Tübingen: Mohr Siebeck, 1919.
Dickson, J. P. (2005), "Gospel as News: Εὐαγγελ- from Aristophanes to the Apostle Paul." *NTS*, 51: 212–30.
Dillon, R. J. (1981), "Previewing Luke's Project from His Prologue (Luke 1:1-4)." *CBQ*, 43: 205–27.
Docherty, S. (2004), "*Joseph and Aseneth*: Rewritten Bible or Narrative Expansion?" *JSJ*, 35: 27–48.
Donahue, J. R., and D. J. Harrington (2002), *The Gospel of Mark*, SP 2, Collegeville: Liturgical Press.
Doole, J. A. (2013), *What Was Mark for Matthew? An Examination of Matthew's Relationship and Attitude to His Primary Source*, WUNT 2/344, Tübingen: Mohr Siebeck.
Doty, S. E. H. (1989), "From Ivory Tower to City of Refuge: The Role and Function of the Protagonist in '*Joseph and Aseneth*' and Related Narratives," PhD diss., The Iliff School of Theology and University of Denver.
Dronsch, K. (2010), "Transmissions from Scripturality to Orality: Hearing the Voice of Jesus in Mark 4:1-34," in A. Weissenrieder and R. B. Coote (eds.), *The Interface of*

Orality and Writing: Speaking, Seeing, Writing in the Shaping of New Genres, 119–29, WUNT 260, Tübingen: Mohr Siebeck.

Dronsch, K., and A. Weissenrieder (2010), "A Theory of the Message for the New Testament Writings or Communicating the Words of Jesus: From Angelos to Euangelion," in A. Weissenrieder and R. B. Coote (eds.), *The Interface of Orality and Writing; Speaking, Seeing, Writing in the Shaping of New Genres*, 205–35, WUNT 260, Tübingen: Mohr Siebeck.

Du Plessis, I. J. (1974), "Once More: The Purpose of Luke's Prologue (Lk 1:1-4)." *NovT*, 16: 259–71.

Dué, C. (2006), *The Captive Woman's Lament in Greek Tragedy*, Austin: University of Texas Press.

Dundes, A. (1999), *Holy Writ as Oral Lit: The Bible as Folklore*, Lanham: Rowman & Littlefield.

Dunn, J. D. G. (2013), "Altering the Deafault Setting: Re-Envisaging the Early Transmission of the Jesus Tradition," in J. D. G. Dunn (ed.), *The Oral Gospel Tradition*, 41–79, Grand Rapids: Eerdmans.

Dupont, J. (1968), "Les paraboles du trésor et de la perle." *NTS*, 14: 408–18.

Edwards, J. R. (1989), "Markan Sandwiches: The Significance of Interpolations in Markan Narratives." *NovT*, 31: 193–216.

Edwards, J. R. (2002), *The Gospel according to Mark*, The Pillar New Testament Commentary, Grand Rapids: Eerdmans.

Eisenstein, Elizabeth L. (1979), *The Printing Press as an Agent of Change: Communications and Cultural Transformations in Early Modern Europe*, 2 vols, Cambridge: Cambridge University Press.

Elder, N. A. (2016), "Of Porcine and Polluted Spirits: Reading the Gerasene Demoniac (Mark 5:1-20) with the Book of Watchers (*1 Enoch* 1–36)." *CBQ*, 78: 430–46.

Elder, N. A. (2016), "On Transcription and Oral Transmission in Aseneth: A Study of the Narrative's Conception." *JSJ*, 47: 119–42.

Ellingworth, P. (1995), "The Dog in the Night : A Note on Mark's Non-Use of KAI." *BT*, 46: 125–28.

Elliott, J. K. (1993), *The Language and Style of the Gospel of Mark: An Edition of C.H. Turner's "Notes on Marcan Usage" Together with Other Comparable Studies*, NovTSup 71, Leiden: Brill.

Evans, C. A. (2001), *Mark 8:27–16:20*. WBC 34B, Nashville: Thomas Nelson Publishers.

Evans, C. A. (2005), "How Mark Writes," in M. Bockmuehl and D. A. Hagner (eds.), *The Written Gospel*, 135–48, Cambridge: Cambridge University Press.

Evans, C. A. (2008), "'The Book of the Genesis of Jesus Christ': The Purpose of Matthew in Light of the Incipit," in T. R. Hatina (ed.), *Biblical Interpretation in Early Christian Gospels*, Vol. 2: The Gospel of Matthew, 61–72, LNTS 310, New York: T&T Clark.

Eve, E. (2016), *Writing the Gospels: Composition and Memory*, London: SPCK.

Fanning, B. M. (1990), *Verbal Aspect in the New Testament*, Oxford: Clarendon.

Farmer, W. R. (1974), *The Last Twelve Verses of Mark*, SNTSMS 25, Cambridge: Cambridge University Press.

Fink, U. (2008), *Joseph und Aseneth: Revision des griechischen Textes und Edition der zweiten lateinischen Übersetzung*, Fontes et Subsidia ad Bibliam Pertinentes 5, Berlin: de Gruyter .

Finnegan, R. H. (1988), *Literacy and Orality: Studies in the Technology of Communication*, Oxford: Blackwell.

Fitzmyer, J. A. (1981), *The Gospel according to Luke*, 2 vols, AB 28-28A, New York: Doubleday.
Fitzmyer, J. A. (1997), "The Language of Palestine in the First Century A.D.," in J. A. Fitzmyer (ed.), *A Wandering Aramean: Collected Aramaic Essays*, 29–56, Grand Rapids: Eerdmans.
Fitzmyer, J. A. (1997), "The Study of the Aramaic Background of the New Testament," in Joseph A. Fitzmyer (ed.), *A Wandering Aramean: Collected Aramaic Essays*, 1–27, Grand Rapids: Eerdmans.
Fleischman, S. (1990), *Tense and Narrativity: From Medieval Performance to Modern Fiction*, Austin: University of Texas Press.
Fludernik, M. (1991), "The Historical Present Tense Yet Again: Tense Switching and Narrative Dynamics in Oral and Quasi-Oral Storytelling." *Text: An Interdisciplinary Journal for the Study of Discourse*, 11: 365–97.
Fludernik, M. (1992), "The Historical Present Tense in English Literature: An Oral Pattern and Its Literary Adaptation." *Language and Literature*, 17: 77–107.
Fludernik, M. (1996), *Towards a "Natural" Narratology*, London: Routledge.
Foley, J. M. (1995), *The Singer of Tales in Performance*, Bloomington: Indiana University Press.
Foley, J. M. (2002), *How to Read an Oral Poem*, Urbana: University of Illinois Press.
Foley, J. M. (2010), "Plentitude and Diversity: Interactions between Orality and Writing," in A. Weissenrieder and R. B. Coote (eds.), *The Interface of Orality and Writing; Speaking, Seeing, Writing in the Shaping of New Genres*, 103–18, WUNT 260, Tübingen: Mohr Siebeck.
Fowler, R. L. (1987), "The Rhetoric of Desperation." *Harvard Studies in Classical Philology*, 91: 5–38.
Fowler, R. M. (2001), *Let the Reader Understand: Reader-Response Criticism and the Gospel of Mark*, Harrisburg: Trinity Press International.
France, R. T. (2002), *The Gospel of Mark*, New International Greek Testament Commentary, Grand Rapids: Eerdmans.
Freedman, D. N., ed. (1992), *Anchor Bible Dictionary*, 6 vols, New York: Doubleday.
Frey, J. R. (1946), "The Historical Present in Narrative Literature, Particularly in Modern German Fiction." *The Journal of English and Germanic Philology*, 45: 43–67.
Galen. (1997), *Galen: Selected Works*, trans. P. N. Singer, The World's Classics, Oxford: Oxford University Press.
Gamble, H. Y. (1995), *Books and Readers in the Early Church: A History of Early Christian Texts*, New Haven: Yale University Press.
Genette, G. (1997), *Paratexts: Thresholds of Interpretation*, trans. J. E. Lewin, Lecture, Culture, Theory 20, Cambridge: Cambridge University Press.
Goodacre, M. S. (2002), *The Case against Q: Studies in Markan Priority and the Synoptic Problem*, Harrisburg: Trinity Press International.
Goodacre, M. S. (2012), *Thomas and the Gospels: The Case for Thomas's Familiarity with the Synoptics*, Grand Rapids: Eerdmans.
Graham, W. A. (1987), *Beyond the Written Word: Oral Aspects of Scripture in the History of Religion*, Cambridge: Cambridge University Press.
Gray, B. (1971), "Repetition in Oral Literature." *Journal of American Folklore*, 84: 289–303.
Grenfell, B. P., and A. S. Hunt, eds. (1908), *The Oxyrhynchus Papyri*, Vol. 6, London: Egypt Exploration Fund.
Gruen, E. S. (1998), *Heritage and Hellenism: The Reinvention of Jewish Tradition*, Berkeley: University of California Press.

Guelich, R. A. (1982), "'The Beginning of the Gospel': Mark 1:1–15." *BR*, 27: 5–15.
Guelich, R. A. (1989), *Mark 1–8:26*, Vol. 34A, Word Biblical Commentary, Waco: Word Books.
Hägg, T. (1983), *The Novel in Antiquity*, Berkeley: University of California Press.
Hagner, D. A. (1995), *Matthew*, 2 vols, WBC 33A–B, Dallas: Thomas Nelson.
Haines-Eitzen, K. (2000), *Guardians of Letters: Literacy, Power, and the Transmitters of Early Christian Literature*, Oxford: Oxford University Press.
Hansen, M.-B. M. (1998), "The Semantic Status of Discourse Markers." *Lingua*, 104: 235–60.
Harris, W. V. (1989), *Ancient Literacy*, Cambridge: Harvard University Press.
Havelock, E. A. (1984), "Oral Composition in the Oedipus Tyrannus of Sophocles." *New Literary History*, 16: 175–97.
Hawkins, J. C. (1909), *Horae Synopticae: Contributions to the Study of the Synoptic Problem*, Oxford: Clarendon.
Hays, R. B. (1989), *Echoes of Scripture in the Letters of Paul*, New Haven: Yale University Press.
Hays, R. B. (2005), *The Conversion of the Imagination: Paul as Interpreter of Israel's Scripture*, Grand Rapids: Eerdmans.
Hays, R. B. (2016), *Echoes of Scripture in the Gospels*, Waco: Baylor University Press.
Hays, R. B., S. Alkier, and L. A. Huizenga, eds. (2009), *Reading the Bible Intertextually*, Waco: Baylor University Press.
Heine, B. (2013), "On Discourse Markers: Grammaticalization, Pragmaticalization, or Something Else?" *Linguistics*, 51: 1205–47.
Helmreich, G., J. Marquardt, and I. Müller (1891), *Claudii Galeni Pergameni Scripta Minora*, Vol. 2, Leipzig: Teubner.
Hengel, M. (1985), *Studies in the Gospel of Mark*, Philadelphia: Fortress.
Herder, J. G. (1880), "Vom Erlöser der Menschen: Nach unsern drei ersten Evangelien," in B. Suphan (ed.), *Herders Sämmtliche Werke*, 135–252, Vol. 19, Berlin: Weidmannsche Buchhandlung.
Hester, D. W. (2015), *Does Mark 16:9–20 Belong in the New Testament?* Eugene: Wipf & Stock.
Hezser, C. (2001), *Jewish Literacy in Roman Palestine*, TSAJ 81, Tübingen: Mohr Siebeck.
Hezser, C. (2010), "Private and Public Education," in C. Hezser (ed.), *The Oxford Handbook of Jewish Daily Life in Roman Palestine*, 465–81, Oxford: Oxford University Press.
Hicks-Keeton, J. (2014), "Rewritten Gentiles: Conversion to Israel's 'Living God' and Jewish Identity in Antiquity," PhD diss., Duke University.
Hicks-Keeton, J. (2018), *Arguing with Aseneth: Gentile Access to Israel's "Living God" in Jewish Antiquity*, Oxford: Oxford University Press.
Hock, R. F. (1988), "The Greek Novel," in D. E. Aune (ed.), *Greco-Roman Literature and the New Testament*, 127–46, Atlanta: Scholars Press.
Hofius, O. (1971), "Eine Altjüdische Parallele zu Röm 4:17b." *NTS*, 18: 93–94.
Holmes, M. W. (2001), "To Be Continued ... The Many Endings of the Gospel of Mark." *BR* 17: 12–23.
Holmes, M. W. (2013), "From 'Original Text' to 'Initial Text,'" in B. D. Ehrman and M. W. Holmes (eds.), *The Text of the New Testament in Contemporary Research: Essays on the Status Quaestionis*, 637–88, 2nd ed., NTTS 42, Leiden: Brill.
Hopper, P. J., and E. C. Traugott (2003), *Grammaticalization*, Cambridge: Cambridge University Press.

Horsfall, N. (1995), "Rome without Spectacles." *Greece & Rome*, 42: 49–56.
Horsley, R. A. (2001), *Hearing the Whole Story: The Politics of Plot in Mark's Gospel*, Louisville: Westminster John Knox.
Horsley, R. A. (2008), *Jesus in Context: Power, People, and Performance*, Minneapolis: Fortress.
Horsley, R. A. (2010), "The Gospel of Mark in the Interface of Orality and Writing," in A. Weissenrieder and R. B. Coote (eds.), *The Interface of Orality and Writing: Speaking, Seeing, Writing in the Shaping of New Genres*, 144–65, WUNT 260, Tübingen: Mohr Siebeck.
Horsley, R. A. (2010), "Oral and Written Aspects of the Emergence of the Gospel of Mark as Scripture." *Oral Tradition*, 25: 93–114.
Horsley, R. A., J. A. Draper, J. M. Foley, and W. H. Kelber, eds. (2006), *Performing the Gospel: Orality, Memory, and Mark*, Minneapolis: Fortress.
Hort, F. J. A. (1898), *The Epistle of St. Peter 1:1–2:17*, London: Macmillan.
Humphrey, E. M. (2000), *Joseph and Aseneth*, Guides to Apocrypha and Pseudepigrapha, Sheffield: Sheffield Academic.
Hunt, A. S., and C. C. Edgar, trans. (1932), *Select Papyri*, Vol. I: Non-Literary Papyri Private Affairs, V vols, LCL 266, Cambridge: Harvard University Press.
Hurtado, L. W. (1989), "The Gospel of Mark in Recent Study." *Them*, 14: 47–52.
Hurtado, L. W. (2014), "Oral Fixation and New Testament Studies? 'Orality', 'Performance' and Reading Texts in Early Christianity." *NTS*, 60: 321–40.
Incigneri, B. J. (2003), *The Gospel to the Romans: The Setting and Rhetoric of Mark's Gospel*, BibInt 65, Leiden: Brill.
Iverson, K. R. (2006), "A Further Word on Final Γάρ (Mark 16:8)." *CBQ*, 68: 79–94.
Iverson, K. R. (2009), "Orality and the Gospels: A Survey of Recent Research." *CurBR*, 8: 71–106.
Iverson, K. R. (2016), "Oral Fixation or Oral Corrective? A Response to Larry Hurtado." *NTS*, 62: 183–200.
Jaffee, M. S. (2001), *Torah in the Mouth: Writing and Oral Tradition in Palestinian Judaism 200 BCE–400 CE*, Oxford: Oxford University Press.
Jeremias, J. (1952), "The Last Supper." *ET*, 64: 91–92.
Jeremias, J. (1954), "Die Missionarische Aufgabe in der Mischehe (1 Cor 7:16)," in W. Eltester (ed.), *Neutestamentliche Studien für Rudolf Bultmann: Zu seinem siebzigsten Geburtstag am 20. August 1954*, 255–60, BZNW 21, Berlin: Alfred Töpelmann.
Jewett, R. (2006), *Romans: A Commentary*, E. J. Epp (ed.), Hermeneia, Minneapolis: Fortress.
Johnson, S. R. (2005), *Historical Fictions and Hellenistic Jewish Identity: Third Maccabees in Its Cultural Context*, Berkeley: University of California Press.
Johnson, W. A. (2010), *Readers and Reading Culture in the High Roman Empire: A Study of Elite Communities*, Oxford: Oxford University Press.
Kautzch, E. (1990), *Die Apokryphen und Pseudepigraphen des Altens Testaments*, 2 vols, Tübingen: Mohr Siebeck.
Keck, L. E. (1978), "Oral Traditional Literature and the Gospels: The Seminar," in W. O. Walker (ed.), *Relationships Among the Gospels: An Interdisciplinary Dialogue*, 103–22, San Antonio: Trinity University Press.
Kee, H. C. (1975), "The Function of Scriptural Quotations and Allusions in Mark 11–16," in E. Earle Ellis and E. Grässer (eds.), *Jesus und Paulus: Festschrift für Werner Georg Kümmel*, 165–88, Göttingen: Vandenhoeck & Ruprecht.
Kee, H. C. (1977), *Community of the New Age: Studies in Mark's Gospel*, Philadelphia: Westminster.

Keith, C. (2009), *The Pericope Adulterae, the Gospel of John, and the Literacy of Jesus*, NTTSD 38, Leiden: Brill.
Keith, C. (2014), *Jesus Against the Scribal Elite: The Origins of the Conflict*, Grand Rapids: Baker Academic.
Keith, C. (2014), "Prolegomena on the Textualization of Mark's Gospel: Manuscript Culture, the Extended Situation, and the Emergence of the Written Gospel," in T. Thatcher (ed.), *Memory and Identity in Ancient Judaism and Early Christianity: A Conversation with Barry Schwartz*, 161–86, SemeiaSt 78, Atlanta: SBL Press.
Kelber, W. H. (1974), *The Kingdom in Mark: A New Place and a New Time*, Philadelphia: Fortress.
Kelber, W. H. (1979), "Mark and Oral Tradition," *Semeia*, 16: 7–55.
Kelber, W. H. (1983), *The Oral and the Written Gospel: The Hermeneutics of Speaking and Writing in the Synoptic Tradition, Mark, Paul, and Q*, Bloomington: Indiana University Press.
Kelber, W. H. (1994), "Modalities of Communication, Cognition, and Physiology of Perception: Orality, Rhetoric, Scribality," *Semeia*, 65: 193–216.
Kelber, W. H. (2005), "The Works of Memory: Christian Origins as MnemoHistory—A Response," in A. Kirk and T. Thatcher (eds.), *Memory, Tradition, and Text: Uses of the Past in Early Christianity*, 221–48, SemeiaSt 52, Leiden: Brill.
Kelber, W. H. (2010), "The History of the Closure of Biblical Texts," in A. Weissenrieder and R. B. Coote (eds.), *The Interface of Orality and Writing: Speaking, Seeing, Writing in the Shaping of New Genres*, 71–99, WUNT 260, Tübingen: Mohr Siebeck.
Kelber, W. H. (2013), "In the Beginning Were the Words: The Apotheosis and Narrative Displacement of the Logos," in W. H. Kelber (ed.), *Imprints, Voiceprints, and Footprints of Memory*, 75–101, Atlanta: Society of Biblical Literature.
Kelber, W. H. (2013), "Jesus and Tradition: Words in Time, Words in Space," in W. H. Kelber (ed.), *Imprints, Voiceprints, and Footprints of Memory: Collected Essays of Werner Kelber*, 103–32, Atlanta: Society of Biblical Literature.
Kelber, W. H. (2017), "The Comparative Study of Oral Tradition," in T. Thatcher, C. Keith, R. E. Person Jr., and E. R. Stern (eds.), *Dictionary of the Bible and Ancient Media*, 252–59, New York: Bloomsbury T&T Clark.
Kelhoffer, J. A. (2004), "'How Soon a Book' Revisited: EUANGELION as a Reference to 'Gospel' Materials in the First Half of the Second Century," *ZNW*, 95: 1–34.
Kelly, B. (2011), *Petitions, Litigation, and Social Control in Roman Egypt*, Oxford: Oxford University Press.
Kennedy, G. (1978), "Classical and Christian Source Criticism," in W. O. Walker (ed.), *The Relationships Among the Gospels: An Interdisciplinary Dialogue*, 125–55, San Antonio: Trinity University Press.
Kilpatrick, G. D. (1952), "The Last Supper," *ET*, 64: 4–8.
Kilpatrick, G. D. (1977), "Historic Present in the Gospels and Acts," *ZNW*, 68: 258–62.
Kilpatrick, G. D. (1990), *The Principles and Practice of New Testament Textual Criticism: Collected Essays*, ed. J. K. Elliott, Leuven: Leuven University Press.
Kilpatrick, G. D. (1993), "Some Notes on Markan Usage," in J. K. Elliott (ed.), *The Language and Style of the Gospel of Mark: An Edition of C.H. Turner's "Notes on Marcan Usage" Together with Other Comparable Studies*, 159–74, NovTSup 71, Leiden: Brill.
Kingsbury, J. D. (1975), *Matthew: Structure, Christology, Kingdom*, Philadelphia: Fortress.
Kinman, B. (1994), "Lucan Eschatology and the Missing Fig Tree," *JBL*, 113: 669–78.

Kirk, A. (2008), "Manuscript Tradition as a *Tertium Quid*: Orality and Memory in Scribal Practices," in T. Thatcher (ed.), *Jesus, the Voice, and the Text: Beyond the Oral and the Written Gospel*, 214-34, Waco: Baylor University Press.

Kirk, A. (2011), "Memory Theory and Jesus Research," in T. Holmén and S. E. Porter (eds.), *Handbook for the Study of the Historical Jesus*, 809-42, Vol. 1, Leiden: Brill.

Kirk, A. (2012), "Orality, Writing, and Phantom Sources: Appeals to Ancient Media in Some Recent Challenges to the Two Document Hypothesis." *NTS*, 58: 1-22.

Kirk, A. (2016), *Q in Matthew: Ancient Media, Memory, and Early Scribal Transmission of the Jesus Tradition*, LNTS 564, London: Bloomsbury.

Kirk, J. R. D. (2012), "Time for Figs, Temple Destruction, and Houses of Prayer in Mark 11:12-25." *CBQ*, 74: 509-27.

Kirk, A., and T. Thatcher (2005), "Jesus Tradition as Social Memory," in A. Kirk and T. Thatcher (eds.), *Memory, Tradition, and Text: Uses of the Past in Early Christianity*, 25-42, SemeiaSt 52, Leiden: Brill.

Kleist, J. A. (1936), *The Gospel of Saint Mark Presented in Greek Thought-Units and Sense-Lines with a Commentary*, New York: Bruce Publishing Company.

Koester, H. (1990), *Ancient Christian Gospels: Their History and Development*, Philadelphia: Trinity Press International.

Kraemer, R. S. (1991), "Women's Authorship of Jewish and Christian Literature in the Greco-Roman Period," in A.-J. Levine (ed.), *"Women Like This": New Perspectives on Jewish Women in the Greco-Roman World*, 221-42, EJL 1, Atlanta: Scholars Press.

Kraemer, R. S. (1992), *Her Share of the Blessings: Women's Religions Among Pagans, Jews, and Christians in the Greco-Roman World*, New York: Oxford.

Kraemer, R. S. (1998), *When Aseneth Met Joseph: A Late Antique Tale of the Biblical Patriarch and His Egyptian Wife, Reconsidered*, New York: Oxford University Press.

Kraft, R. A. (2009), "The Pseudepigrapha in Christianity," in R. A. Kraft (ed.), *Exploring the Scripturesque: Jewish Texts and Their Christian Contexts*, 3-33, JSJSup 137, Leiden: Brill.

Kraft, R. A. (2009), "The Pseudepigrapha and Christianity, Revisited: Setting the Stage and Framing Some Central Questions," in R. A. Kraft (ed.), *Exploring the Scripturesque: Jewish Texts and Their Christian Contexts*, 35-60, JSJSup 137, Leiden: Brill.

Kraus, T. J. (2007), "(Il)literacy in Non-Literary Papyri from Graeco-Roman Egypt: Further Aspects to the Educational Ideal in Ancient Literary Sources and Modern Times," in T. J. Kraus (ed.), *Ad Fontes: Original Manuscripts and Their Significance for Studying Early Christianity*, 107-29, TENTS 3, Leiden: Brill.

Kürzinger, J. (1960), "Das Papiaszeugnis und die Erstgestalt des Matthäusevangeliums." *BZ*, 4: 19-38.

Kürzinger, J. (1977), "Die Aussage des Papias von Hierapolis zur literarischen Form des Markusevangeliums." *BZ*, 21: 245-64.

Labov, W. (1972), "The Transformation of Experience in Narrative Syntax," in W. Labov (ed.), *Language in the Inner City: Studies in the Black English Vernacular*, 354-96, Philadelphia: University of Pennsylvania Press.

Labov, W. (1973), *Language in the Inner City: Studies in the Black English Vernacular*, Philadelphia: University of Pennsylvania Press.

Lane, W. L. (1974), *The Gospel of Mark*, NICNT, Grand Rapids: Eerdmans.

Larsen, M. D. C. (2017), "Accidental Publication, Unfinished Texts and the Traditional Goals of New Testament Textual Criticism." *JSNT*, 39: 362-87.

LaVerdiere, E. (1999), *The Beginning of the Gospel: Introducing the Gospel According to Mark*, Vol. 1, Collegeville: Liturgical Press.

Leander, H. (2013), *Discourses of Empire: The Gospel of Mark from a Postcolonial Perspective*, Atlanta: Society of Biblical Literature.
Le Donne, A. (2009), *The Historiographical Jesus: Memory, Typology and the Son of David*, Waco: Baylor University Press.
Liddell, H. G., R. Scott, and H. S. Jones. (1996), *A Greek-English Lexicon*, 9th ed., with revised supplement, Oxford: Clarendon.
Liebers, R. (1993), *"Wie Geschrieben Steht:" Studien zu einer besonderen Art Frühchristlichen Schriftbezuges*, Berlin: de Gruyter.
Lord, A. B. (1960), *The Singer of Tales*, Cambridge: Harvard University Press.
Lord, A. B. (1987), "Characteristics of Orality." *Oral Tradition*, 2: 54–72.
Loubser, J. A. (2013), *Oral and Manuscript Culture in the Bible: Studies on the Media Texture of the New Testament – Explorative Hermeneutics*, Biblical Performance Criticism Series 7, Eugene: Cascade.
Luz, U. (2007), *Matthew*, trans. J. E. Crouch, 3 vols, Hermeneia, Minneapolis: Fortress.
Lyons, J. (1981), *Language and Linguistics: An Introduction*, Cambridge: Cambridge University Press.
Mack, B. L. (1988), *A Myth of Innocence: Mark and Christian Origins*, Philadelphia: Fortress.
Maloney, E. C. (1980), *Semitic Interference in Marcan Syntax*, SBLDS 51, Chico: Scholars Press.
Mandilaras, B. G. (1973), *The Verb in the Greek-Non-Literary Papyri*, Athens: Hellenic Ministry of Culture and Sciences.
Marcus, J. (1993), *The Way of the Lord: Christological Exegesis of the Old Testament in the Gospel of Mark*, Edinburgh: T&T Clark.
Marcus, J. (2008), *Mark: A New Translation with Introduction and Commentary*, 2 vols, AB27–27A, New York: Doubleday.
Marshall, C. D. (1995), *Faith as a Theme in Mark's Narrative*, SNTSMS 64, Cambridge: Cambridge University Press.
Mateos, J., and F. Camacho (2000), *El Evangelio de Marcos: Análisis Lingüístico y Comentario Exegético*, Vol. 1, 2 vols, En los orígenes del cristianismo 11, Córdoba: Ediciones El Almendro.
Maxey, J. A. (2009), *From Orality to Orality: A New Paradigm for Contextual Translation of the Bible*, Biblical Performance Criticism Series 2, Eugene: Cascade.
McDonnell, M. (1996), "Writing, Copying, and Autograph Manuscripts in Ancient Rome." *ClQ*, 46: 469–91.
McLuhan, M. (1994), *Understanding Media: The Extensions of Man*, Cambridge: MIT Press.
Meagher, J. C. (1979), *Clumsy Construction in Mark's Gospel: A Critique of Form- and Redaktionsgeschichte*, Toronto Studies in Theology 3, Lewiston: Mellen.
Meier, J. P. (1991), *The Roots of the Problem and the Person*, Vol. 1 of *A Marginal Jew: Rethinking the Historical Jesus*, ABRL, New York: Doubleday.
Miller, G. D. (2012), "An Intercalation Revisited: Christology, Discipleship, and Dramatic Irony in Mark 6.6b–30." *JSNT*, 35: 176–95.
Miller, R. D. II (2011), *Oral Tradition in Ancient Israel*, Biblical Performance Criticism Series 4, Eugene: Cascade.
Milligan, G. (1912), *Selections from the Greek Papyri*, Cambridge: Cambridge University Press.
Mills, M. (1985), "Sex Role Reversals, Sex Changes, and Transvestite Disguise in the Oral Tradition of a Conservative Muslim Community in Afghanistan," in R. A. Jordan and

S. J. Kalcik (eds.), *Women's Folklore, Women's Culture*, 187–215, Publications of the American Folklore Society 8, Philadelphia: University of Pennsylvania Press.
Morris, N. (1937), *The Jewish School: An Introduction to the History of Jewish Education*, London: Eyre and Spottiswoode.
Moulton, J. H. (1906), *Prolegomena*, Vol. 1, *A Grammar of New Testament Greek*, 4 vols, Edinburgh: T&T Clark.
Moulton, J. H., and W. F. Howard (1929), *Accidence and Word Formation*, Vol. 2, *A Grammar of New Testament Greek*, 4 vols, Edinburgh: T&T Clark.
Mournet, T. C. (2005), *Oral Tradition and Literary Dependency: Variability and Stability in the Synoptic Tradition and Q*, WUNT 195, Tübingen: Mohr Siebeck.
Myers, C. (1988), *Binding the Strong Man: A Political Reading of Mark's Story of Jesus*, Maryknoll: Orbis Books.
Neirynck, F. (1971), "Duality in Mark." *ETL*, 47: 394–463.
Neirynck, F. (1971), "Mark in Greek." *ETL*, 47: 144–98.
Neirynck, F. (1988), *Duality in Mark: Contributions to the Study of the Markan Redaction*, BETL 31, Leuven: Peeters.
Neirynck, F., T. Hansen, and F. van Segbroeck, eds. (1974), *The Minor Agreements of Matthew and Luke against Mark: With a Cumulative List*, BETL 37, Leuven: University Press.
Niditch, S. (2000), *A Prelude to Biblical Folklore: Underdogs and Tricksters*, Urbana: University of Illinois Press.
Niditch, S. (2010), "Hebrew Bible and Oral Literature: Misconceptions and New Directions," in A. Weissenrieder and R. B. Coote (eds.), *The Interface of Orality and Writing: Speaking, Seeing, Writing in the Shaping of New Genres*, 4–18, WUNT 260, Tübingen: Mohr Siebeck.
Nineham, D. E. (1963), *Saint Mark*, Pelican New Testament Commentaries, Philadelphia: Westminster.
Nir, R. (2012), *Joseph and Aseneth: A Christian Book*, Hebrew Bible Monographs 42, Sheffield: Sheffield Phoenix.
Nolland, J. (1989), *Luke*, 3 vols, WBC 35A–35C, Dallas: Word Books.
O'Brien, K. S. (2010), *The Use of Scripture in the Markan Passion Narrative*, LNTS 384, London: T&T Clark.
Ochs, E. (1979), "Planned and Unplanned Discourse," in T. Givón (ed.), *Discourse and Syntax*, 51–80, Syntax and Semantics 12, New York: Academic Press.
Oesterreicher, W. (1997), "Types of Orality in Text," in E. J. Bakker and A. Kahane (eds.), *Written Voices, Spoken Signs: Tradition, Performance, and the Epic Text*, 190–214, Cambridge: Harvard University Press.
Ong, W. J. (1971), *Rhetoric, Romance, and Technology: Studies in the Interaction of Expression and Culture*, Ithaca: Cornell University Press.
Ong, W. J. (1982), *Orality and Literacy: The Technologizing of the Word*, London: Routledge.
Ong, W. J. (1982), "The Psychodynamics of Oral Memory and Narrative: Some Implications for Biblical Studies," in R. Masson (ed.), *The Pedagogy of God's Image: Essays on Symbol and the Religious Imagination*, 55–73, Chico: Scholars Press.
Osburn, C. D. (1983), "The Historical Present in Mark as a Text-Critical Criterion." *Biblica*, 64: 486–500.
Östman, J.-O. (1982), "The Symbiotic Relationship Between Pragmatic Particles and Impromptu Speech," in N. E. Enkvist (ed.), *Impromptu Speech: A Symposium; Papers of a Symposium Held in Åbo, Nov. 20–22, 1981*, 147–77, Åbo: Åbo Akademi.

Painter, J. (1997), *Mark's Gospel*, London: Routledge.
Pantuck, A. J. (2013), "A Question of Ability: What Did He Know and When Did He Know It? Further Excavations from the Morton Smith Archives," in T. Burke (ed.), *Ancient Gospel or Modern Forgery? The Secret Gospel of Mark in Debate: Proceedings from the 2011 York University Christian Apocrypha Symposium*, 184–211, Eugene: Wipf & Stock.
Parker, D. C. (1997), *The Living Text of the Gospels*, Cambridge: Cambridge University Press.
Parsons, M. C. (2015), *Luke*. Paideia Commentaries on the New Testament, Grand Rapids: Baker Academic.
Penn, M. (2002), "Identity Transformation and Authorial Identification in *Joseph and Aseneth*." *JSP*, 13: 171–83.
Perry, B. E. (1967), *The Ancient Romances: A Literary-Historical Account of Their Origins*, Sather Classical Lectures 37, Berkeley: University of California Press.
Person, R. F. (2010), *The Deuteronomic History and the Book of Chronicles: Scribal Works in an Oral World*, AIL 6, Atlanta: Society of Biblical Literature.
Pervo, R. I. (1976), "Joseph and Asenath and the Greek Novel." *SBLSP*, 10: 171–81.
Pervo, R. I. (1991), "Aseneth and Her Sisters: Women in Jewish Narrative and in the Greek Novels," in A.-J. Levine (ed.), *"Women Like This:" New Perspectives on Jewish Women in the Greco-Roman World*, 145–60, EJL 1, Atlanta: Scholars Press.
Pesch, R. (1984), *Das Markusevangelium*, 2 vols, 4th ed., Herders theologischer Kommentar zum Neuen Testament, Freiburg: Herder.
Philonenko, M. (1968), *Joseph et Aséneth: Introduction, Texte Critique, Traduction, et Notes*, StPB 13, Leiden: Brill.
Pick, B. (1913), "Joseph and Asenath." *Open Court*, 27: 467–96.
Poirier, J. C., and J. Peterson, eds. (2015), *Markan Priority without Q: Explorations in the Farrer Hypothesis*, LNTS 455, London: Bloomsbury T&T Clark.
Polak, F. H. (1998), "The Oral and the Written: Syntax, Stylistics, and the Development of Biblical Prose Narrative." *JANESCU*, 26: 59–105.
Porter, S. E., and A. W. Pitts, eds. (2013), *The Language of the New Testament: Context, History, and Development*, Linguistic Biblical Studies 6, Leiden: Brill.
Rawlinson, A. E. J. (1942), *The Gospel According to St. Mark*, Westminster Commentaries, London: Metheun.
Reed, A. Y. (2002), "Εὐαγγέλιον: Orality, Textuality, and the Christian Truth in Irenaeus' *Adversus Haereses*." *VC*, 56: 11–46.
Reiter, C. L. (2013), *Writing in Greek but Thinking in Aramaic: A Study of Vestigial Verbal Coordination in the Gospels*, Lewiston: Mellen.
Rhoads, D. (2010), "Performance Events in Early Christianity: New Testament Writings in an Oral Context," in A. Weissenrieder and R. B. Coote (eds.), *The Interface of Orality and Writing; Speaking, Seeing, Writing in the Shaping of New Genres*, 166–93, WUNT 260, Tübingen: Mohr Siebeck.
Rhoads, D., and D. Michie (1982), *Mark as Story: An Introduction to the Narrative of a Gospel*, Philadelphia: Fortress.
Rhoads, D., J. Dewey, and D. Michie (1999), *Mark as Story: An Introduction to the Narrative of a Gospel*, 2nd ed., Minneapolis: Fortress.
Rhoads, D., J. Dewey, and D. Michie (2012), *Mark as Story: An Introduction to the Narrative of a Gospel*, 3rd ed., Minneapolis: Fortress.
Richards, E. R. (1991), *The Secretary in the Letters of Paul*, WUNT 2/42, Tübingen: Mohr Siebeck.

Richards, E. R. (2004), *Paul and First-Century Letter Writing: Secretaries, Composition, and Collection*, Downers Grove: InterVarsity Press.
Riessler, P. (1922), "Joseph und Asenath: Eine altjüdische Erzählung." *TQ*, 103: 1–22.
Riessler, P. (1928), *Altjüdisches Schrifttum ausserhalb der Bibel*, Augsburg: Filser.
Riley, H. (1989), *The Making of Mark: An Exploration*, Macon: Mercer University Press.
Robertson, A. T. (1919), *A Grammar of the Greek New Testament in the Light of Historical Research*, New York: Hodder and Stoughton.
Rodríguez, R. (2009), "Reading and Hearing in Ancient Contexts." *JSNT*, 32: 151–78.
Rodríguez, R. (2014), *Oral Tradition and the New Testament: A Guide for the Perplexed*, London: Bloomsbury.
Runge, S. E. (2010), *Discourse Grammar of the Greek New Testament: A Practical Introduction for Teaching and Exegesis*, Peabody: Hendrickson.
Ryan, M.-L. (2007), "Toward a Definition of Narrative," in D. Herman (ed.), *The Cambridge Companion to Narrative*, 22–36, Cambridge: Cambridge University Press.
Sanders, E. P. (1969), *The Tendencies of the Synoptic Tradition*, SNTSMS 9, London: Cambridge University Press.
Schams, C. (1998), *Jewish Scribes in the Second-Temple Period*, JSOTSupp 291, Sheffield: Sheffield Academic.
Schenk, W. (1976), "Das Präsens historicum als makrosyntaktisches Gliederungssignal im Matthäusevangelium." *NTS*, 22: 464–75.
Schiffrin, D. (1981), "Tense Variation in Narrative." *Language*, 57: 45–62.
Schiffrin, D. (1987), *Discourse Markers*, Studies in Interactional Sociolinguistics 5, Cambridge: Cambridge University Press.
Scobie, A. (1979), "Storytellers, Storytelling, and the Novel in Graeco-Roman Antiquity." *Rheinisches Museum Für Philologie*, 122: 229–59.
Shepherd, T. (1995), "The Narrative Function of Markan Intercalation." *NTS*, 41: 522–40.
Shin, H. W. (2012), "The Historic Present as a Discourse Marker and Textual Criticism in Mark." *BT*, 63: 39–51.
Skinner, C. W. (2011), "Telling the Story: The Appearance and Impact of *Mark as Story*," in C. W. Skinner and K. R. Iverson (eds.), *Mark as Story: Retrospect and Prospect*, 1–16, SBLRBS 65, Atlanta: Society of Biblical Literature.
Skinner, C. W., and K. R. Iverson, eds. (2011), *Mark as Story : Retrospect and Prospect*, SBLRBS 65, Atlanta: Society of Biblical Literature.
Skydsgaard, J. E. (1968), *Varro the Scholar: Studies in the First Book of Varro's de Re Rustica*, Analecta Romana Instituti Danici 4, Copenhagen: Munksgaard.
Smith, E. W. (1975), *Joseph and Aseneth and Early Christian Literature: A Contribution to the Corpus Hellenisticum Novi Testamenti*, PhD diss., Claremont Graduate School.
Smith, M. (1955), "Comments on Taylor's Commentary on Mark." *HTR*, 48: 21–64.
Smith, M. (1973), *Clement of Alexandria and a Secret Gospel of Mark*, Cambridge: Harvard University Press.
Smyth, H. W. (1956), *Greek Grammar*, revised by Gordon M. Messing, Cambridge: Harvard University Press.
Standhartinger, A. (1995), *Das Frauenbild im Judentum der hellenistischen Zeit: Ein Beitrag anhand von "Joseph und Asenath,"* AGJU 26, Leiden: Brill.
Standhartinger, A. (1996), "From Fictional Text to Socio-Historical Context: Some Considerations from a Text-Critical Perspective on *Joseph and Aseneth*." *SBLSP*, 35: 303–18.
Standhartinger, A. (2012), "Joseph and Aseneth: Perfect Bride of Heavenly Prophetess," in L. Schottroff and M.-T. Wacker (eds.), *Feminist Biblical Interpretation: A Compendium*

of *Critical Commentary on the Books of the Bible and Related Literature*, 578–85, Grand Rapids: Eerdmans.

Standhartinger, A. (2014), "Recent Scholarship on Joseph and Aseneth (1988–2013)." *CurBR*, 12: 353–406.

Standhartinger, A. (2015), "Humour in *Joseph and Aseneth*." *JSP*, 24: 239–59.

Starner, R. (2011), *Kingdom of Power, Power of Kingdom: The Opposing World Views of Mark and Chariton*, Eugene: Pickwick.

Stein, R. H. (1992), "Synoptic Gospels," in J. B. Green, S. McKnight, and I. H. Marshall (eds.), *Dictionary of Jesus and the Gospels*, 784–92, Downers Grove: InterVarsity Press.

Stein, R. H. (2008), *Mark*, Baker Exegetical Commentary on the New Testament, Grand Rapids: Baker Academic.

Strauss, M. L. (2014), Mark, Zondervan Exegetical Commentary on the New Testament, Grand Rapids: Zondervan.

Streeter, B. H. (1924), *The Four Gospels: A Study of Origins*, London: Macmillan.

Strelan, R. (1999), "The Fallen Watchers and the Disciples in Mark." *JSP*, 10: 73–92.

Suhl, A. (1965), *Die Funktion der Alttestamentlichen Zitate und Anspielungen im Markusevangelium*, Gütersloh: Mohn.

Talbert, C. H. (1977), *What Is a Gospel? The Genre of the Canonical Gospels*, Philadelphia: Fortress.

Tannen, D. (1982), "Oral and Literate Strategies in Spoken and Written Narratives." *Language*, 58: 1–21.

Telford, W. (1980), *The Barren Temple and the Withered Tree: A Redaction-Critical Analysis of the Cursing of the Fig-Tree Pericope in Mark's Gospel and Its Relation to the Cleansing of the Temple Tradition*, JSNTSup 1, Sheffield: JSOT Press.

Thomas, C. M. (2003), *The Acts of Peter, Gospel Literature, and the Ancient Novel: Rewriting the Past*, Oxford: Oxford University Press.

Thumb, A. (1901), *Die griechische Sprache im Zeitalter des Hellenismus*, Strassburg: Tübner.

Tilg, S. (2010), *Chariton of Aphrodisias and the Invention of the Greek Love Novel*, Oxford: Oxford University Press.

Traugott, E. C., and R. B. Dasher (2002), *Regularity in Semantic Change*, Cambridge Studies in Linguistics, Cambridge: Cambridge University Press.

Turner, C. H. (1993), "Marcan Usage: Critical and Exegetical on the Second Gospel," in J. K. Elliott (ed.), *The Language and Style of the Gospel of Mark: An Edition of C.H. Turner's "Notes on Marcan Usage" Together with Other Comparable Studies*, 3–139, NovTSup 71, Leiden: Brill.

Turner, N. (1963), *Syntax*, Vol. 3, *A Grammar of New Testament Greek*, 4 vols, Edinburgh: T&T Clark.

van Unnik, W. C. (1973), "Once More St. Luke's Prologue." *Neot*, 7: 7–26.

Urgelles-Coll, M. (2010), *The Syntax and Semantics of Discourse Markers*, Continuum Studies in Theoretical Linguistics, London: Continuum.

VanderKam, J. C. (1996), "1 Enoch, Enochic Motifs, and Enoch in Early Christian Literature," in J. C. VanderKam and W. Adler (eds.), *The Jewish Apocalyptic Heritage in Early Christianity*, 33–101, CRINT III.4, Assen: Van Gorcum.

Votaw, C. W. (1915), "The Gospels and Contemporary Biographies." *AJT*, 19: 217–49. Reprinted as *The Gospels and Contemporary Biographies*, Philadelphia: Fortress, 1970.

Waetjen, H. C. (1989), *A Reordering of Power: A Socio-Political Reading of Mark's Gospel*, Minneapolis: Fortress.

Von Wahlde, U. C. (1985), "Mark 9:33–50: Discipleship: The Authority that Serves." *BZ*, 29: 49–67.

Wahlen, C. (2004), *Jesus and the Impurity of Spirits in the Synoptic Gospels*, WUNT 2/185, Tübingen: Mohr Siebeck.
Walcutt, J. (1977), "The Topology of Narrative Boundedness," in E. O. Keenan and T. Bennett (eds.), *Discourse Across Time and Space*, 51–68, Southern California Occasional Papers in Linguistics 5, Los Angeles: University of Southern California.
Wallace, D. B. (1996), *Greek Grammar Beyond the Basics: An Exegetical Syntax of the New Testament*, Grand Rapids: Zondervan.
Watts, R. J. (1989), "Taking the Pitcher to the 'Well': Native Speakers' Perception of Their Use of Discourse Markers in Conversation." *Journal of Pragmatics: An Interdisciplinary Monthly of Language Studies*, 13: 203–37.
Weeden, T. J. (1971), *Mark: Traditions in Conflict*, Philadelphia: Fortress.
Weiss, J. (1903), *Das älteste Evangelium: ein Beitrag zum Verständnis des Markus-Evangeliums und der ältesten evangelischen Überlieferung*, Göttingen: Vandenhoeck & Ruprecht.
Wengst, K. (1987), *Pax Romana and the Peace of Jesus Christ*, trans. J. Bowden, London: SCM.
West, S. (1974), "Joseph and Asenath: A Neglected Greek Romance." *ClQ*, 24: 70–81.
Whitmarsh, T. (2012), "Joseph et Aséneth: Erotisme et Religion," in C. Bost-Pouderon and B. Pouderon (eds.), *Les hommes et les dieux dans l'ancien roman: Actes du colloque des Tours, 22–24 octobre 2009*, 237–52, Lyon: Maison de l'Orient et de la Méditerranée – Jean Pouilloux.
Wikgren, A. (1942), "ΑΡΧΗ ΤΟΥ ΕΥΑΓΓΕΛΙΟΥ." *JBL*, 61: 11–20.
Wilcken, U., ed. (1963), *Grundzüge und Chrestomathie der Papyruskunde*, Vol. 1, Part 2: *Chrestomathie*, 4 vols, Hildesheim: Olms.
Wills, L. M. (1995), *The Jewish Novel in the Ancient World (Myth and Poetics)*, Ithaca: Cornell University Press.
Wilmshurst, S. M. B. (2003), "The Historic Present in Matthew's Gospel: A Survey and Analysis Focused on Matthew 13.44." *JSNT*, 25: 269–87.
Wink, W. (1986), *Unmasking the Powers: The Invisible Forces That Determine Human Existence*, Philadelphia: Fortress.
Winsbury, R. (2009), *The Roman Book: Books, Publishing and Performance in Classical Rome*, Classical Literature and Society, London: Duckworth.
Winter, J. G. (1933), *Life and Letters in the Papyri*, Ann Arbor: University of Michigan Press.
Wire, A. C. (2011), *The Case for Mark Composed in Performance*, Biblical Performance Criticism Series 3, Eugene: Cascade.
Witherington, B. (2001), *The Gospel of Mark: A Socio-Rhetorical Commentary*, Grand Rapids: Eerdmans.
Wolfson, N. (1978), "A Feature of Performed Narrative: The Conversational Historical Present." *Language in Society*, 7: 215–37.
Wolfson, N. (1982), *CHP: The Conversational Historical Present in American English Narrative*, Topics in Sociolinguistics, Dordrecht: Foris.
Wright, A. T. (2006), "Evil Spirits in Second Temple Judaism: The Watcher Tradition as a Background to the Demonic Pericopes in the Gospels." *Henoch*, 28: 141–59.
Wright, N. T. (1996), *Jesus and the Victory of God*, Christian Origins and the Question of God 2, Minneapolis: Fortress.
Youtie, H. C. (1971), "Βραδέως Γράφων: Between Literacy and Illiteracy." *GRBS*, 12: 239–61.
Zerbe, G. M. (1993), *Non-Retaliation in Early Jewish and New Testament Texts: Ethical Themes in Social Contexts*, JSPSup 13, Sheffield: Sheffield Academic.

Ziegler, J., ed. (1967), *Duodecim Prophetae*, Vol. XIII of *Septuaginta: Vetus Testamentum Graecum Auctoritate Academiae Scientarum Gottingensis Editum*, Göttingen: Vandenhoeck & Ruprecht.
Zumthor, P. (1972), *Essai de Poétique Médiévale*, Paris: Seuil.
Zumthor, P. (1990), *Oral Poetry: An Introduction*, trans. K. Murphy-Judy, Theory and History of Literature 70, Minneapolis: University of Minnesota Press.

SUBJECT AND AUTHOR INDEX

Ahearne-Kroll, Patricia 56–8, 95–7
Alexander, Loveday 164
aorist tense 23, 86, 101, 146, 150
apposition
   Joseph and Aseneth 64–5
   oral residue 19
Assmann, Jan 26–7, 75 n.127

Bakker, Egbert J. 12–13
bilingual influence 58–61
book 161–2
Bultmann, Rudolf 115 n.98
Burchard, Christoph 8 n.30, 9 n.31, 54–5

composition by dictation 28–32, 97, 176
cultural texts 26–7

Deissmann, Adolf 59
Dewey, Joanna 5
Dibelius, Martin 115 n.98
direct discourse
   Joseph and Aseneth 86
   Mark 92
   Oral residue 21
   P.Oxy. 903 42–3
discourse markers
   characteristics of 80–4
   εὐθύς 79–84
   Joseph and Aseneth 86
   Mark 79–84, 92, 153–6
   oral residue 84
   present tense with 42–3
   Synoptic Gospels 153–6

ecclesiastical testimony
   Mark's composition 48–50, 177
equiprimordiality 23–4, 97, 102, 168–9
εὐθύς 79–84, 153–6, 174–5

Finnegan, Ruth H. 11
Foley, John Miles 13–14, 27

Genette, Gérard 156–7
Gerasene Demoniac 126–8, 129–31
gospel 157–61, 175
Great Divide 3, 4 n.18, 5 n.20, 133–34
Greek romance novels 110–15, 169

historical present tense
   John 89
   Joseph and Aseneth 85–6
   Mark 87–91, 101–2, 145–9, 175
   oral residue 87–8
   speech margins 88–9
   Synoptic Gospels 145–9
   vividness 90
hitching post 64–5

indicative mood 34
   Joseph and Aseneth 84–5
   Mark 92
   P.Oxy.903 42
idea unit
   Mark 68–71
   oral residue 17–18
   properties of 17 n.25
inexplicit references to writings 121–3
intercalations
   Joseph and Aseneth 74–7, 169–70
   Mark 77–8, 151–3
   Synoptic Gospels 151–3
intertextuality
   Joseph and Aseneth 104–15
   Mark 115–32, 176
   oral and literary discourse 25–8

Kelber, Werner H. 3–5, 23 n.51
Kraemer, Ross 55–6

Larsen, Matthew D. C. 15–16, 44 n.147, 103
Latinisms 60 n.54
literacy 30
longer ending of Mark 99–103, 175–6

Markan style 1, 7
Mark as Story (Rhoads, Michie, and
    Dewey) 1–2
miscited and misquoted texts 118–21, 176
mixed media 11–16
Moulton, James H. 59–60
Mouvance 24–5, 97
multiform tradition
    Joseph and Aseneth 95–7
    Mark 98–103

narrative criticism 1
non-retaliatory ethic 109

oral
    composition 2
    literature 2–3
orality and textuality
    interface between 2, 6, 11–16
    intertextuality in 25–8
original ending of Mark 99–103

parataxis
    BGU I.27 34–5
    Joseph and Aseneth 62–4, 135–7
    Mark 66–8, 101, 137–40
    oral residue 16–18
    P.Oxy. 903 39–40
    revelation 66–7
    Romans 67
passive voice
    Joseph and Aseneth 85
    literary discourse 22
    Mark 101, 150
    P.Oxy. 903 42
    Synoptic Gospels 150
past tense
    literary discourse 21–2

Philonenko, Marc 54
present tense
    oral residue 21, 101
primary orality 26
prologue 163–5

relative pronouns 65
repetition
    Joseph and Aseneth 72–7
    Mark 78–9, 150–6
    oral residue 19–20
    P.Oxy. 903 40–1
residual orality 2, 4, 10 n.34, 61–93
Rodríguez, Rafael 5–6

secondary orality 26–7
shorter ending of Mark 99–100
Standhartinger, Angela 55–6
Synoptic Gospels 14–16, 67, 92, 119,
    120, 122, 124 n.134, 129, 137–40,
    145–56

textual recensions of *Joseph and
    Aseneth* 53–8, 168–9
Thomas, Christine M. 24
Thumb, Albert 59

ὑπομνήματα 43–7
verbs
    Joseph and Aseneth 84–6,
        140–4
    Mark 87–93, 145–50
    P.Oxy. 903 41–3

Wire, Antoinette C. 68–9
writing by hand 29

Zumthor, Paul 13–14

INDEX OF SCRIPTURE AND OTHER ANCIENT LITERATURE

Hebrew Bible/Old Testament

Genesis		4:10	159 n.132	51:9-11	125
2:4	162	18:19-20	159 n.132	52:7	159 n.132
3:14	131 n.164	18:26	159 n.132	60:6	159 n.132
5:1	162	18:31	159 n.132	61:1	159 n.132
41:38	106				
41:46-49	105–6	1 Kings		Jeremiah	
		1:41	159 n.132	20:15	159 n.132
Exodus					
2:17	131 n.164	2 Kings		Daniel	
23:20	118	7:9	159 n.132	7	122
33:2	131 n.164				
		1 Chronicles	67		
Numbers		10:9	159 n.132	Joel	
22:6	131 n.164			3:5	159 n.132
		Job			
Joshua		38:1-11	125	Jonah	67
24:18	131			1:1-15	123–5
		Psalms		1:4	124
Ruth	67	18:15	123 n.133	1:5	124
		39:10	159 n.132	1:6	125
1 Samuel	67	40:10	122	1:10	124
17	75, 106–9	67:12	159 n.132	1:11-12	125
17:33	107 n.64	89:9	125		
17:37	108	95:2	159 n.132	Nahum	
17:40	107 n.65, 108	104:7	123 n.133	2:1	159 n.132
		106:8-12	125		
17:42	107 n.64	106:9	123 n.133	Zechariah	
17:45-46	108	107 (106 LXX)	125–6	13:7	120–1
17:48-51	108	107:23-29	123 n.133		
17:49	107, 107 n.66, 108	107:23-32	125	Malachi	
		117:22-24	116	3:1	118
17:51	109 n.69, 109 n.71				
		Song of Solomon		**New Testament**	
21:2-10	119–20, 130	1:1	159 n.132		
31:9	159 n.132			Matthew	
		Isaiah		1:1	157, 161–2
2 Samuel		29:13	116		
18:20-25	159 n.132	40:3	118	3:3	119
1:20	159 n.132	40:9	159 n.132		

Index of Scripture and Other Ancient Literature

3:15	148	1:2-3	118–19	7:35	81
3:16	155 n.112	1:3	118	8:10	82
4:1	154	1:12	90, 154	8:22	91
4:1-11	147	1:21	82	9:11-13	58 n.37
4:20-22	155 n.110	1:21-28	69–70	9:12	115, 121, 122
4:21	60 n.54	1:23	82, 83		
4:23	160 n.134	1:28	82	9:13	115
8:3	155 n.110	1:32	79	10:4	115
8:16	79	1:35	79 n.141	10:5	115
8:27	124	1:42	81	10:35-45	58 n.37
8:28	129	2:20	140 n.39	11	153
9:18-26	152	2:23-28	119–20	11:12-21	77
9:35	160 n.134	2:23–3:6	58 n.37	11:12-25	74 n.119, 152
10:5-16	152	2:26	130		
12:4	120	3:20-25	152	11:17	115
12:22-30	152	3:20-35	74 n.119	12:10	115
12:46-50	152	3:27	140 n.39	12:10-11	116, 117
13:5	155 n.110	4:2	79 n.141	12:15	60 n.54
13:20-21	155, 155 n.112	4:16-17	155	12:19	115
		4:35-41	123–6	12:24	115
13:24-52	147	4:37	124	12:42	60 n.54
13:44	147, 148	4:38	124, 125	12:44	79 n.141
14:1-14	152	4:39	79 n.141	13:14	140 n.39
14:22	155 n.110	4:41	125	13:21	140 n.39
14:27	155 n.112	5:1	129	13:26-27	140 n.39
17:11-12	122	5:1-20	126–9, 129–31, 176	14:1-11	74 n.119, 152
20:34	155 n.110			14:5	60 n.54
21	153				
21:3	155 n.110	5:2	127, 129	14:12-26	58 n.37
21:18-22	152	5:3-4	128	14:18	122
21:23-46	153	5:9, 15	60 n.54	14:21	115, 122
21:28-32	153	5:13	129	14:27	115, 120–1
21:33-41	153	5:14	129		
24:14	160 n.134	5:15	79 n.141	14:43	82
26:3-16	152	5:19	79 n.141	14:49	115, 122
26:12	160 n.134	5:21-43	74 n.119, 152	14:53-72	74 n.119, 152
26:24	122				
26:25	146 n.61	5:25-27	71	14:61	79 n.141
26:31	121 n.118	5:25-29	70	15:39	60 n.54, 82 n.157
26:36-46	148	6:6-30	74 n.119, 152		
26:47	83 n.161			15:44	60 n.54
26:49	155 n.110	6:17-20	109 n.69	15:45	60 n.54
26:56	122	6:26	79 n.141	16:8	6, 99, 102, 175
26:57-75	152	6:27	60 n.54		
		6:37	60 n.54	16:11	101
Mark		7:4	60 n.54	16:13	101
1:1	6, 157–61, 175	7:6	115	16:18	101
		7:6-7	116, 117	16:9-20	99, 101, 176
1:2	115	7:33	79 n.141		

Luke		Colossians		21:6	128
1:1-4	163–5	1:5	160 n.134	22:11	128
3:5-6	119	1:23	160 n.134		
4:1	154			*Joseph and Aseneth*	
4:40	79	1 Thessalonians		1:1	106 n.60
6:4	120	2:2	160 n.134	1:1-3	76
6:49	155 n.112	2:9	160 n.134	1:3	105–6
7:36-50	152			1:3-5	65
7:40	146 n.57	2 Thessalonians		1:4–2:20	76
8:19-21	152	1:8	160 n.134	1:6-8	111
8:25	124	Revelation	66	1:9-11	112 n.81
8:40-42	152	1:3	67 n.86	2:3-5	73
8:49	146			2:16	73
9:1-11	152	**Deuterocanon/Apocrypha**		3:1-6	76
11:14-23	152	Tobit	67	3:4–4:4	73
11:37	146 n.57			3:6	73 n.116
11:45	146 n.57	Judith	67	3:9	63, 73 n.116
13:6-9	152			3:10	73
13:8	146 n.57	3 Maccabees	68	4:1	73 n.116
16:7	146 n.57			4:5	173 n.26
16:23	146 n.57	**Pseudepigrapha**		4:5-8	86
16:29	146 n.57	*1* Enoch	67	4:7	173 n.26
19:22	146 n.57	1–36	126–9	4:11-15	76
19:45-48	152	6–16	127	4:12	173 n.26
22:1-3	152	6	128	4:13-14	106 n.60
22:22	122	6:4	128	5:1–6:8	76
22:53	122	6:4-6	128	6:1	113, 124
22:54-71	152	7:1	127 n.142	6:1-8	113
24:12	146 n.57	9:4	128	6:2	174, n.26
24:36	146 n.57	9:8	127 n.142	6:2-8	113
		10	127	6:4	114 n.94
Acts		10:4	128	6:5	114 n.94,
26:12	160 n.134	10:5	128		174 n.26
		10:8	127 n.142	6:6	174 n.26
Romans	67	10:11	127,	6:8	114, 114 n.94
			127 n.142,	7:1-7	76
1 Corinthians			127 n.143	7:8	173 n.26
9:14	160 n.134	10:11-22	127	7:10-11	76
9:17	160 n.134	10:12	128	8	173
15:1	160 n.134	10:14	128	8:2	173 n.26
		10:20-22	127	8:5	73
2 Corinthians		12:4	127 n.142	9:4	173 n.26
11:7	160 n.134	13:1	128	10	73
		14:5	128	10:1	137 n.19
Galatians		15:3	127 n.142	10:2	79 n.139
1:10	160 n.134	15:4	127 n.142	10:19	79 n.139
		15:7-10	128	10:4-5	63
Ephesians		18:16	128	12:1–14:2	86
1:13	160 n.134	21:3	128	13:9	173 n.26

Index of Scripture and Other Ancient Literature

13:10	86, 174 n.26	29:1-7	76	Eusebius	
		29:3	75 n.129, 76 n.130	*HE*	
14:8-10	142–3			2.16	48–9
15	173	29:3-4	109		
15:2-12	86			Irenaeus	
15:6	168, 169 n.25	*Letter of Aristeas* 68		*Adv. Haer.*	
				3.1.1	49 n.164
16:2	173 n.26	**Philo**			
16:6	173 n.26	*De Abrahamo*	67 n.91	Jerome	
17:1	173 n. 26	1	162 n.144	*Comm. On Matt.*	
18:3	142			Pref.	49 n.164
20:1	173 n.26				
20:7	101 n.60	*De aeternitate mundi*		Origen	
21:1	174 n.26	19	162 n.144	*De Vir.*	
21:8	101 n.60			8	49 n.164
22:1-6	101 n.60	*De Josepho*			
23:1–24:9	77	245	160 n.133	Papias	
23:9	76 n.130			*Apud* Eusebius *HE*	
23:10	173 n.26, 174 n.26	*De Mosis*	67	3.39.15	49–50
		2.38	72 n.109	3.39.16	49 n.163
24:4	173 n.26				
24:12	173 n.26	*De posteritate Caini*		Tertullian	
27	136	127	162 n.144	*Adv. Marc.*	
27–29	75–6, 106–9, 170			4.1.1	49 n.164
		De Somniis		4.2.1-2	49 n.164
27:1	107 n.64	2.281	160 n.133	4.3.4	49 n.164
27:1-5	76, 107			4.5.3-4	49 n.164
27:2	107 n.64	*Legatio ad Gaium*	67 n.91		
27:3	107, 107 n.66, 108			**Classical Literature**	
				Achilles Tatius	
27:4	107 n.65	**Josephus**		*Leuc. Clit.*	
27:5	108	*Ag. Ap.*		1.4.4-5	112 n.83
27:6	76 n.131, 137 n.19	1.1-18	163–4	Apuleius	
27:6–28:3	76			*Metam.*	
27:7	75	*J. W.*		5.22	112 n.83
28	73, 109	1.17	163–4, 164 n.158	Chariton	
28:1-2	136–7	4.487-489	131	*Chaer*	
28:4	76 n.130			1.1	113
28:4-16	76			1.1.1-3	112 n.79
28:5	75	**Patristic/Early Christian Sources**		1.1.2-3	112 n.81
28:6	108			1.1.6	112
28:10	76 n.130	Clement		1.1.10	113 n.84
28:11	108	*Adumbrationes* on 1 Peter	49 n.164	1.1.14	113 n.85
28:13	76 n.130			1.14.1-2	112 n.80
28:14	75 n.129, 108	*Apud* Eusebius *HE*		2.3.8	112 n.80
		2.15.1-2	48–9	3.3.5	112 n.80
29:1	75	6.14.6-7	48 n.161, 49 n.164	3.6.3	113 n.85
29:2	109 n.71				

3.9.1	112 n.80	10.28-55	126 n.138	10.3.17-18	29	
4.5.9	113 n.85			10.3.25-27	29	
7.6	114 n.95	Isocrates		10.3.31-32	29 n.85	
8.2.5	159 n.131	*Panath.* 12.158	49 n.162			
				Vergil		
Demosthenes		Lucian		*Aeneid*		
On the Crown		*Hist. cons.*		1.81-142	126 n.138	
18.323	159 n.131	16	46-7			
		48	43 n.142,	Xenophon		
Diodorus Siculus			47 n.157	*Anthia and Habrocomes*		
The Library of				1.2.5	112 n.79	
History	159 n.131	Lycurgus		1.2.6	112 n.79	
		Against Leocrates		1.3.1	113	
Diogenes Laertius		1.18	159 n.131	1.4.1	113, 114,	
Lives					114 n.94	
1.5 (Bias)	126 n.138	Philostratus		1.4.2	114 n.92,	
8.2 (Empedocles)	43 n.143,	*Life of Apollonius*			114 n.94	
	126 n.138	8.27.2	159 n.131	1.4.6	114 n.92	
		Lives of the Sophists		1.4.6-7	113	
Galen		1.508.14	159 n.131	1.5.1	113 n.86	
De libris propriis				1.5.5	113	
8-9	46 n.154,	Plutarch		1.7.4	113	
	100	*Moralia*		Xenophon		
9	100, 176	347.D	159 n.131	*Hellenica*		
9-11	44	*Phocian*		1.6.36	159 n.131	
9-10	45 n.153	23.4	159 n.131			
10	100 n.35	*Pompeius*		**Papyri**		
12-13	46 n.155	66.3	159 n.131	BGU I.27	32-6	
14-15	45	*Sertorius*		P.Cair.Zen. 199.5	49 n.162	
23	45 n.152	11.4	159 n.131	P.Oxy. 729.17	49 n.162	
				P.Oxy. 903	36-43,	
Homer		Quintilian			122	
Odyssey		*Inst.*				
5.291-390	126 n.138	1.0.7-8	46			

www.ingramcontent.com/pod-product-compliance
Lightning Source LLC
Chambersburg PA
CBHW052042300426
44117CB00012B/1938